The Monster in the Mirror

THE ROBERT H. WAUGH
LIBRARY OF LOVECRAFTIAN CRITICISM

THE MONSTER IN THE MIRROR

Looking for H. P. Lovecraft

Robert H. Waugh

Hippocampus Press
New York

Copyright © 2005 by Robert H. Waugh
This edition copyright © 2006, 2021 by Hippocampus Press.

Early versions of Part I, Part II, and Part III appeared in
Lovecraft Studies, Nos. 17, 25, 32, 34, 35, 36, 37, 38, 39, and 40,
published by Necronomicon Press. A shortened version of
"Documents, Creatures, and History" appeared in
The H. P. Lovecraft Centennial Conference Proceedings,
S. T. Joshi, ed. (Necronomicon Press, 1991).

Published by Hippocampus Press
P.O. Box 641, New York, NY 10156.
www.hippocampuspress.com

All rights reserved.
No part of this work may be reproduced in any form or by any means
without the written permission of the publisher.

Cover art and frontispiece by Josh Yelle, pencilmancer.com.
Cover design and series logo by Daniel V. Sauer, dansauerdesign.com.
Hippocampus Press logo by Anastasia Damianakos.

First Edition
Second Printing
3 5 7 9 8 6 4 2

ISBN-10: 0-9761592-7-9
ISBN-13: 978-0-9761592-7-8

> Shine out, fair sun, till I have bought a glass,
> That I may see my shadow as I pass.
>
> Shakespeare, *Richard III* 1.2.262–63

> Ubi es quando tibiipsi non es? [Where are you when you are not present to yourself?] (Thomas à Kempis 2.5.2)

> Men are really so weak that it is absolutely necessary for them to know sorrow and pain, to be in their right senses. (Addison 4.54; No. 312)

> "I can't explain *myself*, I'm afraid, Sir," said Alice, "because I'm not myself, you see." (Carroll 35)

Contents

Introduction 9

PART I:
First Principles

Lovecraft's Hands 17

Documents, Creatures, and History 52

PART II:
Sorties

"The Picture in the House": Images of Complicity 69

At the Mountains of Madness: The Subway and the Shoggoth 79

PART III:
Meditations on "The Outsider"

"The Outsider," the Terminal Climax, and Other Conclusions 111

Lovecraft and Keats Confront the "Awful Rainbow" 127

The Outsider, the Autodidact, and Other Professions 162

PART IV:
Materialism, Theology, and Imagination

Lovecraft and Leopardi: Sunsets and Moonsets 201

Lovecraft Born Again: An Essay in Apologetic Criticism 241

Works Cited 283

Index 297

Introduction

Why H. P. Lovecraft? Why a book of this size, let alone its complexity, devoted to an author published during his lifetime in the most callow of pulps, derided by Edmund Wilson, and still today accused of being the center of a mere cult following? The book is, of course, its own gradual answer to this question. A provisional answer would be that he simply refuses to go away. But not only does he remain in publication; his recent acceptance into the Penguin Classics series and the Library of America is an indication that he has moved into the canon. Another answer would be that as a part of this canonization he is even more in argument, as the biographies by L. Sprague de Camp and S. T. Joshi show. Any study of the literature of horror, whether historical or theoretical, has to pay attention to him; and in these studies we find a debate about Lovecraft that, like him, will not go away. It is that very difficulty about Lovecraft, his elusiveness, which this book attempts to address.

These essays represent a variety of closely connected approaches to Lovecraft's fiction. The two essays that form the first part lay down certain basic concerns and assumptions that the later essays return to under various forms. If we are to take Lovecraft's most basic theme as the place of humanity in an indifferent universe, it could be said that the first essay examines Lovecraft's vision of the problematically human in such a universe, whereas the second essay examines his vision of the universe from the viewpoint of the questing human. The first essay also introduces the overarching theme of the entire collection, the theme that I believe is central to all of Lovecraft's work, his anxiety with authenticity, his fear that nothing he does and nothing that humanity can do will establish the self as original; we are always a copy, whether in trivial or non-trivial ways.

The two essays of the second part examine two different works, but keep in mind to a greater or lesser extent this Lovecraftian anxiety of the copy and raise the aesthetic question of his work. The first deals with "The Picture in the House," the several different perspectives which that short work moves among and the surprising filiations of its patriarchal vision of racial hybrids, the next with *At the Mountains of Madness;* each investigates from a different angle the problem of Lovecraft's racism and anti-Semitism and thereby the moral difficulty of the work. When I began these essays I did not foresee the extent to which Lovecraft's anti-Semitism informs his fiction, although his anti-Semitism is patent in his letters; in the light of these essays we can now say with full conviction that although very few of his stories are anti-Semitic almost all of them are constructed from anti-Semitic materials.

All the essays in the third part take their starting point from one story, "The Outsider," and use the motifs and themes discovered in it as a way to investigate the other stories. But the overarching theme the essays concern themselves with is still his anxiety with authenticity. Without making any claim to therapeutic or theoretical precision, these essays also become meditations on the modulations of the Oedipal career in Lovecraft's works. This aspect of the essays is an exemplification of the re-visioning advocated by James Hillman, an extension of the mythological figure in confronting Oedipus and others with the various figures of Lovecraft in order to see the implications of his figures more clearly. This re-visioning is not an attempt to psychoanalyze Lovecraft or his characters but to see more clearly their autonomy as semi-articulated aesthetic objects that move as it were through their own continually recreated psychic space. I employ Freud, Bersani, Calasso, and the characterology of phobias in the same way.

The essays of the last part form a pair: the first confirms the atheistic pessimism of Lovecraft's thought, comparing his career to that of the Italian poet Giacomo Leopardi; the second probes the aesthetic affirmation of his stories through the mode of a Christian apologia. These last two essays insist upon an implicit theme of all the essays, that Lovecraft is not a consistent person and that his work possesses fault-lines energized by profound tensions and contradictions. I have written these two essays, at least in their first drafts, as it were in tandem.

Several of these essays have the peculiarity that, having been written over a number of years, they do not bear the mark of premeditation. The argument they pursue I did not understand when I began them; the discoveries they make I did not aim for. Although I have rewritten all the essays for this collection, I have attempted to rewrite them in such a way that the development and surprise that I experienced in writing them have not been affected. I have tried to resolve certain contradictions that arose as I proceeded, but not in such a way that the opening assumptions have been changed. One of the dangers of modern theory, it seems to me, is that it leaves the critic in the position of proving what has been proven and demonstrating what theory insists must be demonstrated. My study of Lovecraft has been wayward, following the paths suggested by a number of methodologies, but I have tried to make them evident; and so from the beginning it must be confessed that I was raised as a New Critic and remain one. Upon occasion I allow the connections among these materials to be implicit rather than explicit because I believe that we must all work upon these connections in the faith that they exist rather than in their explicit demonstration.

Not that I am innocent of theory or of bias. Frequent use shall be made in these pages of Heidegger, Freud, Bersani, Hill, Huet, Young-Bruehl, and Julius; but the essays are about Lovecraft, not about ways of reading him. In addition, I frequently place Lovecraft within a variety of literary contexts, one of the most frequent that of the authors of the eighteenth century, especially Newton, Addison and Steele, Pope, Thomson, Cowper, and Young, as well as in the context of his favorite classical authors, Lucretius, Virgil, and Ovid.

I have many people to thank for their help in the gradual growth of these chapters, first of all the Lovecraft community, above all S. T. Joshi without whose labors on the text and life of Lovecraft and without whose generosity and critical eye this argument would have been impossible—and who is not responsible for any of the more bizarre speculations of this work. I am grateful to David E. Schultz for his editorial assistance. I am also grateful to Peter Cannon, Norm Gayford, and Judith Johnson for their encouragement and presence through the years of my work. My colleagues have also helped me and forbore me graciously, above all Dan Kempton, Jan Schmidt, Tom Olsen, and Ernelle Fife; my students have warmly taken part in this work, above all John Paul Langan; and the College of New Paltz has granted me sabbaticals through the years without which this book would not have been possible. I am grateful to the libraries of New Paltz and Vassar, and of course to the resources and courtesy of the John Hay Library of Brown University with its enormous collection of Lovecraftiana.

Without the research skills and editorial eye of my wife Kappa this work would have been much more chaotic than it must still seem.

Abbreviations

AG	*Letters to Alfred Galpin and Others* (2020)
AT	*The Ancient Track: Complete Poetical Works* (2013)
CE	*Collected Essays* (2004–06)
CF	*Collected FictionL A Variorum Edition* (2015–21)
CLM	*Letters to C. L. Moore* (2017)
DS	*Dawnward Spire, Lonely Hill* (2017)
DW	*Letters with Donald and Howard Wandrei* (2019)
EHP	*Letters to E. Hoffmann Price and Richard F. Searight* (2021)
ES	*Essential Solitude* (2008)
ET	*Letters to Elizabeth Toldridge and Anne Tillery Renshaw* (2014)
FFF	*Letters to Family and Family Friends* (2020)
FLB	*Letters to F. Lee Baldwin, Duane W. Rimel, and Nils Frome* (2016)
IAP	S. T. Joshi, *I Am Providence* (2010)
JFM	*Letters to James F. Morton* (2011)
JVS	*Letters to J. Vernon Shea* (2016)
LL	S. T. Joshi and David E. Schultz, *Lovecraft's Library* (2017)
MF	*A Means to Freedom* (2009)
MWM	*Letters to Maurice W. Moe and Others* (2018)
OFF	*O Fortunate Floridian* (2007)
RB	*Letters to Robert Bloch and Others* (2015)
RK	*Letters to Rheinhart Kleiner and Others* (2020)
SL	*Selected Letters 1911–1937* (1965–76)
WBT	*Letters to Wilfred B. Talman* (2019)

The Monster in the Mirror

PART I

FIRST PRINCIPLES

Lovecraft's Hands

I

> This living hand, now warm and capable
> Of earnest grasping, would, if it were cold
> And in the icy silence of the tomb,
> So haunt thy days and chill thy dreaming nights
> That thou would wish thine own heart dry of blood . . .
> (Keats, "This Living Hand" ll. 1–5)

Among the many stories that a reader might think of as typical of Lovecraft's writing, "The Outsider" is one of the least. Relatively early in his career, it has nothing to do with those stories identified with the Cthulhu cycle; the *Necronomicon*, the secret book that he invented, is not mentioned; and nothing overtly horrible happens to the protagonist, though something very mysterious does happen. Raised without human contact, yearning to escape the ruins within which he has grown up, the narrator climbs a tower to search for a way out, only to discover that those ruins are the underground world of a tomb. That discovery is not the climax of the story, however. Blundering through the country around the cemetery he comes to a castle, strangely familiar, where in an archway he sees "a leering, abhorrent travesty on the human shape" and touching the hand of the monster feels between them "*a cold and unyielding surface of polished glass*" (*CF* 1.272). He is that thing in the mirror. This moment presents a paradigm of Lovecraft's most authentic fiction: at the climax of these stories ambiguous hands reach out; the narrators to whom the hands belong are part ghoul, part exhibitionist, part confidence-man, part dunce, and often nameless; and in response to the narrators monstrous objects rise from water, mirrors in which the self is reflected or identified as a travesty.[1] In addition, the recognition that occurs in the climax occasions a release of emotive words that derive from Lovecraft's vocabulary of horror, words dispersed throughout the stories that suddenly become focused at this point. The analysis of these elements offers a first step in outlining what is truly fearful and authentic in Lovecraft's fiction.

Hands frequently carry the point in these stories. Almost the last words of an early tale, "Dagon," are "God, *that hand!*" (*CF* 1.58). In "The Shadow over Innsmouth" the fingers of the citizens, "strikingly short," with "a tendency to curl closely into the huge palm," tell of their origin in the water to which they shall re-

---

[1]. Donald R. Burleson also treats the conclusion of "The Outsider" as exemplary of HPL's fiction. For him it "brings to focus what is going to be the broad thematic concern of Lovecraft's entire *oeuvre*: the nature of self-knowledge, the effects of learning one's own nature and one's place in the scheme of things" ("On Lovecraft's Themes: Touching the Glass" 135).

turn (*CF* 3.170). In "The Hound" the narrator knows he will die because the monster whose grave he has robbed still clutches the stolen amulet "in its gory, filthy claw" (*CF* 1.348). All that is left of Wilbur Whateley are his face and hands, the only parts of him that ever approximated the human (*CF* 2.441); and, more horribly, Albert Wilmarth only realizes what has befallen Henry Akeley when he sees the perfect waxen copies of the man's face and hands (*CF* 2.538). In the late story, "Through the Gates of the Silver Key," the white mitten of the Swami Chandraputra falls off to reveal a black, insectile claw, that thus assures either the identity of Randolph Carter, an alter ego that Lovecraft has distanced in the story by inserting a new alter ego, the Providence author Ward Phillips, or the identity of Zkauba, the wizard of Yaddith; the revelation, like so many in the stories, is incomplete. Like the Duchess of Malfi these are characters "Plagu'd in Art," even though the terrifying objects, for all the melodrama, "are but fram'd in wax" (4.1.134–35); nor is this an idle comparison, for in "Supernatural Horror in Literature" Lovecraft had spoken with approval of Webster's "horrible gruesomeness" (*CE* 2.86). The several hands of these characters, even their severed hands, lead lives of their own. Even the shipboard hands who appear as occasional supernumeraries, as in "The Call of Cthulhu" (*CF* 1.53), support the motif through the inadvertent pun.

Frequently these hands either write or draw pictures—worth a thousand words, in part because they must yet be handled in words. The manuscripts of "The Call of Cthulhu" carry the story forward significantly; and in describing the apparition of the monstrosity, "poor Johansen's handwriting almost gave out" (*CF* 1.53). Wilbur Whateley's diary, in his odd cipher, is significant enough to be burned (*CF* 2.466), as is a piece of paper in "Cool Air," scrawled though it is "in an awful blind hand" (*CF* 2.20). Erich Zann communicates through notes, notes which he plays on his violin, notable for never being repeated, and handwritten notes that become manuscripts of explanation, unfortunately blown out the window when the wind bursts the pane in (*CF* 1.283–86); thus he fails to communicate that "mocking note" heard through the window pane (288). Especially fearful is Professor Peaslee's recognition of his own calligraphy, his own hand, in that alien book written before the birth of humanity (*CF* 3.450); and it is a pathetic moment when Danforth and the narrator of *At the Mountains of Madness* find "an empty ink bottle" and "a broken fountain pen" (*CF* 3.124). The threatening old man of "The Festival" writes with a stylus and tablet "in a very ancient hand" (*CF* 1.415). Various hands and calligraphies play a significant role in *The Case of Charles Dexter Ward;* Dr. Willett's hand trembles like his voice when he attempts to write of what he has seen (*CF* 2.219); and the common identity of Simon Orne and his son whom he has posed as is revealed through the man's penmanship (267). A scrawl left by a decomposing victim, a person dead but still able to write, forms the climax of both "Cool Air" and "The Thing on the Doorstep," just as manuscripts outlive the narrators of "Dagon," "The Temple," and "The Haunter of the Dark." The only scribal act that a character ever refuses, if he does refuse it, is Keziah Mason's demand that Walter Gilman write his name in her book with a "huge grey quill," his own blood providing the ink (*CF* 3.254). But if hands can no longer write they can employ sign language, as do the creatures in "The Shadow over Innsmouth" (*CF* 3.195). It is hardly necessary to mention the importance that such volumes as the *Necronomicon* play for Lovecraft in arranging the frameworks and allusions of his stories, despite the bogus nature of the book. Plutarch's *Lives* convinces Jervas Dudley in "The Tomb" to be as patient in waiting for his ancestral sanction as Theseus had been (*CF* 1.42), *Paradise Lost* provides the narrator of "Dagon" with images that help him imagine his experience (*CF* 1.55), and the Bible provides entertainment for the old man in "The Picture in the House" (*CF* 3.215). Since in these stories little is discoverable unless through a hand or a hand's extension, writing is crucial.

The significance of a person's hand, however, can lead to difficulties. Hands need to be decoded; the language may be so peculiar that a context needs to be constructed in order to ascertain the true meaning at hand. A typewriter, that model of contemporary clarity, may be used to disguise the identity of the author, as in "The Whisperer in Darkness." But Lovecraft would have been aware of Isaac's words when Jacob disguises himself as his brother Esau to delude their blind father: "The hands are the hands of Esau, but the voice is the voice of Jacob" (Gen. 27:22).[2] Disguised hands can be seen through, even by the blind. These qualities of a hand, the openness of its disguise and its opacity, suggest something uncanny about it. The thaumaturgic quality of hands appears in "The Dunwich Horror" when one of the men confronting Wilbur Whateley's brother "seemed to be raising [his] hands over [his] head at rhythmic intervals" (*CF* 2.462). These hands possess that seductive and miraculous appeal so striking in Heidegger's defense of Hitler when Jaspers charged that the man was totally uneducated: "Education is quite irrelevant . . . just look at his wonderful hands!" (cited in Safranski 232).

The work of our hands, paintings and photographs, even sculptures, abound in these stories. At the end of *The Case of Charles Dexter Ward* confirmation of the horror comes when Ward, that is to say Joseph Curwen, disintegrates to a fine, bluish-grey dust, as had "his accursed picture a year before" (*CF* 2.366). In "Pickman's Model" the recognition turns upon the painting that has been made of "*a photograph*

---

2. The hand in the Bible functions in a number of ways. In the Old Testament the hand of God often represents his anger: the hand is heavy (1 Sam. 5:11), and God will not stay it (Dan. 4:35). The famous sermon by Jonathan Edwards, "Sinners in the Hands of an Angry God," well expresses this usage. The little cloud like a man's hand at the confrontation between Ezekial and the prophets of Baal is an apocalyptic symbol of his victory at the coming rain (1 Kings 18:24). In the New Testament the phrase "at hand" is often used to express the imminence of judgment: the kingdom of God is at hand (Matt. 3:2 et al.), as is the end of all things (1 Peter 4:7). In the middle of Galatians Paul calls attention to his affection for the people by saying, "You see how large a letter I have written unto you with mine own hand" (6:11), for it was usually his custom simply to sign the epistles at the end—a habit of authentication which someone took advantage of in attempting to authenticate the forgery of 2 Thessalonians (Meeks 112n8). The hand functions as an authenticator when Jesus asks Thomas to place his hand upon the scars left by the nails and the spear at the crucifixion.

from life" (*CF* 2.272). Photographs play an evidentiary role in *At the Mountains of Madness*. In "The Whisperer in Darkness" photographs strike the naïve Wilmarth as "the product of an impersonal transmitting process without prejudice, fallibility, or mendacity" (*CF* 2.481). The clumsy illustration of cannibals in "The Picture in the House" requires a similar authentication from "a small red spattering" that falls from the second-floor abattoir (*CF* 1.217). The sculpture of Henry Wilcox offers tactile confirmation in "The Call of Cthulhu," even though he has no responsibility for it since he finds himself working at it as he wakes up (*CF* 2.25). The fascination that the tiara exerts upon the narrator of "The Shadow over Innsmouth" causes him to visit the town. With either immense skill or a woeful ineptitude, attempting to trace a horror that still eludes words, colors, and Euclidean perspective, these hands belong to artists; and frequently an identity is established between these artists and the narrators of the tales.

But the narrators may be more than simply artists. They are ghouls, whether actual or metaphoric; the word *ghoulish* runs throughout Lovecraft's career, often without any apparent appropriateness. In "The Statement of Randolph Carter" the protagonist and his friend Warren behave as ghouls when Warren descends into the depths of a graveyard; the word does not occur, but the recherché phrase "necrophagous shadows" does (*CF* 1.139). The narrator of "The Nameless City" finds himself at the end of the tale alone in "the ghoul-peopled blackness of earth's bowels" (*CF* 1.247). Whatever the narrator of "The Outsider" may originally be, by the end of the tale he rides with "friendly ghouls" (*CF* 1.272). The protagonists of "The Hound" are grave-robbers, "neurotic virtuosi" (*CF* 1.340), as is the magician they plunder. The narrator of "The Lurking Fear," rather like Wilcox in "The Call of Cthulhu," is a "connoisseur in horrors" (*CF* 1.352). And "supreme ghouls" (*CF* 2.343) are rife in *The Case of Charles Dexter Ward*. The corpse-eating cult of Leng decorates the fringes of Lovecraft's mythology. Metaphoric ghouls may be recognized by the interest these narrators often show in genealogical lore, like Ward who was "an antiquarian from infancy" (217), the young bicyclist in "The Picture in the House," the poor gentleman in "The Shadow over Innsmouth," or even the surveyor for the reservoir in "The Colour out of Space." The ghoul is Lovecraft's most authentic protagonist.

"Pickman's Model" is the classic development of the ghoul in Lovecraft's fiction. Not only does Pickman paint ghouls, he is himself a ghoul, as the derivation of the word, *to take, to seize*, suggests: *pickman* translates the Arabic *ghûl*. A ghoul is such by virtue of its long-fingered hands. One of the earliest uses of the word seems to have been in Beckford's *Vathek;* by 1824 the word was common enough that Washington Irving could use it metaphorically in "The Adventure of the German Student," a tale with which Lovecraft was familiar (*CD* 2.86).[3] The stu-

---

3. The word does not occur in Lovecraft's vade mecum to the English language, the dictionary of Dr. Johnson. Thus it is a rather modern word in the language, one of those significant moments of contemporary taste in Lovecraft's work.

dent, the protagonist who discovers at the conclusion that he has slept with a woman who has lost her head to the guillotine, "was, in a manner, a literary goul [*sic*], feeding in the charnal-house of decayed literature" (32). As a sign of the story's authenticity, one that is questioned, the narrator adds that it must be true since he heard the story from the protagonist, our literary ghoul, in a madhouse (36). Irving's "goul" is hardly an authentic author; and we wonder about Irving's spelling, whether he has been tempted into the false etymology of deriving the word from the Latin "gula," a rather low term for throat or gullet, and by extension appetite. Pickman is of course an old New England name, as are so many of the Whateleys, Dyers, Peaslees, and Danforths Lovecraft selected for the names of his protagonists, but he did not select them without thematic possibilities in mind; symbolism shines darkly through his realism. In *The Dream-Quest of Unknown Kadath* Pickman has become an actual ghoul (*CF* 2.134); and he presides as a patron of the Miskatonic University Expedition to the Antarctic in its sponsor, the Nathaniel Derby Pickman Foundation, undoubtedly named for a relative (*CF* 3.15). Lovecraft exhumed him repeatedly. But he had no need; the ghoul is always present at these stories. When the narrator of "The Picture in the House" invites a reader to taste the tale he is about to tell, his flattery of "the true epicure in the terrible," identifies the reader as a ghoul, a decadent, insatiable connoisseur of the bizarre (*CF* 1.206).

This notion of the ghoul as Lovecraft's prototypical figure puts a new light on the first story, "Hands," in Sherwood Anderson's *Winesburg, Ohio*. In the 1920s Lovecraft had dropped the book "half through from sheer boredom" (*SL* 1.283), distressed by its "dreary realism" (*DS* 48), but by the 1930s he confessed that Anderson was "one of those figures whom I respect as real & important artists"—though Anderson still put him to sleep (*JVS* 119). "Hands" tells the story of Wing Biddlebaum, a ridiculous pseudonym hiding his real name of Adolph Myers, a man disgraced because of the creativity and affection that his hands express, hands now forced to live a secret life of their own, "slender expressive fingers, forever active, forever striving to conceal themselves in his pockets or behind his back" (6–7). His innocence—or his inability to recognize his own impulses—fails to prevent him from keeping his hands to himself as he touches his students, an unconscious erotic language that almost leads the parents of the children to kill him. In Winesburg, after his fall, when he tries so hard to hide the shame of his hands, the hands as though with a life of their own have now "made more grotesque an already grotesque and elusive individual" (7). The sign of his paralyzed desire, his hands can no longer caress or instruct; when he forgets himself and they begin to play on the head of the narrator, he jams them back into his pockets and runs away, leaving the boy to think, "There's something wrong, but I don't want to know what it is" (9); the man becomes complicitous in trying to ignore the hands, the desire. So dead affection, the dead past, and the threat of death that stands in front of the man with no name every time the hands begin to live their own life again, this is the life of the ghoul that the man carries with him: "Although he still hungered for the presence of the boy, who was the medium through which he expressed his love of the man, the hunger became again a part of his loneliness and his waiting" (12). The last lines of the story describe him as a priest telling his rosary, but in fact his fingers are picking up crumbs of bread "with unbelievable rapidity" (12), an image of voracity, of subverted desire, rather than of sanctity. In reading Lovecraft's ghouls, we must be ready to perceive the furtive attempt to satisfy a transformed desire. For is not the ghoul, in the horror story de rigueur, an acceptable way to translate desire?

Not only are the narrators ghouls, feeding on the dead and on the expressions of the dead, on their vital salts and on their words, these narrators hardly make a secret of their own secrets. Though they deny any wish to speak out, they flaunt themselves in their secrets, often aggressively, for the secrets are the source of their pride. A phrase describing the slums of New York, "blatant, evasive" (*CF* 1.482), reveals the oxymoronic nature of this quality. The man in "The Lurking Fear" boasts, "I, and I only, know what manner of fear lurked on that spectral and desolate mountain" (*CF* 1.350), and the aesthete of "The Hound" seems to echo him: "I alone know why, and such is my knowledge that I am about to blow out my brains" (*CF* 1.339).

The secret frees the narrators from social restraints: Wilbur Whateley, who as well as Dr. Armitage could have been the narrator of "The Dunwich Horror," threatens, "it 'ud be a mortal sin to let a red-tape rule hold me up [from reading the forbidden *Necronomicon*]. . . . Maybe Harvard wun't be so fussy as yew be" (*CF* 2.435). The horror for which he searches releases him from the protocols of polite institutions. Surely even the sober, nameless narrator of *At the Mountains of Madness* bears a chip on his shoulder when he remarks, "It is an unfortunate fact that relatively obscure men like myself and my associates, connected with a small university, have little chance of making an impression where matters of a . . . highly controversial nature are concerned" (*CF* 3.13). Like Wilbur Whateley, albeit with some professional restraint, he now chafes at the protocols and hierarchies of the institutions society has erected to routinize knowledge, as he never would have before his experience had set him outside of usual experience.

This narrator must also strike us, as several of these narrators do, unjustly no doubt, as something of a confidence-man; for he asserts the authenticity of his photographs by admitting "the great lengths to which clever fakery can be carried" (*CF* 3.12). Twice he insists upon his veracity in his monograph, which "will shortly appear in an official bulletin of Miskatonic University" (94); his narrative, as we have it, may be regarded as an advertisement for that forthcoming monograph, whose publication will remain eternally imminent. The authoritative nature of higher education reveals its authoritarian aspect in his words. Peaslee in "The Shadow out of Time" exhibits a similar aggressive reticence: "It was . . . a frightful confirmation of all I had sought to dismiss as myth and dream. Mercifully there is not proof, for in my fright I lost the awesome object which would—if real and brought out of that noxious abyss—have formed irrefutable evidence" (*CF* 3.363). It is, of course, difficult for anyone dealing in such materials to seem credible; it is no wonder that Thurston at one point believed that Wilcox "had been imposing" upon his grand-uncle (*CF* 2.28). In one of the last stories a hard-headed lawyer accuses the indirect teller of the main narrative of being a faker, a forger, and a common crook (*CF* 3.318–20), though the man appeals to "the unmistakable style of Randolph Carter" (319); despite this appeal, however, and no matter how much sympathy the reader is tempted to show that style, the style of the story itself is no longer the style of the early stories in which Carter had appeared, because time, Lovecraft's time, has blurred the authenticity of his alter ego.

This quality of the bogus is not, however, confined to Lovecraft's narrators, but runs through other aspects of his work. Behind a pseudonym Lovecraft frequently employed lurks Lewis Theobald of the "monster-breeding breast" (Pope, *The Dunciad Variorum* 1.106), the original king of the dunces (Boerem 36–39). Lovecraft as well as Pope was aware that the word *dunce* derived from the Renaissance distrust of Duns Scotus. Years later in *The Dunciad* the whiff of plagiarism still hangs around Theobald:

> A past, vamp'd, future, old, reviv'd, new piece,
> 'Twixt Plautus, Fletcher, Shakespear, and Corneille,
> Can make a Cibber, Tibbald, or Ozell.   (1.284–86)

Abdul Alhazred, the author of the *Necronomicon,* was Lovecraft himself, a pseudonym he had adopted as a five-year-old in his first passion for *The Arabian Nights* (*SL* 1.122). In his essay on interplanetary fiction he wrote, "We should work as if we were staging a hoax" (*CE* 2.179). He uses the same language in his letters, as when in 1930 he claimed that "no weird story can truly produce terror unless it is devised with all the care & verisimilitude of an actual *hoax*," working to "build up a stark, simple account, full of homely corroborative details, just as if he were actually trying to 'put across' a deception in real life" (*DS* 244). Nevertheless, almost none of his typical stories, though full of regional and homely detail, are stark or simple. It is as though the act of the hypothetical lie were determined to complicate itself, to demand of its author a disjunction and displacement of those materials. This convolution had to befall a writer who tried to "devise a lie as carefully as a crooked witness prepares a line of testimony with cross-examining lawyers in his mind" (*DS* 244). Lovecraft is not one of the unacknowledged legislators of the world. A person who from an early age had considered all religions bunk, he finds himself compelled to use the language of guilt to describe his occupation. If caught out he is prepared to be held in contempt of court, so perhaps it is no surprise that the court of mainstream literary opinion did condemn him when Edmund Wilson sat upon that bench.[4] Though Lovecraft indignantly protested that he was not involved in the charlatanry that "concoct[s] the artificial junk which 'successful' commercial hacks pour forth to such financial advantage" (*WBT* 276), he did write

---

4. For more on this subject see the chapter "'The Outsider,' the Autodidact, and other Professions."

for *Weird Tales* and *Home Brew*, albeit without much remuneration.

One of the creatures central to his pantheon, Nyarlathotep, as Lovecraft described him in the letter that recounts his original dream of the figure, "was a kind of itinerant showman or lecturer who held forth in publick halls ... with his exhibitions" (*RK* 174). As a mighty messenger in "The Whisperer in Darkness" he is invoked to "put on the semblance of men, the waxen mask and the robe that hides, and come down from the world of the Seven Suns to mock" (*CF* 2.487). The suspicion Lovecraft expressed in 1923 that *The Waste Land* might be a hoax (*CE* 2.64) did not prevent him from using the pattern of those fragments shored against our ruin to help him construct the conclusion to "The Rats in the Walls" (St. Armand, *The Roots of Horror* 50), for which he also frankly lifted phrases from Fiona Macleod's "The Sin-Eater" (*SL* 1.258). And it could be argued that in that story the Exham Priory which Delapore is reconstructing functions more as a hoax than he realizes; "every attribute of the Middle Ages was cunningly reproduced," he assures us, as he adopts once more what he believes to be the original spelling of his name (*CF* 1.380–81); even an oak door is a replica of the original, although "with slits for ventilation" (387). He commits a hoax on his own dreams of ancestral glory, attempting to become an English gentleman through restoring the house to the former glories that he imagines it possessed, only to discover that those glories are a prettification, a facade that conceals the actual horrors of the place. The extreme of this forged quality are the shoggoths: "Formless protoplasms able to mock and reflect all forms and organs and processes—viscous agglutinations of bubbling cells— ... infinitely plastic and ductile—slaves of suggestion, builders of cities—more and more sullen, more and more intelligent, more and more amphibious, more and more imitative!" (*CF* 3.142). I shall later argue that despite the way in which Lovecraft represses any discussion of shoggoths they are yet his most central invention. And in this light he is very American: questions of authenticity had plagued Poe, Melville, and Clemens in the nineteenth century and still persist in our literature, for instance in Gass and Pynchon. Whether Lovecraft's narrators are ghouls, exhibitionists, pedants, hoaxers, or dunces, above all artists, it is a difficult group in which to repose confidence.

Finally we should notice that several of these narrators have no name. It might be argued that this device ensures the identification of the reader with the narrator; but that it is much more than a device is evident from its frequency and from the self-conscious way in which Lovecraft overtly probes it in "The Unnamable." In the short fiction and in the long fiction, "The Hound," "Dagon," "The Outsider," "Pickman's Model," "The Picture in the House," "The Colour out of Space," *At the Mountains of Madness*, or "The Shadow over Innsmouth," for which Lovecraft rejected the name Robert Olmstead which he had originally invented for the narrator (*The Shadow over Innsmouth* 106–7)—none of the protagonists have names. And in some stories the names prove to be ciphers, such as Pickman in "Pickman's Model," or such as Delapore or de la Poer in "The Rats in the Walls" (*CF* 1.374–75), whose name could as well be de la Peur, *of the fear*, and thus a mask rather than an identity; or perhaps we should take the word *pore* seriously and understand that the family is porous, with nothing of the solidity which the narrator imagines, as hollow as that unknown crypt beneath the house.[5] There is clearly a point in many of these stories where words do not function, a point often referable to the narrators.

Many of these narrators seem to be bending over water at crucial moments in their stories, a rather odd detail if we consider how often it is graves and earth-mould around which the classic horror story moves, unless the River Styx is more pervasive a myth than we realize. This element is clear in "Dagon" and "The Call of Cthulhu." The underground of "The Festival" is "washed by a wide oily river" (*CF* 1.413). But even in that early story "The Tomb" the ten-year-old Jervas Dudley discovers the tomb that shall transform him during the summer when "intoxicated with the surging seas of moist verdure" (*CF* 1.40). In "Facts Concerning the Late Arthur Jermyn and His Family," "The Hound," and "The Shadow out of Time" the narrators must cross the sea to discover the monstrous; and not only does Joseph Curwen traffic with the sea and marry the daughter of one of his captains, the first name of his antagonist, Dr. Marinus Bicknell Willett, identifies his marine antecedents. This story shares with "The Whisperer in Darkness" the motif of rivers pouring down ancient death, also present in *At the Mountains of Madness*. Madness trickles from the stars (*CF* 2.483), out of the abyss that hangs over the human world as well as from the abyss below that world. In "From Beyond" Tillinghast claims that the waves generated by his machine "will open up to us many vistas unknown to man" (*CF* 1.194). Madness comes in waves from every side.

Other waters in these stories include those of wells and marshes. Wells figure prominently in "Pickman's Model," "The Colour out of Space," *The Case of Charles Dexter Ward*, and out of all proportion in the underground sea of *At the Mountains of Madness*, a remarkable detail in the Antarctic landscape. A slight but telling example is the well into which the empty, authenticating locket is cast at the end of "Facts Concerning the Late Arthur Jermyn and His Family" (*CF* 1.183). The nightmare materials of "The Horror at Red Hook" pour "from unsealed wells of night" (*CF* 1.499). The catastrophe of "The Moon-Bog" is triggered by an attempt to defy "the curse awaiting him who shall dare to touch or drain the vast reddish morass" (*CF* 1.257).

Lovecraft's most interesting variation on this theme is the sea-marsh. "The Hound" is set in Holland, always threatened by the waters; and Innsmouth seems to be eternally crumbling and sagging into the ocean that it faces and the salt-marsh that cuts it off from the rest of New England. Even "The Dunwich Horror," which seems an exception to the pattern, is not, for the name of the village probably derives from a poem of Swinburne's, "By the North Sea," a paean to

---

5. Barton Levi St. Armand has pointed out that Lovecraft very probably had in mind Sarah Helen Whitman; a fiancée of Edgar Allan Poe, she had traced his name and her maiden name back to de la Poer: "So HPL's subtle naming device calls attention not only to his main theme of family degeneration and decline but also to the presiding high Gothic ancestry of his tale, and that hint of incest which characterizes both" (19). Lovecraft chose names for their several thematic resonances.

Death which concerns an English Dunwich that sank into the sea (Burleson, "Humour Beneath Horror" 7); the name signifies a town set next to a bay. Swinburne's "Dedicatory Epistle" addresses "the dreary beauty, inhuman if not unearthly in its desolation, of the innumerable creeks and inlets, lined and paven with sea-flowers, which make of the salt marshes a fit and funereal setting ... for the supreme desolation of the relics of Dunwich" (101)—might this not be Innsmouth? Perhaps Lovecraft had been sensitized by Poe's treatment of the imagery in "The City in the Sea." For a man raised in Providence, the ocean seems the natural place into which all returns, even an inland Dunwich. In any case, another model for Dunwich, Greenwich, Massachusetts, was flooded by the Quabbin Reservoir (Murray, "In Search of Arkham Country" 58–62); Dunwich had returned to the waters before Lovecraft ever wrote of it.

Several of these waters appear as mirrors. The narrator of "The Shadow over Innsmouth" recognizes his fate "that morning the mirror definitely told me I had acquired *the Innsmouth look*" (*CF* 3.229). And the poor ghoul of "The Outsider" can play with his kind beside those old waters of the Nile (*CF* 2.272), but the most significant water of that story is the implicit mirror, which at first he cannot see. Lovecraft's entry in his *Commonplace Book* recording the germ of "The Outsider" associates water and mirrors explicitly (*CE* 5.221; #42). Thus Charles Dexter Ward, after his ancestor has broken the mirror of his portrait and stepped forth, must appropriately become Charles Sinister Ward (*CF* 2.276–77); and we may wonder, reconsidering the imagery at the end of "Dagon," what it is that the protagonist in fact sees: "*That hand!* The window!" (*CF* 1.58). Windows are also important in "The Music of Erich Zann," "He," and "The Haunter of the Dark," at the conclusion of which another moment of confusion between the outside and the inside occurs.

It is clear that waters and mirrors function in something of the same way as windows, pictures, and photographs. But because these images are not stable, we cannot pluck out one of them, the mirror for instance, and treat it as the overarching category for the rest. In fact, as we have seen, the water imagery preponderates over mirror imagery, though the mirror and the double that is seen in it have long been considered central to the gothic enterprise; in Lovecraft the water imagery emphasizes that in the mirror the same is not the same; or rather that which is not the same, is. All these images are portals of discovery, both that through which something is uncovered and that by which it is uncovered; it is port and portage, the harbor and the way to the harbor, the burden and the person who carries the burden, both transparent and substantial. The danger the images bear a protagonist is their ability to transform themselves. Again "The Outsider" is one of the most significant of these stories, for the climactic moment occurs when the arch becomes a mirror. In "Pickman's Model" the painting, a work of the imagination, an internal discovery, becomes a photograph, an external discovery. Panes of glass shatter, waters stir, oceans sink to dry land; none of these portals remains stable, but always return a protagonist to the unexpected. The reasons and rationalizations for such transformations vary from story to story; character type as Elisabeth

Young-Bruehl[6] understands it, narcissist or obsessive or hysteric, is probably at play with the thematic and constructive needs of the story itself, so that it is difficult to say whether the images are pathological or literary. That is a part of the elusive delight, though also of the secretive, complicit guilt, of Lovecraft's fiction.

These waters and mirrors, pictures and hands, portals of discovery, are emblems both of the self and of the universe from which the self breaks off; as such a common emblem, the waters are random and infertile, salt waters, tainted wells, rivers of death, which represent the mechanistic materialism of Lovecraft's philosophic position (Joshi, *H. P. Lovecraft* 14). The waters mediate and divide the self and the universe, "wherein we have no part," as his essay on supernatural horror puts the case (*CE* 2.82). Peripheral to that world, in our logical constructs and representations, in our cultures and moralities and arts, we are the abnormal. Our "inner biological heritage" (83), to which Lovecraft so often recurs, our exile from our origins in the waves, assures our monstrosity through which we will always be discovered and pointed out by an awful hand. In these stories we have to see "the things that float and flop about you and through you every moment" (*CF* 1.199). And reflected in those waters we must be even less what we are. Ceaselessly questioning and authenticating ourselves, stepping back from ourselves and approaching ourselves, reaching out our hands, we are travesties. We are pastiche. Writing forgeries, we are forgeries ourselves, assured of our authenticity only insofar as we can point to our inauthenticity, the sense that we have that we do not fit.

And yet, in all finality, we are not broken off from the universe; a connection remains through which we are always returning to the break, fearful that we have not overcome it, not become an autonomous self but not capable either of discovering an authentic self. Like Oedipus we discover that our past is with us and of us, a connection that needs to be accounted for but which will not fully yield itself to our reason. Contingency and accident, the swirl of the atoms or the presence of the loving shepherd who rescued us from the exposure our father Laius threatens, accompany the break to forbid our fully dealing with our past. What is the style of Oedipus? Who has a hand in his identity? No text seems connected with his fate, but his father wrote the child's name in the child's flesh, the wound that shall become his name, puncturing the skin of his ankle to tie his feet together when exposed. Style is of the *stylus*, the pen; and Oedipus, Swelled Foot as Shelley translates the name, receives his fate, identity, and name, the self that he takes such pains to discover, from the same punctuation of the penknife, the pain so ancient he can no longer remember it; the pain leaves the scar, however, which he is accustomed to overlook. The self there amazes us by its standing off from us, of us and not of us at the same time. Like Narcissus and Tarzan, when we look into the waters we suffer a transformation at the moment of discovering the self. Like the House of Usher we discover a tendency to collapse into our own reflections and

---

6. See the chapter "*At the Mountains of Madness:* The Subway and the Shoggoth" for more details.

shatter them as we become one with them, just as Roderick and his sister collapse into one another's arms. Monsieur de Miroir barely lets us go before we return to him for further, incomplete information; when he releases us we depart, but at a loss without that inverted image.[7]

It is no wonder that Lovecraft's fiction plays so frequently with the Double and with the narrator's complicity in and final identity with the monster. Dr. Willett's superior comment, "It is no business of mine if any man seeks duality" (*CF* 2.364), which attempts to brush aside Joseph Curwen's claim that he was merely disguising himself, would be a prevarication in Lovecraft's mouth, for in his fictional world the most authentic characters do seek duality, trying to penetrate the disguise by which the self complicates itself through the simplicity, the camouflage, of quotidian living. The ghoul robbing the ghoul in "The Hound," the complicity of aesthete and Pickman, and the ecstatic degeneration of the narrators at the end of "The Shadow over Innsmouth," "The Rats in the Walls," and other tales are obvious examples of the doubled character who has found the self in the monstrous. Such stories of possession as *The Case of Charles Dexter Ward*, or "The Shadow out of Time," or the remarkable one flesh of the marriage in "The Thing on the Doorstep" also come to mind. The grotesque imitation of Akeley's hands and face is striking. And the last words of "The Dunwich Horror" have an especial plaintiveness in suggesting Wilbur Whateley's failure, both as man and monster: *"It was his twin brother, but it looked more like the father than he did"* (*CF* 2.466).

But we have to return to "The Outsider," an overt travesty of horrific materials, to face the full scope of this theme of imitation. In an overheated story, the language of the narrator at the moment of self-recognition, the moment in which the tongue finds itself released for an ultimate expression, is revealing: "It was a compound of all that is unclean, uncanny, unwelcome, abnormal, and detestable. It was the ghoulish shade of decay, antiquity, and desolation; the putrid, dripping eidolon of unwholesome revelation; the awful baring of that which the merciful earth should always hide" (*CF* 1.271). This is the style so many critics have found unbearable and unjustified. And though Lovecraft was capable of laughing at such a style while defending it, in such a story as "The Unnamable" (*CF* 1.397–99) or *The Dream-Quest of Unknown Kadath* (Joshi, *H. P. Lovecraft* 62), we must still ask how he intended that style to be understood.

Peter Penzoldt once wrote that Lovecraft "was influenced by so many authors that one is often at a loss to decide what is really Lovecraft and what some half-conscious memory of the books he read" (Joshi, *Four Decades* 64); we are reminded of Washington Irving's description of the author as ghoul. Lovecraft has in fact several styles (Joshi, *H. P. Lovecraft* 62–65), which for the purpose of a swift survey may be distinguished as the memoir, the documentary, the regional, and the fantas-

---

[7]. In writing "The Outsider" Lovecraft quite probably was influenced as much by Hawthorne's story as by his own notebook entry (see Schultz, "Commentary" to H. P. Lovecraft, *Commonplace Book* 2.28).

tic. The memoir belongs to the first-person voice which holds together much of his fiction, with such important exceptions as "The Dunwich Horror"; this is the voice of admonition, publicity, and justification. But there is no one tone to this voice. As several commentators have said, it changes during Lovecraft's career from the extravagant and fantastic to the meticulous, but is seldom one or the other. "The Outsider," as we noted, is extravagant, very much so in its vocabulary, but its opening paragraph is rhetorically sober. An example of the meticulous is the description of the alien bodies in *At the Mountains of Madness*: "Six feet end to end, 3.5 feet central diameter, tapering to 1 foot at each end. Like a barrel with five bulging ridges in place of staves. Lateral breakages, as of thinnish stalks, are at equator in middle of these ridges" (*CF* 3.37). The passage continues for another two pages, insistent on what is really there. This style shades off into the documentary, be it of diaries, letters, newspapers, paintings, or photographs, and most extremely the garbled tapes of "The Whisperer in Darkness," in which a "feeble, fiendish buzzing" can be barely distinguished (*CF* 2.488). Such is the transcription of the medieval hand in *The Case of Charles Dexter Ward* (*CF* 2.350). If the words of the memoir are insufficient to describe the actual horror, the narrators have recourse to indelible records, albeit, as they confess, such evidence may be forged.

The documentary shades off into the third style in several of the tales, the regional, often a dialectal record of such direct souls as the people of Dunwich, Ammi in "The Colour out of Space," or Zadok Allen in "The Shadow over Innsmouth," whose Yankee twang asks, "Haow'd ye like to be livin' in a taown like this, with everything a-rotting' an' a-dyn', an' boarded-up monsters crawlin' an' bleatin' an' hoppin' araoun'?" (*CF* 3.199). Dialect is difficult to render, difficult to decipher, and sometimes as difficult and opaque as the words of the *Necronomicon*: "Iä! Iä! Cthulhu fhtagn! Ph'nglui mglw'nafh Cthulhu R'lyeh wgah-nagl fhtagn—" (*CF* 2.33). How can we claim we pronounce the formulas properly? The regional thus shades off into the fantastic and the gorgeous hoax, those fragments from such documents as the Pnakotic Manuscripts or the *Book of Dzyan*, or such collaborations as the *De Vermis Mysteriis* introduced by Robert Bloch, *Unaussprechlichen Kulten* by Robert E. Howard, or the *Cultes des Goules* by August Derleth (Lauterbach, in Joshi, *Four Decades* 96); the foreign languages are de rigueur. This style may remind us of the more extravagant passages in the memoirs, before the narrator's dissolution into fear, incoherence, and oblivion.

Lovecraft is a flexible author with several styles, who can deploy his hand for several purposes. These styles shading into one another form a wheel: from the extravaganza or sobriety of a memoir, through documentaries, regionalisms, and fantasies, and thus back to the extravaganza. If any style has priority it might be the memoir, which is the most constructed, the most evident forgery on the part of the author, embracing and framing the others; this is the priority of the first-person narrative, with its various layers of confidentialities and deceptions. But the relation of the styles might be more truly described as that of Chinese boxes, one of which can enclose another, and that another. Each style attempts to deliver up the horror, to fix it in its essence, and each is a failure that *in extremis* seems a pastiche, perhaps even a hoax, for sometimes the style seems to say that it does not really mean it, that it is not serious; and insofar as the styles will not own up to their purposes they are not authentic. All these words seem mere copies and travesties, never the original horror; thus the quality of play arises that Arthur Jean Cox and others have perceived in the writing (52). In "The Outsider" and so much else of Lovecraft's fiction, it is a play that by circling on a central horror at once distances and mediates it.

We can put this problem of Lovecraft's styles in another way, however. A naïve analysis would claim that he has only two styles, one of them the style of his favorite authors of the eighteenth century, measured and sober and given to frequent parallelisms which suggest that the material of the story is in absolute control, but the other style a parody of Poe, ecstatic, gross and repetitious in adjectives, a style that is not in control at all. The problem is that we have no means of deciding which has priority. Are we to say that stylistic order is maintained only to break down, or that the ecstatic style, the true indication of Lovecraft's themes, is contained and betrayed by Augustan complacencies? This stylistic aporia is one reason for the difficulty of reading Lovecraft and coming to any conclusion about him, and it is probably one reason for the difficulty that he had about himself.

In the maze of these styles Lovecraft is looking for himself; but only in "a single and fleeting avalanche of soul-annihilating memory" (*CF* 1.272) does he seem aware that he finds himself in the climax of each and every story, for such a revelation is always a shocking event, one that erases itself from consciousness. The discovery is a momentary event, so swift that it seems to occur outside of time. It is an apocalyptic moment, and as such it is associated with death, one of the events of human life that seems to us most assuredly outside of time since it is that event which we have no time to express.

II

I will mock when your fear cometh. (Prov. 1:26)

This narrativizing of Lovecraft's stories, my apparent reduction of them to a monomyth, can take us only so far toward achieving a perspective upon his fiction. And this short account of his styles is frankly impressionistic. If the word is the man, we need to examine the vocabulary Lovecraft deploys in order to refine our perspective. For Lovecraft does have his own vocabulary to deal with the weird, the vocabulary to which he turns in the moment of release.

Some of that vocabulary he shares with other horror writers, such as *weird* or *ghastly;* some of that vocabulary seems peculiar to him, such as *foetor* or *eldritch*. To arrive at a better sense of that vocabulary I have made a survey of the stories, noting the words that he employs. Over time his vocabulary changed, but certain words remain constant and represent those aspects of the horrible that he wished to bring before the eye of the reader. Before surveying these words in detail, I would like to summarize two results: first, the vocabulary is considerably larger and more varied than we thought, a vocabulary within which the most peculiar words, like *eldritch*, actually play a small part; nevertheless, it is a finite vocabulary, with certain words artfully repeated in a single story and not so greatly in others and with certain words, background words such as *dread* and *fear* or thematic words such as *ghoul* and *mocking*, repeated in almost every story. Since this finitude of the vocabulary does become noticeable, it seems reasonable that one purpose of the documentary style that Lovecraft increasingly employed during his career was to expand the vocabulary.

Fortunately some of this analysis has already been performed by Steven J. Mariconda, who has written on the extent to which Lovecraft uses such spatial words as *kaleidoscopic, phantasmagoric, prismatic,* and *pageant* to signify the more cosmic aspect of his horror, that view of the universe that finds it random and indifferent, but ultimately beautiful ("Lovecraft's Cosmic Imagery"); in temporal imagery he uses such words as *rhythm, pulse, cycle, incarnation, aeon,* and *epoch,* words that despite the random nature of his universe suggest a pattern within it, at least an aesthetic pattern. Other words that deal with the total outside of the universe are *outside, outer, beyondness, cosmic, abysm,* and *chaos,* words that emphasize the ungrounded quality of Lovecraft's universe; so pervasive are these words, however, that the *outside* at which they point increasingly seems *alongside* or *inside*, words that he refuses to use. A word that seems purely affective, *vortex*, points at the aspect of the universe that he sees within the context of Democritus, Epicurus, and Lucretius; by extension, for Randolph Carter a phrase like "the atom's vortex" belongs to contemporary science, not to magic or marvel (*CF* 3.74).

The other side of this universe is that in its indifference it seems to behave as though it were in opposition to human desires. It is this aspect that justifies a liberal use of such words as *malevolent* and *malignant,* or the infrequent *nefandous* (but not even Herbert West earns that word of the melodrama, *nefarious*) or *infandous*. Only on occasion do the random and the intentional combine in an oxymoron such as "purposeful caprice," the course that a road takes in "The Whisperer in Darkness" (*CF* 2.520). More colorfully, there are the words that Lovecraft used merely for emphatic effect, perhaps unsupported by the course of the story to that point: *gruesome, grisly, ghastly,* or *grim,* exhibiting a pronounced taste for the consonant *g* or *gr, frightful* and *forbidden,* especially books; *outré, daemonic, diabolic,* and *appalling* (*shocking* indicates another level entirely); such words of self-accusation as *shameful, ignominious, putrid,* and *repulsive;* and such all-purpose background words as *portentous* and *ominous, horrible* and *horrifying, abominable, panic, dread, terror,* and *fear,* with its derivatives *fearful* and *fearsome.* These words are often used in connection with the *grand guignol* or the *conte cruel,* which Lovecraft considered a mere "dark realism," given to a "wrenching of the emotions . . . accomplished through dramatic tantalisations, frustrations, and gruesome physical horrors," a literature that is "less a part of the weird tradition than a class peculiar to itself" (*CE* 2.99). All of the words upon this level of Lovecraft's vocabulary are aimed at keeping a reader sensitized to that general anxiety he considered an appropriate response to the indifference of the material universe. We are always and only thrown upon ourselves.

Another level of the vocabulary occurs in such words as *ancient, archaic, antediluvian, immemorial, primal, primeval, primordial, old, elder,* and *eldritch,* which indicate other sources of fear, whether it be the enduring fatality of origins or the imminent threat of the body's falling apart in age. Unconsciously we inherit genetic propensities that appear at birth and compel us toward death, propensities that because they are unconscious always seem not to belong to us. *Eldritch,* one of the words most associated with Lovecraft, means primarily weird, with a possible connection to the word *elvish,* but the sound of the word, a very important element for his purposes, associates it with the imagery of age. These words place the weird at the temporal limits of human life. The weird itself finds expression in such words as *odd, queer, absurd, strange, uncouth, uncanny, curious, unorthodox, exotic, subtle, anomalous,* and *alien.* But *weird,* that all-important word, may be used dismissively, as when Francis Wayland Thurston describes his uncle's collection as "a weird bunch of cuttings, all told" (*CF* 2.30). But Thurston is not yet an initiate into the actuality of the weird. Perhaps the word is tainted because of its connection with the commercial exploitation of the weird in *Weird Tales,* an exploitation that Lovecraft is complicit in. All these words seem to function most often upon the level of the bodily response to the monstrous. The boundary of these words is formed by such words as *unnamable* or *unutterable,* indicating not simply the ineffability topos but the constraint or restraint that a character or the author suffers against speaking. The words point toward boundary experiences revealed in or symbolized by the basic experiences of birth and death, which everyone goes through but no one experiences.

This bodily response may take another form, one that finds the monstrous not so much an intrusion into the everyday world as a perversion of it. This response generates the vocabulary of disease that fills the pages of Lovecraft's stories, such words as *disease, blemish, blight, taint, mildew, infection, contagion, consumption, festering, fevered* and *febrile, anaemia, misshapen, nausea,* and *miasma.* Disease is an important detail in "The Shadow over Innsmouth," which initially gestures toward the *plague, pest,* or *epidemic* that has left the inhabitants with their "scabby" skin (*CF* 3.163); *scabrous* and *leprous* also appear. This group of words functions in three ways. First, it presupposes a condition which is healthy, proper, fit for humanity, at least a health that we imagine is proper, perhaps a health upon which we have communally agreed; but it asserts that such a normality is threatened by the disease that *bubbles, seeps,* or *slithers* outside or alongside everyday life. Imminent deformation always awaits the healthy life; we shall *decline* and *waste away.* Second, this threat is more than a matter of hypochondria, for in these stories the disease is very real, in some cases more real than the boring life which health leads. But third, we should note that several of these words are a part of a traditional anti-Semitic vocabulary, a code that may or may not display an ulterior motive (Julius 46–49).

Diseases can have several symptoms, but Lovecraft emphasizes one symptom to the exclusion of almost all others, the symptom of a bad smell. Evidence of wrongness may be a *musty*, *offish*, or *sickish* smell;[8] worse, it may be *fishy*, in the purely physical sense, *nitrous*, *mephitic* (not very often), *redolent*, *foul*, *poisonous*, *venomous*, *noxious*, *obnoxious*, or *noisome*, or it may have an *odour* (a word highlighted in the text through Lovecraft's preference for the English spelling); more bluntly it may be *malodorous*. Then we have the *stenches*, *reeks*, and *foetors*, a code word in the anti-Semitic vocabulary for the *foetor Judaicus* (Julius 20). One of the most intense references to this imagery may be the moment in *At the Mountains of Madness* when the shoggoth "oozed tightly onward through its fifteen-foot sinus" (*CF* 3.150); the neutral, erudite meaning of the word *sinus* does not rescue this passage from disgust, to say nothing of a touch of the ridiculous. Earlier the smells of the corpses of the Old Ones are *pungent*, *offensive*, and *acrid* (43).

Disease of the body is not the full horror, however, for words of mental disease infect the stories, at first *eccentric*, *unbalanced*, *overwrought*, *unstrung*, *nervous*, *anxious*, *uneasy*, or *disquieted*, suffering sometimes from *awkwardness*, *freakishness*, *vertigo*, or *epilepsy*, frank *idiocy* or *cretinism;* worse, a character may be *mad*, *insane*, *crazy*, *fevered*, *raving*, subject to an *aberration*, a *mania* or *monomania*, *seizure*, *frenzy*, *delirium*, *somnambulism*, *delusions* or *illusions*, *visions*, *hallucinations*, *phantasmata*, *possessions*, even *displacements* as the psychological metaphor becomes in the stories literal fact, *confusions*, and *hysterias*. A character or a landscape may be *blind* or *mindless*. For a materialist understanding of the world *myths*, *legends*, *dreams*, and *nightmares* are suspect, diseases of the imagination or impostures of clerical self-interest, though in the stories dreams often mirror a startling reality. The *amnesia* that Peaslee suffers in "The Shadow out of Time" is a special case, in which "fragments of some hideous memory, elaborately blotted out" disturb him (*CF* 3.375), fragments which are *disconnected* or *disjointed*, though characters are also subject to *forgetfulness*, *lapses*, *opiates*, *pseudo-* or *quasi-memories*, and *oblivion*. The wealth of this part of the vocabulary is quite striking. Another special case is *alienage* or *alienation*, easily derived from *alien*, a word that on the one hand is related closely to a special concern of several plots in the planetary alien, but on the other hand a word that reminds his contemporaries that the psychoanalyst is an *alienist*, such as those called in to treat Charles Dexter Ward. But though those alienists are failures because they cannot admit to a literal possession, the word is still effective in the fiction not only because an alienist forces the patient to reflect upon consciousness and to develop self-consciousness but also because an alienist forces the patient into self-division, into becoming a Double, and thereby of becoming fissured and wounded as well as aware that the wound, the trauma, was always present as a constitutive part of consciousness. The pressure of the spatial and temporal limits that we earlier discussed may find some expression

---

8. Lovecraft has a preference for words, mainly adjectives, ending in *-ish*. Colors are *blackish*, *greyish*, *yellowish*, *bluish*, or *greenish*. So much is *ghoulish*, *wolfish*, *vampirish*, *jellyish*, *freakish*, *feverish*, *dwarfish*, *sluggish*, *fiendish*, *hellish*, and *nightmarish;* it is no surprise that in such a world characters speak *gibberish* and have a tendency to *vanish*. This clumsy vocabulary refuses to assert anything directly, while cumulatively it functions with an onomatopoeic force that accompanies the water imagery of the fiction.

in this language, though it may have another source in the Oedipal apprehension of the monstrous.

Another threat to everyday life besides madness lies in another group of words, connected to the group of disease in two ways. This threat lies in *composite* or *amphibious* creatures, whether we are speaking of the monsters, so often described in terms that must appeal to a variety of earthly creatures, or speaking of the *half-breeds* that populate the world outside of Providence or Boston or Arkham where most of Lovecraft's protagonists live. These *half-breeds* are *mongrels, hybrids, half-castes,* of *mixed blood, mulattos,* or *mestizos.* In "The Call of Cthulhu" they are Kanakas and Lascars, sailors, and "waterfront scum" (*CF* 2.48), just as in other stories they are *spawn,* another anti-Semitic code word rather like *rat* (Julius 45–46, 103). In *The Dream-Quest of Unknown Kadath* the slaves of the merchants of the moon are only "approximate human beings" who, "without turbans or shoes or clothing, did not seem so very human after all" (*CF* 2.115). Brown Jenkin, the rat with the bearded face, is one of the "quasi-animals and queer hybrids" that witches employ as familiars (*CF* 3.260). Some of the monsters in the fiction are frankly hybrids, the tentacular Wilbur Whateley and his brother and the people with gills who bear the Innsmouth look. One of the first signals of danger in "The Shadow over Innsmouth" are the monsters, "half ichthyic and half batrachian" upon the tiara in the museum (*CF* 3.168), a muted suggestion of the miscegenation that follows. The hybrids are both less than his protagonists insofar as they are only half, divided and incoherent, but also more insofar as they embody a broader experience.

Not only is the body diseased, but so is the language, a *babel* of *polyglots, patois, mouthings, jargon, dialects* which both monsters and protagonists *babble, slaver, gibber,* and *cachinnate,* with a vocabulary that is often *guttural, stilted,* or *archaistic,* a vocabulary that is only partially intelligible. Sometimes the voices are *raucous,* other times they *crack* and *croak;* Wilbur Whateley's brother can only achieve "acoustic perversions" (*CF* 2.463). The voices of the creatures in "The Shadow over Innsmouth" are "slopping-like" (*CF* 3.164). The entities in Joseph Curwen's underworld *whine, howl,* and *yelp,* words that suggest the bestial and thus refer to the theme of the composite being. Most hybrids and creatures are not equipped to produce a human sound, though they seem eager to attempt it. In the *Necronomicon,* "the wind gibbers with [the Old Ones'] voices, and the earth mutters with Their consciousness" (*CF* 3.434); Dr. Armitage, however, mutters also (*CF* 3.436), as does the Miskatonic next to Arkham (*CF* 3.326). Peculiar to "The Shadow over Innsmouth" is the bleating, howling, and barking of the frog-fish. "The Whisperer in Darkness" also contains a special case, not only the *whisper* of the title—and Joseph Curwen also speaks in a "husky, ... hoarse whisper" (*CF* 3.310, 315)—but also the buzz or drone which is both human and inhuman, spoken by the Mr. Noyes who is not only full of noise but also noisome; that buzzing, however, is an exception to most of the alien voices in the fiction which seem to verge upon the liquid. *Whisper* resembles *whistle,* the sound of terror in "The Shadow out of Time," and both of the words are related to the *pulsing* and *piping* that accompany the celebration conducted around Azathoth at the center of the universe. Degraded as these sounds are, they do occasionally partake of the spatial and temporal patterning of the universe.

Above all, in a word that recurs frequently, these tongues, sounds and much else within the landscape are *blasphemous,* tongues that like disease depend upon a notion of rightness or sacrality or health; blasphemy exists because God and a right way to speak about God exist Blasphemy transgresses or parodies the sacred; but not only the sacred of orthodoxy, it also parodies and mocks the habits, preconscious beliefs, and trusts that humanity places in the stabilities of its everyday life, just as the *obscene* or the *impious* attack the moral sense. This notion of the blasphemous has application to Lovecraft's frequent mention of *non-Euclidean angles* which are *crooked* or *slanting,* off the true of a normative, everyday experience. In "The Call of Cthulhu" these are "crazily elusive angles of carven rock where a second glance shewed concavity after the first shewed convexity. . . . One could not be sure that the sea and the ground were horizontal, hence the relative position of everything else seemed phantasmally variable" (*CF* 2.52). The sickness and hybridism infect space itself and the vocabulary through which we render it, the geometrical truisms inherited from Euclid, so that space becomes a blasphemy upon the world as humanity lives it. Geometry and mathematics, however, are not innocent in themselves. When Walter Gilman asks what has seduced him, mathematics leads the list (*CF* 3.266). Beyond the question of Lovecraft's own difficulties with algebra (*IAP* 127), he certainly expresses the repugnance to quantitative rather than qualitative knowledge that so many of the Romantics expressed, a repugnance he does not overcome despite his objective awareness that a contemporary view of the universe was thoroughly dependent upon mathematics. Mathematics represents a world divorced from sensory experience, and thereby a world at odds with everyday experience, a world that is blasphemous.

Disease, hybridism, and a blasphemous tongue and space are related to another theme, the *amorphous* or *formless* condition of the monsters that appears with such monotonous, obsessive regularity. They are a *protoplasm* or *jelly, polypous,* a *viscous, porous, gelatinous,* sometimes *agglutinative, oily, elastic,* or *spongy liquefaction* which exhibits an odd *plasticity;* they *wallow, splash, surge, seethe, bubble,* and *lap.* To allow for such qualities the landscape becomes *damp, dank,* and *humid,* a *marsh* or a *swamp,* which like *spawn* and *hybrid* can also function as anti-Semitic code words (Julius 45–46). Alluding to the image of the vortex, which in this mode is a *whirlpool* or *hurricane,* the monsters *engulf* or *suck* their victims; the "maelstrom" of the slums through which Charles Dexter Ward walks is a manifestation of the same imagery (*CF* 2.224). The threat the monsters represent may be one of the reasons for Lovecraft's insistence upon the thoroughly considered structure of each story, despite his insistence upon the story's atmosphere; structure articulates what otherwise might dissolve into mere atmosphere, represented by the purely emotive words with which we began this survey. The threat is real in the stories, for the characters are often reduced to the state of the monsters, puddles upon the floor, a *mass, slime,* or *pool,* a "liquescent horror" at the conclusion of "The Thing on the Doorstep" (*CF* 3.357). Perhaps the only character spared this fate, because of his own personal dignity, is Joseph Curwen, who dissolves into "fine bluish-grey dust" (*CF* 2.366)—yet even that dissolution is also a *transformation* or *recapitulation,* words that point once more toward the language of the swamp from which humanity has arisen as well as toward the boundary experience of birth. It is to this unachieved form that the *"unfinished"* thing with its "deficiencies" refers in *The Case of Charles Dexter Ward,* a thing that is "neither thoroughly human, nor wholly allied to any animal" (261), lacking as both a human and a beast, a hybrid that cannot fulfill itself as either beast or human. The *fog, cloud, mist,* or *vapour* that curls, thickens, and *spirals* after the narrator of *At the Mountains of Madness,* in other works the *haze, exhalation,* or *emanation,* is a version of this imagery of the plastic and the insufficient, as is the "slippery-looking substance" which Walter Gilman sees in his dreams (*CF* 3.249). So omnipresent and so powerful is this liquidity that the characters may become those waters into which they stare and which reflect them. Moreover, as we have earlier suggested, as these characters *dissolve* their hands dissolve also, *scrawled, blotted,* or *smeared,* at the conclusion of "Cool Air" written with a "blind hand" (*CF* 2.20), at the conclusion of "The Thing on the Doorstep" quite "awkward, coarse, and shaky," properly written on "paper impaled on the end of a long pencil" (*CF* 3.355). As bodies deliquesce, hands do also.

III

"It goes to the very soul of me to speak what I really think of my face." (Addison 4.20; No. 306)

All these words, this vocabulary that pervades the stories and is released in a sudden, dense outpouring when the moment of recognition occurs, suggest the background to Lovecraft's dread: a dread of the spatial and temporal chaos that randomly falls into apparent patterns, and a dread of the indifference of that universe; a dread of the genetic possibilities manifested in birth and death, and thereby a dread of life itself; a dread of physical and mental disease, and a dread of the repulsive symptoms, especially of hybridism; a dread of language when it sickens and of the blasphemy that erupts from it; and finally a dread of the deliquescence toward which all these experiences tend. Now we need to describe in more detail the figure that walks out of this background and embodies it, the ghoul. If disease, the half-breed, and the half-breed's language live off health, the ghoul lives off death, a life that has lost its health and wholeness; and the ghoul is the fetish of Lovecraft's imagination. He appears forthrightly in "Pickman's Model," but he is mentioned albeit as though simply a figure of atmosphere in many other stories—in "The Outsider" as a character mentioned, for no clear reason, at its conclusion, in "The Picture in the House" as a near relation to the old man. But the word *ghoulish* appears as a free-floating adjective in most of the stories; the ghoul infects the air that Lovecraft's characters breathe. Yet the ghoul does not seem to represent a great threat, for *weak, feeble, clumsy, furtive,* and *lurking* are words often associated with it. Either it lives off the dead because it does not have the energy to deal with the living, or it is so frail and half-lifeless because it feeds only on the dead. Yet this description is not complete, for the ghoul has also a secret, aggressive energy, a paradox developed in the old cannibal of "The Picture in the House" and in Pickman.

The ghoul, however, wishes merely to engorge the dead body—the simplicity of its desires allows it to function with such metaphoric power in the stories. A more particular kind of the ghoul is the psychic ghoul who attacks the human protagonist through imitation. The very early story "The Tomb" concerns a man from the past who psychically possesses his descendant; yet that story cannot avoid an oblique reference to the simple delights of the ghoul in the phrase "charnel conviviality" (*CF* 1.48). Nyarlathotep is, among other roles, such a psychic ghoul in "The Whisperer in Darkness," for he is the apparent object of that story's peroration, the "sorcerer, emissary, changeling, outsider" who has achieved the "resemblance—or identity" of Akeley (*CF* 2.538). The entity in "The Colour out of Space" is described in similar language, fastening itself upon the Gardners and draining the life from them (*CF* 2.384); clearly there is something of the vampire about this creature, and a form of the vampire appears in "The Shunned House." Curwen and Asenath's father are two other of these creatures, preying upon the identity of the protagonist by either imitating or overwhelming it. With a certain elision of the cannibal and the ghoul, Delapore in "The Rats in the Walls" devours the plump Norrys, whereas Ephraim Waite and his daughter devour the flabby Edward Derby. And when any of these creatures achieve the goal of devouring the substantial Other, the achievement reveals the frailty of the creature. In all these metamorphoses of the ghoul, however, let us never forget Washington Irving's "literary goul," who presides as the author, the only begetter, over all these others.

The imagery of the ghoul is scattered throughout the fiction. The *cormophytic* or *saprophytic* fungus, feeding off a dead log or off dead, rotten matter is a sign of a ghoulish presence, even in so striking a phrase as "the bloated, fungoid moon" that appearing near the conclusion of "The Shadow out of Time" surely means more than that the moon looked like a mushroom (*CF* 3.448). Giving off a slight phosphorescence, the grotesque fungi of "The Shunned House" are "detestable parodies of toadstools and Indian pipes" (*CF* 1.455), an indication that most of Lovecraft's fungi are not those of the waking world.

It is no accident that so many doorways are *mouths* that *yawn* and *gape*. The word *grotto* appears only in two stories, perhaps because of the connection of the word with a Augustan culture of politesse: in *The Dream-Quest of Unknown Kadath* (*CF* 2.131); and in "The Rats in the Walls," where it takes the form of the vaguely solipsistic clause, "not Hoffmann nor Huysmans could conceive a scene ... more Gothically grotesque than the twilit grotto" (*CF* 1.393), a grotto that lies beneath the Abbey the narrator has reconstructed at great cost. But in contrast to *grotto*, the word *grotesque* is ubiquitous. Other words of the underworld are very present, however, the *mazes, labyrinths, warrens* (the word does not occur in "The Statement of Randolph Carter," but Harley Warren, the polyglot who descends into a graveyard and is absorbed by the earth, carries his warren with him), *passages* with *groined ceilings, burrows, tunnels, crypts,* and *catacombs* which suggest as much the peristaltic action of the underground as its enigmatic nature; and the fact that it is so often *honeycombed* indicates how hollow and hungry it is. This landscape is embodied in the death of Walter Gilman, who has "virtually a tunnel through his body—something had eaten his heart out" (*CF* 3.271). It is no accident that the ruins over which characters clamber in several stories are *Cyclopean,* an allusion rendered explicit in "Dagon" when "Polyphemus-like" the creature clambers across its Cyclopean monolith (*CF* 1.57–58), or when Cthulhu "on the masonry of that charnel shore . . . slavered and gibbered like Polypheme cursing the fleeing ship of Odysseus" but "bolder than the storied Cyclops" pursued the ship into the waters (*CF* 2.54). Not only is Polyphemus a cannibal, but his eye, the symbol of his relation to the sun god, is extinguished by a nobody, an *outis,* and his appeal to his father Poseidon is effective only in part; someone always escapes, the I-only to escape, to relate the story of the "storied," perhaps "storeyed," creature that pursues us. Yet, in truth, all that really escapes in most of these stories is the story itself, the untrustworthy words. The ghoulish mountain pursues us across the ghoulish sea, while the gibbering of these creatures leers from the misshapen, *gibbous* moon.

This landscape does not only ingest; sometimes it also vomits and utters. "The Whisperer in Darkness" concerns a Vermont landscape where, it is rumored, "a hidden race of monstrous beings . . . lurked somewhere among the remoter hills—in the deep woods of the highest peaks, and the dark valleys where streams trickle from unknown sources"(*CF* 2.469). A variety of sources are active, however. Some stories come from newspapers, but "one yarn had an oral source" (468), and some "reports from different sources tended to coincide" (469). These sources, however, do not all coincide, and the streams bring down bizarre kinds of matter, some of them, perhaps, "the battered and bloated bodies of human beings" (469), whereas others bring down "organic shapes not quite like any . . . ever seen before" (468). The significant word of both passages is *trickle;* so often rumors or creatures or deadly knowledge *trickles, seeps,* or *filters* down from the stars, oozing into human life from outside experience and infecting it with something deformed. The most concrete symbol of this possibility is the *well.* In each case something is being reported that disrupts experience and language. These two modes, the descriptive and the narrative, combine in a later passage when Akeley gradually tells Wilmarth "of the pits of primal life, and of the streams that had trickled down therefrom; and finally, of the tiny rivulet from one of those streams which had become entangled with the destinies of our own earth" (483). The same rhetoric occurs in "Herbert West—Reanimator" when the awful source of a warning turns out to be "a large covered vat in [the] corner" (*CF* 1.319). The landscape is in pursuit, but it is also admonitory, a voice that warns the protagonist that as the food of a ghoul he is already dead.

Perhaps nowhere is this animated landscape so clear as in the dream landscape of *The Dream-Quest of Unknown Kadath*, perhaps because it is so patently the landscape of a dream, especially in the landscape of mountains that "squatted . . . like wolves or ghouls, . . . those dog-like mountains carven into monstrous watching statues" (*CF* 2.169), surrounding Randolph Carter's approach to the "squat windowless building" where sits the Priest of Leng (172). The entire passage is a reminiscence of the climactic moment to Browning's poem, "Childe Roland to the Dark Tower Came": that tower is a "round squat turret, blind as a fool's heart," surrounded by hills that "like giants at a-hunting lay, / Chin upon hand, to see the game at bay" (ll. 182, 190–91). It is a landscape that the narrator almost does not recognize: "Dunce, / Dotard, a-dozing at the very nonce, / After a life spent training for the sight!" (ll. 178–80). Browning's paranoid desert is heightened in Lovecraft's narrative by the mitred double heads of these creatures that later receive an apotheosis in the monstrous mountain, certainly alive also, at the top of which rests the onyx castle and the mocking presence of Nyarlathotep (*CF* 2.169, 197), another version of the composite creature imagery, by all of which Carter, though a trained dreamer, is also caught off-guard.[9] In addition, the tower and the mountains are described in the word *squat,* whether as verb or noun, a word that Lovecraft frequently uses to describe his mongrels and which he often applies to Jews in his letters (*FFF* 534). The racist undertones of the word are evident in the "squat, hellish, yellow fiends" (*CF* 1.67) that threaten an ideal culture in "Polaris." In the clumsy early tale "The Lurking Fear" the degenerates are "squatters" (*CF* 1.351), the rubbery-looking body of Cthulhu that Wilcox has sculpted squats upon its pedestal (*CF* 2.31), and the New England houses of "The Picture in the House" squat upon the landscape (*CF* 1.207). The mongrels, monsters, and monstrous landscapes are firmly opposed to the upright Nordic ideal. Despite the vertical quests of Lovecraft's characters, the figures they encounter are almost always hugging the earth.

The mockery involved in the climactic scene of Browning's poem (l. 184) is also typical of the Lovecraftian landscape; for *mockery* and several other words like it appear in a great number of the stories for no clear reason. The "synthetic mockeries" that Herbert West concocts are an early example of this motif (*CF* 1.321). As a late, more complex example, in "The Shadow out of Time" Peaslee when possessed speaks with a "veiled mockery" (*CF* 3.368), as though he were an incarnation of the Priest of Leng to whom Lovecraft alludes in other stories. Often the mockery appears simply in the *sardonic* or *saturnine* face or the *sardonic stare*. But faces, windows, and houses also *titter, leer, chuckle, grin, grimace, peer,* and *stare shyly* or *repulsively* or, like the portrait of Joseph Curwen, *blandly*. Of these words *mock* and *leer* are especially significant. *Mock* may mean to ridicule or deride verbally, but the word has come to mean more broadly a wide range of non-verbal aggressions. A simple jest or scoff may be implied, as when Cowper writes in *The Task*:

---

9. In *Supernatural Horror in Literature* Lovecraft speaks with great admiration of Browning's "hideous poem" (*CE* 2.84).

> Here grotto within grotto safe defies
> The sunbeam: there emboss'd and fretted wild,
> The growing wonder takes a thousand shapes
> Capricious, in which fancy seeks in vain
> The likeness of some object seen before.
> Thus nature works as if to mock at art.   (5.117–22)

But more seriously *mock* can mean to ridicule by imitation or by counterfeit, to deprecate through duplication. This meaning occurs in this passage from Young's *Night Thoughts*:

> For what live ever here?—With labouring step
> To tread our former footsteps? pace the round
> Eternal? to climb life's worn, heavy wheel,
> Which draws up nothing new? to bid each wretched day
> The former mock? to surfeit on the same.   (3.329–33)

Except for such different purposes, this passage has the ring of so many atheistic sermons in Lovecraft's letters. The combination of mockery and feeding in the last line is subtly compacted in Shelley's "Ozymandias." The artist of the monument to the king mocks the passions that he reads upon that face and thereby the heart that fed upon those passions, "The hand that mocked them, and the heart that fed" (l. 8), though the collapsed syntax suggests that the artist himself feeds upon those passions too in order to make the work, whether upon those passions of his patron or those of his own heart; mockery and feeding are complicitous. But besides these critical connotations, *mock* can mean to deceive, to impose upon, or to delude; at worst it can mean to defy, to denigrate, or to set at naught, as though the thing mocked had no right to exist. It is at this last level that the persistent mockeries of Lovecraft's world function, for it is as though the large-scale and the small-scale structures of the universe, revealed within the level of human experience, were in conspiracy to set every human value and aspiration at naught; the human has no right to exist here. "Either I was dreaming," Peaslee says of his hand upon the ancient page, "or," he adds ambiguously, "time and space had become a mockery" (*CF* 3.442), categories that denied him or categories that denied themselves.

More sinister than the word *mock* is the word *leer*, since it as much suggests sexual temptation or aggression as it does mockery; the *leer* mocks you with your own unconfessed desires. When Satan first comes upon Adam and Eve, watching their embraces, his reaction is clear: "Aside the Devil turn'd / For envy, yet with jealous leer malign / Ey'd them askance" (*Paradise Lost* 4.502–4). That leer overleaps his own nature, suddenly sexualized and eager to accuse their affection, "Imparadis't in one another's arms" (506), because he knows that one aspect of his hell is his "fierce desire, / Among our other torments not the least, / Still unfulfill'd with pain of longing pines" (509–11). The leer of the accuser represents the attack of nothingness upon the possibility of human tenderness. As Peaslee scrambles through the rubble of the dead city to meet himself, "Physical sensation was dead, and even fear remained as a wraith-like, inactive gargoyle leering impotently at me" (*CF* 3.426). Buildings, windows, carvings, mountains leer upon the characters. It is as though the entire landscape shared a joke that the protagonist knows nothing of, probably because the protagonist is in fact the object of the joke, obscurely knows that, and wishes not to know it. The landscape may be *suggestive* or *provocative;* aspects of it may be *provoking,* challenging or merely annoying, depending on the response of the character. The houses of Arkham "leered mockingly" at Walter Gilman (*CF* 3.234). Brown Jenkin, a "diminutive hybrid" that sucks blood "like a vampire" and can "speak all languages," has "a kind of loathsome titter" and thus combines the themes of the ghoul, the babel, and the mocker (236).

One product of this *leer* is a particular kind of irony. "The Thing on the Doorstep" draws a distinction between "the profound and very genuine irony" of Asenath, an irony that was "grim, basic, pervasive, and potentially evil," and "the flashy, meaninglessly jaunty pseudo-irony" which Derby had once practiced (*CF* 3.342); a few pages later this "deep irony" is associated with "the competent personality" so foreign to Derby's true nature (351), as though the inauthentic were associated with competence and the authentic with incompetence, as though the authentic personality were the one in which Lovecraft's several protagonists, whether Derby, Ward, or Carter, experience failure. But simple capability is not itself a sign of inauthenticity, for Peaslee at the opening of his story, erudite, married, trusted, is certainly capable—and boring, leading a life of everyday inauthenticity. We recognize a much greater degree of authenticity in Peaslee when that dull capability is shattered, just as Ward has more authenticity when he realizes that he shall be destroyed by the Double he has summoned, overlooking the possible consequences. For Joseph Curwen is a touchstone; one of the points of his "sardonic arrogance" is that he seems "to find all human beings dull" (*CF* 2.230), and this arrogant condemnation has a certain rightness to it, because whether he is authentic or not he has the ability to see through the inauthentic in others. Peaslee, a man who had enjoyed "no flaw in [his] original personality," now feels "that some artificial psychological barrier" had been created against his painful quasi-memories (*CF* 3.373), a barrier which he cooperates in when he constructs "a really effective bulwark" that rationalizes those memories (*CF* 3.392). This barrier and bulwark, however, still represent the division from which he suffers; and the story represents the moment in which he overcomes the barrier. Capability and competence is also *self-possession*: the narrator of *At the Mountains of Madness* tries to keep a "tight hold" upon himself as he and Danforth escape (*CF* 3.155); his failure to keep a hold on himself indicates where true authenticity lies, in his failure and admission that the self-possession of the everyday world is a chimera.

Authenticity, let us admit, is a word that, given the contemporary critique of essentialism, we use in this study with some skepticism, especially insofar as we wish to avoid its optimistic associations. We do not want to use it as "a blessing from above" (Adorno, *The Jargon of Authenticity* 11). If in any way achievable, authenticity has to be worked out from within the human condition; it is not a value in and of itself. The attempt to be *eigentlich,* Heidegger's term which is translated as "authentic" or "self-possessed," runs the danger of being *eigenheitlich,* idiosyncratic, or *eigensinnig,* willful or obstinate, as Lovecraft is when he implies that New York, where "values are forced & arbitrary, mental fashions are capricious, pathological, or commercial" (*DW* 48), is inauthentic—because of the Jews. Yet we do not wish the skepticism of our treatment to be taken as a denial of the moral force of the search for authenticity, a search which is rendered quite problematic in the case of Lovecraft's fiction if we understand by authentic that which is not counterfeit, since it is the very possibility of the authentic which this fiction seems to attack. As commonly understood, the authentic either proceeds directly from its author or is traceable to its author with no disjunction; a manuscript is authentic if Lovecraft wrote it *propria manu,* not if an amanuensis did, or a story is authentic if Lovecraft wrote it, not if August Derleth did. In Heidegger's analysis, existence belongs to the subject but it may be inauthentic if the subject lets it slip, overlooks it, or behaves in a mechanical manner. If I am authentic, I possess myself or, as Heidegger later understands the matter, allow myself to re-possess the self-possession that was always mine, whereas I am inauthentic if I become dispossessed or possessed by another (Zimmerman 243–76); I am inauthentic especially if I am possessed by the unexamined beliefs of my ancestors or of my contemporaries in everyday life. In Lovecraft, the other who possesses me is often a powerful individual who denies vulnerability and disclosedness, an individual who from the protagonist's point of view is deeply committed to the lie. And this inauthentic character is ubiquitous, even in the mocking landscape. How can the authentic exist in this fiction if the hoax is everywhere? How can the fiction be serious if mockery arises so often at its climax? The authentic is very hard to come by.

Authenticity, Heidegger argues, must also be understood in a person's relation to time and place, the conditions of existence within which a person makes choices. An authentic act lies in the recognition of one's time and place and owning them, perhaps even owning up to them (Zimmerman 19); so one of the most authentic acts in Lovecraft's life may well have been his recognition that New England, its traditions, its present, and its possibilities, tragic in his view, was indeed his home and his subject, a place and time for which he had to answer. But Heidegger further argues that authenticity is severely limited today by *Technik,* a science and technology that reduces the world to objects which humanity strives to dominate (Zimmerman 219–24), a world in which no relation exists and in which the unprotected individual is always departing (Heidegger, *Holzwege* 270–71). In this regard Lovecraft's authenticity suffers because though he develops themes he found in Joseph Wood Krutch's *The Modern Temper* and Edward J. O'Brien's *The Dance of the Machines*[10] and condemns the ubiquitous machine culture that threatens tradition, he nevertheless does believe in the scientistic vision; the individual is an object, no

---

10. We will examine Lovecraft's relation to O'Brien's book in detail in our last chapter.

more than an object, which a world of contingent objects sweep aside. Taking this stance in his letters Lovecraft mocks any possibility of taking a resolute attitude toward an individual death, the extreme point at which Heidegger perceives a chance for the most authentic act a person is capable of.

If we ask why this mockery is so pervasive, within the landscape and within Lovecraft, our answer shall be quite provisional, not because we do not have a sense of the inauthenticity that seems so spontaneously to arise in our lives but because that inauthenticity has so many means by which to disguise itself. The reason for the mockery is easy to discover, but its terms neither easy nor simple; the inauthentic is a master of involution, indirection, and misdirection. In only a few situations does something or someone openly *laugh* at a character: the stare is *sly*, ghouls are *furtive* and *evasive*, often like so much else in the stories *lurking*. Ghouls are not only thieves but thieves filled with a perverse appetite, yearning for what others find sickening, abhorrent, and taboo; so *lurking* involves not only thievery but sexual ambush. Milton's usage is telling: Gabriel vows to find Satan "In whatsoever shape he lurk" (*Paradise Lost* 4.587); Adam calls Satan "the lurking Enemy / That lay in wait" for Eve (9.1172–73); and Satan himself accuses Belial of the amours of Jove—"how thou lurk'st / [. . .] to waylay / Some beauty rare" (*Paradise Regain'd* 2.183–86).

Inauthenticity, then, is not simply a lack or an overlooking as Heidegger would have it; as an evil it is not privative but positive, driven by desire and aggression, by *imposition* or *imposture,* by *charlatanry* or *counterfeit,* by a *trick, fakery, fraud, forgery,* or *hoax*. The *masquerade* is the ceremonial occasion of the *mask*. *Chimerical* is used at least once to mean *fraudulent* (*CF* 2.326), for it is a composite creature, a quality that led Horace to allude to it at the beginning of the *Ars poetica* as an example of bad art. The giant black slaves of Nyarlathotep carry wands with tips carven into "leering chimaeras" (*CF* 2.204). The characters themselves are *parodies* or *travesties*. In the climax of "The Moon-Bog" the narrator sees "a monstrous resemblance—a nauseous, unbelievable caricature—a blasphemous effigy" of Denys Barry, the man who had dared attempt the emptying of the bog (*CF* 1.264). In an episode of "Herbert West" the dead Dr. Halsey is resurrected as "a malformed ape or anthropomorphic fiend . . . the mocking, unbelievable resemblance" to himself (*CF* 1.302), his philanthropy belied by a murderous rage from the other side of death. His counterpart in the next episode is a Black, "a gorilla-like" boxer whose "abnormally long arms" seem to the narrator "fore legs," altogether a person who "must have looked even worse in life" (306) but whose resurrection is in fact "misshapen, . . . a glassy-eyed, ink-black apparition" with a hand between its teeth (308). In these two episodes the powerful being, whether in brain or in brawn, is revealed as the ghoul. Brown Jenkin's skull is a "degraded parody" of a human skull (*CF* 3.275), presumptively because its face, that male, bearded face, bore a "mocking resemblance to old Keziah's" (266). One person *echoes, mimicks, imitates,* or *apes* another, which is to say that a person *feigns* the disguise of another person's body and thus demonstrates how much that body does not belong to the person or is not at all to be identified with that person; it is clear that this motif is another aspect of the ghoul. So threatening is this mockery that a character *faints*—but perhaps that involuntary disowning of the self is merely a *feint*.

The motif of the *mask* is a concrete example of the parody to which Lovecraft often recurs. Sometimes the mask is only a metaphor, as when Weeden claims that Joseph Curwen's behavior is a mask concealing his true goals, an hypocrisy (*CF* 2.240). This traditional imagery can be used, however, with an irony that sees through even authenticity:

> The world grown old, her deep discernment shows,
> Claps spectacles on her sagacious nose,
> Peruses closely the true Christian's face,
> And finds it a mere mask of sly grimace,
> Usurps God's office, lays his bosom bare,
> And finds hypocrisy close-lurking there,
> And serving God herself through mere constraint,
> Concludes her unfeign'd love of him, a feint.
> (Cowper, *Conversation* ll. 341–48)

The yellow, silken mask of the Priest of Leng has a share in this imagery, though in the case of the Priest the mask signifies more than simply hypocrisy.[11] More often, Lovecraft insists these masks are of *wax*. The wax head with which a character in "Herbert West" returns, "a wax face with eyes of painted glass," is beautiful, not so much a mask perhaps as a complete substitution (*CF* 1.322). The mask in "The Festival," "a fiendishly clever mask" made from wax, gives the thing who writes "with the stylus and wax tablet" (*CF* 1.409) a bland face, so bland that its very blandness terrifies the narrator (409); and this blandness may suggest to us that the bland expression of Joseph Curwen itself functions as a mask (*CF* 2.279).

Theosophy, according to Frances Thurston, masks "strange survivals" like Cthulhu with "a bland optimism" (*CF* 2.22). The necromancer in "He" has a "waxy face" (*CF* 1.514), one which strikes the narrator as "too white, or too expressionless, or too much out of keeping with the locality" (509). This incongruence and repression of emotion reaches an extreme point when the face of Henry Akeley strikes Wilmarth as "immobile, ... damnably abnormal and corpse-like" (*CF* 521–22). When possessed by the shadow out of time Dr. Peaslee wears a "mask-like" face (*CF* 3.372), both more powerful and more enigmatic than the face he wore as a professor of economics, a face most people regard with loathing. The Chandraputra face that Randolph Carter wears is also "singularly immobile," too perfect (*CF* 3.282). The wax head has an historical context, of course, given the fame of Madame Tussaud, her connection with the heads of the French Revolution and her establishment of the Chamber of Horrors. Beyond that resonance, wax may signify a variety of different experiences; it may be both stiff and ductile. Erased, it is nothing; incised, it is a text, and it may be a seal upon that text also,

---

11. Cf. Waugh, "Landscapes, Selves, and Others in Lovecraft."

protecting the text and assuring its authenticity. As a verb, it often points at the waxing of the moon and tides and thus at a growth; but since the moon of imagination in the fiction is so often diseased, sometimes gibbous and squat, and since the waxing tides simply raise those threatening waters closer to the people that it would engulf, neither waxing should be regarded as a good thing. Not insignificantly, in the passage clumsily translated from Low Latin that concludes "The Festival," we read that "dull scavengers of earth wax crafty to vex it" (*CF* 1.417).

A different kind of mask is revealed in the faces of Lovecraft's childhood nightmares, the night-gaunts, whose *rubbery* faces have no eyes, mouths, or noses whatever. They wear the ultimate mask by bearing a mask that is no longer a mask at all, simply the erasure of any feeling; the monstrousness of the polymorphous becomes the monstrousness of the void and the blank. All they can do is horrify through that erasure—and tickle. This tickling may strike us as a silly, childish detail, but it is something of an ultimate invasion for a fiction which most of the time refuses to admit the presence of sexuality; and as the old man in "The Picture in the House" confesses, as he leans across the picture of butchery and cannibalism, "Thet feller bein' chopped up gives me a tickle every time I look at 'im" (*CF* 1.215). *Rubber* is another sort of *wax*, modern, industrial in its implications. Cthulhu has a rubbery body, and Pickman's ghouls "a kind of unpleasant rubberiness" (*CF* 2.64). Most of the counterfeits and parodies in Lovecraft's world are horrifying in that they distort and thus reveal how capable of distortion the human form is; they are thus the other side of the mask, which is almost always too perfect, a perfection which reveals and assures the imperfections of the human. In "Hypnos" the narrator perishes from the "hideous duplication" of the perfect sculpture that so much resembles his own face (*CF* 1.332), as though that duplication were revealed to be a mere mask-like parody.

Why are these characters sick? Because they have a secret. But just as we have seen that they find themselves forced to confess their secrets, the language is forced to confess the existence of a secret by the richness of its *secret* vocabulary. So much is *cryptic, enigmatic, occult, veiled, hieroglyphic,* and *undecipherable* that no time exists in the narrative to disentangle every secret. Neither the characters nor the narrative can ever be cured of so many secrets, and so the trauma continues; the masks are too many.

The great secret is the attraction of the *grotesque*, of the *macabre, bizarre, arabesque, caricature,* and *picturesque*—so much in the fiction offers itself as a delight for contemplation despite its being a distortion or deformation of the human. These words are quite striking in themselves, for in contrast to most other words in Lovecraft's vocabulary of the weird these words are not Anglo-Saxon or Latin in origin but French or Italian and pertain to the fine arts; derived from Poe's language, they suggest that the weird is predominantly a genre of observation, although only in terms of minor genres. The words suggest a theatricality, perhaps a "cheap imposture" (*CF* 2.488); the words deprecate their subject. Although Lovecraft affectionately distances himself from this aspect of the Gothic, its "infinite array of stage properties" (*CE* 2.88), he knows that his work forms a continuity with the genre. That theatricality appears in some of his characters, Erich Zann for instance, who in his own way acts like a zanni from the Commedia dell'arte, but a zanni who has lost his "i." Something of what these words imply appears in this passage from "The Picture in the House," describing the illustration that gives the story its title:

> The especially bizarre thing was that the artist had made his Africans look like white men—the limbs and quarters hanging about the walls of the shop were ghastly, while the butcher with his axe was hideously incongruous. But my host seemed to relish the view as much as I disliked it. (*CF* 1.215)

The "incongruity" points at a part of the pleasure; the picture is a hybrid, combining black men and white men in one figure, but even more incongruously combining the butcher with limbs which ought not to be his work at all. The relish of the host, the incitement to his taste and appetite, is the willful joining together of what does not fit, of what is not fitting on both the factual and the moral levels. It is this relish and irony, this moral discrepancy, that the reader sees in the U-boat commander's record of a hit, "The ship sank quite picturesquely" (*CF* 1.156).

Grotesque is one of the most frequent words of fear in the vocabulary, present from Lovecraft's early efforts—in "Dagon" the bas-reliefs are grotesque (*CF* 1.56)—to the last pages of "The Haunter in the Dark." Originating in Italian but then adapted to French, the word connoted decoration, "representations of portions of human and animal forms, fantastically combined and interwoven with foliage and flowers" (*OED* s.v. "Grotesque"); the style tends to be anti-realistic and decorative. The association of the word with grottoes is evident enough, though obscure in its origin and significance; it is an association to which Lovecraft pays tribute every time that he describes the *frescos* which ornament the walls of his underground worlds. He accentuates the decorative aspect when Walter Gilman describes a dream balustrade upon which "were ranged at short intervals little figures of grotesque design and exquisite workmanship," so delicate that the arms of the figures "like the arms of a starfish" are liable to be snapped off (*CF* 3.250). The varied aspect of the style, its willingness to combine with others, appears in Popean lines which Dr. Johnson had used to illustrate the word in his Dictionary: "Palladian walls, Venetian doors, / Grotesco roofs, and Stucco floors" (*Imitations of Horace* 2.6.193–94). The grotesque is first of all a style interested in and easily lent to a variety of contents and styles, a style of styles that never achieves unity, because it does not want to, though it certainly attempts to devour other styles. Its tendency to be discounted because it is often perceived as comic is well expressed by Edmund Burke in the essay on the sublime, though he believes so because he argues that painting cannot render the details of the terrifying because painting cannot render an idea of the infinite: "All the designs I have chanced to meet of the temptation of St. Anthony were rather a sort of odd, wild grotesques, than any thing capable of producing a serious passion" (Pt 2, sec. 4). Richard Steele deprecates the style when he suggests that a painter has been employed "more in Grotesque Figures, than in Beauties" (*OED* s.v. "Grotesque"). The word is as liable to be used for the absolutely ludicrous as for the mildly inappropriate.

Lovecraft's usage reflects this spectrum. He was perfectly aware of the word's pejorative connotation, as when in his essay "Supernatural Horror in Literature" he claimed that the archaic language of Hodgson's novel *The Night Land,* a work that he otherwise praised, was "even more grotesque and absurd than that in *'Glen Carrig.'"* Wilbur Whateley's trip to Harvard is "grotesque" (*CF* 2.437); and Randolph Carter, in "The Silver Key," is bored and oppressed by the "grotesque claims of solid truth," in this case the assertions of Christianity (*CF* 2.75). The prevailing mode of *The Dream-Quest of Unknown Kadath* is a serio-comic version of the grotesque: zoogs flutter; when Randolph Carter "wickedly" loosens the tongue of a "guileless host" with drink, the man hiccoughs his information; a merchant smirks sinfully before shaking and laughing "in epileptic mirth"; ghouls meep and glibber (*CF* 2.102, 106, 111, 133). This tone is capped by Carter's relief when the ghouls leave him, "for a ghoul is a ghoul, and at best an unpleasant companion for men" (143). In addition, much of the *Dream-Quest* is studiedly decorative, most oddly in the way that the cats who aid Carter in the south of the dream-land are balanced by the dog-like ghouls who aid him in the north. One of the worst aspects of the grotesque, with its hybrid and derogatory possibilities, is its aptness at mocking and denying authenticity. The picture on the wall in an old tavern, carven in haste and crudity, makes Carter most doubt whether it gives an authentic idea of the gods because it is "wholly overshadowed by a crowd of little companion shapes in the worst possible taste, with horns and wings and claws and curling tails" (123). The model for such a description is very likely the art of medieval cathedrals, into which "grotesque carvings [were] slyly introduced . . ., the daemoniac gargoyles of Notre Dame and Mont St. Michel" being the most typical (*CE* 2.85). The grotesque makes cracks in reality.

A further context upon Lovecraft's concept of the grotesque may be found in Anderson's introduction to *Winesburg, Ohio,* the sketch called "The Book of the Grotesque," which with some indirection draws a moral for the stories to follow. Based upon a dream of "a long procession of figures" (2) in which "all the men and women the writer had ever known had become grotesques," some of whom "were not at all horrible," but some "amusing, some almost beautiful, and one, a woman all drawn out of shape" (3), the stories of these people, the never-published book of grotesques, proposed that "the moment one of the people took a truth to himself, called it his truth, and tried to live his life by it, that person became a grotesque and his truth became a falsehood" (4).[12] Anderson's collection

---

12. Ray Lewis White notes how ubiquitous the concept of the grotesque was among Anderson's contemporaries, a milieu which to some extent Lovecraft shared. Given the international nature of the silent film, he saw some of the masterworks of German Expressionism, works described by others as grotesque (xxix–xxx).

portrays people who have single-mindedly denied the fullness of their lives; at least, it means that much, unless by meaning only that much it becomes itself a falsehood, as Anderson must have realized by writing so old-fashioned an allegory.

It is in that light that we should consider Lovecraft's complaint about the collection—the stories do not achieve truth, truth in its fullness and authenticity, because its figures are not sufficiently grotesque, the book's account of their denial of reality not sufficiently extreme, too content despite its condemnation of small-town life to step outside that life into a true outsidedness. Anderson's grotesques deny their reality, but they do not break it apart into pieces that suggest a truly horrifying otherness. If Anderson is a therapeutic author, probing the human wound, his hope that we might heal, even though minuscule, is still present; Lovecraft probes the wound to make it hurt and by that hurt to make it palpable, but he does not believe that it shall heal.

These doubts about reality, however, whose symptoms are such cracks and wounds, are not conclusive; without denying the forgery, reality may be more than the forgery. When Carter at last comes to Kadath he discovers that the great mass of the mountain upon which the onyx castle sits makes his own entourage, the ghouls and night-gaunts, seem ridiculously small; the grotesque may be prophetic, an assertion of a truth which we do not wish to believe, but it does not measure up to our true fears. In one of his wartime broadcasts Ezra Pound made a breathtaking claim about *The Protocols of the Elders of Zion:* "Certainly they are a forgery, and that is the one proof we have of their authenticity" (cited in Julius 239n22). Despite distortions, fakeries, and garblings which attempt to conceal the reality of the threat of the monstrous Outsider, such fakeries and garblings become the seal upon that threat to which they point, as though the naked threat, the monstrous or the Jew or the weird text, in and of itself would seem too preposterous to be believed. In fact, the inauthenticity of the Jew, dispersed through the landscape, may be the great forgery of this fiction. We have seen how such words as *squat, spawn, marsh, leprosy, foetor,* and *rats* form a part of anti-Semitic vocabulary. To them we should now add the themes of Jewish imitation and Jewish free-thinking (Julius 101–2, 146–48). Ghettoization and assimilation form in the Christian community an anxiety about whether one could recognize the Jew, who is either condemned as a bad imitator or condemned as so cunning that he or she cannot be detected, and therefore feared as all the more dangerous; in Lovecraft's terms, the hoax which is either clumsy or successful precludes any possibility of authenticity. The cunning of the Jew is all the more dangerous because of the free-thinking that is ascribed to the people, a free-thinking that is demonized as a ridicule or laughter. This language is one that the free-thinker Lovecraft employs thoroughly in the stories, another source I suspect of the leering mockery that reaches out of his creatures and his landscapes. Since I discuss the anti-Semitism of Lovecraft's work at length in later chapters, the point now is that one of the inauthenticities of the work is its inability to recognize or to confess its compulsive utterance of these words, words upwelling from the most crucial moments of the fiction, seldom allowing this atmosphere of anti-Semitism—and atmosphere was important very important to Lovecraft's aesthetics—to become defined.

Lovecraft's style, then, his dissociated hand, is all-important to a judgment on him, because it is a hybrid, grotesque style, ceremonial and hysterical, artful and clumsy, feline and canine. In its attempts at sobriety and in its meretricious extremes, its desperate, clumsy clamoring for a reader's attention becomes the assurance that its fears and despairs and their objects, whatever their objects may truly be, are real. No one could write so badly as this text seems to have been written unless pressed for time by the danger. The ridiculous moment at the end of "Dagon" when the protagonist is dragged off by the monstrous, while still writing, is paradigmatic of Lovecraft's strategy; the writing is a true extension of the monstrous, for if no one can believe this text the monstrous must be truly present.

Do we dare to say anything of the psychological or moral conditions of a writing of this sort? Heidegger denied that authenticity had anything to do with psychologism (Zimmerman 116), but we are left with the problem whether a person is authentic who plays out the inner structures of the soul in such questionable fictions. Even if the belief in the earth, in tradition, and in the Führer-principle is a profound part of one's argument before aware of National Socialism and its Führer, is a need to dominate truly authentic? None of the yearning for certainty manifested in these themes seems consistent with being thrown toward death or with an awareness of the *ab-Grund*, the bottomlessness of being. If Stephen Mulhall is right that in *Being and Time* Heidegger represses his dependence upon the call of conscience to authenticity and thereby creates "a fundamental mutilation of the potential wholeness and integrity of his text" (136), can we say that Heidegger's support of National Socialism, complex as it was, rendered himself and his further philosophic labors inauthentic because he failed to answer the call of conscience that Husserl and Arendt offered? Did Lovecraft's anti-Semitism and misogyny that he carried with him in his return to New England render him and his fiction inauthentic because he failed to answer the call of his wife Sonia Greene and his friend Samuel Loveman, both of them Jews? This mutilation, wound, and split in himself, this inauthenticity, he does come to delineate fully in the stories, but it was a wound that he could not admit or heal.

Lovecraft did write authentic stories, stories that no one else could have written, stories that disclose a vulnerability that has no chance of coming to closure. Yet even the best stories contain self-betrayals, obsessions, possessions, and dispossessions that imprison the self, at the same moment that even his horror of the monstrous often confesses his identity with it. He also wrote inauthentic stories, stories that almost anyone could have been written, mechanical stories that try to disclose nothing. Yet even the most debased of these stories, "Herbert West" for instance, cannot prevent the ghoul from stalking, the figure who gloats over "charnel picturesqueness" though he also aspires to be "a fastidious Baudelaire" (*CF* 1.316); still, the magazine that requested the story, *Home Brew*, is in charge of the voice in "the large covered vat in that ghoulish corner of crawling shadows"

(319). Authenticity always circles back to undisclosure; that which wishes to remain covered is always struggling with the iron gate of the tomb, motions which are so often in danger of being confounded with one another, like the dimensions of space surrounding Cthulhu.

Consciously the Outsider goes forth to find light and revelry[13]; but if his search is one directed toward the self, he most certainly does not go forth to discover himself as he actually is. And none of Lovecraft's characters go forth to discover themselves as they are, or as Lovecraft was. Though as St. Armand argues he might have been a New England decadent, he was certainly not a French decadent, an image with which he dallied for a time. Nor was he in any serious way an objective genealogist, though several of his characters are and though he enjoys flaunting some details of genealogical lore in his letters. Nor was he an old man like Professor Angell, in touch with traditional wisdom or knowledge. Nor was he a professor in an established university. The glaring falseness of these researches suggests one reason why the self that is at last discovered seems so shocking. The discrepancy between the discovery and the explicit goal is too great to be bridged.

But once the Outsider finds himself, he immediately, before he will confess that the reflection represents his own being, identifies it as someone else or, more subtly, as a travesty, a creature dressed as a human but not one. And so, for a moment, he can almost turn away from himself—before he compulsively falls into himself, falling into the mirror. For that is one of the points of identifying the self as a travesty, a parody, a hoax, and of also identifying the story as a travesty, a parody, a hoax. If the self and story are hoaxes, they can be denied or at the least discounted, emptied of meaning because they are merely decorative grotesques; the assurance of the style that we have noted dwells upon a level far away from the intention of the author. And so the writer and the reader as well can begin looking for themselves once more, stretching out their hands in the darkness once more, looking for the self in the horror, as we shall do in the chapters that follow. As far as the Outsider is concerned, in looking for himself he carries himself, the rotting corpse that he is, out of the castle just as he unwittingly carried himself out of the grave; he can join the ghouls because he feeds upon himself, inexhaustible, bitter food. He is the vulture upon his own Promethean breast.

In this first chapter we have circled on the horror, edged away from it at the same time that we approached it. What is that horror? What does it seem to be in the light of this first study? Human complicity in the unoriginal and inauthentic, our inability to be central or real to the universe: our being engrossed in the peripheral. The first step into authenticity is the confession of contingency. To the climactic question of "The Thing on the Doorstep," "Who was this foul, stunted parody?" we must each answer that we are (*CF* 3.355). We are those "blind, voiceless, mindless gargoyles whose soul is Nyarlathotep" (*CF* 1.205); for gargoyles gargle, like the rivers in *The Case of Charles Dexter Ward* and "The Whisperer in Dark-

---

13. This theme is developed in the chapter "The Outsider, the Autodidact and Other Professions."

ness," pouring out waters from their mouths in waste noise. We are the ghouls whose appetites reflect our emptiness and weakness. Our reflection, that our hand has set forth, gives back only a distortion, and we fear there is nothing else but that distortion. But Lovecraft, with his several styles that embody and refer to this inauthenticity, is in his fiction remorselessly inventive exploring the mirrors, in touching his own reflection; and his reflection is ours.

Documents, Creatures, and History

> The gaps I mean,
> No one has seen them made or heard them made,
> But at spring mending-time we find them there.
>   (Frost, "Mending Wall," ll. 9–11)

The problems of authenticity in Lovecraft demand that we say something more about the role of a document and of a documentary style in his fiction. Perhaps it should be no surprise that a lover of books like Lovecraft delights on occasion in a documentary style, though his having such a style in at least a few stories still disconcerts readers who expect the powerfully emotive style of the early stories. But the closer we look at the uses to which he puts documents, the more aware we become of subtleties in his materialist understanding of history and its participants.

Passages that we might agree are documentary include the letters, diaries, and formulae of *The Case of Charles Dexter Ward,* the accounts of "The Call of Cthulhu," the descriptions of creatures found in "The Colour out of Space" and *At the Mountains of Madness,* the gibberish of Zadok Allen in "The Shadow over Innsmouth," its oral history, the disks of "The Whisperer in Darkness," and the materials of "The Shadow out of Time." The last story presents us with a peculiar case. The protagonist is a scholar transported into a scholar's dream, an ancient library more complex and more destroyed than the Biblos of Alexandria, where he is allowed to function as a scholar; but he can neither translate nor comprehend more than very loosely any of the materials, though he assures us that when there, moving his tentacles over the documents, his comprehension was close indeed. This last case suggests an insufficiency inherent to documents that is central to Lovecraft's treatment.

Derived from the Latin *docere,* to teach or to show, a document suggests a proof, indication, warning, or example. It is something inscribed, obviously in something else though we generally ignore its material basis. It may be a manuscript, a law or decree, a speech (in notes, in memory, or on tape), a deed, letter, or diary. It may be logocentric, with all the ambiguity that Derrida has pointed out. Or it may be almost anything, a picture, epitaph, or coin, even the drop of blood in "The Picture in the House." When we think of a document we are often considering its uses for history. But we also have in mind documentaries, which provide a further context for Lovecraft's purposes: the films on public television are often instructive, whether for technologies, for natural history, or for human history. Though it would seem that most documents are not meant to move us, whether in their original or secondary purpose, as evidence, documents are indeed accompanied by persuasion, beauty, and bias. Historians realize the skepticism they should bring to a document, which whether a factual, cultural, instructive, or numerical item bears a consciously and unconsciously excluding intent to show something.

The Indo-European root of *document* means "to point" and produces such words as *digit* or *token* and several words in Greek, *paradigm* or *apodictic*, derived from *deiknunai, to show,* and akin to *dikein, to throw* (*American Heritage Dictionary* 1511). A document has a double significance: it claims to be factual, as self-evident as a finger, a part and extension of ourselves, or as self-evident as the pen which the finger holds and the paper on which it inscribes an image of our thinking mind; but it is significant only through pointing beyond itself at something else whose validity it thus evidences and attests. A document is only useful through transcending itself.

One of the qualities of the document is the authority that it exerts upon the apparent authenticity of an object. We may take as an example of such authority the scene in Philip K. Dick's novel *The Man in the High Castle* in which Mr. Wyndam-Matson argues that no object possesses authenticity and to prove it shows his mistress Rita the cigarette case worn by Franklin Roosevelt when he was assassinated (this novel concerns a complex system of parallel histories that cast into doubt any idea of a privileged authenticity); it doesn't look or smell authentic, but it is, for within this history the authenticity of the cigarette case is founded upon a document that Mr. Wyndam-Matson presents, what antique dealers now call its provenance, which traces the object back to its origin—for the people who deal in the cash value of an object, no authenticity without an unsevered umbilical cord. "The paper proves its worth, not the object itself" (64). To his own satisfaction Mr. Wyndam-Matson wins his argument, but the narrative makes clear that he loses it, for both cigarette case and document may be forged, placing us into an infinite regress of documents. More particularly, authenticity belongs to Rita, who mourns Roosevelt and her contingency and who repossesses herself and leaves self-possessed. Authenticity belongs or does not belong to people, not to objects, but is nonetheless a desirable state. Rita transcends the object and the document by suffering the historical tragedy of which the object is a relic.

Does Lovecraft think we can transcend objects or documents or, for that matter, our own tragedy? One of the most recurring of images in his writing is the barrier, the wall, which frequently seems to imply a sublimity overawing and fulfilling human desire. *Fungi from Yuggoth* concludes with such a perception: "In that strange light I feel I am not far / From the fixt mass whose sides the ages are" (*AT* 95). His journey concludes; there is no need to go beyond this vision. We can compare to these lines a passage in a letter written at this time: "The constant discovery of different peoples' subjective impressions of things, as contained in genuine art, forms a slow, gradual approach, or first approximation of an approach, to *the mystic substance of absolute reality itself*—the stark, cosmic reality which lurks behind our varying subjective perceptions" (*SL* 2.301). Is there another side to this wall? In "Ex Oblivione," when "the antique wall" at last presents an open door, the narrator dissolves "into that native infinity of crystal oblivion" composed of "neither land nor sea, but only the white void of unpeopled and illimitable space" (*CF*

1.220). There is no other side; there is nothing but the wall. Thus it is "real externality" that he aims to achieve in his stories (*SL* 2.150), for it is only that surface, only that wall, only that "outsideness" (*SL* 3.294–96), possessing no other side, which conveys existence. To do so the author must "cross the line to the boundless" (*ES* 776), trespass the line which is not a line. Lovecraft is forced to bracket the "outside" with irony (*ES* 288).

The image of the wall is a paradox. The usual significance of a wall lies in its excluding us from a definite thing on the other side; most of the time it is built because someone wants to go beyond it. Every wall gives existence to a space and shapes it, so that what lies on one side of the wall is more delectable than what is on the other; paradise is a walled garden. But a wall that has no structure, that is merely a wall for no purpose, which is endless, extending infinitely without meeting itself, has nothing on the other side and does not define an inside and an outside, as a real wall does. Confronted by such a wall, we cannot know whether we are inside or outside or whether we want to escape or to enter. But such a notional wall we usually do not call a wall, but a mass, a rock, a mountain, a heap, stuff—it is simply stuff and matter we cannot trespass. The wall provokes a complex of thought and language insofar as the intention that we give it, of which it seems constructed, is a blank; but we cannot help addressing it. Every background provokes rhythm and meaning. But Lovecraft's protagonists tend to be dubious whether that meaning actually has substance. As Peaslee says, "the efforts of the subconscious mind to fill up a perplexing blank with pseudo-memories might give rise to strange imaginative vagaries" (*CF* 3.376).

What experience do we have of such a wall? For Lovecraft the answer is simple enough: the resonant phrase of Lucretius, "flammantia moenia mundi" [the flaming walls of the world] (1.73), represents the ethereal walls of our coherent cosmos beyond which lies the infinite rain of the atoms. This is a real wall, for we live within it as within an Eden, while an irrational state inimical to our lives rages outside. Only one person has strode beyond that barrier and broken the doors of nature, Epicurus, through his intellection of the atoms by the dialectic; he has not, however, in fact passed those walls (1.66–75). The "finita potestas denique cuique / quanam sit ratione atque alte terminus haerens" [limited power given to each by reason and the fixed frontier] are infrangible (1.76–77). There is nothing beyond or within the atoms, by definition indivisibly all that exist. Surrounded by their ceaseless fall reason finds no end, neither to them nor to the infinite space through which they fall (1.958–64). With no boundary, space can be neither left nor entered; we are one with the wall and bear it with us.

But reason reveals a peculiar condition of the atoms, that they must exist "sponte sua forte offensando" [striking each other by chance of their own will] (2.1059): the only significant event is a sudden swerve of individual atoms, uncertain in place and time (2.218–19). That "exiguum clinamen" [slight swerve] (2.292) causes the great swirls, twists, and vortexes out of which infinite worlds arise (2.83–215), imagery that had its impact on the Kantian and Laplacean theories of the history of the solar system—an imagery, furthermore, that Lovecraft was not to outgrow imaginatively, though during the 1920s he was to find it insufficient intellectually (Joshi, *Decline* 16). The vortex mediates between the human, experiential world within the ramparts and the unimaginable chaos outside. The philosopher transcends the accidents of the world, all that lovely shimmer of a dove's neck changing from ruby to emerald (2.801–5) or the glitter of a distant army (2.332). But not even the walls of the coherent cosmos are privileged, free from change, because even for them the door of death will not remain closed, "sed patet immani et vasto respectat hiatu" [but it lies open and faces {them} with an immense yawning chasm] (5.375). Under the secondary qualities lies the abyss, the *ab-Grund* in which the *Grund* of things is revealed as meaningless (Heidegger, *Being and Time* 194); outside of Eden lies death.

Powerful rationalist and antagonist of mystification though he is, Lucretius uses the language of religion because he is forced to use the language of paradox. Rational transcendence is difficult to achieve, not least because of two verbal dilemmas (1.136–39). One is the problem of dealing with the Greek technical language, a topos often sounded in Latin literature (Cicero, *De Natura Deorum* 1.2). But the other deals with the concepts, because atoms are devoid of secondary qualities and their events are random, opaque to reason (Lucretius 1.830–52). The conceptual dilemma remains valid for any author dealing with these matters, including Lovecraft.

A document represents multiple appearances that do not exhaust reality but point to it. As a wall, a document assumes complex functions. The wall is the background of the world, what merely is, which we would not think of transcending because we are so accustomed to it. When we become aware of it, we demand that it present a door that becomes, when we enter, a terrifying abyss of the imperceptible and irrational, recalcitrant to any totalizing conception. The wall presents a significant access to death; against such accesses, however, we have to erect another wall, a "bulwark" in its place (*CF* 3.392), as Peaslee says of his rationalizations. We perceive the wall and write on it a document that points toward the "outside." A document is a piece of background that claims to have access to more than background. Because a document claims to be more than background, it is pretentious, open to play, parody, and extravagance.

In early stories Lovecraft more often documents a natural history than a history, though he aspires toward the latter. In the later stories, besides passages that describe creatures, details of bodily existence with all the peculiar articulations and feeding habits that alien creatures indulge in, which are essentially factual and unintelligible, he tries to develop a history proper that would include a development and dialectic of cultural worlds. Thus in late works like "The Shadow over Innsmouth," "The Mound," *At the Mountains of Madness*, and "The Shadow out of Time," we find an increasingly complex and rationalized history of different cultures, with an implication of judgment that would clearly be out of place in a natural history. Concomitantly it becomes more difficult to call these stories horror fiction; the possibility that we can identify them as science fiction becomes attractive because of the possibility that we can make better sense of them thereby. The kind of document Lovecraft creates is involved in the question of genre. Two works which constitute this spectrum are "The Colour out of Space" and "The Shadow out of Time," though we shall also glance at *The Case of Charles Dexter Ward*, "The Shadow over Innsmouth," and *At the Mountains of Madness*.

"The Colour out of Space" is a study in natural history, but because the object of the study proves unintelligible the people of the area frame it in a precise context, calling the landscape the "blasted heath," a phrase that seems "very odd and theatrical" to the narrator, especially given the Puritan background of the neighborhood (*CF* 2.368). Theatrical indeed, for the dramatist who coined the phrase is Shakespeare, at the moment when Macbeth and Banquo meet the three weird sisters (1.3.77).[1] Well Banquo may say of them, or of what bursts from the nodules of the meteor, "The earth hath bubbles as the water has, / And these are of them. Whither have they vanished?" (1.3.79–80). What has arrived remains, infecting the landscape so intimately that not even the reservoir will cleanse it; the narrator's biblical hope, "I shall be glad to see the water come" (*CF* 2.399; cf. Ps. 69:1 and 1 Pet. 3:20), which expresses an apocalyptic yearning for the flood, is probably futile. Lovecraft's characters would concur with Macbeth:

> Will all great Neptune's ocean wash this blood
> Clean from my hand? No, this my hand will rather
> The multitudinous seas incarnadine,
> Making the green one red.   (2.2.60–63)

This imagery of the tainting dye continues into the scene of Lady Macbeth's handwashing. Banquo is killed, Lady Macbeth goes mad, and Macbeth himself is devoured, wading into more blood until he drowns (3.4.136–38)—actually, until he is beheaded by a man "from his mother's womb / Untimely ripped" (5.8.15–16), as much an omen as the stone ripped from space. Birnam Wood comes to Dunsinane; and in Lovecraft's story the trees seem to become marvelously sentient outside the besieged farmhouse, tipped by pentecostal fire (*CF* 2.393). Just as Duncan's horses after his death break out and devour one another (2.4.17), the horse of the democrat-wagon breaks free (*CF* 2.393–94). The immaterial event that the several characters must unriddle infects them. The wealth of references to *Macbeth* would seem, despite Donald R. Burleson's arguments on this passage's ludic play of uncertainty (*Lovecraft* 111–13), to make the drama more significant for our explication of the landscape and the creature infecting it. The allusion points to the various trespasses of the tragedy: trespasses of authority, nature, time, and Oedipal

---

1. S. T. Joshi believes that this phrase may owe more to Lovecraft's reminiscence of a passage in *Paradise Lost* (1.612–15), a description of divine wrath in Hell ("Annotations"). The overdetermination of Lovecraft's passage is surely significant, but I consider *Macbeth* the work most at work in the story.

tension. The allusion is not in documentary style, but it is an unmistakable document attesting to an alien corruption.

No document is trustworthy unless we test its author; the author should be authoritative. But the author of this story is repeating what he has heard others tell him and tell each other. Ammi Pierce is the most important, another of Lovecraft's locals who although "very worn and dismal" is "brighter and more educated" than the engineer had expected (*CF* 2.370). Ammi has seen a "white noontide cloud" and a "pillar of smoke" reminiscent of the numinous cloud leading Israel into the desert to confront the law-giver on the mountain (Ex. 13:21); and he has heard of "the great rock that fell out of the sky and bedded itself in the ground" (*CF* 2.371), like the meteor that rests at the center of the cult in Mecca. He also tells of how "the three [. . .] wise men" came from Arkham to witness the stone (371–72). All this happened in June of '82. These details, the descending star, the three wise men, the leading cloud, suggest an injection of the divine into human history—except that its advent in June, on the other side of the year from Christmas, suggests the advent of an Antichrist. The motif of the falling star also recalls the star Wormwood, one of the signs of the seventh seal (Rev. 8:10–11); so potent is the family of this plant that Gerard says of the "fantasticall devices invented by Poëts" concerning it, "tending to witchcraft and sorcerie, and the great dishonour of God," that he does "of purpose omit them, as things unworthy of my recording, to your reviewing" (254). Possibly we witness a bleak understanding of the kenosis by which the incarnation empties godhead (Phil. 2:7); at the crucifixion godhead complains of self-desertion (Matt. 27:46). Various heresies perceive the incarnation as an insult to divinity, a trespass against the original father. But whether the stone appears as a guide into the desert and the law, as a prohibition against its own trespass, as Antichrist, as a sign of the end of the world, or as degenerate son, we realize how charged are the terms by which Ammi perceives the event.

There are other observers, however. The three detectives, the coroner, the medical examiner, and the veterinary constitute with Ammi a cohort of seven who witness the climactic ascent of the creature. There are also the five people in the Gardner family—Nahum, his wife Nabby, and the sons Thaddeus, Merwin, and Zenas—but they are devoured: the only witness they provide is the blank of the wife, Nahum's fragmentary sentences, and the sons' bones in the well. To this list we should add the dreams of the foreigners who have come to live around the heath, with an "insight beyond ours" (*CF* 2.398).

The text that assembles these witnesses unfortunately assimilates to some extent the language of Mrs. Gardner, in which "there was not a single specific noun, but only verbs and pronouns" (*CF* 2.380). But there are a few nouns that describe what the Colour seems to exist in or to transform, and a list of them may be significant: the heath that we have discussed, haze, element (369), cloud, smoke, rock, mound (372), properties, the "shining bands" of a spectrum, the Widmannstätten figures (373), space, globule, hollow, piece (374) and detached piece (379), the vegetation around the farm—skunk-cabbages, saxifrage, mourning-cloak butterflies,

Dutchman's breeches, and bloodroots "insolent in their chromatic perversion" (378), and later the asters, goldenrod, roses, zinneas, and hollyhocks (381)—luminosity, phosphorescence (379), colours (378), collapses, disintegrations, virus, disease (382), wreckage, stench, cloud, current, colours (385), monstrosity—these words apply to Mrs. Gardner, Eve transformed—vapour, noise, suction (386), fragments, parody (387), nothin', colour, well, smoke, seeds (387), specimens, vestige, ooze, slime (390), pit, colour, current, splash, tint (391), beyond, iridescence (392), radiance, St. Elmo's fire, the pentecostal tongues of flame, constellation, a "glutted swarm of corpse-fed fireflies," intrusion (393), no bottom, column, suggestions (394), blend, tongues of flame, fire, amorphousness, rainbow, chromaticism—with a nod to Wagner and Debussy—Deneb in the constellation Cygnus (396), fragments, darkness (396), blight, splotch, dreams (398), gas, daemon, messenger (399), and in the last paragraph Ammi, monstrosity, and sleep (399). We should add the pictures of Salvator Rosa and Fuseli that are cited as examples (369, 395). Undoubtedly this list is subjective, but I could find no rule for developing it that would not prejudge our interpretation of the creature. But I have prejudged, or in fact postjudged, the result, since the list suggests so strongly that the Colour is not an object but only present insofar as it exists within our everyday things, projected or, as Lovecraft says of his attitude toward the abrogation of physical law, extruded from them. It is pure wall challenging transcendence. Lovecraft has chosen the perfect words for his purpose. "Chromatic" derives from the Greek word for "skin."

Much more needs to be said about the most important word, "Colour," which derives from the Indo-European root that means "conceal"; a few of its cognates are Calypso (a concealing or covering), "apocalypse" (an unconcealing), "occultism," "hollow," "hole," and "hell" (*American Heritage Dictionary* 1521; cf. Burleson, *Lovecraft* 108). The root has had a tendency to alternate between convex and concave meanings, like the buildings that surround Cthulhu, simultaneously concealing and revealing. The dynamic has much in common with Heidegger's analysis of truth, that which is covered up, or that which is not overlooked, that which is retrieved from our habit of consigning those things which we want dead to Lethe (cf. *Being and Time* 56–57, 256, 262–63). The well of Democritus to which Lovecraft refers is the abyss in which truth is hidden (*CF* 1.100; cf. Democritus 318–19), so Lovecraft's frequent image of "the wells of night" is quite apt (*CF* 1.499). For Lovecraft the truth exists in a profoundly other place than humans normally have access to; but that truth, destructive because of its otherness, has the power to seep or, sometimes, to pour into our lives, shifting and changing like the Colour, not something that we can grasp or contain. No wonder Lucretius claims, "Omnis enim color omnino mutuatur in omnis" [every color can change into every other] (2.749). The thing, the Colour, is both nothing and a mediation of nothing. If we can put any name to it, I would guess that its being a "stony messenger" and "a piece of the great outside" (*CF* 2.374) discloses its affinity to Nyarlathotep, as does its shifty color, for he is both the shifting look of the phenomena and a type of the Antichrist (Waugh 236).

These preliminary readings are substantiated by the adjectives: white, great, weird, brownish, soft, plastic (*CF* 2.372), magnetic (373), vacant, brittle, hollow (373), cryptic, stealthy, bitter, sick (375), hectic, prismatic, overgrown (378), swollen, grey, brittle (373), dwarfed, tasteless (381), not foetid, not salty, tainted, meagre, ill-cooked, thankless, monotonous, aimless—this series has to do with the life of the family, a description of the nothing as it were from inside—dry, noisome (382), shrivelled, compressed (382), blank (384), blasphemous, clammy, sticky (386), liquid, dry, cleft, cold, wet (287), porous (390), black, queer, hateful, insidious, daemoniac (391), epileptic (392), lambent (395), nefandous, eldritch (397), fat, extra-cosmic (399), and in the last paragraph, the refrain, grey, twisted, brittle (399). This is a considerably shorter list than that of nouns, probably because Lovecraft packs most of his adjectival effects into the nouns, so often metaphoric in nature. But the list could be longer given its repetitions, especially of the key words "grey" and "brittle." For though the thing is a color out of space—how odd a title if we take it seriously, as Steven J. Mariconda illustrates (*Emergence* 22)—few colors are mentioned, and the effect of this color is to leave all earthly things grey, without color; we see it in the absence it leaves, just as it leaves the life of the Gardners meaningless. "Brittle" is cognate to "bore," "perforate," "broken up," and "brothel," a deterioration corroborating the fragmentary and empty quality of the thing (*American Heritage Dictionary* 1510). I have not listed, but a number of these adjectives give a sense of, the many negatives that fill the narrative.

But though empty the Colour is not impotent. A list of the verbs by which it empowers its space is long: blast (*CF* 2.368), fall, bed, shrink, linger, glow, refuse (372), fade (372), burst, leave (374), grow (375), move, inhere, stir (379), change, flutter, take away, drain, fasten, shift, crawl—Mrs. Gardner reduced to all fours—puff, crumble (385), creep, wait (384), eclipse (385), brush, drag (386), scale, bulge, burn, suck, beat down, draw (388), cave in (388), bubble (394), shoot up, belch (391), twitch, claw, scratch, wriggle, pour (393), go, flare, weave (394), shimmer, run, coruscate, infect, strengthen, leave, strain, trickle, seethe, feel, lap, reach, scintillate, strain, bubble, shoot—this is the climax—(390), rise, sink down, lurk (394), eat, spread (397), feed, escape, shine, move, throw open (399), persist, and trouble (399). Except for a very few, the words are basic to the Anglo-Saxon center of the language. Lovecraft packs many of his best effects into his verbs, full of the orgasmic excitement which the Colour projects onto its staid observers who have arrived in their democrat-wagon to put things right on the Gardner farm. But nothing stays right. Even the narrator, the surveyor who will never return to the blasted heath, in his worry for Ammi, who cannot move away because of the insidious influence of the thing (399), is himself becoming possessed by a dream of the thing overwhelming Ammi. The observer is beginning to be assimilated to the void that he observes beyond the wall of his documents.

To this story we may contrast such tales as *The Case of Charles Dexter Ward* and "The Shadow over Innsmouth," which seem to deal purely with history. The novel provides documents that enlighten us on the secret history of Providence. But by doing so it casts doubt on the public history; we need to be skeptical about the pertinence of such documents as have survived. The secret documents, however, are not sufficient for the purpose of an obsessed knower like Curwen, who needs to obtain his knowledge *viva voce* from the essential salts of the dead whom he tortures into life; and the reader only gains such knowledge through the protagonist, whom Curwen displaces. In this novel knowledge and history are a branch of genealogy, a point that is made all the more strongly in "The Shadow over Innsmouth."

Though genealogy does not enter into "The Shadow out of Time," it is a more complex story than these because of the peculiar status of its chief observer, as he learns piecemeal how much he is the thing that he is observing; but it is also more complex because two objects are being observed, the Great Race who incorporate a history in their identity, and an elder race, ungraced or undistinguished by capital letters, who are much less intelligible to the observer and much more repulsive. The documents of the first pertain to history, the documents of the other, like those of "The Colour out of Space," to natural history. This difference also means a difference in the categories of observers we have. A local population is much less prominent; in the place of Ammi, Zadok Allen, or the denizens of Dunwich, we have only the natives of Australia on the periphery of the narrative, rather like the foreigners with their dreams in "The Colour out of Space." In their place the story has more scholars: Nathaniel Peaslee, a political economist who becomes a psychologist; his son Wingate, a psychologist; Peaslee's wife and other children, whose judgment bring them to divorce him; Dr. Wilson, who certifies his return; a plethora of psychologists, anthropologists, and mental specialists, who allow him to deny his hermeneutics (*CF* 3.374), to whom we should add the legends, dreams, and historiographies of the theosophists, which he would have found in books like Blavatsky's *Isis Unveiled* (385, 390, 398); himself as a captive of the Great Race; the Great Race, with its documents; the other captives, writing their documents, like Yiang-Li, Bartolomeo Corsi, a king of Lomar, Nug-Soth, Titus Sempronius Blaesus, Khephnes, a priest of Atlantis, James Woodville, a pre-Incan astronomer, Nevil Kingston-Brown, an archimage of Yhe, Theodotides, Pierre-Louis Montmagny, Crom-Ya (398–99), a list that documents the spaciousness of human and ahuman time—captives, rather like Curwen's captives needed because of a similar distrust of documents to deliver their witness *viva voce* and afterwards *viva manu*, of special importance because only they can trespass the taboo that prevents the Great Race from confronting their fears about the creatures that lie beyond them; Mackenzie and Boyle, with their photographs that cut through the legends—and the blocks themselves—with Dyer, Ashley, and Freeborn, representing geology, ancient history, and anthropology; and finally, the document in his own hand, observation confronting observation. It is a formidable list, from which we would hope to gain some precise information.

The description of the Great Race, however, is more technical than expected of creatures with such a complex experience: "Immense rugose cones ten feet high, and with head and other organs attached to foot-thick, distensible limbs spreading from the apexes. They spoke by the clicking or scraping of huge paws or claws attached to the end of two of their four limbs, and walked by the expansion and contraction of a viscous layer attached to their vast, ten-foot bases" (*CF* 3.387). This neutral language differs from the powerful verbs and metaphoric nouns of the earlier story; here the most repeated word is the unemotional "attached." A longer passage is similar: "They seemed to be enormous, iridescent cones, about ten feet high and ten feet wide at the base, and made up of some ridgy, scaly, semi-elastic matter. From their apexes projected four flexible, cylindrical members, each a foot thick, and of a ridgy substance like that of the cones themselves" (*CF* 3.394). The passage proceeds to a description of "appendages . . ., claws or nippers . . . antennae or tentacles," and eyes that surround a "central circumference" (394). The cautious narrator attempts precision to the best of his verbal ability; though he believes himself horrified by them and by his being one of them, the tone suggests only a dispassionate observation.

    This passage is not isolated in Lovecraft's later fiction. In *At the Mountains of Madness* there is the message Lake sends, of which this citation is a small part: "Six-foot five-ridged barrel torso 3.5 feet central diameter, 1 foot end diameters. Dark grey, flexible, and infinitely tough. Seven-foot membraneous wings of same colour, found folded, spread out of furrows between ridges . . . Around equator, one at central apex of each of the five vertical, stave-like ridges, are five systems of light grey flexible arms or tentacles found tightly folded to torso but expansible to maximum length of over 3 feet" (*CF* 3.38). Another passage is Wilmarth's summary of the newspaper articles in "The Whisperer in Darkness": "They were pinkish things about five feet long; with crustaceous bodies bearing vast pairs of dorsal fins or membraneous wings and several sets of articulated limbs, and with a sort of convoluted ellipsoid, covered with multitudes of very short antennae, where a head would ordinarily be" (*CF* 3.469). In addition that story has a complex apparatus of other documents in the form of letters and remembered tape-recordings. Each of these passages employs the language of geometry and thereby reduces the living anatomy of the creatures, with their historical and cultural life, to that of beasts or machines. Through such descriptions they become symmetric objects, cones, with no possibility of change. The peculiarity of these passages may be related to their dealing with two orders of creatures, one much more like us than the other, as far as historicity is concerned. "The Whisperer in Darkness" presents a special case, for it seems to suggest that the creatures which present themselves as so sane, even sympathetic (Cannon, *H. P. Lovecraft* 91), with an intelligible communal history, are in fact raveners; the story represents a complex transition from the earlier model of alien as absolute other to Lovecraft's later work in which the possibility exists that within this time and space continuum, where matter is recognizably our matter, some alien life might experience knowledge and culture similar to ours; but if such creatures do exist, beyond them whirl raveners which they repress, ineffectually.

    To return to "The Shadow out of Time," though both a trained political economist and a trained psychologist, Peaslee ascribes an odd kind of history to the Great

Race. We find none of the details we might expect. It forms "a single, loosely knit nation or league, with major institutions in common," the political and economic system of the subgroups characterized "as a sort of fascistic socialism, with major resources rationally distributed, and power delegated to a small governing board" (*CF* 3.404). There are more details about governance, culture, technology, crime, and war, but they occupy no more than two pages in this sixty-page novella. The details devoted to the history proper are no more satisfying. The vagueness of the geography is matched by the vagueness of any verbs we might associate with historical process. The third and fourth chapters contain two versions of the history. The first with some elasticity sets it in the framework of the "Permian or Triassic" age (*CF* 3.382) and suggests that the race had "reared towers to the sky and delved into every secret of Nature" (385); there is a whiff of Babel about them. They "came down from the stars" and "conquered the secret of time," thus learning all things known and to be known by projecting themselves into the past and future (386). Having accomplished omniscience, they "chose from every era and life-form such thoughts, arts, and processes as might suit its own nature," though the past is more difficult to comprehend and embrace than the future (386). Their cultural identity is oddly passive; they resemble more islanders in the Pacific suffering culture shock under colonialism than the conquerors of time that they are; having discovered the sweep of time they are conquered by it, as Peaslee is. They have to some extent been changed by their intrusion on different points of time, rather as are the aliens of Samuel R. Delany's *The Einstein Intersection;* "templated on man" they have become more complex and now find it difficult "to remain perfect" because of the differences in which the ancient myths of human behavior have become involved (129). Imitation initiates transformation. After the Great Race tries to probe its own origin, it migrates in order to escape the irruption of the elder race which it knows will come (*DH* 391); cut off in time, they will not interact with it. Their reaction to the elder race that they discover on earth is to subdue it (407), drive it down, seal it away, and erase every allusion to it (407). It is hard not to wonder whether this event recalls the relation of the European to the Native American; Lovecraft's New England did not originally belong to the Puritan nor to the Enlightenment. Having done so, having gone through the only prominent historical event of their existence, the Great Race "maintain a cautious vigilance" (*CF* 3.408), waiting until it will be time for them to leave the earth again to the "utterly alien" race which had dominated it in the past (447).

Late in life Lovecraft accused himself of being concerned only with "the *externals* of history and antiquarianism, the *abstract* academic phases of philosophy," without regard for "the inside facts of history, the rational interpretation of periodic social crises, the foundations of economics and sociology, the actual state of the world today" (*CLM* 217). But it is one thing to perceive the intellectual necessity of a detailed discipline, quite another to embody it imaginatively or to believe in it. The history presented in "The Shadow out of Time," though exhibiting a touch of utopianism based on Lovecraft's engagement with the problems of the 1930s

(Joshi, *Decline* 144–45), suggests little of the language of historical change, nor does it indicate either energy or specificity. The history seems still-born.

Two other patterns of time parallel this history. One is the time that Peaslee experiences within his dreams, representing his daily life in the time of the Great Race. "All were the merest misty, disconnected fragments . . .," he comments, "not unfolded in their rightful sequence" (*CF* 3.400), so that other than the vaguest notion of traveling over the planet he cannot remember the give-and-take particularity of his encounter with individuals of the Great Race or with the captives; all that is left is the obsessive memory of writing in the archives. The other time exists in the six- or seven-year cycle of Peaslee's private history. In 1895 he becomes an instructor at Miskatonic University, beginning a quiet career disrupted by his amnesia in May 1908, which lasts until September 1913; but our own imaginations are liable to stretch this time to the world-historical date of August 1914. After the material of his dreams and of legends possesses him, he puts his research into order in 1920 and by 1922 is able to begin academic work again. His first publication of his findings occurs in 1928–29, coinciding with the end of Coolidge's administration and the beginning of the Great Depression, after which his life is uneventful until Mackenzie's letter arrives in 1935. Paralleling certain important events, the events of his history also occur with some regularity, not as we usually perceive in history, if we understand with Gadamer historical cognition not as the attempt to measure events by the standard of a progressive regularity but as the attempt to understand how this person, people, or nation came to be as it is concretely, once for all time (*Wahrheit* 10)—though we should note that several historiographers since Vico, especially Spengler whose influence on Lovecraft is demonstrable (Joshi, *Decline* 133–35), have attempted to impose such a pattern upon time.

In contrast to the Great Race, the elder race though weakening has an immense energy that its plasticity, lapses of visibility, and fragmentary whispers and whistles render difficult to contain (*CF* 3.408). But of its history we can say that it came down, built towers—in this aspect like the Great Race—preyed upon other beings, and driven down would again irrupt, a word used frequently. Very little to go on.

We learn more about the "elder things" (*CF* 3.407) from Peaslee's direct encounter, recorded by the document we are reading, written for his son. The encounter begins with the whistle he hears behind him and the panic he feels. The encounter is rendered by these nouns: avalanche, chaos, fragment (444, 445), wind, blast, noose, lasso, tug, shriek, tide (446), nightmare, vortex, fall, darkness, babel, pits, voids, horrors, crags, oceans, cities, towers, planet, aeons, vapour, whirlpool, flashes, struggles, tentacles, cyclone (447), and hurricane (448). The verbs are similar: slip, mangle, slide, split, plunge, trip, scramble, whistle (445), pipe, belch, leap, lurch, curl, twist, strike, hinder, hamper, dull, surge (446), struggle, plunge, engulf, writhe, and burrow (447). The striking detail is the several references to spirals, as though a cone were made dynamic. The two races have the same structure, but the terrifying one is still potent in our time, sucking the observer into its structure, so that while he seems to go forward he is in fact being drawn back. And this action parallels the discovery that Peaslee reveals in the last paragraph, having discovered it some four pages of narrative earlier. He documents the shape of an experience.

Another form of his encounter has happened earlier, in his researches after the war when he discovered in a copy of Junzt's *Unaussprechlichen Kulten* the hieroglyphics of his dreams, a volume in which the librarians assure him he must have written during his amnesia (*CF* 3.370). This page is mirrored by the document in his own hand, in English, which he finds in the Triassic ruins unearthed in the Australian desert. A captured history testifies to its indifference and identity *viva manu*. This shadow to human understanding could not exist in the form that it does were it not outside the dynamic structure of time.

Our observer cannot remain objective; he never was. We have noticed a tendency for an observer to be assimilated into the thing that he observes, as Ammi is into the Colour and the surveyor into Ammi. And Peaslee is assimilated to the Great Race, with a feeling horrible to him but which we feel cannot, for a scholar allowed into the greatest deposit of documents the world has ever contained, be an experience so very terrifying; we cannot imagine it being anything but an adventure to the bibliophile Lovecraft—and the temperature is lovely during the Triassic age. But is Peaslee assimilated to the elder race? He approaches the ruins at night impelled by a "lure and driving of fatality" (*CF* 3.426). He has to be there. He wrenches aside a fragment of stone so that a "trickling upward" of cool air beginning to "stream" out (424–25) wells up from the earth and the gulf which it suggests (425). This action was paralleled two pages earlier when, as he walked through the desert, his "dreams welled up into the waking world" (422). The entity willing its release from the earth, which we experience as one of the elder race, has its counterpart within Peaslee as he realizes that "something was fumbling and rattling at the latch of my recollection, while another unknown force sought to keep the portal barred" (422). The wall is within him, as is the assimilating gulf. And if we can put a name on the Colour, so we can on the elder race and the gulf it impersonates; the whistling, the piping, and the chaos we certainly recognize as the prerogative of Azathoth, to whom we have perhaps come closer than anywhere else in Lovecraft's fiction, in this Lucretian language of the curl, twist, and vortex, possibly mediated through Pope and Milton (cf. Quayle 24–27). Still-born, disconnected and jumbled, mechanical, conquering, random, the time that Peaslee encounters, though one of origins, exhibits neither the "initial fullness" nor the therapy which Lévy regards as potential (111). Time in "The Shadow out of Time" is as friable as the space exhibited by the stone in "The Colour out of Space"; and Peaslee is in fragments too.

We have come some distance from the nature of the document, but only in order to demonstrate how difficult the notion of the document in Lovecraft is. Above all, the document is a point of trespass beyond the unbreakable wall of nonsense. Behind history stands natural history, which for Lovecraft signifies the unintelligible creature; he only uses the language of science when the creature being described is capable of history, though that history itself seems to us episodic and static, without any nodes of complex uniqueness to individualize it; and that scientific language suffers from a mechanical quality that does harm to the living creature. But Lovecraft no more means to vivify or individualize the creature than its history; he does not believe in the significance which history seems to deliver to the human race. For him history only bursts into significance at a small number of points, Republican Rome, Augustan England, and late-Colonial New England, the eras that overshadowed and nourished his lost childhood, points that are ineffective in the contemporary world except within his own embattled self. The only document which he considers effective goes through the blank of human history into the thorough chaos which lies on the other side, which is no other side, raging against the unstable walls of the world.

PART II
Sorties

"The Picture in the House": Images of Complicity

> The Creator, who made man such that he must eat to live, incites him to eat by means of appetite, and rewards him with pleasure. (Brillat-Savarin 13)

In the anthology *An Epicure in the Terrible* I developed a theory that encompassed many levels within Lovecraft's fiction, arguing that landscapes, gods, and characters could be regarded as doubles. In order to develop that analysis, I would like to apply those concepts to Lovecraft's story, "The Picture in the House," a short work written in 1920 before he had developed most of the materials of his world. In the process other aspects of his thought will become clearer.

In brief, the theory concerned four modes of perception: the personal, the ideal, the shadow, and the double. The personal is identified with the accustomed, insignificant, unquestioned world in which we live, neither more nor less than what it seems; the personal is a neutral mode. The ideal is that world that suddenly seems more than usual, expansive of promise. The shadow is the world that suddenly seems less than usual, meaningless; but the nothingness that it seems to project is powerfully aggressive. The double perception fuses the ideal and shadow worlds; it is a vision of the personal world as though it were full of ambiguous meaning through the modes of the ideal and the shadow, which otherwise seem fragments of the personal in which they began. Different kinds of imagery are representative of the different modes, especially of the ideal and the shadow: the imagery of the personal world is unaccented, commonplace, for Lovecraft the fact of New England; the imagery of the ideal comprises such objects as windows, doors, mirrors, wells, plays of light; the imagery of the shadow is underworld, always on the other side of the ideal and a distortion of it, and though barren always filled with energy; the imagery of the double recurs to the personal imagery in the light of the ideal and the shadow, subtly synthetic of the world as we know it (Waugh 221–26)..

In the first paragraph of "The Picture in the House" the protagonist offers his story to ideal readers, the "searchers after horror" and "the true epicure in the terrible" who exist for "a new thrill" (*CF* 1.206). This language is charged, in retrospect, introducing as it does a story of cannibalism. And it is not a language foreign to Lovecraft himself, who wrote in 1920, "The utter emptiness of all the recognised goals of human endeavour is to the detached spectator deliciously apparent—the tomb yawns and grins so ironically" (*RK* 158), equating the spectator and the tomb in an oral imagery. The shadow ghoul is present in this language. The narrator, however, makes his offer with some irony, as though those ideal readers were not quite everything they seem, having never understood the world for which they are searching; as Stefan Dziemianowicz points out, it is not impossible that Lovecraft is indulging in critical self-parody here (174). Two kinds of readers are implicit in this offer: the first kind includes the ideal searchers of "strange, far places" (*CF* 1.206); the second kind includes the readers of *Weird Tales,* who suppress their personal mode of existence through reading the magazine for the sake of the vicarious thrill and the vicarious journey, both of which are ideal modes because they offer "the chief end and justification of existence" (206). To these readers the narrator offers a new thrill that is closer to them; he offers to reinterpret a personal landscape both as ideal, because of its thrill, and as shadow, because of its threat. It might seem that this narrator were claiming to take his readers on a tour of at least three of the modes, perhaps in order to leave them within the fusion of the double. As cognoscenti full of knowledge, however, he is prior to the shadow, apparently unaffected, and therefore an ideal narrator; he is untouched by the uncertainty inherent to the double mode. He is "at once the rationalist and the romantic" (Cannon, *H. P. Lovecraft* 38), but these aspects are not coordinated. He is a bit too sure of himself, too much the literary critic perhaps, and therefore we may question whether he will be capable of the double vision that he seems to offer the reader. The story begins in an act of bad faith, an act of inauthenticity since the narrator is apparently incapable of engaging his own promise.

Later details, however, suggest that the narrator is merely a personal self, a pedant looking for "genealogical data" who has taken a short-cut to Arkham on his bicycle and become lost when overtaken by a storm (*CF* 1.208). The search for data is not an act of uncovering the truth but of seizing hold of documentary facts without being aware of the ambivalence of the document. After the portentous beginning, his presence becomes accidental for a short time. And though the old man later calls him a "young Sir," the impression of a pedant is reinforced when his look reminds the old man of a schoolmaster he knew years earlier (216).

One detail of this material about the narrator requires closer scrutiny, the bicycle he rides. Lovecraft rode his own bicycle from 1900 to 1913, "perhaps forming in this way that close acquaintance with rural New England which made me a local antiquarian" (*MWM* 303). The bicycle gave him an "intimate contact with the country" (*RK* 156). It was also connected with his discovery of astronomy, since he used it to ride to the Ladd Observatory in 1903 (*RK* 71). Biographically the bicycle has personal and ideal reverberations. Later Lovecraft was to recall that he rode his bicycle in 1904 while contemplating suicide after the death of his maternal grandfather Whipple Phillips: "That summer I was always on my bicycle—wishing to be away from home as much as possible, since my abode reminded me of the home I had lost" (*JVS* 222). Unable to imagine how "an old man of 14" (*JVS* 221) could adjust his life, he contemplated drowning himself in "the warm, shallow, reed-grown Barrington River down the east shore of the bay" (*JVS* 222). It was his grandfather who, "observing my taste in reading, used to devise all sorts of impromptu original yarns. . . . He was the only other person I know—young or old—who cared for macabre & horrific fiction" (*JVS* 218–19). What pain the death of such a grandfather can cause! Surely a demonized grandfather Phillips, whose library did so much to influence the young Lovecraft, lurks in the preternaturally old man of the story, as surely as Lovecraft lurks in the young man, old beyond his years, who constructs the story. The bicycle extends to several aspects of the story: a relic of the books to which grandfather Phillips had introduced him, an emblem of the pain of his grandfather's death, it offers an escape which only leads in the story to the threat of death. Personal, ideal, and shadow, the bicycle is also a potential double that the rest of the story activates.

This old man, however, is not the only old man whom Lovecraft treats at this time, for in January 1920 he had written "The Terrible Old Man," with the powerfully contradictory diction which Donald R. Burleson so ably laid forth: "Is the old man 'reserved,' withdrawn, friendless, weak, vulnerable, helpless? Or is he possessed of *reserves*—is he covertly strong, capable, powerfully allied, potentially dangerous?" (*Lovecraft* 29–30). To this description we should add that his eyes are yellow, cat-like by implication, a detail revealed as though it had more significance than it can immediately bear, and that despite his presence in the town no one seems to know how old he is or when he arrived. The last sentence, in referring to "his unremembered youth" (*CF* 1.144), implies that his age is absolutely out of the ordinary.

Contradictions of this sort surround the old man of "The Picture in the House." His age contradicts every expectation. Though "white-bearded," with a "thin, weak voice full of fawning respect," he is "tall and powerful" and "abnormally ruddy," and his "blue eyes, though a trifle bloodshot, seemed inexplicably keen and burning" (*CF* 1.212). The contradiction implied in that last detail is rather odd, inexplicable indeed as Lovecraft underlines, for blue eyes seldom burn. If the detail is reminiscent of the eye in Poe's "The Tell-Tale Heart," the opaque, "pale blue eye, with a film over it," the eye "of a vulture" (792), "all a dull blue, with a hideous veil" (795), an "Evil Eye" (793) that pursues the murderer before he ever turns the beam of the dark lantern on it, Lovecraft has taken an image that Poe rationalizes through his plot and condensed it for its own sake; and this high-handed manipulation of an image for its own sake is symptomatic of much else in the story. The impotence that shrouds the old man of Lovecraft's story barely conceals the intense shadow beneath it that vividly re-interprets the past in his oblique comments on the schoolmaster, the captain, and the parson, figures of the Puritan establishment (*CF* 1.213–14). Though the narrator considers him an "ignorant old man" (214) who can only look at the pictures in his book, this old man is able to set the past in a new light. His love of the past is more vital than the genealogical lore that the pedantic young man means to research; and his telling such intimate stories, filled with rumor but also a sort of affection (the affection a gourmand has for a good meal), stories of men who otherwise inhabit only the pages of a chronicle, makes them ambiguously alive; and insofar as he can accomplish this vivification he is more authentic than the narrator. Little relation exists so far between the personal self of the narrator and the shadow self of the old man; each, however, combines opposites in an original way that has to do with age and youth and authenticity and inauthenticity.

Parallel to this confrontation, an increasingly meaningful series of detail indicates a profound mediation in various ideal images. This series begins in the conventional imagery of the mound, "catacombs," "mausolea," and "towers" (*CF* 1.206), displaced by the windows of old houses and of the house of the old man, "bleared" and "opaque," that "stare at travellers so slyly"; more intensely, they "stare shockingly, as if blinking through a lethal stupor which wards off madness by dulling the memory of unutterable things" (207). The ideal quality of these images, however, is undercut by the diction of slyness that as we have seen suggests anti-Semitic imagery that for Lovecraft is the language of the shadow (Waugh 241–42). The characteristics of the old man's eyes, opaque though piercing and ironic, are foreshadowed in the landscape that he shares with his Puritan community. The windows serve the function, as windows so often do, of concealing and half-revealing. That lethal stupor, the narrator supposes, finds its correlative in the old man's, waking "from a sound sleep" (*CF* 1.211), as the old man confirms when he says, "I need a paowerful sight o' naps naowadays" (212): how odd a phrase, as it combines vision and sleep! Let us never say that Lovecraft could not achieve special effects with his use of dialect.

The third paragraph uses identical ideal terms to describe the Puritans, in a passage remarkable in this early story for its complexity as it juggles visual and kinetic imagery with the threat of oral imagery: "Divorced from the enlightenment of civilization, the strength of these Puritans turned into singular channels; and in their isolation, morbid self-repression, and struggle for life with relentless Nature, there came to them dark furtive traits from the prehistoric depths of their cold Northern heritage" (*CF* 1.207). This remarkable blend of Darwin and Freud contrasts the inward urges of self-isolation and repression to the outward urges of hunger, which are also represented by the "dark furtive traits" so obscurely alluded to. These suggestions of cannibalism Lovecraft might have associated with witchcraft following the example of Sir Walter Scott (231–32). The passage follows the person, rather than the traits, downward: "Erring as all mortals must, they were forced by their rigid code to seek concealment above all else; so that they came to use less and less taste in what they concealed" (*CF* 1.207). Here also the oral imagery basic to the story appears and denies the concealment it affirms, to give way quickly to the visual material once more: "Only the silent, staring houses in the backwoods can tell all that has lain hidden since the early days; and they are not communicative, being loath to shake off the drowsiness which helps them forget" (207). But if speech does not occur, space is made for the oral function to reappear. The passage is a knot of approach and avoidance. The shadowy hints of hunger are staved off, the threat of the material, accidental, irrational body tempered; but hunger and body shall reappear all the more powerfully as the story proceeds.

The other component of this passage is its faint use of the background, personal imagery of the Mother, which Lovecraft associates with the origin of New England history. When he wrote the story in December his mother had only six more months to live, the mother whose father's death had caused such a trauma earlier in Lovecraft's life. The narrator sets his scene in this fashion: "Most horrible of all sights" in New England "are the little unpainted wooden houses remote from traveled ways, usually squatted upon some damp, grassy slope or leaning against some gigantic outcropping of rock. Two hundred years and more they have leaned or squatted there, while the vines have crawled and the trees have swelled and spread" (*CF* 1.207). This is language Lovecraft will later associate with the Crawling Chaos Nyarlathotep—of whom he had the dream in which that figure originates during the month that he wrote this story—and with the various toad divinities, above all Clark Ashton Smith's Tsathoggua that Lovecraft found so congenial to his imagery. But the Mother is not only present in the landscape; she is also present in those "dark furtive traits" of cannibalism that Scott discovered in witchcraft. This personal, enveloping imagery shall crystallize as a threat later, like the oral imagery.

Finally in regards to this so singularly rich third paragraph, we must pay attention to its frankly essayistic style; for a short time we could believe that we were not reading a narrative but an analysis and synthesis of several documentary accounts of backwoods Massachusetts and its culture. Lovecraft writes in this fashion at the beginning of several stories, most obviously at the beginning of "The Call of Cthulhu," and it behooves us to recognize the double nature of such a stance as it attempts to cope, futilely of course, with the complex nature of the story it is about to recount.

Let us take up again the series of ideal images we are examining, which indeed seem to accent even more heavily the maternal imagery just examined. The "suggestive and secretive door" of the house reveals a room "rich in relics," a "collector's paradise" (*CF* 1.209)—ideal for this collector of data—including the greatest treasure, a book that belongs in a museum or library and makes the wonder of the narrator increase as the ideal aspect increases (213). In the book, in the last paragraph of the story, a "picture staring repulsively upward" (217) at the protagonist, personal self or ideal other, and at the shadow recalls the staring windows of the opening. We thus move through a sequence of tombs, windows, Puritan landscape (with its knotted visual, oral, kinetic, and maternal imagery), door, book, and picture (or window), the dirty glasses of the old man (214), and the implication of the staring eyes of the protagonist and antagonist, a sequence that promises more and more significance. The climactic image, however, is the lightning-flash in the rain (216) and the "small red spattering" that gives a picturesque vividness, a reality, to the picture; on the ceiling the drop changes to "a large irregular spot of wet crimson which seemed to spread" (217), the only image that represents the second flash that the narrator does not see, because he has to shut his eyes—or because that flash and the revelation it bears overwhelms human comprehension and destroys the "house of unutterable secrets . . . bringing the oblivion which alone saved my mind" (217). Through this series of images the narrator becomes identical with the stupor of those windows "which wards off madness by dulling the memory of unutterable things" (207) and by implication identical with the old man whose community those windows represented. The old man's last words, *"more the same"* (217), make solipsistic sense upon several levels, not least that he and the narrator and the reader are the more than the same in their need to live through incorporation.

These considerations, of course, raise the question of the conclusion of the story, which may well strike readers as "entirely gratuitous" (Schweitzer, "Abnormal Longevity" 12) through its failure to deal reasonably with the plot; but there can be no doubt about the imagistic necessity of the story's last paragraph, given the way that it fulfills the several passages throughout the story that have prepared for it. Windows and eyes, lightning and blood, speech and oblivion, young man and old man are converging.

Parallel to this series of ideal images, various oppositions occur that imply the process by which the ideal world and the shadow world become the double world through a Chinese-box series of oxymorons. Lovecraft implicitly contrasts the odd fertility of the landscape, with its "lawless luxuriances of green and guardian shrouds of shadow" (*CF* 1.207) and its "rain of such chilling copiousness," to the "leafless elms," "rocky hill" (208), and dirty, dusty, bare house, the house with its "rusty latch" (209) on the one hand and the abnormal energy in the upstairs room on the other. Hardly to be differentiated from their landscape in this regard, the Puritans "indeed flourished free from the restrictions of their fellows, but cowered in an appalling slavery to the dismal phantasms of their own minds" (207). This double landscape is clearly more than either ideal or shadow and modulates their simple particulars. The house itself is divided. The young man chooses between closed doors leading to rooms on the right and the left. Though of course it makes sense that he choose the sinister door, where the fateful *Regnum Congo* rests on the table, I cannot but feel an irrational anxiety caused by the pattern we have noted that the same book rests on the same table in the same room on the right side, its mirror image, "more the same."

Within that mode of the double, the narrator feels a disturbing complicity with the old man, a "desire to turn the pages" and a shame "at my susceptibility to so slight a thing," that is to say the wretched picture that he feels compelled to belittle because it moves him (*CF* 1.210); and he wonders "if my host could help me in the task at which I was labouring" (213), so rich in the past the old man has become through feeding upon it. Both narrator and old man seem compelled; the old man's "tickle" (215) and *"cravin'"* (216), his slavery to the taste and trespass that his idea of "new life" (217) merely rationalizes, correspond to the narrator's desires. At this stage the narrator is no longer accidental to his story but an integral part of it. It is unimaginable that the old man would talk so confidentially to a person who showed no sign of being interested in the same curious matters as he; the narrator must be self-revealing in order for the old man to be self-revealing. Otherwise a simple crack over the head would end both the young man and the possibility of his ever telling the story, which is now his story as it always was, and as it is ours, reading it as we do. It is through our existence and our nature, because we want to turn the pages and because we blush at so slight a thing as these pictures and at our weakness in reading so contrived a story as this, that the book and story gain their existence. Bacon's words are à propos: "Some books are to be tasted, others to be swallowed, and some few to be chewed and digested" ("Of Studies," 130). The *Regnum Congo* savors of Eve's apple.

As S. T. Joshi has demonstrated ("Lovecraft and the *Regnum Congo*"), the old man's volume raises interesting questions of authenticity and imitation given the fact that Lovecraft knew of it only through the secondary source of Thomas Huxley's collection, *Man's Place in Nature and Other Anthropological Essays* (13), a work that with its emphasis upon the continuity between ape and human renders dubious the question of any discontinuity between Caucasian and African, though both Lovecraft and Huxley would deny such a hint. But all evidence is hard to come by. Huxley's essay on the man-like apes that opens and closes on the Pigafetta material concludes also with Paul Belloni Du Chaillu's description of gorillas, in which it is unclear whether the beasts make the sound Kooloo or, "according to that eminently trustworthy observer Dr. Savage, . . . a sound like 'Whoo-whoo'" (71). Huxley decides that "as long as [Du Chaillu's] narrative remains in its present state of unexplained and apparently inexplicable confusion, it has no claim to original authority respecting any subject whatsoever" (72), an opinion we should keep in mind whenever considering the question how to pronounce the name of that anomalous entity Cthulhu. "Tulu" is the approximation in Lovecraft's ghost-written story "The Mound." In 1934 he wrote that "Khûl´-hloo" would be as correct as the human mouth could manage (*FLB* 194). I now believe that our efforts should bear a French accent, an amalgam of the sounds "Kooloo," "Whoo-whoo," and "Chaillu," as the various orthographies indicate. If this is so, the story loses something of its integrity and becomes a part of the Cthulhu mythos—that inauthentic creation of August Derleth—which may explain why the young man is taking a short cut to Arkham (*CF* 1.208). But to realize the possibility that Du Chaillu's narrative "has no claim to original authority" is also to realize a further significance to the pictures that the narrator and the old man examine with such care, their iconic significance. The cannibals represented in the Pigafetta volume are the gods of the story, to which we are tempted to ascribe such meanings as Lovecraft develops in his later fiction.

These gods are explicated by the book, the ideal mediator, which contains important drawings of "half monkeys an' half men," "a sort of dragon with the head of an alligator" (*CF* 1.214), and "negroes with white skins and Caucasian features" (210), a detail sufficiently important for the narrator to repeat it: "The especially bizarre thing was that the artist had made his Africans look like white men" (215). This description is purely Lovecraft's, not Huxley's, in whose account the only basis for it is elsewhere in the essay, in the report that the face of the mandrill is "covered with white skin" (16) and the story which a Mr. William Smith told of the creature in 1744, having been made a present of one:

> It was a she-cub, of six months' age. . . . I gave it to one of the slaves, who knew how to feed and nurse it, being a very tender sort of animal; but whenever I went off the deck the sailors began to teaze it—some loved to see its tears and hear it cry; others hated its snotty nose; one who hurt it, being checked by

the negro that took care of it, told the slave he was very fond of his countrywoman, and asked him if he should like her for a wife? To which the slave very readily replied, "No, this no my wife; this a white woman—this fit wife for you." This unlucky wit of the negro's, I fancy, hastened its death, for next morning it was found dead under the windlass. (16–17)

It is unclear whether the unspoken, ambivalent horror of this detail consists of the possibility that the African cannibal can pass for white, that the white can so easily be imitated that the difference is negligible, indeed in an ideal world non-existent, or that the white can regress to cannibalism, as the old man does—to say nothing of the sexual threat and the triumph that the man's witticism had accomplished. These pictures exist within the double mode where opposites are so liable to exchange qualities, to combine, to confuse and to fuse, to demonstrate the difficulty of the lines that are drawn within the ideal and shadow modes. But we must also admit along with the narrator and the old man the allure latent in the various ambivalences of this passage that makes male pass for female, native pass for colonist, animal pass for human, black pass for white; such ambivalence becomes the domain of Nyarlathotep in the later fiction. And we must note the possibility that all of this anxiety about imitation is simply a displacement for Lovecraft's anti-Semitic anxiety that a Jew could assimilate Western culture, assimilate and digest.

The gods in this story are embedded in a pantheon for which we can write a genealogical record. On the one hand, Grandfather Phillips begets Howard Phillips Lovecraft, who begets the old man and the narrator, who begets in his narrative the old man (it is hard not to think of Buck Mulligan's parody of Steven Dedalus's theory of Hamlet, "He proves by algebra that Hamlet's grandson is Shakespeare's grandfather and that he himself is the ghost of his own father" [*Ulysses* 1.555–57]). Lovecraft also begets Cthulhu and Nyarlathotep, who we find present by analogy in this story; Lovecraft is as it were in labor for them. But we may also consider Huxley one of Lovecraft's begetters; and in regard to this story Huxley on the one hand owes his birth to Pigafetta, who owes his to Eduardo Lopez, who owes his to the Anziques—on the other hand Huxley owes his birth to Du Chaillu, who owes his to the Ape (whether Kooloo or Whoo whoo it is hard to say). In addition to begetting Huxley, Pigafetta begets the imagination of the old man through the intermediaries of Captain Ebenezer Holt and the Brothers De Bry with their illustrations, though we should remember that the "Scripter about slayin'" has a part in begetting him (*CF* 1.215); and bypassing the old man, the Brothers De Bry have an immediate effect upon the narrator. Finally we must admit that the old man begets Parson Clark and the schoolmaster who resembles the young man; the ghoul gives a narrative life to the people he devours. The author himself, in relation to all these forebears, is a clearing-house of deity. We have already seen that to lift such stories off the page one must have a taste for them, be as the narrator has said in his prologue a "true epicure" (206) for whom "utter emptiness" is "deliciously apparent" (*RK* 158). Only such energetic involvement makes the stories alive. This genealogy, so obviously different from that which the young man had imagined, is a much more authentic uncovering than one concerned with mere data.

A problem with this genealogy, however, is its being a mere filiation; the mothers, wives, and daughters are apparently excluded as human characters in the drama. But they are not absent. In Huxley's essay they appear as the mandrill, "fit wife for you." In Lovecraft's story they appear as forests, houses, rooms, libraries, books, ships, even languages, the various mother tongues of Italian, French (in Du Chaillu), Kooloo, and the pre-Revolutionary dialect of the old man. They also appear as the pond of Parson Clark, the rain, and the meditation into which "the tone of the old man now sank very low" (*CF* 1.216) immediately before the final revelation. The female, which the incestuous male genealogy attempts to exclude, returns dispersed through the landscape and the language.

I believe that we can characterize the gods adumbrated in the story further. The attempt of the old man to become like the cannibal certainly suggests their identity. And the young man's complicitous reaction, his desire and shame, hints at the possibility that anyone dealing with such material might regress. What, then, of the author by second-hand, for the book is "per Philippum Pigafettam, olim ex Edoardo Lopez acroamatis lingua Italica excerpta, nunc Latio sermone donata" (Huxley 2). Did Pigafetta yearn for long pig? Did, by the trivial accident of the name, Lovecraft's grandfather Phillips, whom we have already recognized as involved in the figure of the old man? And did grandfather Phillips devour the autonomy of the young boy when he died? What do we mean by the cannibalism of the story? The custom of the Anziques is remarkable for keeping a butcher's shop. Are they cannibals, ghouls, or thrifty Yankees? What is happening in the old man's second story? Is that a shambles or, rather, an orderly system of exsanguination? Lovecraft's reticence invites us to imagine various narratives for the gods of the upper room.

It is the power of these gods to fuse the narrator and the old man, the timorous genealogist and the cannibal-ghoul, in a series of images of expansion. The narrator has discovered a significant, preserving landscape, not yet witch-haunted but certainly so by implication, before he has ever arrived in Arkham, while he was merely riding his bicycle on way to Arkham, by a short-cut, in this out-of-the-way house with its suppositious shambles upstairs and its bookish spareness downstairs. Lovecraft we might say has also arrived at his true Arkham by not arriving at the hunger-driven Arkham that the young man had begun to fear lay behind his genealogical research. But the young man was not wrong, for he has come upon many more begetters than he had any right to expect; so far does this story anticipate Lovecraft's stories in which protagonists confront their powerful, devouring ancestors. But to say so much is to say more than the blank of the lightning allows, more than "more the same" allows.

But we cannot take refuge in the lightning without examining the ashes. The young man opens his eyes "in a smoky solitude of blackened ruins" (*CF* 1.217). The Jupiter-wielded lightning, "the titanic thunderbolt of thunderbolts" (217), so often associated in tradition with justice and retribution bears more of a relation in this story with the imagery of the burning eyes of the old man. Jupiter becomes conflated with Saturn his father, as perhaps he ought since he was the only one of his siblings to escape his father's hunger and to assume the old Titan's throne. When Lovecraft refers to a painting by Goya in "Pickman's Model" the context makes it probable that the work is *Saturn Devouring One of His Sons* (*CF* 2.58). The burning eyes of the old man devour his house and himself—in his solitude he has become a cannibal of his own heart (Bacon, "Of Friendship," 72). But the narrator survives to beget and to feed on the reader.

At the Mountains of Madness:
The Subway and the Shoggoth

I

> The apparition of these faces in the crowd;
> Petals on a wet, black bough. (Pound, *Personae* 111)

One of the most impressive scenes in *At the Mountains of Madness* is the moment when a shoggoth bursts forth upon the narrator and his friend Danforth, who in an attempt to contain the utterly alien within a familiar context suddenly begins to chant the stations of the Boston–Cambridge subway line, so much does the entire scene resemble the arrival of a subway car at a station (*CF* 3.146–50). In certain ways this scene is not out of the ordinary in Lovecraft's fiction, for the flight through a tunnel forms a frequent, ecstatic climax. But the scene in the small novel is imaginatively impressive for the extended particularity of its imagery in addition to being remarkable because it is one of the few allusions to the daily life of a metropolis in Lovecraft's fiction. S. T. Joshi is justified to exclaim, referring to both this scene and one in "Pickman's Model," "Here, then, is certainly one example of a modern—even prosaic—device inspiring Lovecraft's imagination!" ("Topical References" 250), but the imaginative weight of the scene increases its impact, above all because the tunnel at the bottom of the world and the other tunnels which criss-cross Lovecraft's fiction provide a way of understanding the prejudices which terrified him but which he could not do without.

Subways were not that recent an innovation, the first subway line having been constructed in London in 1863 (Bobrick 101). But by the time the Paris Metro was opened in 1900 (154) and the New York system in 1904 (232), the Boston line, the first in North America, had already been opened in 1897 (223). Though a certain amount of opposition was mounted against the subway because of its underworld associations, its frequent damage to the landscape, and anxiety for the safety of the people who might use it, it quickly became a part of the normal background of the megapolitan scene; after all, it was the majority of people, the working and middle classes, who used the underground lines. It is both the popular and the modern aspect of the subways that forms the context of Ezra Pound's imagist poem, "In a Station of the Metro," but the poem also concerns mortality. Not surprisingly Wells's Morlocks, the proletariat in revolt, were underground creatures.

In his letters Lovecraft refers to the subway neutrally, as a part of the background. He had quite possibly used it in his visits to Boston in 1910, 1916, and 1919, the memorable event of his hearing Dunsany lecture (*RK* 146). His account of his subway ride in 1921 is quite off-hand—"Arrived at South Station, I took subway and car to Allston and was soon at the now familiar 20 Webster Street"

(*FFF* 31)—as is his account of his first visit to New York to visit Sonia Greene and Samuel Loveman, "By means of subway and taxi, we beat Loveman to 259 Parkside" (*MWM* 85); on the same visit he was proud to discover a copy of *Home Brew* at a subway station and show them the latest installment of "Herbert West" (*MWM* 91). On another visit when a subway tie-up delayed him "hopelessly" he took it in stride (*FFF* 193), like the experienced urbanite he had become. On a visit in 1928 he was still speaking well of the transport: "From [Flatbush], New York seems remote and incredible indeed—and it is difficult to believe that the howling bedlam of 42nd St. is only a half-hour away on the subway. That is the one mitigating thing which makes it possible for me to remain here for any continuous time. I have not yet . . . been above ground in the crowded mid-town district, save for one trip to the public library" (*SL* 2.239). A few years later he pointed out that the subway has the immense advantage of protection from the January cold (*JFM* 307). In December 1934 he said of another visit that "the weather will be a troublesome factor, but in N. Y. the subway system forms a convenient way of getting around without much exposure" (*ET* 286). This detail is of interest as far as *At the Mountains of Madness* is concerned, for since one reason for placing the story in the Antarctic is the intense cold, a positive aspect of the tunnels in that story is the protection they offer from the cold. But that protection harbors worse dangers than the cold.

Only in retrospect, comfortably back in Providence that never felt the need of a subway system, did Lovecraft imagine "hurtling through interstellar blackness in cryptic subways, never knowing on just what planet or within just what universe I would next emerge to overwhelming light" (*JFM* 223); only in retrospect did the subway become material for the imagination. Whatever his other phobias, Lovecraft seems never to have suffered from claustrophobia, though he did suffer from "a distinct fear of *very large enclosed spaces*" (*CLM* 324), what he called a combination of claustrophobia and agoraphobia. Since the examples that he gives, "the shadowy interior of a deserted gas-house—an empty assembly-room," have emptiness in common, it is doubtful that the subway ever aroused this fear. But his linking of the fear with "with the black abysses" of his childhood nightmares does resemble his imaginative phrase, "hurtling through interstellar blackness," and confirms that the subway, once it is emptied of people, becomes available as a landscape of terror.

But the people of the subway may be a source of threat also. Sonia Davis recalled in the addendum to her memoir that the subway was not always a neutral place, for "whenever he would meet crowds of people—in the subway, or, at the noon hour, on the sidewalks in Broadway, or crowds, wherever he happened to find them, and these were usually the workers of minority races—he would become livid with anger and rage" (148). Since the subway was the transportation par excellence of the working class it is hard to imagine how Lovecraft could have avoided this rage when he rode the lines. In a subway, moreover, a person is exposed to the inspection of strangers. Samuel Loveman recalled an occasion when Lovecraft remarked, because a woman had as Loveman put it given Lovecraft the eye, presumptively on account of his odd appearance, "My one desire . . . is to remain inconspicuous and unnoticed" (241), a desire difficult to satisfy in a subway. It is difficult to remain inconspicuous, moreover, when livid with rage.

But Lovecraft has many prejudices. In 1925 he wrote to his aunt how he and a friend escaped from a park invaded by African-Americans: "Wilted by the sight, we did no more than take a side path to the shore and back and reënter the subway for the long homeward ride—waiting to find a train not too reminiscent of the packed hold of one of John Brown's Providence merchantmen on the middle passage from the Guinea coast to Antigua or the Barbadoes" (*FFF* 310). The subway can, unfortunately, resemble a slave ship. With such a vision it is not strange that Lovecraft's racism enters into his fiction. The casual description of blacks in "Medusa's Coil" (*CF* 4.298–99) is a blotch on the work, for the miscegenation of the last paragraph is clearly tacked on, a mere appendage. The conclusion was an original element of the story that the ghostwriter Lovecraft received from Zealia Bishop; but he developed so much else in the story that the conclusion became a formal accident. Lovecraft shared his prejudices about African-Americans with the rest of America, but they did not energize his imagination, perhaps because the entire society felt so secure in the stereotypic character it projected; as Elisabeth Young-Bruehl suggests, caged securely within "the American national household fantasy" (35) African-Americans did not obtrude into Lovecraft's own fantasies. Both "Facts Concerning the Late Arthur Jermyn and His Family" and "The Picture in the House," which trace the evil to Africa, are early stories, more concerned with Darwinian anxieties than with cultural invasion. Only in "The Shadow over Innsmouth" does he pick up the theme again, though the evil there is a volatile compound of the threats of devolution, immigration, alienage, sexuality, and the family drama (Lovett-Graff 180–89). The climax that these four stories share, the cleansing by fire, surely represents a violent reaction to miscegenation and devolution but one that, given its finality, affirms the original racist view. If an African-American attempted to transgress the narrow boundaries that the nation had drawn, Lovecraft's reaction was violent; "The Picture in the House" is such an interesting story in part because the African-Americans it fantasizes, or rather that the illustrator of the book fantasizes, have "white skins and Caucasian features" (*CF* 1.210). Nevertheless, the descriptions of Jews and Italians in the New York stories, of Central Europeans in "Dreams in the Witch House," and of Italians in "The Haunter in the Dark" are more complex and violent, although the raving against Poles and Italians, a prejudice with some historical context in the changing population of New England, seems present in the stories because they were swept into the maelstrom of the ahistorical anti-Semitism. Pathological fantasy takes precedence over historical data.

In his letters Lovecraft consistently drew a line between his racism and anti-Semitism. Blacks were racially inferior, Jews culturally alien. Shortly after returning to Providence from New York he closed an analysis of the Jewish situation in this way:

What, then, shall we do with our Jews? Absorb a few as Aryans—well and good—it has been done to some slight extent without ill effect; for most Jews hold like mules to their beliefs, and most are racially unfit for amalgamation anyhow. What of this alien majority? Well—as with the negro, there is only one thing we can do as an immediate expedient to save ourselves; *Keep them out of our national and racial life.* With the negro the fight is wholly biological, whilst with the Jew it is mainly spiritual; but the principle is the same. (*SL* 2.67)

A propos of the Nazis in 1933 he wrote, "It's hardly accurate to compare the Jewish with the negro problem. The trouble with the Jew is not his blood—which can mix with ours without disastrous results—but his persistent & antagonistic *culture-tradition*" (*JVS* 133); and a few months later he reiterated, "It isn't *religion*—all religion is a negligible factor today. It is only slightly *race*—half the Jews in existence are of very superior stock, as their ability to undermine our culture shews; and only a fraction are more physically repulsive than many races whom we hate less. The real, impassible barrier is *cultural*" (*JFM* 324). The difficulty in seeing the problem clearly, according to this passage, is the confusion of Christianity with Northern, Germanic culture, for Christianity is itself a "silly, alien, decadent Jewish by-product" that extends "the Hebrew slave-psychology" (*JFM* 324–25). Lovecraft had adopted Nietzsche's analysis, just as he adopted another part of Nietzsche's views, that of supporting the free male's prerogative against "hair-splitting old slave-women" (*JFM* 325); sexism and anti-Semitism join hands in a fantasy of weakness, because the crucial point for Lovecraft is his desire for strength and power. His insistence upon tradition and culture masks the meaning of the Nordic tradition for him, an exaggerated insistence upon strength and freedom. In opposition to his fantasy of the Jew he upholds a fantasy of the Teutonic race, one about which he wavered for only a moment during the Great War when he lamented the division of Anglo-Saxons against the Hun (*RK* 98); more characteristic of his attitude is his rant of power, "We are strong men, for we make men do what we want" (*SL* 1.274). This stereotype for Lovecraft is the other component of anti-Semitism, the desire for strength that accompanies the fear of weakness; but this passage, a parody of desire, almost allows him to see the ridiculousness of the complex and dismantle it, if fear and hatred did not blind him. He calls these strong men different names at different times; but whether Hun, Teuton, Aryan, Caucasian, Viking, Anglo-Saxon, Norman, English gentleman, even Roman, the object of his desire maintains itself by floating among fantasies that refuse to be defined.

As for Jews, the object of Lovecraft's hatred, he claims to have two kinds of Jews in mind:

> We must not forget that the normal & successful assimilation (*full* assimilation to *our* culture, without any compromise or concession on our part) of a *few* Spaniards & Jews has nothing to do with the totally different problems presented when *hundreds of thousands* of Cubans & Eastern European ghettoes begin pouring in & actually changing the predominant blood-composition of whole sections of our territory. (*JVS* 157–58)

Once more his problem is cultural—but it does not remain cultural when an alien culture and appearance begin to make massive claims upon his Anglo-Nordic society. At that point the problem becomes racial, which is to say biological, and the temperature of the writing rises. In New York, for instance, "the Jews are of an inferior strain, & so numerous that they would essentially modify the physical type" (RB 201). Numbers, not strength, achieve the victory of lesser peoples; Lovecraft is not that interested in the anti-Semitic fantasy of financial invasion. It is what he calls a biological heritage, that is to say race, which is never to be ignored (JVS 154). In the middle of one of his longest arguments for assimilation he still claims that the Jew "has been content to cringe and fawn and scheme along with sickly smirk and greasily rubbed palms as everybody's door-mat.... It is the eternal East—you can see it in the Hindoo fakir and Chinese coolie as well" (SL 2.65). And thus, imperceptibly, the further East Lovecraft looks and the more people he sees, the hotter his language: "The more one learns about India the more one wants to vomit" (JVS 158–59). As his feelings overwhelm his rationalizations, contradictions arise. Though Lovecraft demands that Jews who are able to assimilate should, he clearly despises Jews who are able to assimilate, characterizing them as persons of low cunning. In this matter Lovecraft is fantasizing through a stereotype that stigmatizes Jews as imitators (Julius 101–2), whether as bad imitators, in which case they are open to scorn, or as imitators so cunning that they cannot be detected and thereby all the more dangerous because at that moment the biological threat arises. This contradiction in Lovecraft's fantasy of Jews has a good deal to do with his own ambivalent feelings about imitation and originality.

In fact, Lovecraft's attitude toward Jews is inseparable from his attitude toward the Chinese, whom on his strolls through a city and in his stories he is liable to confuse as Mongoloids—though he would have defended his language as scientific, appealing to the example of Thomas Henry Huxley. As with Jews he insists that the cultures of the East are all very well in their place, but once he begins to describe the people themselves the note of loathing begins to enter his language, because he believes in the American myth of the yellow peril. In 1915 he refers to "the rising power of Slav and Mongolian" (CE 5.14); in 1919 he speculates that the "numerous Chinese ... will probably be the exterminators of Caucasian civilization" (*Letters to Alfred Galpin* 57) and in 1937 that "the oldest of all civilizations" might "survive its younger rivals" (SL 5.393). But he believes in the power of China, at least in its numbers, at the same time that he believes "it isn't in Anglo-Saxons to accept the kicked-around squalor & brokenness of ghetto Jews, or the paralytic lethargy of the defenseless, opium-soaked Chinese, without such a fight as the world never saw before" (JVS 176). Western civilization is beleaguered on every side by an immense weakness, a conflation of Jewish and Chinese stereotypes that shall overcome it.

His treatment of Asians has a literary background in the stereotypes and popular literature of the day. From the establishment of Chinatown in San Francisco it was believed, with some basis in fact, that a vast underground lay beneath the area: "Actually an ingenious labyrinth contrived out of connecting basements and narrow passageways one level below the street, it grew in legend until practically every stranger as well as most of the natives of San Francisco repeated marvelous tales of how it burrowed down five, six, seven, *eight* stories underground" (Dobie 245), a legend that the great earthquake did little to modify for still in 1926 it was believed by "even police sergeants who probably had been regaling bar-flies and the home circle with tales of their explorations into the bowels of the earth" (246). This popular legend lies behind a good deal of the fiction of the turn of the century. In 1899 Mary E. Bamford's sympathetic novel *Ti: A Story of San Francisco's Chinatown* uses the legend (Wu 104–07). In 1908 a rather more baroque underworld appears in Frances Aymar Mathews's novel *The Flame Dancer* (128–29). By 1913 when Sax Rohmer published his first Fu Manchu novel and fixed the legend in its mythic form, the difficulty of distinguishing the truth of the matter had increased enormously. A trap drops Petrie into a sewer off the Thames where he has to fight off "terror of the darkness about me, of the unknown depths beneath me, of the pit into which I was cast amid stifling stenches and the lapping of tidal water" (40). One of the confrontations with the evil genius begins in the middle of a dream of drowning among "impenetrable walls of darkness" to give way to "an apartment of such size that its dimensions filled me with a kind of awe such as I never had know: the awe of walled vastness" (83). In novels in which the action is often repetitious, ill-connected, and ludicrous, the decor assumes much of the meaning.

And this scene of "walled vastness" and those other scenes of an underground with several levels, intricate in its articulation and alien in its purpose, so often associated in contemporary fiction with the Chinese, are just the sort of scenes that Lovecraft thought he saw played out in the subways and streets of New York. "The New York Mongoloid problem," he explodes in 1926, "is beyond calm mention"; the city has become a "stew of Asiatic filth," a place of "the nameless spawn," a situation in comparison to which the African-American problem is nothing because here the phobic personality must deal with "yellow, soulless enemies whose repulsive caresses house dangerous mental machines warped culturelessly in the single direction of material gain by stealth at any cost" (*SL* 2.68). And thus he concludes, remarkably, "There are two Jew Problems in America—one national and cultural, and to be met with firm resistance to all those vitiating ideas which parasitic subject-races engender; and another local and biological—the New York Mongoloid problem, to be met God knows how, but with force rather than intellect" (*SL* 2.68–69). To Lovecraft the description of the Golem in Meyrink's book must have seemed familiar: "bartlos, von gelber Gesichtsfarbe und mongolischem Typus" [beardless, with a yellow face of Mongolian type] (48). Reality and literary convention, the New York subway and the basements of the Chinatown in the pulps, the fear of the Jew and the fear of the Chinese, the fear of the flesh and the fear of the machine, fused for Lovecraft into a totally new landscape with a totally new monster inhabiting it.

As far as Lovecraft's feelings for African-Americans are concerned, a survey of his remarks, even in so offensive a poem as "On the Creation of Niggers" (*AT*

389), does not reveal a language that matches in intensity the language he uses in connection with Chinese, Central Europeans, and Jews, especially considered within the cultural context of the 1910s and 1920. His language for African-Americans, "beast," "semi-human," or "vice" (*AT* 389), is not as emotively charged as this well-known passage from 1924:

> The organic things—Italo-Semitico-Mongoloid—inhabiting that awful cesspool could not by any stretch of the imagination be call'd human. They were monstrous and nebulous adumbrations of the pithecanthropoid and amoebal; vaguely moulded from some stinking viscous slime of earth's corruption, and slithering and oozing in and on the filthy streets . . . in a fashion suggestive of nothing but infesting worms or deep-sea unnamabilities. . . . The individually grotesque was lost in the collectively devastating; which left on the eye only the broad, phantasmal lineaments of the morbid soul of disintegration and decay . . . a yellow leering mask with sour, sticky, acid ichors. . . . (*SL* 1.333–34)

In 1930 he speaks of "the cowed, cringing Jews" (*SL* 3.114). In 1933 he accuses the newspapers of "Jew York" (*JVS* 154) of being run by the Jews and, paradoxically, of being too sensitive to "the whole pack of synagogue-hounds" (*JVS* 170–71; cf. *ES* 133 and *JVS 143–44*). The Jews of this culture "repudiate the past & proclaim that the sole logical province of the poet & novelist is the pathology of neuroses & the sewer system of New York City. That is the 'new Americanism'" (*JVS* 138). The racist language he applies to African-Americans is, comparatively, abstract and general; the anti-Semitic language is specific, concrete, direct in its sensory offense.[1] In Young-Bruehl's terms, his racism is an ethnocentricism that looks to the past—the New Englander Lovecraft has a fondness for the Confederacy—whereas his anti-Semitism is an ideology of desire, constructed by an obsessive personality that emphasizes differences, delegitimizes and dehumanizes, represses and projects guilt, regards the body not the mind as the source of otherness and marks the part of the body where the difference starts, and yet identifies with the victim (184–99). Lovecraft's racism is notional, stereotypic; his anti-Semitism is personal, something he felt in his bone, so deep that he himself probably did not know its causes. And I do not think he ever freed himself from it; though he dissociated himself from the Nazis, he remained condescending, and condescension is all the worse in the context of the genocide that the Nazis planned. He may have transferred some of his feelings to the Bolsheviks, for though he often speaks well of aspects of Communism he describes the Russian people as "already mongrelised with Mongol blood" (*RB* 199) and fears "the imported Russian-Jewish radicalism of New York City" (*JVS* 243). He believed firmly that "blood is thicker than doctrine" (*RB* 199).

---

1. Maurice Lévy felt that Lovecraft's racism was more significant than his anti-Semitism, though Lévy saw the pertinence of the prejudices to a reading of the monsters and though he noted "how Lovecraft *dreamed his repugnances* and with what verbal richness he ranted from purely sensory data" (29; cf. 61).

I have not been exhaustive in listing Lovecraft's derogatives, simply indicative of the sort of rhetoric he indulged in, what Anthony Julius has described as the conventional language of anti-Semitism. In this regard it is clear that despite Lovecraft's anglophilia he was thoroughly American; rather than simply despising Jews, he affected the patrician attitudes exemplified by Henry Adams and T. S. Eliot, a violent attack combined with self-disgust (12–14). This language often recurs to imagery of shit, swamp, disease, infection, and disfigurement, a fear of the power of Jews en masse despite their individual weakness (16–18), pullulating from slime, protozoic morasses, gutters, and decaying buildings like vermin, lice, or rats (20, 44–46, 103), fixating the world with protrusive eyes (125). Lovecraft inherited a vocabulary to exploit. Like most prejudiced people he was not inventive when generating such lists, certainly not in his vocabulary—in his fiction he is at least inventive in syntax, rhythm, and symbol; and in the fiction such words become generalized, more available for the use of any reader, perhaps more dangerous because they do not exhibit or identify anti-Semitism but rehearse it. They engage the reader, challenging and forcing a response.

Lovecraft's experience of other minorities differed from his experience of Jews, for though he knew very few African-Americans or very few Southern- or Central-Europeans he did know Jews; he married Sonia Greene, and Samuel Loveman was one of his best friends. It could be argued that Lovecraft sought out Jewishness. He was familiar with Jewish and Yiddish works, such as *The Dybbuk*, and appreciated them; one of his late discoveries, Meyrink's *Der Golem*, is a remarkable evocation of the old Jewish quarter in Prague.

We must take his relations with Sonia Greene as symptomatic of his entire attitude, and the wedding service itself as thoroughly remarkable. His description of it in the *United Amateur* devotes more attention to the church, "a noble colonial structure built in 1766 and dignified by the worship of such older figures as General Washington, Lord Howe, and that Prince of Wales who later became successively the Prince Regent and King George the Fourth," than to the bride, and no attention is paid to her ethnicity (*CE* 1.352). In his letter to Frank Belknap Long describing the wedding he also emphasizes the church and ritual:

> Outside, the antient burying ground and the graceful Wren steeple; within, the glittering cross and traditional vestments of the priest—colourful legacies of OLD ENGLAND'S gentle legendry and ceremonial expression. The full service was read; and in the aesthetically histrionick spirit of one to whom elder custom, however intellectually empty, is sacred, I went through the various motions with a stately assurance which had the stamp of antiquarian appreciation if not of pious sanctity. Your Grandma [Sonia], needless to say, did the same—and with an additional grace. (*FFF* 105–6)

How chivalric the final sentence, and how anti-climactic! We may suspect that although his insistence upon an Episcopalian service was motivated to some degree by his respect for Anglicanism, since his father was Episcopalian though his mother was Baptist (*IAP* 11) and since he seldom expressed admiration for any religious tradition except for its effect upon the mob, to a greater degree he was motivated by his desire to impress an Anglo-Saxon tradition upon his Jewish bride, i.e. to encourage her assimilation. And she acquiesced: "I let him have his way" on assimilation (13, 22). Would she have let him have his way, would she have married him if she had heard his comment three years earlier about her incomprehension of his prose poems, "Teutonic mysticism is too subtle for Slavs" (*RK* 183), or his jest two years earlier about a fictitious flirtation, "I regret such cavalier treatment of a pure Anglo-Saxon by a foreigner" (*MWM* 89)? Sonia's problems were compounded by Lovecraft's attitudes toward women, assertions that they were not imaginative (*SL* 1.238); even Dorothy Roberts, whose abilities he strongly admired, had the "unfortunate failure to belong to the superior gender" (*SL* 1.254). By 1934 he grants much more innate equality to women (*DS* 583), but by that time the marriage had dissolved. Sonia had tried to act like a man, running a business and writing for the *United Amateur,* but she had failed; and she was still Jewish. In 1929, after the marriage had ended, without mentioning the marriage at all Lovecraft wrote, "From our attempt to assimilate Semitism we have gained nothing but misery—and the attempt itself has not succeeded, because it was based upon impossibility" (*JFM* 191).

Lovecraft's insistence that Sonia assimilate by going through the forms of the Anglican Church, therefore, calls into question his own assimilation, attempting to assert through the rite that he was a loyal subject of the king, without allowing himself to notice that the Episcopal Church of America partially owes its existence to the distance it placed between itself and Canterbury after the Revolution. He co-opts the ritual for the sake of his own pretension to being an English gentleman. Beyond being a marriage service, the event was an attempt to assimilate a Jewess and to alter the identity of a déclassé atheist. It should be no surprise that both attempts were failures; Sonia refused to be assimilated as much as he expected, and Lovecraft could never achieve the character of an English gentleman that he believed his father had fulfilled, though he insisted upon wearing such a suit as his father had worn. Instead, he would live and die a lower-middle class American with no faith in religious institutions.

Given all these details, might we not suspect that among other reasons for the dissolution of Lovecraft's marriage one might have been that it brought him too close to the acts of imitation? For not only did Sonia become in his eyes an imitator of Anglo-Saxon culture, he himself in their relationship became more obviously an imitator. What was he doing in a church, atheist that he was? in the metropolis of a democratic nation rather than in Providence? in the street trying to sell things, a gentleman like him? in the bed, in the subway? All of these acts overlooked the truth of his existence. Though we should not deprecate his love for Sonia, for surely a component of that love was the very risk of imitation that she offered him, in terms of the definition of anti-Semitism that Anthony Julius offers, "the malevolence of the confined unable truly to emancipate themselves" (120), Lovecraft never emancipated himself from the social attitudes of Providence. The malevolence that he displayed for Jews before the marriage he continued to display after the marriage had failed and he had returned to the city of his ancestors.

It is possible that a further component of that love was Lovecraft's complex feelings for Samuel Loveman, a man associated with the course of Lovecraft's courtship after Sonia had arranged their meeting in New York in 1922 during Lovecraft's first visit to the city, though he had been acquainted with Loveman through letters and amateur activities for some five years (*IAP* 290, 419). Before Sonia entered Lovecraft's life Loveman had been a part of its imaginative awakening, above all by introducing Lovecraft to the ambiguous figure of Nyarlathotep in a dream.[2] A good deal of speculation has already been written about how consciously Lovecraft was aware of Loveman's homosexuality; Joshi thinks it unlikely (*IAP* 930). I believe that Lovecraft would have had to have a very powerful defensive structure, naïve to an extent that it is difficult to accuse him of being, to have avoided such an awareness. Through Loveman he met a man of whom he said, with a violent wit, "I didn't know whether to kiss it or kill it!" (*JFM* 63). He became acquainted with Hart Crane through Loveman and probably knew of Crane's orientation, as de Camp believes (221), though Joshi thinks this unlikely also (*IAP* 930).[3] Lovecraft did write to Loveman in 1923, "And so the delectable Crane is now wallowing in the underworld of N.Y.? Good idea, your going there, but don't get in his Bohemian, near–Oscar-Wilde sort of circles! Gawd, how I hate that swinish Heliogabalan type!" (*MWM* 498). Though this letter may imply that he was unaware of Loveman's orientation, its warning may imply that he was aware of Loveman's bias. Lovecraft dedicated "Hypnos," with much of its power deriving from an ambiguous relationship, to Loveman. Above all, I do not understand how Lovecraft could have mistaken the drift of Loveman's poem *The Hermaphrodite*, a poem Lovecraft praised as "perhaps the most authentically Greek in spirit of any sustained utterance of recent years" (*SL* 1.176). The poem is an intricate account of the quest of the Hermaphrodite and his kin across time to find acceptance and realization, which the poem suggests can only happen in art, a

---

2. See my explication of that dream and of the involvement that Loveman had in Lovecraft's development of the figure of Nyarlathotep in "Landscapes, Selves, and Others."

3. In 1922 Crane wrote a letter in which he describes an apparently repressed Loveman: "You will like my classic, puritan, inhibited friend Sam Loveman who translates Baudelaire charmingly! It is hard to get him to do anything outside the imagination,—but he is charming and has just given me a most charming work on Greek Vases (made in Deutschland) in which satyrs with great erections prance to the ceremonies of Dionysos" (91). But Loveman was sufficiently uninhibited with Lovecraft to cause this comment to Clark Ashton Smith in 1926, "As to Long's notion that your work systematically contains phallic symbolism—he picked that up at secondhand from Loveman, who seems to have done enough delving in that line to see phalli in most things from church steeples to mushrooms" (*DS* 103). By the late 1960s, if Andrei Codrescu is to be credited, it was commonly assumed that Loveman and Crane had been lovers (132–33).

quest with no end because the Hermaphrodite is "unfathomable" (15). The quest is often compared to that of Dionysos, with an explicit allusion to his encounter with Pentheus (24–27) in a passage that concludes in comparing the tortures of the god and of the ambiguous hermaphrodite to the masochistic sufferings of Christian martyrs:

> "He saw my brethren flee," he said,
> And some they buried with the dead.
> Others in pillared colonnade
> They scourged and crucified and flayed. (27)

But the reason for such suffering, the secret of this godhead, lies in its sexual nature that excites its onlookers "To obscure lust, to inverse night" (16), a "frozen" sexuality (30) that offers "Beauty, in guise of man to men, / Clear, alternate, unveiled to view" (37). Perhaps Lovecraft avoided the implications of the poem by insisting that it "must be read wholly for imagery and not for ideas, as must every other work of art" (*MWM* 443). But how could he have mistaken poems like "Vice," in which "Phaedrus meets Alcibiades— / Two faces, each a poisoned flower" (71) or "Legend," in which "Laertes enters first, then Helion, / Then Phaedrus, lover of both, beloved by each" (81), "Amy Levy" with its reference to "her Sapphic heart" (101) or "Becalmed" with its reference to "the dead sea fruit" (110)? Was it enough for Lovecraft to place this poetry in the context of French decadence, to point at the influence of Baudelaire's Lesbian poems, to disinfect it of any reality? Yet everything that this material implies, Lovecraft denied in a letter to Searight: "No—the main poem has nothing to do with human abnormality, & will doubtless disappoint many smut-hounds who buy the book. It deals with a mythological being typifying pure beauty—the beauty that is *beyond sex*" (*EHP* 403–4). But though the poem is certainly about the nature of beauty, to claim that it "has nothing to do" with homosexuality seems wrongheaded. Upon some level of his being Lovecraft must have understood that Loveman was homosexual and despite that knowledge, perhaps because of it, found Loveman an exciting friend; and when Sonia became a part of their relations something of the same despite-and-because-of took place. And a part of the attraction might have been that Loveman like Sonia was attempting, from Lovecraft's point of view, to imitate what Lovecraft like Sonia was attempting to imitate, the Anglo-Saxon, masculine gentleman of letters, and at some point failing: Loveman was homosexual, and Jewish; Sonia was a woman, and Jewish; and Lovecraft was Lovecraft. They were all shoggoths. Crane writes of a scene in which Lovecraft hiked Loveman through the antiquities of New York until "he groaned with fatigue and begged for the subway!" (quoted in de Camp 221).

It is tempting to outline a psychological account for such prejudices as we see displayed in the letters and the fiction. For such a purpose Young-Bruehl's theory of prejudices is useful because her connection of the obsessional, narcissistic, and hysterical configurations of character with the anti-Semitic, sexist and homophobic, and racist prejudices is both simple to employ and sufficiently complex to discriminate a wide range of traits; and because the theory refuses to identify its subjects as pathological it includes us all within its scope (31–33). In the framework of her theory Lovecraft exhibits a wealth of the obsessional traits that provide the shape of anti-Semitism and a number of the narcissistic traits that provide the shape of sexism and homophobia. He exhibits, however, almost none of the hysterical traits that provide the shape of racism, as we might expect given the unimportance of racism to his daily life and his fiction; he does not indulge in display or theatricality or romanticism and is not intellectually vague, traits common to the hysteric (219–21). Those romantic elements in his style, which early in his career exfoliated under the influence of Poe and Dunsany, he later did his best to erase. On the other hand, though he is certainly given to gastrointestinal complaints that seem more than physical, something of an hysterical trait (225), he harps upon his abhorrence of fish more as an obsessional than as an hysteric; he is very neat, emphasizing his intellectual life though given to repetitive gestures, works with enormous application upon his stories, and identifies himself strongly with certain groups, the amateurs or English gentlemen, whose uniform, the particular suit, he wears just as his father had. He hoards the last remnants of the family's objects and spends much less upon himself than he might have, making his poverty even worse than it surely was. His distinctive hobby becomes a repeated search with a telescope for the perfect antiquarian house, perhaps because the death of his grandfather has dispossessed him from the home in which he grew up; and that search may be one component of the search through the tunnels of the earth for the truth of our prehistory. Even his teetotalism may be seen within the pattern of the obsessional (210–15). His confounding of his fear of the yellow peril with his anti-Semitism fits well with Young-Bruehl's analysis of their affinities (20, 33). Certain narcissistic traits, in addition, reinforce obsessional tendencies, above all the insistence upon boundaries and mental integrity (34); the narcissism of the mind sees others as stupid or uncultured in contrast to a complex cultural elitism (234). As a lover a narcissist is liable to regard the other as unformed, in need of rescue (233)—assimilable, dare we add? But the narcissistic self-regard of intellectual elements, in his own case Lovecraft's increasingly sober use of an eighteenth-century style, allows him to modify the obsessional repetition of his exotic vocabulary and to vary the liturgical character of the descent into the underworld of the subway where he confronts the object of his prejudices. Moreover, the narcissistic identification with the object of a prejudice allows him to overcome partially the rigid prohibition against such an identification that the obsessional configuration constructs; that tension in his fiction, between confessing and not confessing the identity of the self and the other, becomes one of its major themes. It is a glory of fiction that it allows an author not to escape type but to explore all the facets that a complex personality brings to bear, for few people exhibit this or that configuration in any pure form; and thus we certainly have stories that move within the structures of narcissism, above all "The Outsider" with its mirror within which sex becomes fluid. But since Lovecraft's sexism and homophobia are minor in comparison to his anti-Semitism, it is to his obsessional character that we need to look for a guide to the ritualistic nature of his stories.

None of these psychological considerations allows us to avoid the moral knot that we confront in Lovecraft's xenophobic terrors; to understand is not to gloss, nor should it be to gloss over. In general terms, as people of good will but obviously fractured minds—for we are each obsessionals, hysterics, and narcissists, as well as potential slaves of a stereotypic vocabulary—we do wish away the prejudices of the past. But wishing away the past is not effective; it is only now, the present, with which an ethics is concerned. And as far as we care for Lovecraft and his fiction, he would be a very different person and writer if he had overcome his prejudices that are a central energy source and complex theme of his fiction. "The Shadow over Innsmouth," for instance, with its fear of miscegenation, and so much else in his fiction, even the small details of the subway in *At the Mountains of Madness*, are inconceivable without his profound involvement in the structures of such prejudices.

As Julius says in regards to T. S. Eliot, anti-Semitism may not only provide the material for an author, it may also be that author's muse, the inspiration and, I would add, the spur and wound through which the work comes into being (77). This aspect of Lovecraft's work offers an answer to the question of how an author explores the nature of evil. It has to be through what the author believes in, what the author has experience of. And a phobia is not only an evil that a person visits upon others; it is also an evil that a person suffers. Neither Lovecraft nor Wagner in their art specify or rationalize the sources of the evil that they suffer, or only to the extent to which a trace of that evil remains, a residue that provides a complex evidence of that evil's source; Lovecraft does not identify Cthulhu or the shoggoth as a Jew, just as Wagner does not identify Alberich, Mime, or Hagen as a Jew. Pound, on the other hand, harms his art in specifying and rationalizing his evil. When the object of the phobia is unspecified but symbolically present, the reader is forced to suffer it as evil; we project its presence and suffer it, thus becoming complicitous in it, no longer able to condemn it or stand aside from it.

Lovecraft suffers a complex wound in his anti-Semitism. His relations with Judaism are threaded through with love and hatred, affecting how we read his stories now. For if we appreciate the stories, if we are affected by them, we cannot wish that they were other than they are; and so we cannot wish that he were other than he was. Not only can we not wish that he had overcome his prejudices; we cannot wish that he had overcome the violence and irrationality that powered them. Willy-nilly we are forced to align ourselves—not with his anti-Semitism—but with the wound from which his prejudices proceed, and not only to align ourselves with it but to probe it and make it hurt again, because it is so integral a part of his fiction. We are not fully able to will his wound to heal. We need, in any case, to confess that any writing about prejudice and delegitimization labors against the inertia of a wounded mind. Bender's article on the extent of Lovecraft's prejudices, thorough in its quotations from his letters, veers on the one hand upon the edge of voyeurism and on the other, in his frequent disclaimers, upon disingenuousness and naiveté. Lovett-Graff's analysis of "The Shadow over Innsmouth" veers between the clinical and the self-righteous. Hill's meditation on Pound's responsibility for his words is so oblique that it misses the violence in Pound. My assertion that Lovecraft's anti-Semitism is of a different order from his racism deprecates the racism with no other excuse than the rhetorical needs of this essay; and guilt exceeds all comparisons. No way exists to avoid contamination; a clinical stance, a controlled rage or a statistical survey, too much implies our own innocence. But as Hill wrote, "Too near the ancient troughs of blood / Innocence is no earthly weapon," no tool suitable for exploring genocide, no defense against its guilt (61).

What should we do as readers of Lovecraft? Ought we to read critically, with every ounce of our moral sense alive, bracketing and dismissing such imagery as we read word for word? What then becomes of the aesthetic effect that arises from the totality of the story? Is it not more likely, whatever our moral sense may be, that as readers we allow the total story to work upon us and that we translate such imagery into emblems of our own various and individual xenophobias? For how can it be that we are any of us innocent of fears and hatreds like these?

II

> Wir können nur etwas so tief hassen, wie ich es tue, was ein Teil von uns selbst ist. [We can only hate something so deeply, as I do, which is a part of our self] (Meyrink 134)

Lovecraft does not mention subways often in his fiction. Besides *At the Mountains of Madness* only two other stories contain them, "Pickman's Model" and "The Horror at Red Hook." In "Pickman's Model" they have no function as far as the plot is concerned, for Thurber and Pickman arrive at the North End by taking the elevated. But the subway assumes a prominent place in Pickman's paintings. "There was a study called 'Subway Accident', in which a flock of the vile things were clambering up from some unknown catacomb through a crack in the floor of the Boylston Street subway and attacking a crowd of people on the platform" (*CF* 2.66); the subway allows the things of nightmare, a flock of them, as though they were the birds of the underworld, an escape into humanity's everyday lives. The subway also allows the prospect of tunnels beneath North End, Beacon Hill, and Mount Auburn Cemetery to be more plausible. Ghouls, however, are not unsympathetic figures in Lovecraft's fiction. An important question of the story is the extent to which aesthetic strength redeems a questionable moral content; and though the story seems to deny such a possibility, we must keep in mind that the narrator is an extremely unlikable personality.

"The Horror at Red Hook," on the other hand, takes place in New York, with all of Lovecraft's disillusioned detestation of that city on display. In that story one of the signs of Suydam's decadence is that he could be "seen occasionally by humiliated friends in subway stations, or" in a significant parallelism "loitering on the benches around Borough Hall in conversation with groups of swarthy, evil-looking strangers" (*CF* 1.487). But though the story does not deal with subways in any extensive fashion, Kenneth Sterling, who knew Lovecraft in the last years of his life and defended him against the charge of racism, later remembered it as a story "where he talks about subways and squat foreign types, which lumps together various minorities. I guess many of us would feel a little uncomfortable in New York's subways even today" (413–14). The story remains a gauge of Lovecraft's obsessions through his exploitation of the subway.

But shoggoths, the plastic shoggoths, are Lovecraft's central invention connected with subways, and to discover the meaning of the subway we need to say more about the meaning of the shoggoth. Certainly it carries the connotation of the Hebrew suffix -*oth*, a plural ending as in Sabaoth or Yuggoth, which "has a sort of Arabic or Hebraic cast, to suggest certain words passed down from antiquity in the magical formulae contained in Moorish and Jewish manuscripts" (*FLB* 140–41); a shoggoth may not be individual—it is legion. In addition, "shog" is a common English word that Samuel Johnson records: "to shake; to agitate by sudden interrupted impulses." The *Oxford English Dictionary* notes other meanings, "to rouse from sleep," "to upset," "to walk, ride or move with a succession of bumps or jerks," or "to go away, begone" and cites Shakespeare's line in *Henry V,* "Will you shog off?" (2.1.42). Through "shake" the word is possibly a cognate of the vulgar "shag," to copulate (Partridge). Certainly there are points in Lovecraft's stories at which a shoggoth shatters, rouses, moves, or threatens a protagonist in a quasi-sexual manner. A shoggoth is the occasion of Lovecraft's most intense, though often most opaque, *ébranlements*.

As Will Murray has shown ("The Trouble with Shoggoths" 37–38), the immediate occasion of Lovecraft's shoggoth was Clark Ashton Smith's description in "The Tale of Satampra Zeiros" of a black, "semiliquescent" creature that either serves or incarnates the toad-god Tsathoggua, a description that uses words capable of triggering Lovecraft's own anti-Semitic language: "What unimaginable horror of protoplasmic life, what loathly spawn of the primordial slime had come forth" (Smith 74)—it could well have seemed to Lovecraft reading these words that what he had seen in the streets and subways of New York had suddenly taken concrete form. His essential development of this figure lies in its history and its explicit ability to imitate and supplant its masters.

Shoggoths first appear in "Night-Gaunts," sonnet XX of *Fungi from Yuggoth,* where they are associated with the deep underworld landscape of Thok in *The Dream-Quest for Unknown Kadath,* the deadest pit of the dreamworld. In the poem Lovecraft's childhood nightmare figures, rubbery, black, and faceless, snatch the dreamer off to a place "deep in nightmare's well":

> Over the jagged peaks of Thok they sweep,
> Heedless of all the cries I try to make,

> And down the nether pits to that foul lake
> Where the puffed shoggoths splash in doubtful sleep. (*AT* 88)

This is the point at which the dreamworld seems to make contact with the unconscious world of evacuation and matter (Waugh, "Landscapes, Selves, and Others" 225). In the ghostwritten story "The Mound," similar to *The Dream-Quest* in that it concerns an enormous space, so large that it does not seem to be an underworld but an articulated chain of caverns, the shoggoth may also materialize. In the deepest of the caverns, the black N'kai (inky?), creatures appear that resemble shoggoths (Murray, "The Trouble with Shoggoths" 37–38), creatures that the advanced race of the story abhor, "amorphous lumps of viscous black slime that took temporary shapes for various purposes" (*CF* 4.262), and seal them off from their consciousness so thoroughly that they think them mere legend. In these descriptions shoggoths very much resemble excrement, that stuff that children (and adults) produce with such anxiety and pleasure, that stuff of us that we can mould into any shape we wish and that becomes one sign of the obsessional personality. It is in this regard that Geoffrey Hill's analysis of Ezra Pound's failure at the crisis of his life has special relevance, for Pound had thought it possible to demand of poets an "irreproachable skill," an ability to force the aesthetic and the ethical to coincide; but, as Hill sees it, "When the conjunction is bungled we discover the complicity between a solecism and 'a sloppy and slobbering world,'" the world Pound had so resolutely and madly opposed (158). Because in Lovecraft's thought an aesthetic response to the world is more difficult, more questionable than it is for Pound, the shoggoth functions rather directly as an emblem of the dirty world that the obsessional hates but that in fact proceeds from the body and mind itself, as Lovecraft should have recognized since he had, after all, read Swift's anecdote of the Spider, a creature that according to its opponent the Bee "by a lazy Contemplation of four Inches round; by an over-weening Pride, which feeding and engendering on it self, turns all into Excrement and Venom; producing nothing at last, but Fly-bane and a Cobweb" (383), though the more objective voice of Aesop concedes that its very venom, the spirit of satire, may be the only genuine product of the modern age (384). Excrement, dirt, and death have aesthetic and authentic possibilities, but only if the artist recognizes them for what they are and is willing to dabble in them.[4]

To round out this survey, the shoggoth is also alluded to in "The Shadow over Innsmouth" and "The Thing on the Doorstep," stories in which the "bulgy, stary eyes" (*CF* 3.163) that characterize the Innsmouth look become prominent; Asenath's eyes, the eyes of a hypnotist, "blazed and protruded" (330), details that we have noted form a part of the traditional anti-Semitic language. We would include "The Shadow over Innsmouth" in our review of underworld flights if it were not that the shadow that roofs Innsmouth in from the rest of the world is simply

---

4. St. Armand deals with this imagery to some extent in what he calls the Great Dread of the Viscous, which he connects to Lovecraft's Sinophobia (63–77).

metaphoric. The shoggoths of these stories are treated in such general terms that it is also tempting to feel their presence in *The Case of Charles Dexter Ward* (Murray, "Do Shoggoths Lurk . . .?" 37–39) and "The Call of Cthulhu" (Murray, "The Trouble with Shoggoths" 37). Certainly the passage in "The Call of Cthulhu" is intriguing, which recounts "legends of a hidden lake unglimpsed by mortal sight, in which dwelt a huge, formless white polypous thing with luminous eyes. . . . [B]ut it made a man dream, and so they knew enough to" (*CF* 2.35). Within a pantheon of creatures that often resemble one another, this creature would be a shoggoth if it were not for the white skin; shoggoths are pointedly black, though iridescent. Be that as it may, a creature with such an aptitude for imitation seems to have the ability to appear in its foul flesh anywhere.

I have some doubt about these speculations, but I cannot press this doubt too far given my own speculations. I cannot help but note the extent to which the imagery of a multitude of eyes pervades the descriptions of the shoggoths and the descriptions of other, unnamed creatures in Lovecraft's works: in "He" (*CF* 1.516), the most paranoid story of New York; in "The Shunned House" (*CF* 1.475); and in "The Dunwich Horror" (*CF* 2.439), one of the most finished of Lovecraft's works. In each of them, but perhaps most insistently in the shoggoth, the figure of Argus the watchman is alluded to, which we shall examine more closely later. In addition, it seems striking how absolutely Lovecraft insists that a shoggoth is no individual; it is no man, unlike the Old Ones or even the Deep Ones, for a shoggoth never deserves the dignity of a capital letter, just as in some anti-Semitic literature the Jew is merely a jew.

To form a more precise understanding of the shoggoth, however, we need to examine the extent to which a flight through a complex of tunnels forms a climactic scene in several of Lovecraft's works, for this scene is the context of the apparition of the shoggoth in *At the Mountains of Madness*. One of the earliest of these scenes is in "The Nameless City." Its narrator is investigating the temples of a city he has discovered, temples whose walls are so squat that he must crawl through them. At last searching for a subterranean wind that blows at dawn and sunset he finds a temple with an artificial door leading into the abyss. He follows a staircase of "very small, numerous, and steeply descending steps" that resemble "some hideous haunted well" (*CF* 1.237). At last he arrives in a corridor lined with odd coffins and a wall decorated in a pageant history of an ancient reptile race; this leads to an "illimitable void of uniform radiance. . . . Behind me was a passage so cramped that I could not stand upright in it; before me was an infinity of subterranean effulgence" (242–43). In the climax of the story an enormous wind comes, that which had summoned him below and now plummets him into the void.

The next story with a similar event is "The Festival," in which the narrator comes to the ancient city of Kingsport to participate in a family rite. The worshippers enter a church in which a trapdoor in front of the altar opens to a spiral staircase that leads down to a series of side passages like maggoty catacombs. At last they arrive at an underground river in the middle of which burns a pillar of green fire that they worship. In this story the narrator is saved, but only by his casting himself into the river, to be found blown up on the shore the next day.

The underground in "The Rats in the Walls" is entered by a secret door under the stone in the basement. It is an enormous space, vast and articulated, containing such elements as the altar, well, crypt, and wind. The narrator is alive at the end of the story, but his voice has descended the ancestral underground not to return whole; rather than fleeing his ancestral source he has been drawn into it. Though he can say, "I only am escaped to tell you," he has not escaped whole. We need also to add that his escape has brought back from his experience a vocabulary that perforce reminds a reader of the vocabulary of anti-Semitism. The rats are a "scampering army of obscene vermin, . . . lean, filthy, ravenous" (*CF* 1.380), by the end of the story a "viscous, gelatinous, ravenous army" (395). Both a real presence and a presence of the mind, the rats gain a metaphoric power that seems infinitely suggestive but which in the context of American anti-Semitism and in the context of Lovecraft's own language certainly bears an anti-Semitic charge.

"Under the Pyramids" is an anomalous story in Lovecraft's work, ghostwritten for Houdini, but similar elements are present. Upon one of the pyramids the narrator is lowered through a "burial shaft," a well that descends without measure; before he reaches the bottom he is carried upon a wild flight by invisible bat things. Once he comes to himself and tries to escape he trips and falls down a staircase that brings him into a vast area where he beholds a nightmare pageant of hybrid creatures and loses consciousness at the sight of a gigantic sphinx. But, he adds at the anti-climactic conclusion, it was all a dream.

The short underground adventure of Malone in "The Horror at Red Hook" also occurs under the suspicion of being a dream. He enters the tunnels through a cellar door, in the face of "a howling tumult of ice-cold wind with all the stenches of the bottomless pit" (*CF* 1.498). Crypts and "wells of night" (499) confront him, as does a concentration of "the foetor of hybrid pestilence" (499). He comes upon a shore of water where a phosphorescent thing on a throne is worshipped, as the beings untwine a corpse in an attempt to restore it, a procession of hybrid creatures marches before it, and Malone faints.

"Pickman's Model" may not quite fit our investigation; its interiors are not immense, and in the conclusion the narrator leaves quietly. Pickman and Thurber approach the underworld through the secular tangle of alleys in Boston's North End and enter through "an antediluvian ten-panelled door" (*CF* 2.63). Only three rooms remain to be explored, one in the cellar with "a great well in the earthen floor" (68). But this underworld is expanded immensely by the paintings that offer alternate spaces, many of them further underworlds: "old churchyards, deep woods, cliffs by the sea, brick tunnels, ancient panelled rooms, or simple vaults of masonry" (63), the Boylston Street subway as we noted earlier, but perhaps most impressive "a vast cross-section of Beacon Hill, with ant-like armies of the mephitic monsters squeezing themselves through burrows that honeycombed the ground" (66). Most important to the narrator, however, are those monsters, because in the paintings Pickman provided a pageant history of their lives, "in all his gradations of morbidity between the frankly non-human and the degradedly human, establishing a sardonic linkage and evolution" (65).

The Case of Charles Dexter Ward contains one of Lovecraft's most complex underworlds. Charles' father descends with Dr. Willett but has to withdraw when he becomes faint at a "mephitic blast from the crypt" (*CF* 2.239); one of the only specific details in the attack on Curwen had been a "chill wind" and "intolerable stench" (260). An iron ladder allows Willett to descend, to "[make] the plunge," but then he must walk down a staircase in "three abrupt turns" (329). At the bottom he finds himself in a large space surrounded by archways that lead into various rooms, one of them Ward's library. Another tunnel leads to "a vast open space" with an altar in the center of "a circle of pillars grouped like the monoliths of Stonehenge" (333); at the circumference of the space are prison-cells and along the floor a group of flagstones hiding "a vast number" of shafts and wells in which Curwen's incomplete resurrections are imprisoned, "neither thoroughly human, nor wholly allied to any animal" (337). Off this space is his laboratory, with urns containing the essential salts of the Custodes and the Materia, that is to say the coffins of the people whom Curwen and his associates have gathered over the centuries; the laboratory forms the more significant library of the complex, "the mortal relics of half the titan thinkers of all the ages" (343). Another room contains torture instruments, the critical methodology of a reader of that library. But at this point Willett's exploration is ended by a cold wind and a "stench from the far-away wells" (347), driving him out from the labyrinth in a nightmare.

"The Mound" is something of a special case, not simply because Lovecraft ghostwrote it. We will not examine the descent and return of Pánfilo, the core of the story, because the very size of its underworlds, similar to the size of *The Dream-Quest of Unknown Kadath*, their geographical complexities unrolled beneath a sky glowing with a hazy light or beneath a sky with an alien moon, militates against their terror, as does the fact that one is frankly the stuff of the past and the other the stuff of dream; historiography and faerie set the tone of those worlds, not horror, and so their structures differ from the labyrinths that erupt within our everyday world. For an opposite reason we have not included such stories as "The Lurking Fear" and "The Shunned House." The underground of the one is never experienced at first hand; the basement of the other is too simple, with none of the articulation characteristic of the other underworlds, and the protagonists do not flee it but confront its terror.

But in "The Mound" the descent of the narrator that frames the story elaborates some of the motifs we have noted. In pursuit of the stories he has heard the ethnologist approaches the top of the mound where he sees the guardian "with an expression of infinite evil and decadence on his seamed, hairless features" (*CF* 4.223), but the man disappears. As the narrator begins to dig he shivers as though "some perverse gust of wind arose to hamper my motions. . . . As if a half-tangible force were pulling me back as I worked—almost as if the air thickened in front of me, or as if formless hands tugged at my wrists" (*CF* 4.224). It is, of course, a part of the fiction that these are indeed dematerialized people attempting to prevent him. But he discovers Pánfilo's manuscript, hidden beneath the blue sky above the mound, the red sandstone, and "a strange black loam" (224), as though the manuscript were secreted in a model of the underground world at the place of the semi-shoggoths; and the narrator hurries away with the manuscript at "the onrush of night" (227). At the climax he returns to dig further and again feels "the suggestion of a sudden wind blowing against me" (283) and the resistance of the invisible hands. The descent is difficult because of an "up-rushing of a cold wind from below" (284). Carvings appear on the wall, of which the manuscript had told him, but he also begins to glimpse the figures pulling at him, so that he suffers from a moment of "visual chaos" (284). As he descends the "seemingly endless staircase" (285) the carvings begin a narrative of the world below—redundant since he has read the manuscript—and he comes to the circular space in which the statues of Tulu and Yig form a climax to the carvings. As "the adverse winds" (287) increase and he discovers his own pick and shovel, perhaps the equivalent for him of his own hand to Peaslee the scholar, the shapes become more visible: "pushing and plucking—those leprous palaeogean things with something of humanity still clinging to them—the *complete* forms, and the forms that were morbidly and perversely *incomplete* . . . all these, and the hideous *other entities*—the four-footed blasphemies with ape-like face and great projecting horn" (288), all in an utter silence, forms that, given details in the manuscript, suggest hybrids that because of their semi-artificial state displace shoggoths into N'kai and assume the function of shoggoths here, with an explicit racial component in the stereotypic words of "ape-like" and "flat-nosed, bulging-lipped" (259). When the narrator runs, however, in a state of "merciful unconsciousness" (288), it is not from these creatures but from the sight of a figure "quite dead—besides lacking head, arms, lower legs, and other customary parts of a human being" (290), Pánfilo whose consciousness we have inhabited through most of the story in his manuscript, murdered and castrated by the decadent race that lives in the underworld.

Lovecraft's penultimate achievement, "The Shadow out of Time," has one of his most elaborate underworlds, the city of the Great Race. Yet in contrast to Curwen's labyrinth, this space is treated in the most general of terms because Peaslee's compulsion to descend is more dreamlike than Dr. Willett's disinterested will to rescue his young friend. Once more, the entrance is marked by a "violent wind" (*CF* 3.419), then by a trickle and "stream of air" that could only indicate "a hidden gulf of great size" (425); after Peaslee has struggled with stones, "there welled up a strong draught" (425). Rather than a staircase Peaslee follows an incline obstructed with ruinous heaps of stones until he comes to a level where carvings reveal his familiarity with the place in his dreams; the history of the Great Race has already been described and so can be left aside in Peaslee's descent, and in any case he is trying to find his way to the central archives where "reposed the whole history, past and future, of the cosmic space-time continuum" (430). Descending to the next cellars, with some difficulty he passes "a mighty mound of stone reaching almost to the ragged, grotesquely stalactited roof" and "a gaping, ragged chasm" (431). Probably because of the dreamlike nature of his descent the obstructions are emphasized. Once he arrives at the archives he stops to read one manuscript before he resumes his "feverish racing through unending tangles of aisles and corridors" (*CF* 3.436) and passes the vault where the Great Race had buried a creature that certainly seems to fulfill something of the same function here as the shoggoth fulfills in *At the Mountains of Madness*, once more feeling a significant "current of cool, damp air" (*CF* 3.437). After he finds in the archive what he had feared, the bit of paper written in his own hand, he begins to flee, but this flight is confused by a great wind and his own panic. Once more, in an intricate passage of swift forward-and-backward plunging motions, it becomes difficult to say how the protagonist has become the I-only-am-escaped-to-tell-you.

To summarize, a persistent element in these descents is the threatening wind that precedes them, an inverted version of the inspiring wind that opens so many visionary moments in Romantic poetry; accompanied by a cold stench—another aspect of anality—the wind announces the opening of the unconscious, loosens the confidence of the rational ego, and counters the warmth of an expansive inspiration. Often the entrance is associated with a temple, but that detail tends to drop away. Frequently the descent is associated with a history lesson arranged as a pageant, carvings and parades providing the protagonist with an emblem of the past; in addition, the descent probably represents a palaeographic process. In *The Case of Charles Dexter Ward*, "The Mound," and "The Shadow out of Time" the history lesson becomes contained in texts and bodies, fragmentary, mutilated, or inverted; earlier this aspect is represented by a variety of tombs, not only a part of the landscape, that is to say, because of the images of death and burial but because of the images of texts and knowledge. Often the peoples of this underground world are hybrids, sometimes failed imitations. Almost always the image of the well appears. A persistent feature at the conclusion of these stories is the way that the protagonist escapes, whether by water or wind or falling unconscious; very seldom are we told in any detail that he is able to climb the stairs by which he descends. As Bachelard says of the stairs to the cellar of his house of the imagination, "We always *go down* the [stairway] that leads to the cellar, and it is this going down that we remember, that characterizes its oneirism" (25). Faithful to such dreamlike states, Lovecraft continues his characterization of the underworld by rendering its inescapable nature. In a like manner Virgil renders in complex detail the descent Aeneas makes to his father's history lesson, but leaves the ascent problematic when Aeneas and the Sybil pass the gate of false dreams (*Aeneid* 6.893–98).

Confronting Bachelard's dream house of the imagination, we must digress to note that in Lovecraft's fiction no prominence is given to an ascent, to an attic, and this is remarkable because the attic was such a prominent part of his experience of the lost paradise of the house of his childhood; it was in the attic that he found the library that formed the main part of his education. But his description of that experience is significant: "But what did I do? What, pray, but go up with candles and kerosene lamp to that obscure & nighted aërial crypt—leaving the sunny downstairs 19th century flat, & boring my way back through the decades into the late 17th, 18th & early 19th century by means of innumerable crumbling & long-f'd tomes of every size and nature" (*ES* 379). As a crypt into which he bores backward in time the attic is more than simply Bachelard's place where the fears of the night are rationalized (19). In fact Bachelard's attic shares a quality of the stairs that go down: just as with them the dreamer does not remember an ascent, so with the attic stairs the dreamer does not remember a descent (26). But for Lovecraft, the ascent and the descent are homologous; the way up and the way down are truly the same. Perhaps more truly, the attic is collapsed into the cellar. I believe that St. Armand's speculation is correct: 454 Angell Street was the model for Lovecraft's psychic home (17), and its loss, its terrible loss, meant a profound loss of the self that these descents in the fiction are always an attempt to undo; the mind bores through the ancient self and the ancient home trying to find the root that shall stabilize them.

With these various considerations in mind let us review the descent in *At the Mountains of Madness* and the climactic appearance of the shoggoth. By any account this descent is the most remarkable in Lovecraft's work, for it fills almost half the work, some fifty pages, and in it we find passages that remind us both of Dr. Willett's descent into Curwen's labyrinth, for this passage is developed in a good deal of specific detail, and of Professor Peaslee's descent into the city of the Great Race, for the details are combined in such way that the oneiric treatment prevents us from drawing a map of the route. After crossing a pass in the mountains and comparing the city to the Garden of the Gods in Colorado (*CF* 3.70), the first suggestion of the sacred, Dyer[5] and Danforth land next to a rampart shaped like a star and climb through a window and begin their descent to the city. Since the city lies in the midst of a glaciation the explorers descend several stages before the landscape they traverse is truly underground, yet they are going down almost continuously. Finally, having found an archway that seems to promise a descent through the glaciation, they "[make] the plunge" (84). At this point they begin to leave a trail of torn paper behind them so that they do not become lost, the only explorers in Lovecraft's fiction with such foresight; but it is a trail that in fact they have no need of at the end of the story, for once again the way down leads only down. Also at this point Dyer prefaces his narrative with a disclaimer: "It would be cumbrous to give a detailed, consecutive account of our wanderings inside that cavernous, aeon-dead honeycomb of primal masonry" (85). The details are arranged, as he says at another point, "in a formless, rambling way" (94), a manner that allows Lovecraft to shape the whole artistically.

Having entered the first tower they at first ascend over "stone ramps or in-

---

5. In this analysis I give the narrator the name Lovecraft seems to bestow upon him in retrospect in "The Shadow out of Time" (*CF* 3.414); but it seems apt that this story about a creature that can imitate any form should have a narrator who remains nameless.

clined planes" (*CF* 3.86), similar to those in "The Shadow out of Time," before beginning the descent. They now discover an "almost universal system of mural sculpture" that runs through the corridors they explore (87), an element that Dyer believes represents an "abnormal historic-mindedness" (89)—later in his account he describes the murals as "well-nigh omnipresent sculptures, which indeed seemed to have formed a main aesthetic outlet for the Old Ones" (127). This detail furnishes Lovecraft, of course, with a handy method for the protagonist to discover the history of the lost race, realistic in its resemblance to the walls of the ancient Egyptians, recalled here by identifying the writing as a series of cartouches. But the detail has another significance in representing how we live within our history, bore it, carve it, and are directed and protected by it.

After several circuitous wanderings through the city, often "crossing bridges under the glacial sheet" (*CF* 3 92), they come to "a frightful abyss below even the ancient ground level—a cavern perhaps 200 feet square and 60 feet high" (93), where they learn their first account of shoggoths. Sometime before coming to earth the Old Ones seem to have manufactured "not only necessary foods, but certain multicellular protoplasmic masses capable of moulding their tissues into all sorts of temporary organs under hypnotic influence and there forming ideal slaves to perform the heavy work of the community" (95). It may be important to note from this account that shoggoths are prior to the Old Ones' later creation, humans (100); shoggoths are our elder siblings, and so sibling rivalry, along with the complex dialectics of the master/slave relationship, informs our understanding of the shoggoth and the loathing with which Lovecraft surrounds it, a resentment against that which is enslaved and against that which is prior. This pattern may also suggest the envy of the older children for the youngest, the darling of parental authority, in fairy tales.

The second description of the shoggoth is more complex, for the shoggoth has gained a certain amount of independence, "a dangerous degree of accidental intelligence," at the same time that the Old Ones lost the ability to create life from inorganic matter (*CF* 3.102). The Old Ones' decadence, therefore, for which they are solely responsible, makes them more dependent upon the shoggoths at the very moment that the creatures become, through no merit of their own, intelligent: "They had, it seems, developed a semi-stable brain whose separate and occasionally stubborn volition echoed the will of the Old Ones without always obeying it" (102–3). Is that to say that in some fashion the Old Ones had themselves willed this opposition of the shoggoths, a collusion that they are unable to confess, just as the anti-Semite cannot confess his or her collusion in the fantasized aggression of the Jew? The shoggoths are now able to form "apparent organs of sight, hearing, and speech in imitation of their master, either spontaneously or according to suggestion" (103), so that the only sign of their independence would apparently be the extent of rebellion they exhibit It is hard not to feel some degree of unrecognized complicity in the separation of the shoggoth from their makers.

Only a few paragraphs after this description of the shoggoths' growing resentment against their slavery we find a remarkable suspicion about the Old Ones, one we should keep in mind alongside the famous exclamation, "They were men!" (*CF* 3.143). An account of wars that the Old Ones have fought with beings from other parts of space-time concludes with the possibility that such assumptions of origin might be mere myth:

> Conceivably, the Old Ones might have invented a cosmic framework to account for their occasional defeats; since historic interest and pride obviously formed their chief psychological element. It is significant that their annals failed to mention many advanced and potent races of beings whose mighty cultures and towering cities figure persistently in certain obscure legends. (105)

The Old Ones are quite possibly liars, above all to themselves, conscious liars who have tried to evade the consequences of their own knowledge. Lovecraft's model for this process might be Nietzsche's analysis of historians' temptation to make their will to truth serve their will to power. One of the uses of history is its protection of a labile self-image. But where does the labiality of the Old Ones' self-image proceed from if not from their relations with the shoggoths? And this doubt that arises from their inability to tell the truth to themselves about this external threat infects their entire history. The honeycomb of history in which they live becomes maggot-infested with simulacras of truth with a will of their own. Inauthenticity is not a passive state; the mask and the hand can become autonomous. And if the history is merely a cosmic framework that the Old Ones have invented, what are we to make of the assertion that "this general region was the most sacred spot of all, where reputedly the first Old Ones had settled on a primal sea-bottom" (107)? The sacrality that we have seen associated with these descents lies itself in question.

With these discoveries that reveal a foundation of truth that remains stubbornly suspect, the explorers now find a new goal, for they learn of "the Stygian sunless sea," a "vast nighted gulf [which] had undoubtedly been worn by the great river which flowed down from the nameless and horrible westward mountains" (*CF* 1.110). To build a city there the Old Ones had developed new shoggoths that "grew to enormous size and singular intelligence" and "seemed to converse with the Old Ones by mimicking their voices" (114). A page later we learn that shoggoths are "curiously cold-resistant" (116), unlike the Old Ones, unlike Dyer and Danforth in the colds of the Antarctic, unlike Lovecraft.

The explorers try to find "a steeply descending walk of about a mile" that would bring them "to the brink of the dizzy sunless cliffs above the great abyss" (*CF* 3.117), by "traversing rooms and corridors in every stage of ruin or preservation, clambering up ramps, crossing upper floors and bridges and clambering down again" (119). Once again the connective tissue of the narrative becomes vague. Their tunnel becomes in fact a blind when they discover the remnants of what the Old Ones had stolen from Lake's camp. Confronted by this evidence that the Old Ones are still alive Dyer and Danforth press on, now in the hope of finding "that great circular place" (126) that might provide a way down to the underground sea at the same time that it might provide a short cut to the surface and their plane. When they find it, in so short a time that the compression of the narrative again suggests a dream, it proves to be "a prodigious round space" with walls "boldly sculptured into a spiral band" around which a "titanic stone ramp" (127–28) winds. We cannot miss the sacral appearance of this place of final descent. But here they also discover the body of their friend Gedney.

Before we descend with them further, however, we must pause to consider the significance of that phrase, "the Stygian sunless sea," surely one of several reminiscences of Coleridge's "Kubla Khan" that situates its action

> Where Alph, the sacred river, ran
> Through caverns measureless to man
> Down to a sunless sea. (ll. 3–5)

The city that Dyer and Danforth are exploring is much more than "twice five miles . . . / With walls and towers . . . girdled round" (ll. 6–7), though it has something of the same structure; and it has certainly felt the same threat as had Kubla, for where the river "sank in tumult to a lifeless ocean" he "heard from far / Ancestral voices prophesying war!" (ll. 28–30). One of the triumphs of the poem is that we agree with the bardic voice: "It was a miracle of rare device, / A sunny pleasure-dome with caves of ice!" (ll. 35–36). Though groups of eyeless, albino penguins detain the explorers, they enter "a prodigious open space which made us gasp involuntarily—a perfect inverted hemisphere" whose symmetry is broken by "a black arched aperture" that was "the entrance to the great abyss" (*CF* 3.134), with a waft of warmer wind from it.

In addition to these general similarities, the presence of "Kubla Khan" in the story points at the presence of Lovecraft's prejudice against the Chinese, especially as creators of an immense alien culture that one must admire at the same time as fear. The Old Ones, like the Khan, are archimages and poets who have created this manifold space under the impact of a divine afflatus that remains hidden and unknowable to normal discourse. But it also remains suspect because it has been accomplished through the agency of the so thoroughly assimilable shoggoths. In the poem the poet yearns to build "that dome in air, / That sunny dome! those caves of ice!" (ll. 46–47), and to some extent he has, but only through the afflatus of "honey-dew" (l. 53), which is to say, from Lovecraft's hard-headed, teetotaling point of view, through laudanum, a potent mixture of opium and port. This Coleridgean context, furthermore, suggests one further point regarding the plastic shoggoth, that it not only accomplishes its work at the order of the Old Ones but that its usurpation of command is also a usurpation of what Coleridge calls the shaping, esemplastic power of imagination. The student becomes an autodidact whose powers now mock its teacher, and thus the imagination is recognized to dwell as much below, in the source of that cold wind, as in the heavens.

Two last discoveries remain before the onrush of the shoggoth that concludes this remarkable narrative that has depended for its effect on its rhythmic alternation of small and large spaces. One is the sudden change in the carvings marked by "a degradation of skill" producing work that is "coarse, bold, and wholly lacking in delicacy of detail" (*CF* 3.138), Jewish work an anti-Semite might say. It has no originality in itself but is "a sort of palimpsest formed after the obliteration of a previous design," an artwork based on destruction. "In nature it was wholly decorative and conventional," but it was also "more like a parody" of the Old Ones' style, not a new beginning in any way. Dyer is "reminded of such hybrid things as the ungainly Palmyrene sculptures fashioned in the Roman manner" (138). George Albert Cooke's article on "Palmyra" in the *Britannica* may be responsible for this description, for he says that the style of the ruins is "late classic and highly ornate, but without refinement" (200); and the fact that Palmyra is an Arabic, a Semitic city, is probably not without force in Lovecraft's passage. In addition, Cooke's description of the tomb-towers, built in six stories with room for 480 bodies and an immense vault under the entrance, may have given Lovecraft imaginative material for some of the details of the city. The second discovery confirms the nature of this style, for here are the Old Ones decapitated—it is characteristic of the shoggoth to suck its victim "to a ghastly headlessness" (142), to incorporate the seat of its maker's intelligence into itself. In his shock Dyer allows himself this peroration: "Formless protoplasm able to mock and reflect all forms and organs and processes . . . —more and more sullen, more and more intelligent, more and more amphibious, more and more imitative" (142). The shoggoth, this part of the narrative claims, is a distorting mirror that objects to its slavery and its maker, taking on that intellective capacity with its originating center, hybrid, mimic, lurking in a labyrinth that more and more resembles the subways that Dyer and Danforth left behind them in Boston—and New York.

The comparison arises in so gradual a fashion that it is difficult to fix limits to it. As Dyer says of a slightly earlier stage of recognition, "it is only through later conversations that we have learned of the complete identity of our thoughts at that moment" (*CF* 3.144). Does this sentence mean that only later did they identify what they thought, or that only later did they realize that their individual thoughts resembled one another? Another moment of identity or of identification occurs in the next paragraph when Dyer says of the onomatopeia "tekeli-li" that it was "exactly what we thought we heard" (145), but again we cannot decide whether he means that what they heard was precisely what Poe described or that the word Poe used was precisely appropriate to what they heard. Like Dyer and Danforth we are increasingly in a fog as we approach the moment of revelation; and it is a fog thrust ahead of the approaching shoggoth, a part of its being, and a fog that "driving ahead with increased speed" (146) appears in the narrative as the cold wind we have come to expect, which is to say that the wind is a part of the center of fear.

Two paragraphs later Dyer seems to identify the creature pursuing them, even to describe it, only to retract the possibility of such an identification: "Of the whereabouts of that less conceivable and less mentionable nightmare—that foetid, unglimpsed mountain of slime-spewing protoplasm whose race had conquered the abyss and sent land pioneers to recarve and squirm through the burrows of the hills—we could form no guess" (*CF* 3.146). Despite such an inability—since it is unglimpsed and no guess can be formed—the words "foetid," "slime," "spew," "protoplasm," and "squirm" that form a part of Lovecraft's anti-Semitic vocabulary remain as a means of fixing the creature, a mountain of it, in the reader's mind. Three paragraphs after this moment comes the glimpse itself, also described in terms that take it away. "We actually caught one first and only half-glimpse," Dyer claims. Is that a "one first and only glimpse" or "only a half-glimpse"? He concludes, "If the fate which screened us was benign, that which gave us the half-glimpse was infinitely the opposite; for to that flash of semi-vision can be traced a full half of the horror which has ever since haunted us" (147). Like a series of double and triple negatives, the insistent verbal play on "half," "semi-," and "full half" both widens and narrows the aperture of vision. Such an introduction of the vision, nevertheless, should remind the reader that something half-glimpsed invites projection; the fewer clues, but not too few, that an object presents, the more the observer is compelled to organize it. So the passage that follows should perhaps be seen on the same level as the Old Ones' compulsion to myth.

After a meditation on why they looked back—the instinct of the pursued, the instinct of curiosity, the instinct of smell, the instinct to see with their flashlights and to dazzle the pursuer—Dyer compares them to other lookers backward: "Not Orpheus himself, or Lot's wife, paid much more dearly for a backward glance" (*CF* 3.148). Not the poet who tried to save his wife from the underworld and lost her, whether from too much love or from suspicion or from an inability to obey a divine injunction, and not the wife who looked back to the cities of the plain disappearing in the cataclysm, whether from curiosity or from a longing for their lost perverse delights, and became a pillar of salt—an image James Hillman interprets as a symbol of that love that looks backward into family history to make events into experience, at the risk of fixation (126–27)—neither Orpheus nor Lot's wife were as much involved in acts of loss and compunction and sexual desire as were Pickman and Danforth.

In order to control the horror of what is seen, Danforth begins to "chant an hysterical formula" (*CF* 3.149), though it is unclear when he began the chant. The words form a magical sentence, a liturgy or mantra, perhaps an instance of sympathetic magic, to hold at bay and to hold in mind the out-of-world apparition. Beginning with "South Station Under," where Lovecraft may have arrived in Boston on his first venture, the chant proceeded "Washington Under—Park Street Under—Kendall—Central—Harvard" (149). Such a chant, surprisingly, arising from Danforth's vision of the shoggoth places him within the perspective of the creature or the perspective of the people riding that subway train. Shall we say that the chant imitates the perspective of the shoggoth? These are "the familiar stations," Dyer comments, "of the Boston-Cambridge tunnel that burrowed through our peaceful native soil." But having given a reader this remarkably precise detail, and having with that word *burrowed* cast some doubt perhaps upon the security of that native soil to which he appeals, Dyer retracts: "We had expected, upon looking back, to see a terrible and incredibly moving entity if the mists were thin enough; but of that entity we had formed a clear idea. What we did see—for the mists were indeed all too malignly thinned—was something altogether different" (149). "It was," he writes, appealing to literary criticism, "the utter, objective embodiment of the fantastic novelist's 'thing that should not be'" (149–50). The language is possibly an appeal to the language used in "The Colour out of Space" describing the thing that destroys Mrs. Gardner: "something was fastening itself on her that ought not to be" (*CF* 2.380). Finally Dyer appeals once more to Danforth's chant, justifying it at the same time as he extends the imagery and rounds off the passage: "its nearest comprehensible analogue is a vast, onrushing subway train as one sees it from a station platform—the great black front looming colossally out of infinite subterranean distance, constellated with strangely coloured lights and filling the prodigious burrow as a piston fills a cylinder" (*CF* 3.150). Modernity erupts out of exoticism.

This passage condenses several themes we have already touched on, undoubtedly one of the reasons for its imaginative power. The shoggoth has a "great black front," a detail consistent with the excremental imagery we noted in connection with the poem "Night-Gaunts." The passage resembles one of the fantasias in *Gravity's Rainbow*: "this godawful surge from up the line, noise growing like a tidal wave, a jam-packed wavefront of shit, vomit, toilet-paper and dingleberries in mind-boggling mosaic, rushing down on panicky Slothrop like an MTA subway train" (66). But in Lovecraft's vision shit is transformed, "constellated with strangely coloured lights." This transformation may be related to the colors that play across the stone fallen from the sky in "The Colour out of Space," as though the thing that infects the Gardner farm were a shoggoth of the celestial subway. Nor is this an empty phrase if we recall Lovecraft's daydream of himself, "hurtling through interstellar blackness in cryptic subways, never knowing on just what planet or within just what universe I would next emerge to overwhelming light" (*JFM* 223). The scientists from Arkham who expect a mere stone and, in one of the most neutral phrases in the story, find a "brown lump" (*CF* 2.373) discover also colors of "an unknown spectrum" (374) and later "a monstrous constellation of unnatural light" (393) and "unholy iridescence" (392).

Now all this language, perceived as a transformation of something heavy, dark, and foul into an object of great value, certainly suggests moments in the fantasies of alchemy. Though suspicious of sublimation Norman O. Brown believes that "with the transformation of the worthless into the priceless and the inedible into food, man acquires a soul; he becomes the animal which does not live by bread alone, the animal which sublimates" (258). After all, as he points out at length, anal imagery provides a compacted narrative of the assumption of the world by demonic forces that the dreamer must oppose and ally the self with in order to advance the project of becoming one's own originator (202–33). These lights refer to a terrifying, alchemical moment in which the transvaluation of the matter of the world suddenly occurs and the aggression implied in our descent to the ancestors upon whom our civilization depends is suddenly released. The iridescence signals such a change.

So Dyer's shoggoth reveals itself as a "plastic column of foetid black iridescence" that "oozed tightly onward through its fifteen-foot sinus" (*CF* 3.150), as though it poured from a huge nose. And now, in perhaps his clearest description, Dyer adds that it was "a shapeless congeries of protoplasmic bubbles, faintly self-luminous, and with myriads of temporary eyes forming and unforming" (150). This ocular imagery is oblique but frequent in material surrounding shoggoths. In "The Shadow over Innsmouth" Zadok Allen's reference to the creatures, "Ever hear tell of a *shoggoth?*" (*CF* 3.200) is preceded by what seems to be an irrelevant exclamation, "Curse ye, dun't set thar a-starin' at me with them eyes—I tell Obed Marsh he's in hell, an' hez got to stay thar!" (199), words that only at the end of the story become explicable when the protagonist dreams of a shoggoth for the first time and wakes to see in the mirror that he has the Innsmouth look of his grandmother (229). The story obliquely connects vision and change of identity, a change one is at first not aware of, with a shoggoth; and the dream so often connected with a shoggoth assures us that imagination is its provenance. In the only other story to refer to the creature, "The Thing on the Doorstep," Edward Derby tells how sitting in the library in Asenath's body he suddenly found himself, without transition, in his own body in "the pit of the shoggoths! Down the six thousand steps . . . the unholy pit where the black realm begins and the watcher guards the gate. . . . I saw a shoggoth—it changed shape. . . . I can't stand it" (*CF* 3.338). Vision and alteration, in this case change between male and female, female and male, are again linked. Quite possibly, then, we confront the shoggoth in one other poem of the sonnet cycle, "Antarktos," which concludes, "God help the dreamer whose mad visions shew / Those dead eyes set in crystal gulfs below!" (*AT* 86). The lines continue the theme of "Kubla Khan" in which pleasure dome, caves of ice, and caves in air, archimage and poet and demon mirror and collapse into one another. In the same fashion the constellated eyes along the side of the shoggoth refer out of its darkness to an astral hemisphere. In addition they suggest what we see in subways, the eyes of the passengers looking out, eyes that mirror the eyes of the narrator in this most ocular of Lovecraft's works. The dark productions of the imagination and the objects of desire and loathing are granted an omniscient brightness, a visionary and creative power, probably from the female side of the personality, from which the rational consciousness Lovecraft so much values must continue to flee.

Another reason for the flight is rather complex, for the untransformed excremental images, the residue of the ecstatic language, still remains a threat of impurity, still something to be rid of; and in this situation Young-Bruehl's insight becomes apt that racism for the obsessional white male often develops the fantasy that the black man "is an anal product who must be eliminated" (239). And these aggressive thoughts are countered and further justified by the threat of anal penetration contained in the imagery of the piston.

The chapter is not quite finished, though, for after an emphatic repetition of words like "foetid," "ooze," "plastic," "protoplasmic," "slither," and "pustule," once more placing the monster within an anti-Semitic context, Dyer reminds the reader that shoggoths have no language and no voice except their imitation of the accents of the Old Ones (*CF* 3.150); language and voice have been erased by the ideology of desire and the force of the imagination. Perhaps in the same fashion the Colour reminds the narrator of the tongues of fire that allowed the Apostles to speak to anyone in their own tongue, but the Colour itself has nothing to say; the author must, as it were, speak for the thing, just as he must speak for the shoggoth. And at this point we should wonder whether Lovecraft consciously intends that a reader identify the Chinese, the Women, the Jews, the Blacks, or the Gays as the imitative slaves made by their masters, the Old Ones of New England who project them out of their uneasy dreams to inhabit the houses the Old Ones shall never inhabit again and who project them as threats that have nothing to say because buried in prehistory their divine tongues were stolen. Lovecraft's language compacts the structures of so many fears that it becomes impossible to disentangle them fully.

But the story cannot conclude with so easy a reading. The ascent occurs in the midst of "dream-fragments . . ., as if we floated in a nebulous world or dimension without time, causation, or orientation" (*CF* 3.151); and Danforth, who has looked back and seen the fata morgana of a city more colossal than the one through which they have burrowed, now places the shoggoth in that expanded space, babbling a catalogue of phrases that both confirm our suppositions but also render them dubious: "'the black pit', 'the carven rim', 'the proto-shoggoths', 'the windowless solids with five dimensions', 'the nameless cylinder', 'the elder pharos', 'Yog-Sothoth', 'the primal white jelly', 'the colour out of space', 'the wings', 'the eyes in darkness', 'the moon-ladder', 'the original, the eternal, the undying'" (157). Edward Derby associated the shoggoths with the black pit, and we can sense how the nameless cylinder, the primal white jelly, or the eyes in darkness may be apt; and we have suspected an imagistic relation with the Colour out of space. But what is the relation between shoggoths and the elder pharos or Yog-Sothoth? Or what can we say of all the windowless solids or the moon-ladder? At this point our hermeneutics collapse, and we have to regard Danforth, as does Dyer, as too susceptible to his reading, too deeply read in the *Necronomicon,* so that his learning obstructs his ability to understand his experience. And if we regard such a catalogue as a typical strategy by an obsessive personality to take control of his experience, to deflect his obsessions and avoid being overwhelmed by his prejudices, as a way to live in the world, if we are baffled because we have read too many of Lovecraft's letters, has our reading also obstructed the impact of this chill story? Does the search for authenticity prevent any possibility of an authentic discovery? Lovecraft's language deflects our fears from any definite object; the figure of the shoggoth, its ability to imitate infinitely, glides from one object after another. And we connive at the deflection. So the subway pulls out, leaving us in the dark.

PART III

Meditations on "The Outsider"

"The Outsider," the Terminal Climax, and Other Conclusions

I

Oblivisci ceperam, sed incipio recordari. [I was starting to forget, but I begin to remember.] (Petrarca 106)

H. P. Lovecraft's "The Outsider" is perhaps his best-known short piece, but the reasons for its reputation are elusive because its diction seems, like that of many of his early stories, florid and imprecise; in contrast the final sentence is abruptly sober, concluding a short paragraph that represents a retardando after the orgiastic fury of the penultimate paragraph. Reflectively, in a mirror, the narrator realizes the self: "For although nepenthe has calmed me, I know always that I am an outsider; a stranger in this century and among those who are still men. This I have known ever since I stretched out my fingers to the abomination within that great gilded frame; stretched out my fingers and touched *a cold and unyielding surface of polished glass*" (*CF* 1.272). Why does this passage convey such a sense of necessity and satisfaction? An answer to this question also involves the significance of a typical manner Lovecraft had for concluding his stories, what Fritz Leiber identified as the terminal climax (56). The conclusion of "The Outsider" begs for a close consideration, through which we can examine similar conclusions in order to construct a morphology of the terminal climax.

The words "cold, unyielding, polished glass" need to be understood literally, at the least, for they remain the final words of the story. The speaker is not that rotting hulk seen in an ultimate moment of consciousness; the speaker is that glass at which touch, so much more intimate a sense than sight, comes up short, that into which the "living being resolves itself" (Buchanan 13). The glass is the wall to which Lovecraft's writings so often refer; and the self is that real wall that remains polished, cold, unyielding, at which it comes up short.

Glass is a liquid, much more slow moving than the mass of a glacier, and the liquid of the glass that faces the Outsider is a wall that the creature cannot cross, though having crossed already a river in the approach to the castle, a river that presumptively the self has to cross again in a futile attempt to return to the underworld region abandoned at the beginning of the story.

Has the Outsider crossed the river? Crossed Lethe? The character has experienced an inner oblivion. To cross Lethe and to enjoy its oblivion had two meanings in the classical world. The more ancient meaning was that unconscious descent into the earth from which there was no return except the necrophantic glance that precedes the final dissolution. The more recent meaning appears in the myths of metempsychosis, which demand that the soul lose its memory of its past life—for no other reason is the experience of Pythagoras extraordinary, one of the few mortals to remember the names of the personalities within which he lingered through the ages, but whom in the climax to the *Metamorphoses* Ovid declines to name, as though life after life had rubbed out identity (Ovid 15.161). In the terms of our entire study, to cross Lethe is to hide the self in untruth once more, in an *a-letheia*. But which direction is decisive, to cross the river first or to return across it, to enter the mirror or to flee from it?

It is difficult to say whether the Outsider has drunk from Lethe. This very discussion, on the other hand, throws us back to the beginning of the story in which the creature as it were appears out of the oblivion of a past life, not reborn, but certainly returned not merely to life but suppositiously to life and lands known when formerly alive.

"But in the cosmos there is balm as well as bitterness, and that balm is nepenthe," says the character (*CF* 2.272). The word nepenthe, which means "painless," occurs in the fourth book of the *Odyssey* as Telemachus visits Menelaus and Helen, who as though she were a pharmacologist dispenses the dangerous substance at the banquet (Lovecraft had Pope's translation in his library [*LL* #464]):

> Mean-time with genial joy to warm the soul,
> Bright *Helen* mix'd a mirth-inspiring bowl:
> Temper'd with drugs of sov'reign use, t'assuage
> The boiling bosom of tumultuous Rage;
> To clear the cloudy front of wrinkled Care,
> And dry the tearful sluices of Despair:
> Charm'd with that virtuous draught, th'exalted mind
> All sense of woe delivers to the wind.
> Though on the blazing pile his parent lay,
> Or a lov'd brother groan'd his life away,
> Or darling son oppress'd by ruffian-force
> Fell breathless at his feet, a mangled corse,
> From morn to eve, impassive and serene,
> The man entranc'd wou'd view the deathful scene.
> These drugs, so friendly to the joys of life,
> Bright *Helen* learn'd from *Thone's* imperial wife;
> Who sway'd the sceptre, where prolific *Nile*
> With various simples cloaths the fat'ned soil. (4.301–18)

In an annotation Pope cites opinions that nepenthe was to be understood allegorically as history, music, philosophy, or good conversation, but concludes that Homer's description "agrees admirably with what we know of the qualities and effects of *Opium*" (9.133). As for Thone, he reports the opinion that from the name of that king the Egyptians "gave the name of *Thoth* to the first month of their year" (9.134). Lovecraft would have known that Thoth is also the scribe of the gods, often described as the patron of authors. We meet here another kind of oblivion, one that we must understand upon its own terms before we ask its relation to Lethe.

Yet this oblivion parallels Lethe at least in the sense that the entire scene with Menelaus occurs as though it represented an underworld experience. This Sparta is an underworld, down in its valley as Telemachus approaches at nightfall. Menelaus has an underworld experience to recount in his story of Proteus. And the story of Helen was not to remain unsuspect; during the sixth century B.C.E. her visit to Egypt became understood as a death that was not a death. The poet Stesichorus, struck blind after writing an attack on Helen, wrote a recantation that asserted, "Thou wentest not in the benchèd ships, thou camest not to the city of Troy." To vindicate the daughter of Zeus, he claimed that an eidolon, a phantom, a mere appearance of her, walked the walls of Troy (2.45). Euripides uses the same word, "eidolon," when he writes his play *Helen* (1.468–69). The theme of the underworld Helen and her double, her eidolon, has been a theme of European literature from Stesichorus and Euripides through Goethe. And it is an eidolon that the Outsider faces (*CF* 2.271). This story of Helen is an alternative to the one with which we are familiar. But so, in this regard, is "The Outsider," for it is Lovecraft's only story in which the narrative is seen through the eyes of the monstrous, the already monstrous, instead of through the eyes of our common human face. But who is the Helen, the original Helen or the eidolon, who provides the Outsider a draught of nepenthe?

It is structurally noteworthy that the word *nepenthe* brackets a paragraph that it may be useful to imagine as the oblivion the narrator enjoys. In that paragraph a number of significant names appear: "Now I ride with the mocking and friendly ghouls amongst the catacombs of Nephren-Ka in the sealed and unknown valley of Hadoth by the Nile. I know that light is not for me, save that of the moon over the rock tombs of Neb, nor any gaiety save the unnamed feasts of Nitokris beneath the Great Pyramid" (*CF* 2.272). It is doubtless an act of decorum on Lovecraft's part to make the scene that nepenthe brackets vaguely Egyptian, since Helen obtained the drug in Egypt.

The Valley of Hadoth reappears in *The Case of Charles Dexter Ward*, Nephren-Ka in *Charles Dexter Ward* and in "The Haunter of the Dark." Neb is peculiar to "The Outsider." Nitokris reappears in "Under the Pyramids" as the queen of the "sneering King Khephren *or the guide Abdul Reis";* beside him she kneels, "beautiful Queen Nitokris," with "the right half of her face . . . eaten away by rats or other ghouls" (*CF* 1.448). Nitokris is not Helen, but she does seem to stand in the place of Helen and possibly to bear her significance, which is at the least the incarnation of the greatest beauty that the world has seen. Robert Calasso treats her as a figure related to the courtesan Rhodopis, for each is said to have built the Micerine pyramid, and he cites Manetho who called her "'the noblest and most beautiful woman of her time, fair of skin'" (270–72). Helen and Nitokris make beauty seem possible in a broken world. Beauty can signify health, wholeness, value itself; but such beauty seems difficult in the world where most of us live. And such beauty judges our world, for as Marlowe's Dr. Faustus exclaims "all is drosse that is not *Helena*" (Sc. 17; l. 1774). She simultaneously attracts and condemns.

But we can say more of Queen Nitokris, for her feasts are not in fact "unnamed." Herodotus tells stories of two Queens Nitokris, one of Babylon who made the straight Euphrates crooked in order to protect the city from invaders (1.185), the other of Egypt who, to avenge her brother's death, "built a spacious underground chamber; then . . . she gave a great feast, inviting to it those Egyptians whom she knew to have been most concerned in her brother's death; and while they feasted she let the river in upon them by a great and secret channel. . . . When she had done this she cast herself into a chamber full of hot ashes, thereby to escape vengeance" (2.100).[1] A number of doublings occur here, first of names, then the doubling inherent in a story of a brother and a sister. But also we have the doubling of the rivers—Herodotus, always interested in public works, tells the story of the Egyptian queen in the context of other works on the Nile. A queen makes each river a part of the architecture of the city, in the one case in order to protect her citizens, in the other case to destroy them. And a further doubling occurs simply in the place of Egypt, where Nitokris ruled and where Helen, whether before the fall of Troy or afterwards, abode for a time. We may consider how anathema Egypt was to the Roman civilization Lovecraft idolized, that Egypt—and that other queen, Cleopatra—with its multiform gods that Caesar Augustus defeated at Actium. How attractive and how terrifying such a beauty appears from the perspective of the Outsider.

We have to think, however, that this figure of Nitokris and Helen means something quite complex for the Outsider, since her beauty makes the creature aware of its deformity at the same instant that it erases that awareness from its mind. The abomination it has seen was contained by "that great gilded frame" (*CF* 2.272), described earlier as "the golden-arched doorway leading to another and somewhat similar room" (270). The beauty of the arch is emphasized in both accounts. On the other hand we should note the slight difference between "golden" and "gilded" and consider once more the vision of Queen Nitokris with half her face eaten away. The beauty of Helen contains a horror, for Greek myth presents her as ceaselessly fugitive, passing through the world but not participating in it, and Greek philology preferred to read her name as man-destroyer:

> Who gave the ill-omened name,
> So fraught with terror for the time to be,
> So true to her career of blame?
> War-won, war-wed, war-wakening Helenè?
>   (Aeschylus, *Agamemnon* 681–84)

Approaching the doorway the Outsider touches cold, unyielding, polished glass and becomes a creature capable of destruction.

---

1. Lovecraft was aware of this story both from Herodotus and from Dunsany's play *The Queen's Enemies,* based upon the episode (*RKO* 146). Perhaps Dunsany's play recalled the story to Lovecraft's attention.

It is useful here to remember Mollie Burleson's argument that the narrator of "The Outsider" might be a woman. If we grant the force of her analysis, it is possible for us to react to the narrator as the kore Persephone, the lost anima, the figure that like Helen suffers an underworld experience and is never quite of the living world nor of the dead world thereafter; she becomes a possibly delusive beacon to the world to arrest its errant attention; as Carl Buchanan puts the matter, the Outsider "remains trapped somewhat in the animistic conception of things as living, and of living beings as things" and thus, "never maturing into a true subject-object discrimination, . . . fails to evolve as a sexual being" (14). Since this is a first-person narration, the "I" prevents the specificity of either "he" or "she" from being uttered (as I have tried to avoid those words, though "it" is surely unsatisfying also); we cannot know whether the Outsider is a man, a woman, or a something to which gender is indifferent, yet neither can we avoid supposing that the Outsider is related to the human. The narrator, hidden in an unfathomable identity, like Goethe's Helen who faints when made too aware of the fact that she has been brought back from the underworld, becomes an idol and speculation to itself (*Faust II* 8879–81).

In everything said so far we have been tacitly following the advice of Gadamer that a useful path into a literary work is to begin at the conclusion (*Wer bin Ich* 55); but this advice is most useful if we feel that the conclusion has something to do with the closure of the work or that the work indeed enjoys closure. In the case of "The Outsider" this assumption of closure may be questionable given the structure of the final pages, for Lovecraft has accomplished here the advice that he gave on the writing of horror stories, to arrange the narration in such a way that the climax comes at the very end of the story after the denouement. In his essay, "Notes on Writing Weird Fiction," he advises preparing a synopsis of narration that shall rearrange the chronological order of the plot if such a change will increase "the dramatic force or general effectiveness of the story" (*CE* 2.176). This remark certainly covers the case of the terminal climax, but does not allude to a separate treatment of the conclusion. This reversal of chronological expectations throws into question whether the work has been closed; the climax, the realization, the anamnesis remains undeveloped; it remains very much in the hands of the reader to work out the significance of the final words. In the case of "The Outsider," this working out is difficult given the slight ambiguity of the final word of the story, for quite literally the creature has touched glass. Whether that glass happen to be a mirror must be a work of the reader's rationalizing mind. If the glass is a glass, the outsider has not quite contacted but realized something monstrous that is totally other, totally not the self, and suffered a severe split of the self that the reader has throughout the course of the story come to believe a monstrous self; if the glass is a glass and that other a monster, the reader suddenly has no idea whatsoever what the narrator might be like, so that the narrator becomes not an Outsider but a cipher. Should the reader not then, like the narrator, forget the whole business? Is there nepenthe for us? No, because even glass, if it is only glass, still casts a reflection, and the image of the narrator coincides with the image of the abomination. We are all quite desolate.

We would hardly be discussing the conclusion of "The Outsider" if Fritz Leiber had not commented on what he slily called the terminal climax used in this story. In such a story "the high point and the final sentence coincide.... Use of the terminal climax made it necessary for Lovecraft to develop a special type of story-telling, in which the explanatory and return-to-equilibrium material is all deftly inserted before the finish and while the tension is still mounting" (56–57). But the climax is not postponed. It *has* happened, but it is occluded by various mental acts of repression that the structure and style attempt to mimic and model. In terms of first-person narrative, the climax has happened before the first sentence of the story, which devotes itself to the postponing of its own revelation.

In horror stories we often have not so much a delayed ending as a multiple ending; or rather, what Lovecraft calls a delayed ending is better described as a multiple ending. A delayed ending simply ends; a multiple ending shatters into alternatives, providing the formal equivalent to Todorov's notion of the fantastic. Rather than one ending, whether it is delayed or not, we have a series of endings among which to choose—though we must admit that the final ending in the linearity of the story still bears a priority among them.

There are other reasons for returning to the climax that has happened before the first sentence of the story, for if we are to talk of such allusions as those contained in nepenthe we must for balance discuss the explicit allusion to Keats's *The Eve of St. Agnes* contained in the epigraph to the story:

> That night the Baron dreamt of many a woe;
> And all his warrior-guests, with shade and form
> Of witch, and demon, and large coffin-worm,
> Were long be-nightmared. (*CF* 2.265)

Is this story a dream?—according to Lovecraft's *Commonplace Book* the source was a dream (*CE* 5.224; #42), and William Fulwiler believes that we can only understand it as a dream (4). Is it literally a dream of that night on which Porphyro and Madeline escape, or is it a dream that results from their escape, a dream that the Baron suffers warning him of his loss, his spiritual and material death, and his ungendering? With Madeline's flight the castle has lost its anima, and the carcass that remains becomes a mockery of its living self. Or is it a dream that follows the death, the kind of dream we find described in *The Tibetan Book of the Dead?* From the epigraph we might in retrospect think of the Baron of that poem as the Outsider. The most inside of people, the ruler, has been placed outside, interred, before the story ever began. In any case the last stanza of the poem, Lovecraft's epigraph, declares that everyone in the castle has died, died in the midst of their revels like the victims of Queen Nitokris. From such a perspective we may judge the shock and rejection that the revelers of the story express, for in the middle of their celebration has appeared not simply a *memento mori;* here is a walking symbol of the process of death toward which they are everyone tending. And such a process is a summons.

These several procedures by which we avoid and approach the event contained within the terminal climax and within the gilded arch are represented in the story by the Outsider's own act of confronting the unknown monster from which the revelers flee. The Outsider first turns to face it, approaches the arch, sees the monster, steps back, throws up a hand to cut off sight of the monster, unbalanced stumbles forward, throws up a hand once more to ward off the monster, and thereby, at last, touches it. What others flee, the Outsider approaches; and twice the Outsider is forced to approach through an act of avoidance. Is it any wonder that a reader postulates a narcissistic attraction hidden in the moment of oblivion? The protagonist cannot help approaching, apprehending, and confessing the monstrous self through the very act of repressing it.

II

Aliquantulum evagati sumus, sed iam sensim ad primordia nostra evertimur, nisi forte unde discesseramus oblitus es. [We have digressed a little, but let us gradually return to our first points, unless you have forgotten where we started.] (Petrarca 106)

It is time to consider the extent to which we find the characteristics of "The Outsider" elsewhere in Lovecraft's work. We are not concerned now with simply the question of a terminal climax, which is itself simply a variation of the surprise ending so frequently employed in the history of the short story, itself so like the conventional conclusion of detective stories in which the internal meaning of the clues and motives is revealed. By my own count I would say that of Lovecraft's 64 stories, novels, and revisions 18 of them employ some form of the terminal climax, including "Beyond the Wall of Sleep," "Facts Concerning the Late Arthur Jermyn and His Family," "Herbert West—Reanimator: V. The Horror from the Shadows," "The Lurking Fear," "The Unnamable," "Under the Pyramids," "The Curse of Yig," "The Mound," "Medusa's Coil," "The Dreams in the Witch House," and "The Horror in the Museum," stories from the beginning of his career to its end; but for a number of reasons I would exclude these stories from our consideration of characteristics peculiar to "The Outsider." The stories more central to our interest are these six: "The Tomb," "Hypnos," "Pickman's Model," "The Dunwich Horror," "The Whisperer in Darkness," and "The Shadow out of Time," a relatively small number in the canon. But our categories are not firm, for as Leiber notices the terminal climax may be considered an aspect of the device of confirmation, in which the conclusion makes explicit what the reader may have guessed on the first page of the story (56). My second list, moreover, contains a number of negligible works, and nowhere in it appear such excellent, typical works as "The Colour out of Space," "The Call of Cthulhu," or the novels. The technique is only a technique, not a guarantee of aesthetic interest.

What do I find peculiar to the stories that I group with "The Outsider"? First, the ending must be necessary to our understanding of the plot. The significance of "The Outsider" is unimaginable without that polished glass. But the plot of "The

Mound" has no need of the detail of the watchman at the end; the voice from the vat in "Herbert West" adds nothing to that story. The last paragraph of "The Dreams in the Witch House" is only a confirmation of the reader's apprehensions. With an Aristotelian discrimination of this sort we can separate what is merely gratuitous from what is essential. Some stories that look as though they were ending in this fashion are only offering a confirmation of a part of the plot with which, necessary as it is, we are already familiar.

Second, the ending should imply a transformation in the protagonist, often through a juxtaposition of contexts that forces the character to understand the self in a wholly new way. We might also say that this transformation affects the way in which the human and the other, the ahuman, the inhuman, and the universe, are related. Often a doubling of the character occurs, though given the use of the Double in fantasy we cannot say that it is necessary to only this technique. But the transformation of the character becomes a dramatic justification for the delay; a reluctance, a recalcitrance within being itself refuses to confess itself. This ending represents those moments in the confessional and in therapy when the sick and guilty only mentions going out the door the truly significant event of the last week, conquering as Leiber says a "disinclination" (57). The ending is a sudden, compulsive confession and confrontation, perhaps a reconsideration and transformation of the event and of the self, a *Nachträglichkeit* that once more, and once more, grapples with an unassimilable trauma (Laplanche and Pontalis 184). This peculiar term *Nachträglichkeit* Freud employs at length in his essay on the Wolfman, describing the reaction that the patient has to the primal scene long after the event. In psychoanalytic circles it is often translated as deferred or delayed reaction, though the term has a slight clumsiness that renders it awkward to use. But in addition to this awkwardness, *Nachträglichkeit* is a concept in debate in psychoanalysis. As Freud employs it, the term denotes the mechanism by which a person not only remembers an event but remembers it with an affect wholly absent at the event itself, usually because the person is too young to have either the words or the understanding for the experience—and thus the event is almost always to be understood clinically as the primal event, whether in fact the person has seen the primal event or not, with all of its Oedipal implications[2]—so that the event is remembered both with understanding and with emotion. It is, incidentally, very unlikely that the Outsider, given what it is, whatever it is, has observed a primal event unless it does so in the mirror. Freud describes the moment of remembrance in these words:

> Die Vorgänge, die sich nun abspielen, können wir weder vollständig erfassen, noch sie hinreichend beschreiben. Die Aktivierung des Bildes, das nun dank

---

2. Though in this particular case Freud believed that the child had seen his parents copulating, he also asserts that primal scenes, with the full weight of their seductive and threatening aspects, are "ererbter Besitz, phylogenetische Erbschaft" [inherited possessions, a phylogenetic heritage] ("Aus der Geschichte einer infantilen Neurose" 131).

der vorgeschrittenen intellektuellen Entwicklung verstanden werden kann, wirkt wie ein frisches Ereignis, aber auch wie ein neues Trauma, ein fremder Eingriff analog der Verführung. [The processes which now play out we can neither fully grasp nor sufficiently describe. The activation of the image, which thanks to the intellectual development can be understood, works as a fresh occurrence, but also as a new trauma, a foreign intervention analogous to the seduction {which the patient had presumptively experienced with his sister}.] ("Aus der Geschichte einer infantilen Neurose" 144)

The new trauma and the new understanding do not exhaust the event, for at a later time it may recur once more, within a new context and a new understanding and thus once more as a new trauma; it might be claimed that the new seduction bears with it the implication of a continuous fall. Thus the person is transformed, again and again. "Deferred reaction," therefore, does not carry the full flavor of Freud's German or of his understanding of the mechanism. Derrida points out that a *Nachtrag* is an addendum or a supplement, something that is "folded over" a previous text and thus clear evidence for his concept of *différence:* "c'est l'appendice, le codicille, le post-scriptum. Le texte qu'un appelle présent ne se déchiffre qu'en bas de page" (314); and certainly, given our analysis of the terminal climax, something of repeated deferral does seem to adhere to it. But *Nachträglichkeit* also implies an inertia of the event, a belatedness, a *Trägheit* that remains in motion within a person without any awareness or any defense. We can imagine, indeed, that a person might at last say that this understanding, here and now, is enough, not wishing to suffer that trauma ever again; but owing to the involuntary nature of memory it may very well happen that a fresh understanding and a fresh trauma can break in upon the complacency of an understanding to which the person has become habituated. In our most placid moments we run the risk of remaking.

It is this characteristic, the trauma, the self-confrontation, and the transformation, to say nothing of the implication that in some fashion the primal event is involved, that is so lacking in the stories of our first list. Slattery's fate does not affect the narrator's; the gigantic claw in "Under the Pyramids" does not penetrate the narrator of that story, and its implications, the riddle and eternity of a sphinx and its Oedipal complications, do not seem relevant to him. This moment is highly significant, however, for the Outsider, who in the mirror comes to birth at least in consciousness for the first time, but not as he implies for the last time.

Third, a part of the reaction of the character should involve an ecstatic position, in part because of the release implied in having at last said what must be said—though given the mechanics of the page the expression of ecstasy will often precede the confession. But we should also understand the ecstasy quite literally: the character is beside himself. Given what we have already said it is clear how this characteristic does not function in the first list. A frequent expression of ecstasy is the flight that sweeps the protagonist away; the protagonist flees and flies, helplessly, often as though in a great wind and afflatus of being.

Fourth, a moment of oblivion will be involved in the transformation and ecstasy, which will stand between the self and its realization. This oblivion may be seen in several ways. It may represent an act of repression; it may represent a balm, a pharmakon; and it may be recurrent, a process of oblivion and consciousness that has no end. It may alternate as remorse and nostalgia. It preoccupies what happens after thought. Our meditation on "The Outsider" has underscored the importance of this characteristic twice in the allusions of Lethe and nepenthe. So we shall often find a drink present in the story, in some fashion associated with oblivion, transformation, or rebirth.

Fifth, the ecstasy and transformation may bear the concomitant experience of beauty and art, but also definitely the experience of the artwork's frame being broken. The limit that is formed between the work of art, the way in which it is set apart from the everyday world, shall be violently disturbed; and with that event the everyday world shall experience an invasion of beauty that it finds difficult to bear. This characteristic may be only another way to express the transformation, revolution, and doubling of the protagonist. But it still seems a frequent characteristic of Lovecraft's delayed endings that they are associated with the experience of a work of art with aggressive boundaries. The art may be painterly, architectural; it may be associated with decadence; it may be the art of calligraphy, under the sign of Thoth. It will often be scoptic and skeptic at once, involving sight and an anxiety of sight; so mirrors, glasses, lenses, flashlights, and telescopes become media of the artwork.

Sixth, given this element of art, the conclusion will be short and carefully demarcated from the rest of the story. This element may be simply a question of proportion, but it explains why the novels do not conclude in this way; for them too short an ending would seem abrupt, not able to bear the weight of the material that preceded it. Such a short end might seem a mere trick. But a longer ending would have a tendency to blend into the material before it. If we are to have the click or snap that is a major effect of the technique and a result of the ecstasy, it must be short and adequate. This characteristic may not be necessary, but it appears often enough to seem a sign of the technique. And the demarcation becomes emblematic of oblivion and of the boundaries of beauty.

Finally, we will often find that in the conclusion of the story the reader finds some reason for returning to an earlier point in the story, obviously that point where the delayed action and information ought to have arisen, less obviously there may be a compulsion to return to a point near the beginning of the story, as though remorse and nostalgia would find there a satisfaction that is not granted by a rational contemplation of the story. In "The Outsider" such a moment occurs when we return to the epigraph from *The Eve of St. Agnes,* but our return to that point, inconclusive as it was, may itself be too obvious.

Let us now examine these stories, not in any great depth, to see how these characteristics work out in each. The earliest, "The Tomb," is a nicely plotted piece in which the epigraph from the *Aeneid* is not without its irony, for the request Palinurus makes of Aeneas is impossible for the hero to fulfill; the spirit will not be able to rest in a quiet place in death, but since he was unburied will roam restlessly the further bank of Styx (6.337–83); but he will find rest when in a hundred years the unburied spirits cross the Styx at last, as though it took a hundred years for putrefaction to give the body at last the effect of burial. Jervas Dudley will rest in the tomb of Jervas Hyde and thus the latter, if Dudley is not mad, will find peace. But the reader is cast back and forth on the various uncertainties that compose the story, not least of which is the question whether or not Dudley had entered the tomb and slept in Hyde's coffin on the night when the significant hiatus occurs in the story (*CF* 1.44). The servant's report in the last sentence would seem to confirm Dudley's story retroactively, but the entire telling of the story is retroactive in the mad house. What we cannot doubt is that Dudley has been cast out of himself, as was Hyde on the night of the lightning-stroke. And we cannot but be moved by the sober Dudley's achievement of drunkenness or, if the doctors are correct, by his desire to be drunken and escape the sobriety of his life; we also note in his revelry the connection between drunkenness and sexuality as we recall that drink and revelry are offered, with soothing and with deadly consequences, by Helen and Nitokris. Sobriety and chastity, conversely, function as a means of upholding an integrity of spirit.

Whatever the truth of the matter, all the protagonists of fiction find rest at last, in time, a burial and a peace and an oblivion in our minds, released from the ambivalence of an active and remorseful reading. We reread a book to unbury them, to ferry them back across the Styx and set them wandering again.

"Hypnos" is a slight story that nevertheless reveals traces of the technique we are studying. As drugs, the drink is prominent in this story, not metaphoric as in "The Outsider." Baudelaire and De Quincey, perhaps also the Rimbaud of *Une Saison en enfer*, who wrote, "J'ai avalé une fameuse gorgée de poison.—Trois fois béni soit le conseil qui m'est arrivé!" (220), preside as decadents in this story, causing us to ask what drugs represent in the context of the abstemious habits of Lovecraft. Is a drug the equivalent of art in its ability to change the appearance of the physical world? Ecstasy seizes the narrator, beyond any question of Lovecraft's early style, though it is an ecstasy that his acquaintances call madness. Here, as in "The Outsider," two figures apparently fuse at the final moment, as well as an enigmatic third called Hypnos, a statue that resembles the main figure of Samuel Loveman's poem *The Hermaphrodite* (*CF* 1.333).

In "Pickman's Model," Thurber the narrator is deeply concerned in the fate of Pickman, for he regards the artist as the hope for an aesthetic revolution at the same time that Pickman justifies his elitism; but the photograph reveals the brutal reality of Pickman's aestheticism. In part the doubling of Thurber and Pickman reveals the ecstatic moment, but more profoundly Thurber's inability to find his way back to Pickman's study reveals it. And the shock of the story does not lie in the reality of the ghoul so much as in the implications of its reality. If the ghoul is real, Pickman may be a ghoul also; he is certainly on familiar terms with it. And the narrator, in his familiarity with Pickman, may be a ghoul also, as he is certainly a metaphoric ghoul. He might well consider how assured anyone can be of not being a changeling. But he has little assurance; drinking as he relates his story (*DH* 58, 63, 64), needing black coffee at the end (71), he tries to modulate and control the anxiety and ecstasy that nevertheless escape him.

Given the length of "The Dunwich Horror," several of the characteristics are scattered through the text; and the effect of some are muted. The drink does not seem at work here, unless in the inadvertent pun on the telescope: "the glass was passed around" the group watching the final scene from below (*CF* 2.461), as scoptic control substitutes for a potation. Other references to the motif might be the "black wells of Acherontic fear," the "great tidal wave of viewless force and indescribable stench," and "the lethal foetor" rolling down from the hill (464); the monstrous offers its own drink, like the Nile that Nitokris gives her enemies to drink. But it is Curtis Whateley, "of the undecayed branch" of the Whateleys (464), who sees the apparition of the monster and first speaks of the significance that Armitage only reveals in the last sentence. Curtis cannot; "he collapsed completely before he could say more" (462). But Curtis's attempt to speak leads to Armitage: "There was a brief silence, and in that pause the scattered senses of poor Curtis Whateley began to knit back into a sort of continuity; so that he put his hands to his head with a moan. Memory seemed to pick itself up where it had left off, and the horror of the sight that had prostrated him burst in upon him again" (465). Struck out of himself, Curtis suffers the continual reversion of memory, and Curtis, "of the undecayed branch," provides Lovecraft with a link between the tragedy of the Whateleys and Armitage, who also has the link of erudition with Wilbur; Curtis is a significant double in the story. Invisibility certainly functions as a symbol of oblivion; what is not seen does not exist. But it also functions as a symbol of hesitancy: the monstrous exists but does not want to show the pathos of its divided self, a pathos revealed so movingly in the last sentence.

In "The Whisperer in Darkness" an identification similar to that between Pickman and Thurber is suggested between Akeley and Wilmarth, and Akeley is grotesquely doubled when his head is removed from his body; he is stricken out of his body, displaced from the stances and habits and skin of everyday life; he has lost his mind. Perhaps he drank "that acrid coffee," perhaps drugged, perhaps the prelude to hypnotism, that Wilmarth refused (*CF* 2.535). Wilmarth falls asleep but cannot say, at the beginning of the last chapter, "how long my unexpected lapse into slumber lasted, or how much of what ensued was sheer dream" (528). Two pages later, after describing his escape, he remembers that he has "still to tell of the ending of that terrible night in the farmhouse" and continues, "As I have said, I did finally drop into a troubled doze" (531). He dallies and delays the conclusion; morose delectation, the provocation or pursuit of inordinate passion (Aquinas 1–2.74.6), is a strong feature of this story. When he consents to tell what happened as he crossed the room where Akeley was sitting, he still hesitates to come to the point. He wishes, in retrospect, that he had made the apparatus containing Akeley's head speak. "But then," he counters, "it may be merciful that I let it alone" (537). After some hesitation in the room, he confesses, "Would to heaven I had quietly left the place before allowing that light [of his flashlight] to rest again on the vacant chair" (537). Two paragraphs later, after describing his shriek and, once more, the delirium of his ride, he repeats, "As I have implied, I let my flashlight return to the vacant chair" (538), but now admits that the chair was not vacant. And once more, still without naming the objects on the chair, he reverts to the beginning of the narrative: "As I said at the outset, there was nothing of actual visual horror about them" (538). The final admission that there lay, or did not lay, the face and hands of Akeley cannot happen without elaborate repetitions, hesitations, elisions, and further repetitions. Yet Wilmarth does perforce admire the perfection of the various arts involved in Akeley's transformation and masking.

A significant detail of this passage is its lingering on such phrases as "let alone," suggestive of the Greek verb *lanthanomai* or *lanthanei* that lies at the root of Lethe: to forget and not to notice, to overlook, and to allow to remain hidden lie very close together, and not to overlook, to overcome the human tendency not to notice, to uncover, to bring some special attention to bear against our desire to bury, becomes the sign of truth, of *aletheia* (Heidigger, *Being and Time* 56, 262). We must feel a great respect for Lovecraft's protagonists that they cannot "let it alone" against the immense recalcitrance of their own being. At the same time, however, it must be confessed that the *Nachträglichkeit* of a trauma operates as an obstacle to *aletheia,* for each of its shatterings, each of its reconstructions of the original event, covers that event once more. In the case of this story, for instance, what else is indicated than that Akeley is now headless, that his own truth has suffered a severance and removal?

In "The Shadow out of Time" Professor Peaslee most clearly reveals the pattern of recurrent oblivion and consciousness, for that pattern provides the rhythm of the novella. Given its length "The Shadow out of Time" is wonderfully successful in its click, which forces us to reconsider the involvement of the hand in its act of writing the story we have this instant concluded. And this return is performed in a great anxiety, not least because Peaslee has lived out his life in a great anxiety of his own identity.

The hallmarks of the terminal climax begin considerably before the last paragraph, however, given the length of the novella. When Peaslee's expedition arrives in Western Australia he finds architecture which seemed "to dovetail horribly with something I had dreamed or read, but which I could no longer remember," architecture that excites a "perplexing illusion of memory" (*CF* 3.416). The Outsider had suffered a similar *deja vu* as he approached the castle. The erasure of memory becomes a "mnemonic urge" that propels Peaslee to his exploration of the ruins, where his dreams well up into the world (422), an image of water repeated as the climax approaches (425), so much that the place of the quest becomes "the draught-giving abyss" (442). And as he comes closer he begins to look "nervously down at myself, vaguely disturbed by the human form I possessed" (431); the ecstasy begins. The flight itself, accompanied by nooses of wind that would draw him back into confrontation, experiences those nooses and shrieks as a merciful opiate that dulls him to the gulf that he has to pass (446). Indeed, we should see his experience as a geography of the underworld mind: the gulf contains a gulf that he must pass in order to arrive at the memory for which he searches.

Now that we are near the end of this essay, it cannot be amiss to return to Leiber's phrase, the terminal climax. Much of what we see characterizing Lovecraft's practice may indeed be compared to the *petit mort*. A long, almost exhausting foreplay leads to an orgasm both ecstatic and obliterating, a pharmakon to the spirit doubtless but also a remorse, though only in the sense that we feel compelled to ruminate fruitlessly, finding no end except in the navel of the dream into which Freud found that so much meaning disappeared (*The Interpretation of Dreams* 143, 564).

But we cannot end there either, for we did not quite tell the truth when we thought the Oedipal implications of the sphinx in "Under the Pyramids" unimportant. How could that be, given the figure of Helen so intensively doubled in "The Outsider"? I hesitated to consider "Medusa's Coil," in which the image of the sphinx recurs (*CF* 4.332), "The Curse of Yig," and "The Thing on the Doorstep" relevant to the terminal climax since they did not appear to satisfy our second characteristic, that the climax in a rather direct fashion deals with the transformation of the protagonist or narrator, often through their being one and the same. But the fear of miscegenation does not touch the narrator of "Medusa's Coil." In "The Curse of Yig" it is difficult to find any evidence in the text to identify the narrator with Audrey or with her child, unless we wish to postulate that identification from outside the story. In "The Thing on the Doorstep" Daniel Upton, a Daniel come to judgment, does not resemble his friend the weak-willed Edward Derby—but Daniel may be mad. On the other hand, all these stories have in common the figure of a woman who becomes identified with the monstrous. The misogynist traits are clear. We may feel that whenever Lovecraft began to identify a narrator and a female horror he found himself driven to use a number of framing, distancing devices. The great exception to this tendency is "The Shadow over Innsmouth," which does not have a terminal climax; but "The Outsider" is itself a significant exception.

The stories have two other elements in common, the image of the snake and a paralysis caused by a fascination. In "Medusa's Coil" the references to a lamia (*CF* 4.325, 345) indicate the debt to Keats's *Lamia,* though in Lovecraft's story Lamia has fallen in love with Apollonius—the artist who despises the woman and demon that he reveals—as the references to Tanit and Isis may indicate the kinship the story has to Flaubert's *Salammbô* with its famous scene in which the daughter of Hasdrubal undresses for a black snake; Egypt and Carthage, and the Africa and R'lyeh behind them (334), provide the backdrop to the story. A further indication of this backdrop lies in the reference to Berenice "who offered up her hair to save her husband-brother" (301); Berenice, celebrated in a poem by Callimachus and a translation by Catullus, who uses the word *frater*, was her husband's second cousin but easily confused with his sister, also named Berenice, securing the pattern of doubles that we observed in the story of Nitokris (Fordyce 328–32). But the allure of Marceline is neutralized by the insistence that the story of the father's lust for his son's wife is sheer gossip (*CF* 4.344–45) and that the narrator "can come to no harm" (297). The opiate the old man drinks (319) becomes the visionary goblet that Marceline holds in the painting; we do not know whether she drinks or offers this cup "full of abominations" (Rev. 17:4). In confronting this revelation the old man is "turned to stone at last" as the myth demands (*CF* 4..335), but something of this paralysis is also suggested in the narrator's having overstayed the night for six years (344).

"The Curse of Yig" is a later story, remarkable for its horror being so forthrightly rooted in a common phobia. But the action is triggered significantly by Audrey's killing, for the sake of her husband's peace of mind, "a mass of lazy wriggling which could be no other than a brood of new-born rattlesnakes" (*CF* 4.166), an act to which her husband reacts with "awe and anger" (167). The scene reveals the central crime of these stories, the attack upon fertility that is also present in Perseus' beheading Medusa. The Erinyes, "With Gorgon-faces and thick serpent-hair / Twisted in writhing coils," pursue Orestes for his murder of his mother Clytemnestra (Aeschylus, *Choephoroe* 1051–52). In the crisis both Walker and Audrey suffer a paralysis (*CF* 171–77) from the fascination of the snakes they fantasize surrounding them. When she kills him, she kills the man whose fears had compelled her to kill the snakes, and her own death is involved in her giving birth to snakes that are recompense for those she killed.

In comparison to these two works, done for Zealia Bishop, "The Shadow over Innsmouth" and "The Thing on the Doorstep" regain Lovecraft's complexity and lightly reveal the snake imagery we are discussing. I would hardly mention "The Shadow over Innsmouth" if its mythos were not connected with the latter story and if it did not show the same pattern as the "Facts Concerning the Late Arthur Jermyn" that like "Medusa's Coil" looks back to the heart of Africa; Asenath is Joseph's wife, named after an Egyptian goddess, the daughter of Potiphar the priest of Heliopolis—not the same Potiphar as the one whose wife attempted to seduce Joseph earlier in the story, though the repetition does reverberate with incests, jealousies, and aggressions (Gen. 41:45). The toad-fish of Innsmouth are related to the snakes we are examining, and their eyes are equally fascinating; in "The Thing on the Doorstep," "that female shell that wasn't even quite human" is accounted for by its Innsmouth origin (*CF* 3.339), with eyes that function prominently, Lovecraft says protuberantly, fastening the spineless Edward Derby in place and engorging him. Besides the eyes, this story reveals the central reason for the snake imagery, for Edward Derby continually sloughs himself off to be reborn into new being, injected into the series of metempsychoses that the entity that was Ephraim has entertained for eons. Already in *Gilgamesh* the snake symbolized immortality, for which it may be well worth the moral trespass to stand outside one's skin. And certainly the claim to self-creation strikes at the most intimate sense of our human dependence on our mothers.

To return, conclusively, to "The Outsider," I consider its reputation well-earned. It was a break-through story for Lovecraft, containing a knot in its terminal climax of many of the techniques, motifs, and themes that were to preoccupy the rest of his career. Undoubtedly the oneiric had to be projected through his meticulous love of a concrete New England to be truly effective; his development was real. But in "The Outsider" he was already Lovecraft.

Lovecraft and Keats Confront the "Awful Rainbow"

I

> Zur Burg führt die Brücke,
> leicht, doch fest eurem Fuß:
> beschreitet kühn
> ihren schrecklosen Pfad!
>
> [The bridge leads to the castle, light but firm to your foot: stride boldly its fearless path!] (Wagner 70)

In 1980 William Fulwiler noted the relevance of *The Eve of St. Agnes* to "The Outsider," given the motto Lovecraft had adapted from the last stanza of the poem—a relevance not, however, immediately obvious. But whatever the relevance of the motto, other aspects of the poem have a bearing upon the story also, and in turn the story illuminates certain aspects of Keats's poem. The line, "Of witch, and demon, and large coffin-worm" (374)[1] creates a twofold quest to identify the significance of these figures, the wise or wicked woman, the numen, and the worm or serpent, and to identify the Outsider of Lovecraft's story. But *The Eve of St. Agnes* and "The Outsider" are difficult texts, with very rich imagery and narrative but little self-reflective commentary to guide us. If we begin with *The Eve of St. Agnes* itself we will enter upon our quest out of place, either too late because this is the last stanza of the poem, or too early because this is the poem that inaugurated Keats's annus mirabilis. To clarify the quest it is useful to examine into what thickets Keats and Lovecraft pursued it before we return to the details of the works themselves. The quest shall, therefore, seem erratic. Many digressions lie ahead, investigations of the debates between Newton and Goethe over the nature of light and a proper scientific methodology, probings of the imageries of rainbow, snake, and worm, and extended observations of other poems, above all *Lamia,* and Lovecraft's ghost-written story "Medusa's Coil," a glance at Poe, before we can realize the depth of creation at work in "The Outsider." Several works are in dialogue here as we discuss the dynamic relations between Lovecraft and Keats.

These relations are not symmetrical, for Keats comments on Lovecraft only through Lovecraft's understanding of the English poet, whom he regarded with some reserve. The extravagant praise of "the Musaean Keats" (*CF* 4.24) in his early story "Poetry and the Gods" he qualifies in his letters, in one of which he advises a correspondent to pay more attention to the sciences than to such poets as Keats and Shelley (*RK* 141). He seems to approve of Keats only insofar as his images are

---

1. All citations to Keats's poems refer to lineation.

crystal-clear (*FFF* 34–35). By 1929 he says that he is of Keats's school, but his description of that school as the "aesthete-pagan tradition" is not whole-hearted praise (*ET* 26), for by that time he had disentangled himself from the pleasures of decadence. In a few months, however, he groups Keats with Milton and Chaucer (*ET* 37; cf. *SL* 3.78) and only a month later asserts, "For the soul & substance of poetry, there is no richer source than Keats" (*SL* 2.336), praise he was to repeat, adding Shelley in 1932 (*JVS* 114). His references to Shelley, however, are few and perfunctory in contrast to the rich ambivalence of those to Keats, who stands out among the second-generation Romantic poets. Of course in his most cosmic mode Lovecraft finds Keats indistinguishable from Jack the Ripper, but so are "Beethoven, Plato, & the mythical Christus," high company indeed (*SL* 3.311). In "Supernatural Horror in Literature" he refers to the "more restrained approaches to cosmic horror in *Lamia* and many of Keats's other poems" (*CE* 2.87). Perhaps most apt for our concerns in this chapter is Lovecraft's comment in 1929 on the Keats of "Ode on a Grecian Urn": "It was a glowing, misty-minded young poet, and not a sober man of analytical intellect, who muddled matters by fastening a false linkage of truth and beauty upon the popular consciousness! However—" he immediately adds, "this isn't to say that poets and artists are less important than men of science, for in hard fact we must admit that *truth* is nothing of any intrinsic importance" (*ET* 102).

An obvious attraction Keats held for Lovecraft was his classicism, a "true Hellenism" Lovecraft called it (*JFM* 251), in such poems as "On First Looking into Chapman's Homer," "The Elgin Marbles," *Endymion,* and above all *Lamia,* which we may suppose also attracted Lovecraft because of its heroic couplets; and *Lamia* is crucial to our study. But Keats also attracted Lovecraft insofar as Lovecraft was a writer of science fiction and horror, a writer interested in the themes of awe, expressed both as cognitive estrangement, the description of a physical universe different from the reader's, and as cognitive breakthrough, the realization that that universe is not a full description of reality (cf. Suvin 3–10 and Wolfe 13–16). But at the conclusion of only a few science fiction works do the authors question the content of the breakthrough, whereas Keats frequently questions the order of experience that the poem represents, just as Lovecraft forces the reader to question the conclusion of "The Outsider." Andrew Bennett perceives this questioning when he identifies the presence of the Freudian uncanny in Keats's work (5, 13). Keats is a poet of the moral pressure of knowledge, a poet for whom the possibility and status of truth becomes increasingly pressing. Explorative rather than definitive, his works move through a mist, whether upon Ben Nevis, in the Vale of Soul-making, or in the Chamber of Maiden-Thought.[2] The most remarkable reference Lovecraft makes to Keats is in 1930 while writing "The Whisperer in Dark-

---

2. It was natural for an author like Dan Simmons, who moves easily between the genres of horror and science fiction, to employ the figure of Keats in his trilogy of novels, *Hyperion, The Fall of Hyperion,* and *Endymion.*

ness," as he describes the tremendous impact of the recent discovery of Pluto:

> Its existence is no surprise, for observers have long known that one or more such worlds probably exist beyond Neptune; yet its actual finding carries hardly less glamour on that account. Keats (thinking no doubt of Herschel's discovery of Uranus in 1781, or perhaps of the finding of the earlier asteroids) caught the magic of planetary discovery in two lines of his *Chapman's Homer* sonnet, & that magic is surely as keen today as then. (*ET* 139)

In this kind of event Lovecraft aligns himself with the English poet.

Toward the end of 1930 he expressed his interest in anything Harlow Shapley had to say "about the size and structure of the universe, or what John Keats has to say about the intimations of hidden, tremulous strangeness and beauty therein" (*JFM* 237); Keats's achievement is not only comparable to that of astronomers, it works as an extension of their insights, though from the point of view of practical knowledge he believes that Keats is a prattler in comparison to Newton, Einstein, or such Roman models of integrity as Regulus, Cato, or Scipio (*SL* 3.314). We understand Lovecraft's ire; a year before writing *The Eve of St. Agnes* Keats had prattled against the name of Newton (Bate 270). But the sonnet on Chapman's Homer, by any measure, is a remarkable poem. The speech of the Greek poet and the creation of a landscape through that speech, wide as an archipelagoed ocean and high and deep as an archipelagoed sky, shatters the speech of the English poet, "like some watcher of the skies / When a new planet swims into his ken" (9–10), and silences him; and Lovecraft concurred in the Keatsian silence because he also believed that the universe exceeds words.

But cognitive breakthrough in the later Keats is bleak. As he writes in the epistle to Reynolds, "I have a mysterious tale / And cannot speak it" (86–87). He sees through the landscape of the earlier sonnet, the sparkling surface of the ocean and its several islands, into an abyss of destruction in which every creature, shark and robin, participate. Once again breakthrough causes a silence. The first *Hyperion* is filled with this proto-Darwinian vision, and Keats's struggle to recognize the consequences of a world in which individualities destroy one another is even more difficult in the second *Hyperion* and in *Lamia*.

So *The Eve of St. Agnes* is not the only poem that Keats wrote relevant to a discussion of Lovecraft. In addition, his sonnet about a dream of the second circle of the Inferno, written in the April of 1819, is akin to the romance that was written in the preceding January and to *Lamia* that was to be written during the summer. The three poems share several elements, not least the alexandrine, a line necessary to the Spenserian stanza of the romance; it is not common to a sonnet, however, though Keats used it earlier in "On Sitting Down to Read *King Lear* Once Again," and in *Lamia* it behaves as a distinct experiment, alluding to the ironic formulations of Dryden's narratives. Keats regarded *Lamia* as a revision of the sentimental tendencies that he felt deformed the earlier romances (*Letters* 2.174). Hermes appears in the beginning of the sonnet as he appears in the beginning of *Lamia*, in which both the god and the ambiguous protagonist undergo a descent, a kenosis, and a melting for the sake of love; Hermes, after all, is the psychopomp to the underworld. The Hermes of the sonnet, however, is the conqueror of Argus:

> As Hermes once took to his feathers light,
>   When lulled Argus, baffled, swoon'd and slept,
> So on a Delphic reed, my idle spright
>   So play'd, so charm'd, so conquer'd, so bereft
> The dragon-world of all its hundred eyes;
>   And seeing it asleep, so fled away. (1–6)

This imagery of the eyes will form an important complex in *The Eve of St. Agnes* and *Lamia*, as in Lovecraft's stories. A shadowy figure in Greek mythology, Argus is a hundred-eyed shepherd according to Aeschylus, born from the earth, chthonic, set to guard Io after the jealous Hera has transformed her into a cow; but even after Hermes slays him a gadfly—his eidolon—stings and pursues her (*Prometheus Bound* 566–68). His eyes were set in the tail of Hera's totemic beast, the peacock. Argus is an emblem of the reptilian, ever-observant, critical, compulsive, public world that the poet has internalized, for it is the critic in himself that he must put to sleep in order to experience this dream. Argus may have a peculiar avatar in Wilbur Whateley who shepherds his mother and drives cows for the nourishment of his brother; he keeps his reptilian skin and "rudimentary" eyes clothed until he dies in the library (*CF* 2.439). In *Lamia* eyes are associated with both Lamia and Apollonius, who with such an antecedent as Argus is as reptilian and phantasmic as she; in *The Eve of St. Agnes*, despite Porphyro's assurance that "There are no ears to hear, no eyes to see" (348), Madeline hurries "beset with fears, / For there were sleeping dragons all around, / At glaring watch" (352–54). The eye is consistently public and critical.

In the sonnet the lovers are swept through the "melancholy storm" (14) of "that second circle of sad hell, / Where in the gust, the whirlwind, and the flaw / of rain and hail-stones, lovers need not tell / Their sorrows" (9–12). That chill storm is a part of the landscape of *The Eve of St. Agnes;* it beats against the window as the moon of imagination sinks. Into that storm the lovers are "fled away" at the conclusion (371). The same "endless storm" appears in an earlier treatment Keats had made of the Argus story, in which we find the same "eclipsing eyes" and the same "ravishments" (*Endymion* 2.875–83). And both a growing chill and a sense of imminent starvation appear at the conclusion of *Lamia*. But if the sonnet and *Lamia* are as important for our understanding of "The Outsider" as is *The Eve of St. Agnes*, then *Lamia* is also important for our understanding of another of Lovecraft's stories, that in which the woman central to its horror is called "the accursed gorgon or lamia" (*CF* 4.345). "Medusa's Coil" is near akin to *Lamia*, as are other stories, "The Colour out of Space" and "The Thing on the Doorstep," which move in a similar orbit of imagery.

Before Lamia presents a problem in appearances to Lycius and Apollonius she presents a problem to the reader: "a gordian shape" (1.47), "full of silver moons" (1.51), and "rainbow-sided" (1.54), "She seemed, at once, some penanced lady elf, / Some demon's mistress, or the demon's self" (1.55–56); at one and the same time she appears as a remorseful self, as a woman, and as that in which gender may be various. Much of this language is reminiscent of the serpent in *Paradise Lost:* "Close the serpent sly / Insinuating, wove with Gordian twine / His braided train" (4.347–49). She possesses the ability to veil and unveil the beauty of the nymph whom Hermes pursues and seems to approve the moral neutrality that allows Hermes to capture the nymph. When she endures her transformation at the touch of the psychopomp's wand, her colors grow more intense until she appears to suffer a volcanic eruption that "Eclipsed her crescents, and licked up her stars" (1.160) until she is nothing but suffering. Appearances are erased not to a tabula rasa but to a negativity full of presence.

What kinds of options are open to understanding her? To Apollonius she is only a snake. His explication of her "knotty problem" (2.160) satisfies him because "'twas just as he foresaw" (2.162); it is the solution of Alexander the Great, who cut the knot of the farmer Gordius in order to conquer the world. Keats resembles the sage, as his confession to the difficulty of ridding himself of a prejudice in regards to women indicates: "For an obstinate Prejudice can seldom be produced but from a gordian complication of feelings, which must take time to unravell and care to keep unravelled" (1.342). To Lycius she is at first divine, but later an object of sadistic control. To a reader she might be a demon or daemon, a part of the numinous world as it invades and becomes a part of the world of appearances. "Eyed like a peacock" (1.50) she bears the emblems of Argus and Hera, stamped like the poet with signs of a jealous eye before Apollonius ever sees her. To the narrator, despite his already having told a story that must have left him deeply doubtful what she might be, she is a woman, insistently and only a woman with whom he is perhaps more in love than is Lycius.

But for the narrator she is clearly something else as the movement toward her disappearance and Lycius' death precipitates this famous passage:

> There was an awful rainbow once in heaven:
> We know her woof, her texture; she is given
> In the dull catalogue of common things.
> Philosophy will clip an Angel's wings,
> Conquer all mysteries by rule and line,
> Empty the haunted air, and gnomèd mine—
> Unweave a rainbow, as it erewhile made
> The tender-personed Lamia melt into a shade. (2.231–38)

Besides angel, mystery, and height and depth of the natural world, Lamia is a rainbow, the very specific spectrum that Sir Isaac Newton had measured, to whose mathematics Keats and Lamb drank confusion in 1817 (Bate 270). Three months earlier Keats had deplored his inability to dissect the hues of grass since he missed his triangular prism in its mathematical case (*Letters* 1.162); the animus is clear despite the comedy. In his study of light Newton had addressed himself to several questions of appearance, the nature of white light, of the rainbow, of the colors on the film of a bubble, of the colors that arise from pressing a finger against the eyeball, bright as "those in the Feather of a Peacock's Tail" (*Opticks* 347), the play of light in the eyes of a peacock's tail as well as the shifting colors in a spider's web or in a sheen of silk (252). Poets often listed the peacock and the rainbow as images of varied colors, as Spenser does in the house of the scopophilic Busyrane (*Faerie Queene* 3.11.47.7–8); Milton fuses them in a description of the peacock "coloured with the Florid hue / Of Rainbows and Starry Eyes" (*Paradise Lost* 7.445–46). In *Comus* the Attendant Spirit wears a robe "spun out of *Iris'* Woof" (l. 83). Ovid had regularly used the image of the robe for Iris, "varios induta colores" [clothed in various colors] (1.270); having robed herself in "velamina mille colorum" [veils of a thousand colors] (11.589), she descends to the cave of Somnus, which her "vestis fulgore reluxit" [garment shone and glittered on] (11.617). The image is sufficiently general that according to the *Kalevala* a goddess sits on the rainbow weaving (Grimm 2.611). Though not a language Newton employed—he actively restrained his tongue—the imagery of the woven web, whether applied to the rainbow, the spectrum, or the ether and air, swiftly became a stereotype in his praise: James Thomson invented the lovely phrase, "Twine of light" (*The Seasons* 1.211). Marjorie Nicholson cites a host of poets who use similar imagery (13–14, 26, 31–36, 66–68); damasks and dyes abound.

In a survey of this sort with Lovecraft in mind we must not ignore Pope, who in *An Essay on Criticism* wrote suspiciously, "*False Eloquence,* like the *Prismatic Glass,* / Its gawdy Colours spreads on *ev'ry place*" (311–12). Not much less pejorative is the possibility in *The Dunciad* that Billingsgate may strip the robes of Rhetoric (4.23–26) and that in the apocalypse of thought "*Fancy's* gilded clouds decay, / And all its varying Rain-bows die away" (4.631–32). Pope consistently uses the imagery of the rainbow and the analysis of Newton's spectrum to suggest that language and its object are hopelessly divided. But most influential in the work of later poets was this passage from Thomson's "To the Memory of Sir Isaac Newton" (Nicolson 12):

> Even Light itself, which every thing displays,
> Shone undiscovered, till his brighter mind
> Untwisted all the shining robe of day;
> And, from the whitening undistinguished blaze,
> Collecting every ray into his kind,
> To the charmed eye educed the gorgeous train
> Of parent colours. (96–102)

This is a kindly language. And of a kind with it is an odd description that conflates the generation of snakes and insects in the light of the prismatic sun:

> Waked by his warmer ray, the reptile young
> Come winged abroad, by the light air upborne,
> Lighter, and full of soul. From every chink
> And secret corner, where they slept away
> The wintry storms, or rising from their tombs
> To higher life, by myriads forth at once
> Swarming they pour, of all the varied hues
> Their beauty-beaming parent can disclose. (2.241–48)

Thomson's language treats the relation of white light and spectrum as one of parent and child, the flesh and blood of kind. By 1819, however, Keats like Blake has in mind not the hand-loom but the steam-loom, operated according to the mathematics and mechanics of the Industrial Revolution. From this perspective both rainbow and Lamia seem an emanation of the natural world that many Romantics believed was losing its integrity to the analysis of a quantitative science. At the touch of Newton phenomenon becomes epiphenomenon, the merest glance of skin. When Wordsworth, present that evening of Keats's toast, wrote, "My heart leaps up when I behold / A rainbow in the sky," he hoped that his response redeemed the rainbow. Goethe, no friend to Newton, plays with similar imagery in his *Märchen* as he tells the story of the snake that drinks the golden rain of the will-o'-the-wisps, becomes transparent and glowing and then, transformed to jasper, emerald, and chrysopras, the bridge that unites the two shores (6.225–32)—green and gold lie of course at the center of Newton's colors. Though Goethe is never explicit, it is inviting to understand the transformed snake as a rainbow—the connection of the snake with the will-o'-the-wisps and their gold pieces recalls the folk belief that golden coins are shaken from rainbows (Grimm 2.611)—or to understand both snake and rainbow as mysteries necessary to holding the world together. And surely Lovecraft would be moved by chivalry to protect the rainbow also, for *The Rainbow* was the name of Sonia Greene's amateur publication in the first issue of which appeared his article "Nietzscheism and Realism." When Lovecraft was writing "Medusa's Coil," James Joyce was imagining Bishop Berkeley as Irish Idealism and St. Patrick as Roman Catholic Realism, "through photoprismic velamina of hueful panepiphanal world" (*Finnegans Wake* 611.13), unweaving the clothes of the sun, god the father/son, that "like a heptagon crystal emprisoms trues and fauss for us" (127.3–4). Whether the rainbow and its sun belong to an analytic or a synthetic understanding remains problematic.

This problem manifests itself in several ways, one of which is a problem of language. Newton wrote:

> If at any time I speak of Light and Rays as coloured or endued with Colours, I would be understood to speak not philosophically and properly, but grossly, and accordingly to such Conceptions as vulgar People in seeing all these Experiments would be apt to frame. For the Rays to speak properly are not coloured. . . . Colours in the Object are nothing but a Disposition to reflect this or

that sort of Rays more copiously than the rest; in the Rays they are nothing but their Dispositions to propagate this or that Motion into the Sensorium, and in the Sensorium they are Sensations of those Motions under the Forms of Colours. (*Opticks* 124–25)

It is more proper to speak of the sines of incidence than of the color that so affects us, which is itself "nothing but" a sensation of motion. Or, as Addison was to put the matter in his essays "On the Pleasures of the Imagination," referring for a moment to Locke, "Light and colours, as apprehended by the imagination, are only ideas in the mind, and not qualities that have any existence in matter" (5.42; No. 413). The world outside the chamber of the mind, as far as Newton was concerned as he worked in his chamber at Cambridge upon his *experimentum crucis*, is a white blur of motion, nothing but the motion of corpuscular bodies in an elastic ether. Popularizing the Newtonian and Lockean world, Addison influenced several of the eighteenth-century poets—an abstract world animated by our sensuous imagination that, like an enchanted knight, wakes up when the spell is past, "disconsolate . . . on a barren heath, or in a solitary desert" (5.42; No. 413), like the knight-at-arms in Keats's "La Belle Dame sans Merci," written within the week of his sonnet on the second circle. But not only did Keats read Addison, Lovecraft did, comparing himself to Addison's persona of the spectator (*Letters to Rheinhart Kleiner* 55).

Lovecraft is not insensitive to Addison's analysis. Though references to Newton and Locke are perfunctory in Lovecraft's letters, Newton is clearly a hero. What more, Lovecraft implies, can anyone say? But the extent to which he adhered to an eighteenth-century epistemology may be measured by his one reference to Kant, "whose name might be quite readily commenced with a lower-case 'c', . . . whose revered mouthings and dialectics would evaporate if examined without the deafness and blindness of irrational veneration" (*ET* 365). Lovecraft never refers to Schelling, Fichte, or Hegel,[3] and he is not interested in Coleridge's esemplastic power; the only admirable successors to Kant are Schopenhauer and Nietzsche, though not for the sake of their analysis of knowledge. German transcendentalism is a closed book to him. Much more dear to his heart are Addison and Thomson, from both of whom, as did the authors of the eighteenth century, he probably imbibed the principles of Newton and Locke (Nicolson 12, 148). Thus Lovecraft writes in 1929:

> All reason unites to prove that we can apprehend the cosmos only through our five senses as guided by our intellect and intellectually tinged *imagination* (not *fancy*) and that there is nothing in any living being's head which he did not get through those channels, either directly, unifiedly, and consciously, or indirectly, subconsciously, and fragmentarily. The inner mind can rearrange, select, com-

---

3. Among his "pet aversions," according to a summary of one of his letters in the *Haldeman-Julius Weekly*, January 20, 1923, were "*Kant, Hegel* and other founders of Nineteenth Century metaphysical mystification" (Lovecraft, *Letters to Samuel Loveman and Vincent Starrett* 37).

bine, dissociate and recombine, re-proportion, re-stress, and so on, till the "subjective" idea loses all resemblance to its unconscious sources; but it cannot create anything wholly new because the human mind is a blank apart from what sensory intake gives it. (*SL* 2.273)

Lovecraft agrees with Keats: there was an awful rainbow *once* in heaven, but according to the authority of early eighteenth-century thought we are no longer permitted to believe in its numinous existence.

The consequence is a tremendous emptiness that gapes where the world had once been full of an unquestioned significance, an emptiness where matter and space threatened to flounder. To save matter Bishop Berkeley invoked God; to save space Newton invoked God and the ether, in both his General Scholium to the *Principia* and the final paragraphs of the *Opticks,* where he spoke of God's ability "to move the Bodies within his boundless uniform Sensorium" (403). As Addison put the matter, "Infinite space gives room to infinite knowledge, and is, as it were, an organ to omniscience" (6.250; No. 565)—God is an Argus, a public expedient to save the appearances, but Addison asserts this as a response to his anxiety "of being overlooked amidst the immensity of nature, and lost among that infinite variety of creatures, which in all probability swarm through all these immeasurable regions of matter" (6.248; No. 565). More unobtrusively than Berkeley or Newton, very aware how cold the world was becoming, Keats invoked plenitude through the remarkable density of the style that he constructed through 1818 and 1819 and that in writing *Lamia* he then simplified because of his anxiety about the Miltonic influence the style betrayed and, in the light of these remarks, because he felt that such a plenitude was intellectually and emotionally dishonest; but in both poems and letters he also invoked Newton's ether as a model for poetic creation, though by the time of *Lamia* that use may seem parodistic (Sperry 269–75, 276–77). More confidently Goethe invoked a plenitude of images as an insistence that the language of inside and outside, with its implication of distance and objectivity, is improper when applied to Nature and our relation to her (cf. the poem "Allerdings: Dem Physiker," 1.359). A part of his debate with Newton concerned the quality of the language we use for scientific enquiry, the degree to which Newton's purified language diverged from the language of experience; in contrast, Goethe advocated the use of imagery because it is open-ended (12.356) and because "eine Sprache eigentlich nur symbolisch, nur bildlich sei und die Gegenstände niemahls unmittelbar, sondern nur im Widerscheine ausdrücke" [language is only symbolic, only pictorial, and never expresses objects directly, only through reflection] (13.491) and the use of irony because it admits the insufficiency of any language in the investigation of Nature's wholeness (13 317). And both he and Keats relied on a kinaesthetic language that provided muscle for a dynamic world (13.337, 379). Lovecraft, intimate with the emptiness that had opened in the world, dealing with a world that is thoroughly decentered, writes of a universe muscled by sloppy, unpurposive monsters; and though the irony of his letters may seem heavy-handed, he does employ it delicately and pervasively in his fiction. But like Keats he is aware that irony will never by itself take the chill off the world.

If Goethe is correct that language, even scientific language, is symbolic, we need to investigate more closely Keats's and Lovecraft's imagery, especially the images of the snake and the rainbow. Certainly the association of rainbow and rain accounts for the climax of the biblical story of the flood, the emergence of a world-snake like Okeanos or the Midgard Serpent, and the explosion of life from the ground after a storm, as in Ovid's story of the birth of Python after the flood (1.416–40). Homer describes the decorations on Agamemnon's breastplate in terms of the rainbow, a passage Lovecraft would have read in Pope's translation:

> Three glittering dragons to the gorget rise,
> Whose imitated scales against the skies
> Reflected various light, and arching bow'd,
> Like colour'd rainbows o'er a showery cloud
> (Jove's wondrous bow, of three celestial dies,
> Placed as a sign to man amidst the skies). (11.33–38)

The conjunction of snakes and rainbows in the context of war is striking. Three scenes in the *Aeneid*, a text familiar to both Keats and Lovecraft, treat these images. Snakes undulate across the Trojan shore to destroy Laocoon, a priest of Neptune, and to rest beneath the shield of Athena. Iris as a rainbow descends at the order of Juno, "mille trahens varios adverso sole colores" [trailing a thousand colors against the sun] (4.701), to snip a lock of Dido's hair, at which "dilapsus calor atque in ventos vita recessit" [her warmth slipped away and her life dispersed in the winds] (4.705)—echoing one another both "calor" and "color" vanish. A line similar to that describing the rainbow describes the snake that inhabits the tumulus and altar of Anchises—"mille iacit varios adverso sole colores" [it cast a thousand various colors against the sun] (5.89); and later in the fifth book Iris descends again—"celerans per mille coloribus arcum / nulli visa cito decurrit tramite virgo" [racing her arch through a thousand colors / but seen by no one the virgin ran down the path] (5.609–10)—to drive the Trojan women into an attack on the ships; and though not cognates, be it noted that *trames*, path, and *trama*, the woof of a web, are very close sonically. In the *Aeneid* the rainbow signifies death and deceit, the messenger of the mother-goddess inimical to the founding of (Roman) civilization, as well as an underworld figure associated with Neptune and the Father who has descended to the underworld; but the rainbow is also full of a beauty not to be denied. Such imagery is foreign to Newton, of course, though at one point he compares the behavior of diffracted light to "a motion like that of an Eel" (*Opticks* 339). But the otherworld motif does operate in the imagery connected with Bifrost, the rainbow bridge between earth and heaven that will shatter at the onslaught of monsters and giants in the Norse apocalypse; guarded by Heimdall, a god of beginnings and conclusions, a primordial god and a god of boundaries (Dumézil 126–30), the fiery bridge combines qualities of transparency, lightness, and firmness.

These motifs of the rainbow, the web, and the snake are significant to several details in Lovecraft's stories. In *The Dream-Quest of Unknown Kadath* the "tall, slim figure" of Nyarlathotep greets John Carter in "prismatic robes" (*CF* 2.204). The metempsychoses of John Carter are associated with the Snake-Den (*CF* 3.278). In "The Colour out of Space" the thing in the meteorite challenges Newtonian presumption, for its "chromatic perversion" (*CF* 2.378) and "shining bands unlike any known colours of the normal spectrum" (372) defeat any attempt the scientists offer with their spectroscopes. As the climax of the story approaches, "the column of unknown colour . . . began to weave itself into fantastic suggestions of shape which each spectator later described differently" (394); the web stubbornly refuses to be unwoven. At this moment the horse Hero dies, to be buried the next day; Anchises and his tomb hover about this detail, for a hero and a snake in the service of the chthonic goddess and her fertile powers are quite possibly identical (Harrison 260–89). The Colour writhes and wriggles (*CF* 2.393). But most significant is the "iridescence" that describes the color (392) immediately before it shoots off in the direction of Cygnus, the Swan, the totemic bird of Aphrodite: "that riot of luminous amorphousness, that alien and undimensioned rainbow of cryptic poison from the well—seething, feeling, lapping, reaching, scintillating, straining, and malignly bubbling in its cosmic and unrecognisable chromaticism" (395–96). Twice called a messenger (373, 399), we should as well understand the Colour as Iris as we have earlier understood it as Hermes; this messenger means death to Mrs. Gardner as Iris had to the suicidal Dido. But besides Virgil's Dido, Lovecraft might have in mind Ovid's Hersilia, Romulus's wife whom Iris conducts to see her husband apotheosized, "Ibi sidus ab aethere lapsum / decidit in terras, a cuius lumine flagrans / Hersilie crinis cum sidere cessit in auras" [Where the star had slipped from the sky / and fallen to earth, catching fire from it / Hersilia's hair departed with the star into the air] (14.846–48). Romulus transfigures her into Hora, a goddess of seasons and fruition. The conjunction of star, rainbow, and hair is important for "Medusa's Coil" and "The Colour out of Space," in which the Colour, "dowered with outside properties and obedient to outside laws" (374), bestows an overwhelming fruition upon the farm.

Another moment in Lovecraft's fiction resembles this pattern of rainbow and snake, the moment when the shoggoth bursts from the Antarctic tunnel, resembling a subway train. "Constellated with strangely coloured lights" like Lamia, it is a "column of foetid black iridescence, . . . a shapeless congeries of protoplasmic bubbles, faintly self-luminous, and with myriads of temporary eyes forming and unforming as pustules of greenish light, . . . slithering over the glistening floor" (*CF* 3.150). One of the problems Newton addresses in the *Opticks* is that of the shifting colors of a bubble. The extent, however, to which the shoggoth is what it seems or sounds like is questionable, for shoggoths have *"no voice save the imitated accents of their bygone masters"* (150). It differs in this respect from the Colour and Lamia, for it is made, artificial; we cannot quite escape the possibility that nature itself is not an original but a mimicry of something else, let us say of the outside, like the Outsider.

The movement from *Lamia* to "Medusa's Coil" registers a radical change of perspective. In *Lamia,* despite the narrator's distance he still exhibits a certain amount of advocacy for Lamia, perhaps excessive or ironic but palpable, whereas in "Medusa's Coil" it is as though the place of the narrator had been usurped by Apollonius, informing both his view of de Russy *père* and of Marsh and bestowing not a shred of sympathy on Marceline. In "The Thing on the Doorstep," also, Daniel Upton assumes the role of Apollonius in judgment over Asenath even before the death of Derby's father; and the futile scientists in "The Colour out of Space" assume the same role.

Apollonius is, then, more conspicuous for Lovecraft than for Keats. He unravels the web of appearances in the natural world and resembles, ironically since he is not at all poetical, the Apollo who usurped the navel of the world after slaying Python, one of the prodigies the earth had born in profusion after the flood (Ovid 1.434–51): "The sophist's eye, / Like a sharp spear, went through her utterly, / Keen, cruel, perceant, stinging" (2.299–301). Lycius is not behindhand in this respect in the sadomasochistic scene that opens the second part of the poem, for the young man seemed in a position "like / Apollo's presence when in act to strike / The serpent" (2.78–80).[4] Apollonius commits the crime of Stesichorus, blinded for his attack on Helen of Troy, another figure of a compound nature; but Apollonius, despite the threat of Lycius, the gods do not blind—he has no qualms and does not recant. Unlike Argus, he stands there, and his "lashless eyelids" (2.288), "without a twinkle" (2.246), never stir; Apollonius never winks. There he stands, and at the letter of his word the pretensions of tradition fly. Immediately before the climax the narrator offers him a wreath of "spear-grass and the spiteful thistle" (2.228), a line reminiscent of Keats's doggerel of the previous year, "There is newton marsh / With its spear grass harsh" (*Letters* 1.250).

With the increased importance of de Russy/Marsh/Apollonius, Marceline/Lamia is thrust into the background of the story. The narrator knows of her only through de Russy's account, through the picture, and as he flees through the sight of a bald, naked figure in the distance and near him a rustling in the weeds and briers, the "cockleburrs and stickers" (*CF* 4.292), *"as if some large, swift serpent were wriggling purposefully along the ground in pursuit of me"* (343). The last detail is an instance of a frequent motif in our study, the doubling of characters, in this case accompanied by the splitting of Marceline into her hair personified as a powerful snake in the brush and into an ugly, scalped body of pain. Before de Russy meets her he hears of her cult in the vaguest of terms. It concerns "prehistoric Egyptian and Carthaginian

---

4. Though no one would imagine that Keats was aware of the fact, Newton did owe some of his mathematical apparatus in the *Principia* to another Apollonius, Apollonius of Perga, to whose analysis of conics he refers (71–78). Professor Peaslee in "The Shadow out of Time," when his consciousness is transferred into the "rugose, iridescent bulk of a vast cone" (*CF* 3.396), may owe his fate to that Apollonius; in "Through the Gates of the Silver Key" Lovecraft refers to conics in an elaborate simile (*CF* 3.304).

magic" (301), pretending to have its source in "the great Zimbabwe, the dead Atlantean cities in the Hoggar region of the Sahara" and possibly containing the "veiled facts behind the legend of Medusa's snaky locks" and the story of Berenice (301). Keeping in mind our earlier discussion of patterns of doubling and incest in the story of Berenice, let us turn to the story of Medusa. According to Hesiod she is one of the three Gorgons, monsters with snaky hair who live at the edge of the world; when Perseus cut off her head Pegasus sprang from her blood—the flying horse associated with the power of poetry (*Theogony* 270–86)—as did the golden swordsman Chrysaor. Her connection with poetry is re-iterated in Pindar's Pythian XII, in which the winner of the flute contest becomes the occasion of telling her story and the dirge that her sisters sang for her. According to other stories, her head becomes the aegis with which Athena terrifies armies in battle; and because her head has the power to turn people into stone, when the rebel angels of Dis invoke her at the opening of the sixth circle of the *Inferno*, the episode suggests that she slays spiritual as well as biological life (9.52–57). In order to protect himself Perseus made a mirror of his shield that would hold her face at a distance. According to Ovid, Minerva changed her into the creature with snaky hair after she had been raped by Neptune inside the temple of the goddess of wisdom—for Medusa had once been a great beauty, "clarissima forma" (4.794); but Minerva is also affronted, according to the version Roberto Calasso tells, because "Medusa looked very much like herself. So she raised the aegis to . . . detach herself from them" (228). Medusa, then, has connections with both wisdom and poetry; besides the power to fascinate and paralyze she exercises the power to terrify and panic. Beautiful and grotesque, her story ranges between the violence of rape and the distance and scopophilic pleasure of the mirror.

The hair has other significance, however. Besides being a sign of transcendence as in the stories of Hersilia and Berenice, it implies Marceline's self-sufficient auto-eroticism and narcissism. "She brushed it incessantly, and seemed to use some sort of preparation on it. I got the feeling once—a curious, whimsical notion—that it was a living thing which she had to feed in some strange way" (*CF* 4.304), says de Russy, and adds, "I never knew of anyone so wrapped up in cosmetics, beauty exercises, hair-oils, unguents" (310). Lovecraft thoroughly exploits the sexuality of hair in the story, familiar as he is with *The Rape of the Lock* in which Belinda says to the Baron who has snipped her tress, "Oh hadst thou, Cruel! been content to sieze / Hairs less in sight, or any Hairs but these!" (4.175–76).

Marceline's background is uncertain: though her name is Bedard, she claims to be a bastard daughter of a marquis and may come from Martinique, perhaps significant because of its exotic attraction for Gauguin whose art Lovecraft distrusted (*JVS* 68) but who is an inspiration for Marsh (*CF* 4.302). It is her first name that is striking, however, a French form of the Latin diminutive Marcellus, the mark or the march, line or border, for her nature does inhabit the borderline; and the name is not widely dissimilar from the marsh that lies near Riverside. Finally, with only the slightest change of letters it is possible to eat your Madeline and have it too; by the time Lovecraft wrote "Medusa's Coil" he had read *Swann's Way* with approval and may have sensed the ambiguous sexuality that was to develop around the figure of the narrator Marcel.

The imagery of the border says another important thing about Marceline, as about Lamia, Asenath, Madeline, even the Outsider: they are beautiful. The border is the area of beauty and terror, which Rilke describes in the moment of heightened consciousness within which the *Duino Elegies* originated, "Denn das Schöne ist nichts / als des Schrecklichen Anfang" [for beauty is nothing / but the onset of terror] (1.4–5). Froh's invitation to cross the rainbow and his assurance that it is "schrecklos," without terror, is enmeshed in dramatic irony when the Rheinmaidens sing, "Falsch und feig / ist, was da droben sich freut" [false and cowardly / is what rejoices above] (Wagner 72). In the border intersect risk, allure, and illusion. Beginning his study with Shelley's fragment on the head of Medusa, Mario Praz demonstrates how the conjunction of beauty and terror was thematized in nineteenth-century literature (25–27), often in authors whom Lovecraft read avidly. In her eyes we behold the exclusivity and aggression of the aesthetic object as it attempts to be taken for the single, physical manifestation of beauty in an observer's consciousness (Adorno, *Minima Moralia* 75). Beauty demands to be framed, not only in its own integrity but as an object that has severed itself from its origins and thus as an object that denies the world. But beauty is also to be understood as something that has a flaw, a hook for the eye. The rainbow, of course, is as fleeting as it is beautiful, in part because, as Goethe argued, an uncountable number of surrounding conditions are necessary for an *Urphenomenon* to spring forth, astonish, accuse, and discomfort (12.367–68). In the "Ode on Melancholy" Keats wrote of "the rainbow of the salt sand-wave" (16) as an emblem of the evanescence of beauty. Beauty is fleeting, as all poets have written; but they are not only asserting the commonplace that we age, that youth passes, and that time "delves the parallels in beauty's brow" (Shakespeare, *Sonnets* 60.10). The evanescence of beauty is a metaphor of the momentary, instantaneous nature of the aesthetic state as it arises from the several particulars of the artwork, which may last for a flash or a wink of an eye; this was a theme Lovecraft found at the center of Proust's magnum opus. The evanescence and particularity of aesthetic contemplation, the pastels and shadows and half-lights, was one of the prizes for which Goethe contended with Newton, concerned as the German was for the colors proper to the painter, "dem zuliebe eigentlich wir uns in dieses Feld gewagt" [for whose benefit actually we dared enter this field] (13.527). Newton's vocabulary is limited and dismissive; he calls white a "middling" color (*Opticks* 159) and admits that his eyes were "not very critical in distinguishing colors" ("Hypothesis" 98). He does not behold beauty in the play of color; he began his study of optics, in any case, in order to eliminate the distortions of color from his telescopic lens (Sepper 61).

All these details of Marceline's beauty are colored by de Russy's experience of her. Though mythological details are not forgotten—"Her complexion called up thoughts of Babylon, Atlantis, Lemuria" (*CF* 4.304), the stock-in-trade of *Weird Tales*—it is her eyes that are filled with significance, "the eyes of some unholy forest creature or animal-goddess" (304), and her hair that "coiled up ... made her look like some Oriental princess in a drawing of Aubrey Beardsley's" (304), Salome perhaps or the incestuous Cleopatra with her "pretty worm" (Shakespeare, *Antony and Cleopatra* 5.2.242). With its "dense, exotic, overnourished growth of oily inkiness," the hair resembles "a great black python" (*CF* 4.304), the phrase varied by the narrator when he sees the painting and says, "It was nothing human, this ropy, sinuous, half-oily, half-crinkly flood of serpent darkness" (339). These are the stereotyped details that prepare for the miscegenetic revelation of the last paragraph: "coil," "oil," "inky," "crinkly" form a chain of semi-contradictory evidence for her African blood, as the narrator claims in the last paragraph. She might as well have had her locks marcelled.[5] Lavinia Whateley, albino that she is, also has crinkly hair (*CF* 2.424).

But Marceline's hair, and possibly she, may be more than human, as we must expect of something on the border. Looking at the picture, the narrator "did not wonder at the myth of the gorgon's glance which turned all beholders to stone"; when the pupils dilate, "the eyes themselves seemed to bulge outward" (*CF* 4.340). Since the narrator sees those eyes, we should consider to what extent they hold him despite his escape. In Lovecraft's fiction exophthalmic eyes are often the hook of beauty; besides Marceline, Asenath and Lavinia look at the world through staring, prominent eyes in which the protagonists find mirrors that reflect them. The protagonist of "The Shadow over Innsmouth" discovers that his ancestors have such eyes, as does he, "the true Marsh eye" (*CF* 3.225). Does Frank Marsh have such an eye? The "brazen glare" of Medusa (cited in Praz 25) became a cliché of the fatal woman in such works as Eugene Sue's *Mystères de Paris,* in which a woman resembles "le serpent qui ... fascine" [the serpent who ... fascinates] with a "régard magnétique" [magnetic stare] (ctd. in Praz 197–98). Lovecraft treats these eyes as a clinician; often a sign of the Innsmouth look, they represent the cold-blooded or the amphibious, the totally other than human or the hybrid, that which inhabits the border.

But de Russy cannot remain as uninfected by Marceline as he would have the narrator believe. His spinal neuritis suggests an atrophy of the Kundalini powers. He resembles Blake's Urizen, the embodiment of analytic reason, whose backbone in the fallen, created world appears "Hurtling upon the world / Like a serpent" (*The Book of Los* Pl. 5.15–16). She has, he confesses, captured "something in [his] shaken will and turned [it] to stone at last" (*CF* 4.335). But she is not only a force that destroys the will; she is also "the key" which "had unlocked [Marsh's] inmost stronghold of genius" (333). She functions as a Pegasus, uplifting the imagination into a time and space that have nothing to do with the experienced world. It is, for instance, not a category of the space she unlocks "whether it's an

---

5. This is the one story in which Lovecraft's racism forms the explicit basis for the horror, in part I believe because the setting of the story is in the South.

exterior or an interior" (334). De Russy asserts, contradicting the rumors of the cult suggested earlier, that the space she inhabits "was *behind* Egypt. . . . It was the ultimate fountain-head of all horror on this earth, and the symbolism shewed only too clearly how integral a part of it Marceline was" (335). From this aspect of feeling that the space is beyond categories, the guess that it might be R'lyeh makes sense, "for life and death are all one to those in the clutch of what came out of R'lyeh" (336).

And as the narrator learns on the next morning of his stay, the time of this house is not his time either. The discrepancy between the time that he has experienced and the time that has passed in the world outside recalls the motif of Rip van Winkle, Thomas Rhymer, or the knight in Keats's "La Belle Dame sans Merci": the experiential time of faery is not the chronological time of the mundane world. But also we should remember that behind Egypt is Africa; the passage may be a hint at the secret revealed in the last line of the story.

The oddity of Marceline's space and time is the context for her ability to send herself forth into the chronological world that is measured by means of Newton's absolute space. To the narrator she seems to reach out, and de Russy claims that she talks from the painting and that her body and her hair will now rise from their separate graves to pursue the father and his guest. In the climax of the story she appears to have engulfed the father. It is fitting to recall the power of Asenath, or rather of Ephraim, with her "overprotuberant eyes" (*CF* 3.329), to send herself forth and ultimately engulf Edward. This power was one that Lamia possessed in an apparently more benign form. She has had a dream of Hermes in Olympus longing for the nymph upon whom he has, lightly, set his heart (1.68–80). The narrator informs us "how she could muse / And dream, when in the serpent prison-house, / Of all she list, strange or magnificent: / How, ever, where she will'd, her spirit went" (1.202–5), whether under the sea, to a feast of Bacchus, or into the underworld; she can even, and thus she discovered and fell in love with Lycius, send her spirit into the world of everyday life. She is, in other words, rather like the poet who participates in every level of ontology.

Lamia and Marceline may have another power in common, a peculiar power over the unity of pleasure and pain:

> Not one hour old, yet of sciential brain
> To unperplex bliss from its neighbour pain;
> Define their pettish limits, and estrange
> Their points of contact, and swift counterchange;
> Intrigue with the specious chaos, and dispart
> Its most ambiguous atoms with sure art.   (1.190–96)

The operation that Newton performs on the rainbow and Apollonius performs on Lamia, she performs on the insoluble enigma of human desire at the same time as she falls in love, that is as she suffers from desire for desire, just as Marceline, who touches upon the utterly unhuman, falls in love with Marsh who because he also touches upon the irrational nature of the mind, the point at which it is unhuman, is able to perform upon her the operation of Newton and Apollonius. Like Marsh, Lamia and Marceline are not innocent of misapprehending and misappropriating desire.

One other detail of the painting furthers our understanding of Marceline and her space: "She was nude except for that hideous web of hair spun around her," with "a monstrously shaped goblet in one hand, from which was spilling fluid whose colour I haven't been able to place or classify" (*CF* 4.334). A part of this description looks to the whore of Babylon, who dressed in scarlet tipples the blood in a great cup in her hand and sits on a scarlet beast with seven heads and ten horns, the two of them next to great waters (Rev. 17:2–19:2); her figure reverberates in such characters as Duessa in *The Faerie Queene* and Sin in *Paradise Lost*. But behind this figure looms Nature, either the natura naturata of the world as it is or the natura naturans of the world as it becomes. Since the space she inhabits is neither exterior nor interior it is impossible to decide which vision of nature this is; de Russy and the genre of the story would persuade us that this horror is the natura naturata, the finished and dead world, but the impossibility to bring a category to bear suggests that Marceline resides, as the story expresses the matter, "behind" the categories. The web belongs to the immanence of an impenetrable Maya that Lovecraft's Apollonius cannot unravel, similar to the veil worn by the Priest of Leng, Lovecraft's version of the Isis of Sais whose veil it is death to remove. Denis dies of his success at separating Marceline from her hair—but she cannot die, and she and her hair remain in touch; Marsh cannot come out of the marsh of his name, the marsh that allowed him to approach, recognize, address, and interpret Marceline—our realization that he can interpret her because he is a horrified extension of her; and de Russy is captured running for the river, the complex world of flux out of which the serpentine and all else of the world of appearance, himself included, had emerged. The flight reveals the omnipresence of the web.

The narrator flees a storm and the conflagration of the de Russy mansion into the November cold (*CF* 4.291, 342), a cold night reminiscent of the weather in *The Eve of St. Agnes*. Lovecraft probably found these conclusions fitting, for to him "only that which is *cold* is supremely associated with evil, horror, and death" (*EHP* 256). So far does the narrator flee that the de Russys are left five or six years in the past, as though their living plantation had never been, just as in *Lamia* the palace of the lovers seems to have been inserted into the reality of Corinth. It may be possible that Keats's Corinth gains sinister reverberations for Lovecraft through being the scene of Goethe's ballad "The Bride of Corinth" in which a young man and a dead bride lie down together (*CE* 2.86).

At the conclusion of *Lamia* a contagion of stone occurs: Lamia turns to stone under the eyes of the philosopher, as though Apollonius were a Gorgon; and "not a man but felt the terror in his hair" (2.268), as though each were a Gorgon also. Lycius wrapped in his shroud resembles a dead snake, without hope of a resurrection. The attempt to slay the snake turns everyone into a snake in a dead, stony world; grappling with the epistemological contradictions of the phenomenal world reacts upon the imagination of the investigator to slay it, as though Perseus had mistaken the head for its image. In "Medusa's Coil" the attempt to slay the exotic intrusion results in the death of the two young friends, then in the complicitous silence of the father, and finally in his embarrassed confession of failure.

The witch and demon and worm have not passed away. But to identify them further we will have to return to our original quest, *The Eve of St. Agnes* and "The Outsider."

II

The lowly worm climbs up a winding stair. (Roethke 108)

So we return to our initial problem, the thematic relations between "The Outsider" and *The Eve of St. Agnes*, beginning where Lovecraft begins at the motto to his story that he takes from the last stanza to Keats's poem:

> That night the Baron dreamt of many a woe,
> And all his warrior-guests, with shade and form
> Of witch, and demon, and large coffin-worm,
> Were long benightmared. (372–75)

"The Outsider" begins where *The Eve of St. Agnes* ends, with a "grotesquerie" (Gradman 79) in sharp contrast to the previous romantic narrative, a contrast Keats had wished to make even sharper (*Letters* 2.162–63). In the context of "The Outsider" the lines might evoke passages in Poe, whether of "The Masque of the Red Death," "The Conqueror Worm," or "The Haunted Palace" with its epithet, "Porphyrogene" (22). And we cannot ignore "The Masque of the Red Death" (de Camp 151; Buchanan 12) because it may have a peculiar relation to Newton's rainbow, our obsession in this study, as described by James Thomson in a passage that follows the one we have cited earlier in his poem, "To the Memory of Sir Isaac Newton":

> First the flaming red
> Sprung vivid forth; the tawny orange next;
> And next delicious yellow; by whose side
> Fell the kind beams of all-refreshing green.
> Then the pure blue, that swells autumnal skies,
> Ethereal played; and then, of sadder hue,
> Emerged the deepened indigo, as when
> The heavy-skirted evening droops with frost;
> While the last gleamings of refracted light
> Died in the fainting violet away. (102–11)

Thomson temporalizes Newton's seven colors—red, orange, yellow, green, blue, indigo, violet—as the year-round and the day-round; and so does Poe in his story, but disordered and distempered as blue, purple, green, orange, white, violet, and scarlet-black, his suite of "irregularly disposed" apartments stretching from the east to the west (2.671). Newton's experiments into the multiple refractions of thin plates and bubbles produced similar distortions of the spectrum: red, orange, yellow, white, blue, beginning of black, black, very black (*Opticks* 233). The implication of the motto and its companion texts is that the Outsider searches for what he has been or what he has lost. Is he the Baron, as Fulwiler suggested (4), or Porphyro, or Madeline herself? Is he, conflated, Prospero or the Red Death? The revelers in Prospero's castle react to the Red Death as those other revelers do to the Outsider, with terror, horror, and disgust (2.674); and when the figure of the Red Death is revealed to be empty, the revel is even more disconcerted than it had been when the clock rang within the shadows where the Red Death stood (2.676–77). If the Outsider is the Baron, is he "the barren, the broken" (*CF* 1.265) as he claims, is he worm or snake with "vermin fangs" ("The Conqueror Worm" 31), death-devourer or phallic hero, or is he "the monarch Thought" ("The Haunted Palace" 5)? The motto and first paragraph of Lovecraft's story provide a wealth of possible identifications.

    Or is the Outsider another Madeline, the Madeline to whom "The Haunted Palace" should alert us, for Poe inserted the lyric into "The Fall of the House of Usher"? Poe's Madeline is morbidly withdrawn; she appears and disappears without noticing the narrator (2.404), just as Keats's Madeline dances "all amort" (70), blind to the appeal of the young men (59–61). The agonies of Usher's sister to escape her tomb are distorted by their projection in the imaginative world of Ethelred the conqueror and the death-scream of the dragon he slays (2.414–16). The possible conflation of these two Madelines in Lovecraft's enigmatic worm alerts us, in addition, to the way that the climax of "The Fall of the House of Usher" may shape the climax of "Medusa's Coil." Indeed, given the background of Keats's reading in Lemprière, who connects lamiae with lemures and larvae that issue from graves at night wearing masks that "terrify all who see them" (De Almeida 188), we may wonder whether we find an antecedent of the Outsider in the figure of Madeline Usher as a lamia. We are forced to realize how much the falls of Riverside and Usher, the incestuous pursuits of the brother/father, and the ambiguous presences of the guest, both the narrator of Poe's story and the narrator of Lovecraft's and the guest Marsh, resemble one another. The resurrection and revenge that Marceline and Madeline suffer for their premature burial is the proper revenge of a nature oversubtly idolized and objectified; and from this perspective the resurrection of the Outsider becomes the interior meditation of a nature that consents to its burial but that cannot, alas, remain inert. The narrator of "The Fall of the House of Usher" remarks that though he did "acknowledge how familiar was all this," he nevertheless "still wondered to find how unfamiliar were the fancies which ordinary images were stirring up" (2.400–401), in a similar manner as the Outsider realizes how familiar the castle seems. And how familiar and unfamiliar the Outsider grows for us! Both stories imply "the hideous dropping off of the veil" (2.397). Even the narrator of Poe's story, then, offers a world for Lovecraft's figure. Here is the casement, the storm (2.412) into which the narrator flees at the end of the story. It is as though Poe's stories and poems, with their genealogy in Keats's poems, converge upon Lovecraft's stories to distort the genealogy that Lovecraft's stories also possess in the poems.

But the story in Poe's work perhaps most significant for our study is "Berenice," the opening paragraphs of which de Camp believes almost paraphrase the opening of "The Outsider" (150). Berenice is, of course, a significant name in the background of "Medusa's Coil"; but as significant as the name and the rhythms of those paragraphs is the simile with which the story opens:

> Misery is manifold. The wretchedness of earth is multiform. Overreaching the wide horizon as the rainbow, its hues are as various as the hues of that arch— as distinct too, yet as intimately blended. Overreaching the wide horizon as the rainbow! How is it that from beauty I have derived a type of unloveliness?— from the covenant of peace, a simile of sorrow? . . . Either the memory of past bliss is the anguish of today, or the agonies that are have their origin in the ecstasies that *might have been*. (2.209)

The rainbow at the portal of "Berenice" signifies the variety of our ill-at-ease place in the world, the transience of beauty, and the hypothetical nature of our perception that is able to understand ecstasy only through the subjunctive mode. The narrator applies to Berenice the same attention as Newton applied to the rainbow or Apollonius to Lamia: "I had seen her . . . not as a thing to admire, but to analyze; not as an object of love, but as the theme of the most abstruse although desultory speculation" (2.214). Especially is he obsessed by "the white and ghastly *spectrum* of [her] teeth" (2.215)—though the compatibility of whiteness with the spectrum is the very question we have seen in debate; the oxymoron sharpens the paradox of the rainbow. The imagery is as bizarre as the grotesque, self-conscious language that describes Lamia: "Her head was serpent, but ah, bitter-sweet! / She had a woman's mouth with all its pearls complete" (1.59–60). But the narrator of "Berenice" longs for this rainbow of teeth "with a frenzied desire" (2.215), and that desire destroys them in the horrendous manner revealed by the last sentence of the story, a sentence as sober in its way as the conclusion of "The Outsider": "There rolled out some instruments of dental surgery, intermingled with thirty-two small, white, and ivory-looking substances that were scattered to and fro about the floor" (2.219). Is the Outsider this dental ghoul, whose desire transforms the rainbow into thirty-two particles of whiteness? Does the story parody Newton's corpuscular theory of light? Possibly the fate of Berenice recalls Madeline's in the small detail of the "trance very nearly resembling positive dissolution" (2.211), but even more clear is her resemblance to the Madeline of "The Fall of the House of Usher": catatonic cousin and sister return to obsess the neurasthenic protagonist.

But if, despite these possibilities, we allow the Baron priority in our quest to identify the Outsider, it is as though at the end of the poem the Baron had become the sort of creature that the Outsider appears to have been revealed as at the end of his story, though it could as well be put that at the beginning of the poem the Baron and his guests form the sort of society that the Outsider wishes to join, the "gay crowds" he imagines (*CF* 1.267) to which later he is drawn, behind a window "gorgeously ablaze with light and sending forth sound of the gayest revelry" (270). The phrase may have been suggested by the line, "At length burst in the argent revelry" (37); but in Keats's poem the bright crowd is muted by a simile that suggests their insubstantiality: "Numerous as shadows haunting faerily / The brain, new-stuffed, in youth, with triumphs gay / Of old romance" (39–41). In such a way is the Outsider's brain unsubstantially stuffed with images from the books in the dark castle.

But the crowd in the poem is despicable. "These let us wish away," says the narrator (41), turning our attention to Madeline isolated in the middle "Of whisperers in anger, or in sport; / 'Mid looks of love, defiance, hate, and scorn" (68–69). It is a society of which Porphyro must beware:

> For him, those chambers held barbarian hordes,
> Hyena foemen, and hot-blooded lords,
> Whose very dogs would execrations howl
> Against his lineage: not one breast affords
> Him any mercy, in that mansion foul. (85–89)

This society is much worse than the Capulets and Montagues who influenced this part of the poem; for Romeo's and Juliet's families are not "hyena foemen," merely human parents who suffer an emotional inertia. Madeline's relatives are hellish and deformed. At the end of the poem, "bloated" with drink (346), they seem "sleeping dragons, . . . / At glaring watch" (353–54). In the underworld, they guard the underworld—but not very well. The dog lets the lovers escape. An ambivalence exists in this Argus. Do Madeline and Porphyro desire each other so intensely because of the hatred that divides them? According to Roberto Calasso the gadfly, Oistrus (whence "estrus"), figures as the inciter of murderous hatred, religious frenzy, and sexual desire (328–32). Argus incites the desire he prohibits.

The revelers of Keats's poem, however, are already dead. When they enter the revels they are part of an underworld, "a fairy rout," and the poem reveals the moral death that they have suffered in their hatred, scorn, and exclusion of the outsider of the poem, Porphyro. This is not quite to say that we should identify Lovecraft's Outsider with Porphyro exclusively, especially since the Outsider has difficulty identifying the relation of the self with the appearance in the glass within the archway. When we read *The Eve of St. Agnes* with "The Outsider" and its various mirrorings in mind, we may be struck by the doublings that exist in the poem: the pair of the young Porphyro and Madeline are reflected in the old Beadsman and Angela. It is these doublings that offer a more satisfying self-image than the people of the revel, especially since the people of the revel, Hildebrand and Maurice, are so exclusively, unpairedly male.

On the margins of this society are the Beadsman and Angela, with whom the poem opens and closes. A part of the cold world out of which he materializes in the first stanza, the Beadsman is preoccupied with professional repentance; full of remorse for the past he is paid to keep in mind, he prays in a chapel next to the tombs and among ashes in isolation for the soul of his employer, presumptively the Baron, for the people who have died, and for his own soul (26–27). "The sculptured dead" (14) of the chapel move him, "Emprisoned in black, purgatorial rails" as they seem (15), oxymoronically "praying in dumb orat'ries" (16). But he is a "weak spirit" (17). Angela is "A poor, weak, palsy-stricken, churchyard thing" (55) with "agues in her brain" (189). They are appropriate progenitors of the Outsider, progenitors and nourishers whom he lacks, unless they are models of the only kind of nourisher that the Outsider can imagine: "I think that whoever nursed me must have been shockingly aged, since my first conception of a living person was that of something mockingly like myself, yet distorted, shrivelled, and decaying like the castle" (*CF* 1.266). Angela appears in this light to Porphyro as she laughs over Madeline's simplicity:

> Feebly she laugheth in the languid moon,
> While Porphyro upon her face doth look,
> Like puzzled urchin on an aged crone
> Who keepeth clos'd a wondrous riddle-book,
> As spectacled she sits in chimney nook.   (127–31)

For the Outsider such a figure represents, not within his conscious memory but certainly within his imagination, the inverted castle, the tomb, that he is trying to escape, as she represents with her closed book everything that he cannot learn, a painful situation for a person who has learned all that he knows from books; for Porphyro, Angela represents all the mysteries of age and the reveling company which he and Madeline shall flee at the end of the poem.

Besides this desire for company the Outsider desires light. It is a frantic "longing for light" (*CF* 2.267) that drives the creature from the castle. Above all the Outsider wants brilliance and the sun portrayed in the books. A picture of the sun, of course, is a poor signifier since the sun at its most brilliant hurts the eyes, as Faust experiences on the morning of his renewal at the beginning of Part II of Goethe's work, forced to look away into a rainbow, since only "Am farbigen Abglanz haben wir das Leben" [only in colored reflection do we live] (4727).[6] Our pictures of the sun, those clear-cut yellow circles in our juvenile books, are modeled on a sun we see reddened at sunset by a thick atmosphere or paled by the fog in the morning, a poor parody of the sun at noon. Instead of the sun the Outsider receives the full moon, but not the moon that

---

6. When referring to *Faust II* I will cite the German text, when referring to *Faust I* the translation by Bayard Taylor that Lovecraft had in his library (Joshi, *Library* #360); there is no evidence that Lovecraft read *Faust II*.

presides over the events of Keats's poem and breaks magically into a spectrum shining through a stained-glass window; this moon, though in it a ruined spire "gleamed spectrally" (*CF* 1.269), does not satisfy "the frantic craving for light" that he still feels (269). At the conclusion of the story he knows, besides what he is, "that light is not for me, save that of the moon" (272).

The Outsider is almost destroyed by a mirror, but long before confronting that mirror he has an anxiety of such things, perhaps most tellingly when his ascent of the tower climaxes in an act that parallels the climax of the story: "All at once, after an infinity of awesome, sightless crawling up that concave and desperate precipice, I felt my head touch a solid thing, and knew I must have gained the roof, or at least some kind of floor" (*CF* 2.267). Lovecraft's sleight of hand allows the reader and the Outsider to misplace the fact that no obstruction, neither roof nor floor, is to be expected since the Outsider is climbing the outside of a tower in order to observe from its peak an open landscape. And that word *concave* is most properly applicable to concave mirrors such as Newton describes for his construction of a reflecting telescope.

A series of arches guides Porphyro's career and the Outsider's. For Porphyro the arch is relatively insignificant, a part of the decor: in an early, discarded stanza "arched ways" are associated with "this high Baronial night" (Keats 28n); Porphyro follows Angela "through a lowly arched way" (109) into the "little moonlight room, / Pale, lattic'd, chill, and silent as a tomb" (112–13) where he plans his approach to Madeline's chamber where the all-important stanza of the stained-glass begins, "A casement high and triple-arched there was" (208). For the Outsider the arch becomes associated with moments of anxiety similar to his anxiety of the mirror. He steps out of the tomb "under an arch" (*CF* 2.269); this image culminates in the "golden-arched doorway" that leads to another room (270), the arch that he approaches, the *"golden arch"* beneath which he touches the outstretched paw that his monstrous reflection holds out to him (271). The shape of the rainbow hangs across his passage.

The rainbow circumscribes a paradox, both as an object and as a symbol that hovers within the poem and the story. As an object it circumscribes the problem Goethe disputed with Newton, the problem that light can be both simple and compound, simple in our experience and compound in our reflection, and the problem of fact, theory, and language. Unlike Newton, who boasted that "hypotheses . . . in *philosophiae experimentali* locum non habent" [hypotheses . . . have no place in *experimental philosophy*] (*Principia* 764) and believed that his work had been as purged of theory as it had, almost, been purged of metaphoric language, Goethe believed that "alles Faktische schon Theorie ist" [everything factual is already theory] (12.432). A fact was itself a construct of the seventeenth and eighteenth centuries' compulsion for certainty; it was, as neither Newton nor Goethe could have been aware, a reified thing rather than a concept and bore the traces of its origin in an interaction with a subject (Sepper 164–67). In the poem and story the rainbow—which we must not forget is only an implicit image—

symbolizes how contraries, innocence and corruption, or joy and pain can cohabit both our experience and our reason. Corruption is represented variously in the poem, in part in the figures of the Baron, the Beadsman, and Angela, in part as a potential loss of love and idealism; in Lovecraft's story corruption is present as the factual, passionate corruption of the body within which the narrator naively matures and which finally becomes a part of the narrator's identity, the decay that appears in the mirror.

But innocence is also part of both poem and story. The creature is immensely innocent; much of the pathos of the story flows from our acceptance of that innocence. Madeline is an innocent, perhaps too much so—yet Keats gave her a name that is a variant of Magdalen, the repentant prostitute so often figured in Christian iconography sitting before a memento mori. In a pointed, ironic, but rejected stanza the narrator says that Madeline would "wake again / Warm in the virgin morn, no weeping Magdalen" (54n), an ambiguous phrase since we cannot know whether to read, "no weeping *Magdalen*," or, "no *weeping* Magdalen." However that may be, her innocence is supported by a number of details, only one strand of which I wish to trace. Devoted to St. Agnes, whose name is a form of "agnus," lamb, Madeline is frequently compared to a lamb; lambs are mentioned early in the poem, the "woolly fold" in the first stanza, a regression to the conventional language of the eighteenth century (4). The ritual of the two unshorn lambs whose fleece is woven into a sacrificial offering at the church St. Agnes fuori le mura (Barnard 624n) is invoked in the poem by Porphyro, "by the holy loom / Which none but secret sisterhood may see, / When they St Agnes' wool are weaving piously" (115–17); the lamb of God suffers a slight conflation with the Fates. For a moment, at his failure to wake Madeline, Porphyro becomes "entoil'd in woofed phantasies" (288).

But this imagery of weaving implies also the weaving of appearances. Madeline is a character who like Lamia has suffered an unweaving in recent years, but the inviolability of her person is safeguarded by two stanzas that have always represented a problem because of their apparent gratuity, the stanza that describes the effect of the moonlight on the stained-glass window of Madeline's chamber and the stanza that describes the feast Porphyro lays next to her bed, a feast that remains uneaten as the lovers turn to each other; on the one hand an exploration of the visual, on the other of the gustatory and olfactory senses, with strong suggestions of the kinaesthetic and the sexual, the two stanzas investigate the evanescence of the senses and their service to the world as appearance. Bennett has argued, indeed, that the poem is "tri-centered" in these two stanzas and in stanza 36, the stanza of the consummation the two stanzas anticipate (108). The juxtaposition of the window to the statement of the previous stanza that Madeline is silent but "Paining with eloquence" like "a tongueless nightingale" (205–06) suggests that the window speaks for her. If it does, it arguably speaks in a manner similar to that by which the tapestry spoke for Philomela after her brother-in-law raped her and cut out her tongue (cf. Stillinger 76–77, 210–11n29), though the violence of silence that Madeline suffers is self-imposed (Gradman 81n). The imagery of the window moves from the relatively innocent fruits and flowers and knot-grass to a more charged language, "diamonded with panes of quaint device, / Innumerable of stains and splendid dyes, / As are the tiger-moth's deep-damasked wings" (211–13), words associated for us with Lamia and the rainbow. But the heraldries, saints, and blood of queens and kings with which the stanza concludes reminds us of the society and revelries within which Madeline first appears; and the entire stanza reminds us of the light and company for which the Outsider begins the quest. Both these aspects of the quest reappear in the feast Porphyro prepares: "lucent syrops" and jellies, especially jellies "soother than the creamy curd"—whether smoother or more true or more true because more transparent—are suggestive of light, whereas the "argosy"—ship and, more distantly, the eyes of Argus—and the cities, Fez and Samarkand, are suggestive of the social world (266–70).

These two stanzas converge in the person of Madeline without overtly referring to her. They are not metaphors; they work as atmosphere, the surround of her that she breathes, or as symbols if we recall the original meaning of a symbol, the two broken parts of a coin that signify that the people who own them belong to a particular order of being. For Madeline the two stanzas, broken off from each other and her person, signify the elusive, unascertainable, indecidable aspect of her presence for Porphyro and for the reader. The oblique revelation of the two stanzas is all the more necessary because, at the moment of fullest revelation as her dress drops from her body, a "teasing veil" (Bennett 108) of non-visual imagery, the epiphenomenal bliss of the engaged imagination, is cast over her, as is the spectrum of the stained-glass window, "rose-bloom" (220), inexplicable and miraculous because scattered, reflected light does not produce color.

We have not abstained, however, from attempting to read Madeline and the stanzas. Intricate analyses have been constructed of their sonic patterns. But one of the most influential readings of the poem was performed by Stillinger, for whom Porphyro is "a peeping Tom and villainous seducer" (82), Madeline a "hoodwinked dreamer" who "gets her reward in coming to face reality a little too late" (86–87), Apollonius a seer who has "done what he had to do" to Lamia, "basically an evil creature," and Lycius like Madeline "hoodwinked" (57–58). With some self-satisfaction Stillinger behaved like Apollonius confronted by Lamia, unweaving her innocence; and since unlike Stesichorus he has not retracted, the smear upon Madeline remains as a commonplace within Keatsian criticism.

Another image connected with her must be striking for us in the context of *Lamia:* her dress like Marceline's hair "creeps rustling" (230) to her knees, and as she pauses she resembles "a mermaid in sea-weed" (231), a half-and-half creature not fully of the land or the sea. The image may remind us of the sirens who enchant men with song until they die for want of food (Lemprière, cited by Barnard 716n). Does such a resemblance account for Porphyro's need to set the feast?

Another range of imagery associated with her emphasizes her indrawn nature. At the dance, because she is following the precepts of St. Agnes' Eve, she behaves as a person thoroughly withdrawn from contact with others. Her sleep is described by a remarkable half-stanza:

> Flown, like a thought, until the morrow-day;
> Blissfully haven'd both from joy and pain;
> Clasp'd like a missal where swart Paynims pray;
> Blinded alike from sunshine and from rain,
> As though a rose should shut, and be a bud again.   (239–43)

She has flown like Lamia and the dreamer of the sonnet but in a different direction, regressing from the contraries of human experience into an enclosed object of desire. Later she wakes to be both unclasped to Porphyro and clasped by him, but at this stage she is entering into her dream of Porphyro, which we may feel sure shall be shaped by her expectations that virgins who have prepared themselves shall "have visions of delight, / And soft adorings from their loves receive / Upon the honey'd middle of the night" (47–49), autoerotic imagery reminiscent of situations we have described in *Lamia* and "Medusa's Coil."

Like Madeline, Porphyro strikes us as a blend of innocence and corruption. His name resembles that of Porphyrion, the giant or titan so formidable that Jupiter inspired him with love for Juno and while the giant was prostrate overpowered him with the help of Hercules (Lemprière, cited by Barnard, 714n). Porphyrion is guilty of the crime of Ixion, an attempt to overcome the goddess, for which the human was crucified on the solar wheel. In his dedicatory poem to the *Principia* Halley had praised Newton's achievement in the language of rape, "Intima panduntur victi penetralia caeli" [The most intimate inner rooms of the conquered sky lie open] (Newton 12), though Newton never made such exaggerated claims for his optics, believing that a microscope would not be able "to see the more secret and noble Works of Nature within the Corpuscles by reason of their transparency" (262). But it is surely an exaggeration to claim that Porphyro rapes or, in the epistemological sense, knows Madeline. The young man of whom Madeline dreams, willing for her sake to risk his life, is sufficiently idealistic to see her in such a way that her beauty transcends herself. But our probe of his character may be indecidable. Are we able to conclude that, as he asserts, he is "no *rude* infidel" or "no rude *infidel*" (342)? Our problem with the phrase in the cancelled stanza, "no weeping Magdalen," is mirrored here more acutely. Is Porphyro an infidel, having come "o'er the southern moors" (351), but not rude? Or is he not an infidel, not a pagan, or is that "infidel" merely metaphoric, his assurance of his faith in her or in love or in the transforming power of love? Her response to his assertion is a tacit answer, but since we do not understand the assertion we cannot understand the answer. Our comprehension shatters at this moment in the poem when speech ceases; we watch the lovers' flight into silence.

Not only is Porphyro double-visioned, he is himself two-sided, for when Madeline wakes she sees him to her own confusion under both aspects and has difficulty resolving them. Like Lamia and Asenath, like a poet, she sends her spirit forth to see her belovèd as in a vision that threatens to engulf the flesh and blood that he also is:

> 'Ah, Porphyro!' said she, 'but even now
> Thy voice was at sweet tremble in mine ear,
> Made tuneable with every sweetest vow,
> And those sad eyes were spiritual and clear:
> How changed thou art! How pallid, chill, and drear!
> Give me that voice again, my Porphyro,
> Those looks immortal, those complainings dear!' (307–13)

These are not only seductive words. Registering her confusion they also register the confusion of the image that she returns to him and the creation of a need in him to resolve that discord. She is the mirror that shatters and recomposes him, just as he shatters and recomposes her.

His response to her words is wordless, pure act and image:

>   like a throbbing star
> Seen mid the sapphire heaven's deep repose;
> Into her dream he melted, as the rose
> Blendeth its odour with the violet—
> Solution sweet. (318–22)

The two ends of the Newtonian spectrum resolve themselves in a synaesthesia of color and scent. As Newton comments, "Thus the Colour of Violets seems to be of that Order, because their Syrup by acid Liquors turns red" (*Opticks* 256). But instantly a cold crystal opposes this warm liquidity: "Meantime the frost-wind blows / Like Love's alarum pattering the sharp sleet / Against the window-panes" (322–24). Their love-making is an *ébranlement*, a self-shattering as Leo Bersani understands it, who places sexuality within the context of a narcissism that accounts for the sublimations of culture and the self-creation of the ego; the compulsion toward totality and the splitting-off of ego-consciousness, narcissistic attentiveness and aggressive negligence, are mutually constitutive and progenitive (*Freudian Body* 19–20; *Culture* 36–46): "The pleasurable-unpleasurable tension of sexuality—the pain of a self-shattering excitement—aims at being maintained, replicated, and even increased" (36), an apt description of the concerns of a poet like Keats so committed to an exploration of the intimate polarities of pain and pleasure. The self upon its way to selfhood continues returning to its creation of new objects and scenes of desire. Hermes, who carries the caduceus, the snake-staff, as Lamia's creation reacts upon her and enables her to accomplish her desire for a time, takes on thereby his own life with his object the nymph, also within the spell of Lamia, to remain an emblem of ceaseless pleasure; March, elevating Marceline into the sublimation and essentialism of art, becomes the object of her desire, which his own narcissism and the envy of de Russy *père* regard as degraded. But it is the pleasure moving within the progressive self that centers and captures the self in its own orbit. Narcissistic desire continues observing itself; the Outsider returns to the mirror, though we have no assurance that what lies there in memory is ever the same. Since, furthermore, Argus and Oistrus meet in the figure of the gadfly, where it is difficult to distinguish the ecstatic and the murderous, then in *ébranlement* we encounter the eyes of Argus once more; the public representations which we need in order to be sexual have their hand in our secret desire (*Freudian Body* 42), at the same time that desire attempts to subvert and evade them.[7]

The appearance of the figure of Narcissus should not surprise us since narcissism is always potential within the imagery of the Double. Ovid's narrative plays with doubling extensively, from the moment that a sinister, insistent doubling, "Si se non noverit" (3.348), warns Narcissus's mother that her son will have long life "if he does not know himself," as though the Delphic command to know one's self were also a warning. And in fact the Delphic answers to problems always presented themselves as problems; Calasso wisely argues that Oedipus's answer to the Sphinx, "Man," itself points at the insoluble problem of human nature (343–44). But the story of Narcissus need not be sinister. Edward Young alludes to it as an emblem of authenticity in *Night Thoughts:*

> Rich from within, and self-sustain'd, the true.
> The true is fix'd, and solid as a rock;
> Slipp'ry the false, and tossing, as the wave.
> This, a wild wanderer on earth, like Cain;
> That, like the fabled, self-enamour'd boy,
> Home-contemplation her supreme delight;
> She dreads an interruption from within,
> Smit with her own condition; and the more
> Intense she gazes, still it charms the more.   (8.926–34)

This truth, however, is clearly solipsistic, absolutely self-referential. Home-truths are self-enjoying.

To the story of the young man who confronts his own enigmatic nature, falling in love with his reflection in a pool and wasting away to a flower, Ovid adds the story of Echo, a nymph too fond of her own voice who from her cave can only court him by echoing the words he utters to court his own image; the figures inter-

---

7. Forrest Jackson has studied the fate of the Outsider as a narcissist in the context of Otto Rank's argument that a Double is often a portent of death since it bears the stigma of unattainable perfection, but then draws the moral that "it is society which creates monsters and the subsequent chaos they propagate" (9). As this chapter and the chapter "*At the Mountains of Madness:* The Subway and the Shoggoth" argue, I regard narcissism as a matter of desire (the individual requires society to foreground taboo objects in order to overcome that taboo) and as one of three kinds of psychic configuration, the other two being obsession and hysteria, configurations which Elisabeth Young-Bruehl believes should be understood as components of any one psyche if our picture is to have any fullness and acuity.

penetrate and excite each other while remaining images of doubling and solipsism. In "Medusa's Coil" Marsh and Marceline are Narcissus and Echo. He places her in her cave of the painting, while admiring himself; she admires herself but is shattered into humanity by her sudden desire for him. The desire of Denis is a pallid reflection of hers, his father's a petrified reflection. The Lovecraftian moral seems to be that it is fatal to shatter the narcissistic absorption into the self, but inevitable. An act of narcissistic aggression, of intense pleasure, is visited upon the self, which passes on. In "The Outsider" the narrator leaves his cave, where he has listened to the disembodied voices of the books and fallen in love with the images of others, only to find that the one he would most love is his own crazed, cracked self, whom he cannot possess; dispossessed but unable to return to the cave, since the self-absorption is shattered, he is forced into a new relation with others, the ghouls and the nameless feasts. But he continues to return in memory to the moment of the mirror, his point of intensest energy.

Narcissus's plight arises in the tension of his unwinking gaze, which he can only break should he be so bold as to reach out his hand and shatter that image floating in the water; the love and voice of Echo do nothing for him (Ovid 3.339–510). Since the Outsider touches glass, the self-shattering is entirely internal. Madeline and Porphyro, however, enjoy a series of shatterings. Her narcissistic descent into the dream is shattered by the music that Porphyro plays. Their "solution sweet" becomes a self-shattering dissolution each within the other, a gap and oblivion after which they both need to put the world together again; but it can in no way return to its paradisal images. Or rather, in Bersani's terms, its paradisal image is now the self-shattering itself.

Within *The Eve of St. Agnes* this self-shattering is to be understood in a number of ways. Porphyro invokes the storm as an invasion from "faery land, / Of haggard seeming, but a boon indeed" (343–44), an invocation akin to the narrator's perception earlier: "Never on such a night have lovers met, / Since Merlin paid his Demon all the monstrous debt" (170–71). Undoubtedly, as Stillinger argues, we dare not acquiesce in Porphyro's interpretation of the storm. But neither is his interpretation denied by the text. Whatever it is that the lovers flee into at the end of the poem, it is other than the life within the castle and other than the lovers' first coming together; it is outside corruption and innocence, but experience is a poor word for it.

It is a flight into which they fling themselves willingly, as the poet in the sonnet had flung himself imaginatively into the second circle where he circles, lip to lip, with the belovèd in the hail-storm of starvation and impoverishment. Porphyro and Madeline leave the feast behind them untasted, through a lane of imaginary eyes; and as they flee the weave of the world rises up around them: "The arras, rich with horseman, hawk, and hound, / Fluttered in the besieging wind's uproar; / And the long carpets rose along the gusty floor" (358–60). The Outsider leaves the castle behind without partaking of the feast, since for him are only the friendly ghouls and the "unnamed feasts of Nitokris" (*CF* 2.272) in which that queen of

Egypt drowned her enemies in a full awareness of her attack; he celebrates the storm of aggression. The celebration into which the lovers flee is the chill repression of a world of pain, a vale of soul-making some might say; but Keats says no such thing within the poem. The Outsider flees into a society partaking of a parody of feasts.

Do the lovers return? Yes, if we assume that they die as do their doubles, "For aye unsought for" (378). All humanity returns to the feast where, as Hamlet says, they shall not eat but be eaten by "a certain convocation of politic worms" (*Hamlet* 4.3.19–20), among which moves that "large coffin-worm" that nourishes the Baron's nightmare. The Outsider returns to the *ébranlement* of the mirror, not soul-creation but soul-annihilation (*CF* 1.272). But a formulation by Bersani is illuminating here: "It is as if a certain split occurred in consciousness, a split that paradoxically is also the first experience of self-integration. In this self-reflexive move, a pleasurably shattered consciousness becomes aware of itself as the object of its desire" (*Culture* 37). The Outsider says that "in the supreme horror of that second I forgot what had horrified me, and the burst of black memory vanished in a chaos of echoing images" (*CF* 2.272); the oxymoron of "black memory" and the synaesthesia of "echoing images," variations of the earlier phrase "vanishing echoes" that describes the revel in flight (270), indicate the charged, dynamic, contradictory nature of that moment. Yet the Outsider also assures us, at the beginning of the story, that the mind persists in reaching "beyond to *the other*" (265); he reaches out to the painful moment that is compulsively attractive precisely because of its pain. Both physically, at the climactic moment of staggering toward the glass, and metaphorically, time and again involuntarily reaching out toward the memory, the Outsider reaches out to the image that responds to its reach. He achieves a condition that Narcissus must envy, for the Outsider always possesses in memory, both with him and beyond him, that image in the mirror that his hand eternally shatters. But the image is faithful; no rude infidel shattered out of shape, it always returns, reaching its hand out. It is as though he were able to invert the words of Narcissus, "Inopem me copia fecit" [Abundance makes me poor] (3.466): the inabundant emptiness of the Outsider's image makes him rich, possessed, potent. And around him the echoes of the revelry and the echo of his own voice—how does he know it is his?—dance back and forth, retreating and approaching like the ripples of a stone dropped in water, an image too apt for Newton not to use, applying one aspect of the wave theory of light that he rejected (*Opticks* 280, 362–70). Beauty and narcissistic sexuality, framed by the golden arch, participate in the Outsider's self-recognition; not foreign to this motif is the Serbian belief that men change to women and women to men when they walk beneath the rainbow (Grimm 2.611). Indeed, to imagine the Outsider as a reptilian self-coupler, an orgasm upon the caduceus of Hermes, is to invoke Ovid's story in which Tiresias strikes two intertwined snakes and changes sex; eight years later, at another blow, "genetivaque venit imago" [and the generating image returned] (3.331). The story of the Outsider represents a compulsion to repeat itself, to compose and be composed, to shatter and be shattered. The composition concerns a self-shattering, and the self-shattering demands a composition; and that moment, with its double motion and double image, represents how consciousness comes to itself. Instead of revelry and light he finds the multitudes of himself, breaking apart like the rays of light in the prism, and the light of the self in the mirror within the golden arch.

Such a shattering of the image does not, however, reduce but increase its power upon our imagination, recalling our attention repeatedly. Madeline as well as Agnes remains a figure to whom we can address our attention, "Agnus dei, qui tollis peccata mundi," as does the Outsider who bears our anxiety over the origin of our consciousness in alienage and the shame of corruption. But the Outsider is also, as we have hinted, worm and snake. The "coffin-worm" of the motto has already given us pause. Keats is naturally familiar with the "wormy circumstance" (*Isabella* 385) of Jacobean and Gothic imaginations, having in *Sleep and Poetry* invented a myth of poetry whose strength, if it isolate itself from the Muse like "a fallen angel," delights in "Darkness, and worms, and shrouds, and sepulchres" (242–44). Furthermore, Keats and Lovecraft are familiar with the ancient identity between worm and snake. Cleopatra bespeaks her asp fondly, "the pretty worm of Nilus there, / That kills and pains not" (*Antony and Cleopatra* 5.2.243–44); in *Cymbeline* Pisanio refers to "the worms of Nile" (3.4.35). The background of Egypt for Marceline's cult takes on a new significance in this connection. In *A Midsummer Night's Dream* Hermia accuses Lysander of being "a worm, an adder" (3.2.71). Speaking of the murder of Banquo and the escape of Fleance, Macbeth says, "There the grown serpent lies; the worm that's fled / Hath nature that in time will venom breed" (*Macbeth* 3.4.29–30). These several passages suggest a figure that is both weak and deadly, small and young but capable of swift attack. And in *Paradise Lost* Adam names the serpent into which Satan crept "that false Worm" (9.1068); it is the Miltonic context to which Keats alludes when he writes that Porphyro, "Stol'n to this paradise" of Madeline's room, gazes entranced "upon her empty dress" and then creeps from his hiding place (244–49). This wide spectrum is present in the twenty-second psalm, "But I am a worm and no man" (6), for the abjection of the speaker is qualified by the New Testament interpretation of the psalm as one of those figurations of the death and election of the messiah (cf. Matt. 27:46). The Red Death had come, as the day of the messiah comes, "like a thief in the night" (Poe 2.676; cf. 1 Thess. 5:2). Given the literary context, we are compelled to regard the Outsider as worm and snake, as the accuser and the appointed. But besides these verbal suggestions, the Outsider also behaves like a snake, issuing from its hole in the hope of finding light and warmth in which to slough its skin in rejuvenation. From this point of view, however, the quest is abortive, for finding no light or warmth, only *"a cold and unyielding surface"* (*CF* 1.272), the narrator remains the rough-skinned creature it began as.

This journey that the snake-like Outsider makes has other overtones. Keats argues that the poetic character is negative, liable to reflect the characters of the subject at hand. If Lamia is a study of the poetic character, as we have argued, then her lack of character may be a part of the reason for our difficulty in identifying and defining her; she is a field of possibilities, destroyed when Lycius and Apollonius force their identifications upon her. Like Pegasus she is a winged creature. When she melts away at the touch of Hermes her words are "borne aloft / With the bright mists" (1.168–69); she flies from Crete to Corinth, from Corinth to who-knows-where? She behaves as though she were a winged serpent, a compound of the elements of earth and air.

But if her form is difficult to distinguish because of its paradoxical and open nature, the Outsider is difficult to distinguish also because unformed. As the poetical character or the possibility of consciousness, Lovecraft's narrator is something always on its way toward definition. The worm that Cleopatra takes to her bosom has an immortal bite according to the peasant (*Antony and Cleopatra* 5.2.246–47), who tells how a woman "died of the biting of it, what pain she felt. Truly, she makes a very good report o' th' worm; . . . the worm's an odd worm" (5.2.252–57). He leaves the stage saying, "I wish you joy o' th' worm" (5.2.288). The passage recalls Lucrece's complaint, "Why should the worm intrude the maiden bud?" (*The Rape of Lucrece* 848). If the Outsider is a snake, he is also a worm in the sense of a foetal creature struggling into birth. Shakespeare's phallic jokes prepare for Blake's usage, in whose poems the worm functions with both phallic and foetal significance. Vala and Orc recapitulate the forms of worm, snake, and dragon before their births (*The Four Zoas* 2.83–92 and *Urizen* 19.20–36). In *Thel* the virgin bends over a worm "like an infant wrapped in the Lillys leaf" (3.4); but upon descending to "the couches of the dead" (4.3) and her own grave she flees in terror at the question, "Why a little curtain of flesh on the bed of our desire" (4.20). The entire sequence presents a compact symbol of the innocence and aggression of sexual knowledge. In "The Outsider" the revelers flee from the consciousness that the unconscious narrator embodies for them, not only of their mortality but also of their origins in darkness and frailty. To this extent his quest is successful, that at the conclusion of the story he rides "with the mocking and friendly ghouls on the night-wind" (*CF* 2.272) as though he were winged; the chrysalis has unfolded its wings to the air.

But to what extent is the Outsider like a worm, a word that remains despite our analysis firmly in the motto with which we began? In the second paragraph he states, "I know not where I was born" (*CF* 1.265), though by the end of the story we may wonder whether he were ever born. But he continues, "save that the castle was infinitely old and infinitely horrible; full of dark passages" (265–66), words that imply a birth from the stuff of castle and ground itself (Buchanan 14), earth-born like Argus whose eyes he internalizes. From the first paragraph we probably infer a certain beauty, for he does deploy an elaborate prose; and he believes that he is as normal as the people he reads of in his books, the young, bright, and gay (*CF* 1.266–67). He mentions his head and arms, several times his hands, and his fingers that in the mirror are blunted and paw-like (271). He never mentions legs or feet, though climbing the tower he clings to footholds (267). The verbs of motion are also enlightening. In the first paragraph he looks and gazes; the eye is all-important. He lies, runs, climbs, clings, and swims; more frequently, however, he crawls, drags, fumbles, stumbles, staggers, stands, and trembles, awkward and maladroit in the extreme. Midway through the story he tests and tries repeatedly. Such specificity as these verbs give, however, is shattered by the extremity of his language as he confronts the mirror. In the final paragraphs he rides, plays, knows insistently, and welcomes, at the same time that he forgets and remembers. None of this language implies the snake, but neither does it represent the fully human.

So far I have narrativized the Lovecraftian protagonist and thus betrayed my own insistence that the subject is unreadable. In this chapter I have attempted what Sepper analyzes as Goethe's method of *Vermannigfaltigung,* to cite manifold instances of the *Urphenomenon* of Lovecraft's protagonist which is everywhere and nowhere in his characters; we have amplified, simplified, and recomplicated our materials, varied, augmented, and enumerated exhaustively (Sepper 70–71; cf. 13.316). We have not analyzed the material quantitatively, and we have not been embarked upon a quest. We have meditated, moving attentively among the materials of our study, the writings, the desires, our methods, and ourselves, taking their spiritual measure. The object of desire is fugitive, a reflex of the mobility of desire, the rainbow of a desirous subject that dodges its own perceptions (Bersani, *Culture* 43). But so we ought to expect of a worm that feeds upon the damned in the garbage heap of Gehenna and dies not (Mark 9:44). Plutarch was wrong, the Outsider insists, to name the feasts of Nitokris, for they are the bodies that feed his own unidentifiable flesh; and if he is a travesty of flesh, which is the central condition of the Lovecraft protagonist, it remains unclear whether he is a travesty of the flesh that was, that shall be, or, unnamable fate, that is. The Outsider never dies, and we never die as long as we continue trying to read that which is before, outside, or after life. The Outsider, in any case, has no ability to name for he has no voice, only the ululation at the moment of self-shattering which is a pre-linguistic moment, incommensurable to language and therefore endlessly productive of words (Bersani, *Freudian Body* 39–40, 67). Who is the Outsider? He is Madeline "asleep in lap of legends old," passive but expectant. He is Porphyro and Lycius: he has crossed the moors and the open country for love, seducer and seduced. He is the Baron from whom they proceed, possessive father, anima, and shadow. He is Apollonius, the skeptic unraveler. He is Lamia, fixated by his own stare. He is the rainbow that moves as he pursues it.

In both Keats's poems and in Lovecraft's stories we are left with the persistent question what kind of a creature Lamia and Madeline may be, what Marceline and the Colour out of space and Asenath may be, what kind of a creature the Outsider may be, only to be presented with a series of insufficient answers. The poems and the stories refuse to come to a conclusion and use a variety of strategies in order to avoid that consummation. Because they refuse to conclude, we must not overreact to such readings as Stillinger's and defend Lamia and Madeline against attack, to say nothing of Marceline, Asenath, or the Outsider. Nor should we, like the narrator of the story of the de Russys from his desire to protect the putative honor of the family and perhaps from a desire to abstain from the Oedipal threat, reject out of hand the notion that "the ol' fellow fell in love with the gal himself and kilt her and the boy" (*CF* 4.344). De Russy had admitted about his son, "I'm not sure yet but that he tried to kill me, too" (330). The eternal quadrangle in "Medusa's Coil" resembles that in "The Rats in the Walls," at the climax of which the father devours his son's close friend. Just as Oedipal dynamics pressure Apollonius into the role of the dominating father whose desire steps between the young man and the enigma he would lie with, in the same way de la Poer *père* peureux attacks the effeminate threat to his son's honor and destroys the attraction he himself feels, all in the name of patriarchal honor, though his madness confesses that he acts at the behest of the great goddess. And the great goddess, in the form of Asenath and Poe's Berenice, has teeth, a spectrum of white teeth. Her more benign form is Angela with "agues in her brain," holding the book of enigmas which Porphyro, a mere boy in this regard, doubts he shall ever read (127–31). Shall we ever read it? The remarkable feat Lovecraft accomplished in "The Outsider" was to create a field within which we see the trace of all these transformations of desire at work upon the polished surface of a single character.

But despite our earlier indecision about the creature's gender, no matter how much the Outsider puts on the garb of Helen, Nitokris, Lamia, and Madeline—as he does—I believe we can now say that he is male, insofar as he engages the female figure of the rainbow within which he attempts to discover himself; in literature flesh and complex take precedence over logic. The Outsider intrudes on the primal scene like Newton who, according to James Thomson, had "untwisted" the robe of day to uncover and discover the "parent colours." Iocaste ran into her room, out of the light of the sun—out of the light of the son, as English allows us to say—wringing her hair. A reflex of woven and unwoven desire, she is hung up like a rainbow off the ground, the enigma out of which our broken enigmas proceed. Though in his version of the tale Seneca allows her to die by a sword, he still implies that those things which the gods "volunt / iterumque nolunt" [wish / and again do not wish] to be recognized (332–33) resemble a flame, "qualis implicat varios sibi / Iris colores" [such as when Iris weaves herself various colors] (315–16). In *Finnegans Wake* Joyce parodies and illumines this moment: "My heart, my mother! My heart, my coming forth of darkness! . . . Yes, there was that skew arch of chrome sweet home, floodlit up above the flabberghosted farmament and bump where the camel got the needle. Talk about iridecencies!" (493.34–494.4). Our indecencies lie in our attempt to read the maternal matrix as it bodies itself forth in the emblematic light of the rainbow; and the more we try, the less chance we shall have of entering into heaven, as little chance as the camel that cannot go through the needle. The riddle of the Sphinx receives a new, more exhaustive answer: the human is that which walks on four legs in the morning, on two at noon, on a prosthesis at sunset, and on none at night; nature is an eternal surround of appearance that a human being cannot see at all, certainly not see through, because it is our only means of sight—neither the personality nor the photon can be seen because of its weightless transparency. The Oedipal reaction includes a reaction against this dependence that lies in every direction. Oedipus meets two women, the Sphinx, his very own Sphinx according to Seneca (641), and the Mother, both of whom die from that encounter; but he goes on, as Lovecraft did, blinded because he knows what is due a carper like Stesichorus. This blinding, however, is itself suspect. We may say that Oedipus now possesses a vision that goes forth ceaselessly searching for a way to create a new object of ecstasy; he becomes the prophet of *Oedipus at Colonus,* a point we shall examine further in the last chapter of this study. Or we may say that when Lycius blinds himself against Apollonius (1.373–74) he attempts to retreat from Newton: "Factum est periclum lucis" [The danger of light is done with] (Seneca 971). But since no retreat from intellect is possible, for either Oedipus, Keats, or Lovecraft, they must proceed blinded and unblinded, returning like the Outsider to the gilded frame of the rainbow within which they find themselves vanishing, appearing, sparkling in restless desire.

The Outsider, the Autodidact, and Other Professions

I

Sensum ipsum, qui communis dicitur, ubi discet, cum se a congressu, qui non hominibus solum sed mutis quoque animalibus naturalis est, segregarit? [Where do you learn what is called common sense if you cut yourself off from that society which is not only natural to humans but to the mute animals also?] (Quintilian 1.2.20)

In his final words upon his condition the Outsider writes that he is "a stranger in this century" (*CF* 1.272). Several people have already noticed the extent to which these words have an autobiographical significance; in 1919 Lovecraft had confessed, "In everything I am behind the times" (*MWM* 47). And before writing the story he had already used its language in his letters, in 1916 writing, "In everything I am an outsider" (*Letters to Rheinhart Kleiner* 55), a month later, speaking of himself as a child, "I had permanently come to feel myself an *outsider*" (*RK* 65), and in 1920 once more, "I was ever an intellectual outsider" (*RK* 167). The reasons for such an alienation were many, but one of them was certainly the extent to which the child Lovecraft was self-educated; and with his failure to attend college the rest of his life became a further experiment in his own education. Such a fate produces remarkable consequences in an age when public education has been well nigh universal since 1865; in Providence the public school system had been established since 1828 (Kelsey 3).

Not that Lovecraft was totally self-educated, far from it, but his education was piecemeal. After a year of primary school he was removed in 1899, not to return until 1902, only to be withdrawn a year later (*IAP* 70–71, 87). His main crisis, however, occurred when his grandfather died and he realized that he would have no more tutors but have to attend high school; but as he contemplated suicide he realized that he knew so little that even high school might have possibilities (*JVS* 222)—despite, he remarked in 1916, "a considerable *Jewish* attendance" (*RK* 72). He was grateful for the education, nevertheless, writing that Hope Street High School had "an admirable staff of teachers, each one of keenest sympathy and understanding for an awkward, nervous and retiring youth" (*MWM* 46). But since he attended intermittently, forced "to piece out as good a special course as pedagogical ingenuity might devise" (*MWM* 46), and since to his own regret he could not attend college, the teachers who stood out in his memory were his grandfather Phillips, his two uncles-in-law, and his neighbor the Rev. James Pyke; most important for his self-image was his grandfather's library, in which he browsed from an early age. His learning he received from his family, in person and in their books acquired over the years; thus his learning expressed family tradition, private instead of public, and his mind became an extension of the family mind. Though "Latin and Greek were [his] delight," he had a lengthy dispute with a teacher over pronunciation because his grandfather "had previously taught [him] a great deal of Latin, using the traditional English pronunciation taught in his day" (*MF* 583). It was hard for the teenager to surrender a tongue learned from the family, even one that he knew his beloved Romans never spoke; and Pope supported him, attacking pedants who "give up Cicero to C or K" (*The Dunciad* 4.222). Physics and chemistry he delighted in, in part because he was already studying them at home with a "pretty well equipped basement laboratory" (*MF* 584). His account gives the impression that high school succeeded when it behaved as though it were an extension of his learning at home. With a certain amount of complacency he says, "All this time I had a very free hand in choosing my pursuits, since ill health kept me from school much of the time" (*FLB* 38). Indeed, he wrote of himself in 1924, "After all, a cultivated family is the best school, and I am singularly complacent about the training this young man did not get" (*SL* 1.297).

Much of his education, then, took place without contact with anyone except his tutors and his family; it was an education between him and the book, unmediated, and led to an immense lack:

> My contacts with mankind—& with its varied aspects, folkways, idioms, attitudes, & standards—have been extremely limited; so that there are probably very few people outside the extreme rustic class who are more fundamentally unsophisticated than myself. I don't know what different kinds of people do & think & feel & say—their lives, languages, values, & technical processes are as remote from me as the manners and customs of the Cingalese. (*EHP* 121)

Education is as much concerned with a community of knowledge as with knowledge. The autodidact does not recognize being within a community. He is always outside it, though he may realize rather slowly how outside he is since at first such an outsidedness does not preoccupy him because people do not. Even if the autodidact is a creature of institutional education, this characterization holds: the authentic relation is between the person and the book, which most autodidacts devour, preferring to bolt their food rather than linger over it. And to gain control over their education many autodidacts learn to read early; Lovecraft was three years old (de Camp 3).

Such an education is difficult. It is now a cliché that education is communal; a personality becomes differentiated through a dialogue that allows the other full respect, attention, intimacy, and love. Schleiermacher's epistemology began with Adam's encounter of Eve: "In dem Fleische von seinem Fleische und Bein von seinem Beine entdeckte er die Menschheit und in der Menschheit die Welt; von diesem Augenblick an wurde er fähig, die Stimme von Gottheit zu hören" [In flesh of his flesh and bone of his bone he discovered humanity and in humanity the world; from this moment he became capable of hearing the voice of divinity] (60).

In Martin Buber's work, addressing the other as Thou accepts the other as alive, self-originating within a mutual reciprocity; mere objects of knowledge in the I-It relation become in the I-Thou relation alive and dynamic (65), meaning itself something worked through continually rather than pointed out (112). In examining the implications of such ideas we must not lose sight of the religious aspect which our myth of education has borne, for today much educational and psychological theory insists upon the communal aspect of education: we learn through a group of peers and through coming into a new social group, learning its language, which Kenneth A. Bruffee following Richard Rorty describes as an alternation of normal and abnormal discourses. Normal discourse is the language of the community, the everyday language upon which everyone is agreed, all of the contexts, facts, and rules of logic out of which knowledge is built (Bruffee 642–43); abnormal discourse is the kind of language which arises as an individual leaves a familiar community for one in which new contexts, facts, and rules are arising, a discourse that reveals the provincial nature of the normal community, a discourse challenging and upsetting, often nonsensical (648). Normal discourse has to do with things that are understood, abnormal discourse with things that require understanding and demand a self-transcending hermeneutic process (Rorty 320–21). Jean Guéhenno made a similar distinction between "savoir" on the one hand, which "refers to knowledge which has become frozen as doctrine, claimed by those who control it to be absolute and exclusive," a normal discourse that is useful for social control, and "culture" on the other hand, which stands for an ideal attitude concerned "with truth and justice" that strikes across class lines, an "attitude relative rather than absolute, because always open to future discoveries and interpretations, ... inclusive rather than exclusive" (Chapman 94). This culture belongs to what Bruffee calls the largest community, which always contradicts the languages of any smaller, provincial group that attempts to maintain knowledge and its self-interest in that knowledge as it is; but the interest of the largest community "is to bridge gaps among knowledge communities and to open them to change" (650). In a critique of Bruffee, lest we interpret such a bridging as a consensus that glosses over difference, John Trimbur makes explicit that the largest community is one committed to "the inexhaustibility of difference" (615). The largest community is thus committed to a language of disruption; the consensus of such a community is one displaced "to a horizon which may never be reached" (616). This largest community that Bruffee postulates and that Guéhenno longs for is not yet; no one belongs to it fully because it is always the community that shall be, the community that is on its way. Autodidacts project their community as a dynamic fellowship out of the books they are reading; and it is a community always about to be, they only need to read a little more, always on the verge of arriving, always on its way over the horizon of the understanding. The soul "Rests and expatiates in a life to come" (Pope, *An Essay on Man* 1.98). For good reasons a dialogical theory of education reverberates to religious overtones.

These considerations of the relation between the autodidact, the family, and the community need to be qualified as far as an autodidact in America is concerned, for autodidacticism is an essential part of a national character that has defined itself by its rebellion against the authority and learning of the old world. The American Adam, "emancipated from history" (Lewis 5), born naked in a world that can only be conquered through experience, is complicated in Lovecraft through his insistence on being a loyal servant of His Majesty, a loyalty personalized in his belief that his father was "something of an Englishman himself" (*RK* 61). For Lovecraft to be an autodidact is to deny the American experience, to bow out of American institutions, and to assert a family loyalty to an extremely hypothetical Oedipal authority, though within his denial and despite it we still see a typical American gesture. His resemblance to Ezra Pound is striking, the great denier of the American experience who spoke as Uncle Ez to the American troops.

But this adherence to the family needs to be qualified also, since the rush to create the self often seems a reaction against the family. How many autodidacts have their families perceived and they themselves perceived as cuckoos, orphans, changelings—inexplicable sports within the stream of a deterministic biological identity? In Lovecraft's fiction the image of the changeling becomes explicit in "Pickman's Model." For such a figure it is a real puzzle to ask where an identity is to be found, if neither in the family nor in society can it be stabilized. For Lovecraft a hypothetical, playful solution was to appeal to a father and an authority that was essentially absent and ineffective, since his father had gone mad and died in an asylum and since the colonies had two hundred years earlier repudiated Britain lying 3,000 miles across the Atlantic; and Lovecraft never went overseas. His solution assured him that he was on his own. "God save the King!" he cried, but he was in no position to bend the knee to either King or God. The only purpose of the ejaculation was to preserve his independence from the American democracy within which he lived. When during the Depression he wrote letters approving of socialism, he tacitly admitted his connection with American problems, but he also wrote less fiction. His pose as a gentleman was another such gesture of independence, an *odi profanum* both cultural and literary, preserving him from the middle-class within which he was born and from the imperatives of the genre within which he wrote, more specifically from the imperatives of Farnsworth Wright who edited the only journal that made such a genre public. Lovecraft was an autodidact who asserted his independence upon every level possible.

Several aspects of his life belie that independence, of course. During the 1920s he was eager to be published. And as he wrote in the opening of "The Picture in the House," he regarded the independence of the Puritans that had produced "an appalling slavery to the dismal phantasms of their own minds" (*CF* 1.207) as problematic. But though he was no Puritan, his independence preserved to some extent from corruption by his skepticism, we must still admit that his private learning did not protect him from the phantasms of anti-Semitism; more positively, his independence was qualified by his love of his childhood landscapes. Above all, his independence was qualified by the ethos of the Lovecrafts and the Phillipses, who were a product of that landscape and its traditions; and family and landscape committed him to Rhode Island, which became a political entity through abstaining from the enforced pieties of Massachusetts—from which, with Roger Williams, Lovecraft took flight.

The autodidact is swept by sudden passions for this or that narrow branch of knowledge and thus often unable to perceive the relevance of that branch within the wider sweep. An autodidact is often narrow. We may sense in some of Lovecraft's letters a defensive bluff about his learning; but late in life he wrote, "Whether a sort of curiosity about things in general—impelling informal dabblings in bits of history, a few of the sciences, and so on—would win me an unofficial or non-commissioned status as semi-student, I really don't know. But my ignorance as always impresses me more than any ill-coordinated acquirements which I may have picked up in an aimless way" (*CLM* 286). And not only are the details lacking; without a mentor an autodidact often has holes in the principles that hold a discipline together. He does not know what facts the community considers important nor why they are important; such things as facts and the justification for their coherence the autodidact may have to create from the ground up, so that in the hands of an American traditional materials have often appeared "lumpy and not altogether digested" (Lewis 144)—"rudis indigestaque moles," as Lovecraft said when he applied Ovid's description of chaos to *The Waste Land* (*CE* 2.63–64). Such lumps and gaps mean that an autodidact is always hungry, conscious of the emptiness within, whereas a speaker of normal discourse feels full and complete, solid in his skin. And such gaps and imbalances for the autodidact lead to a touch of half-baked pomposity that Lovecraft tried to disguise with a clumsy humor. Abnormal discourse is constituted from discourses that do not cohere, that contradict each other; we must not, therefore, expect coherence of Lovecraft.

Not being able to put bits of knowledge into proportion can also lead to a stubborn insistence upon the correctness of a part of that knowledge. Lovecraft's story of a conflict with a history teacher in high school has a number of consequences: "He asked me what the native races of Europe were, and I told him Caucasian and Mongolian. That last didn't suit him, and he began to tell me that *Asia* was the only home of the Mongol. Then I reminded him of the *Lapps,* and of the original stock, at least, of the Finns, Magyars, and Turks. He was doubtful, but slowly began to see the light; and was afterward the most affable of beings" (*MF* 582–83). Imagine the poor teacher who is trying to build up knowledge from the textbook in front of him, only to be confronted with the details of Huxley from the student! The student, moreover, is energized by his emotional investment in the word *Mongol* which will become a part of his rhetorical equipment in the stories—and Lovecraft is telling this story some twenty-five years after the fact, in part as a justification of those stories and their racism. His being correct is disproportionate to the structure of knowledge at that point in the high school cursus and disproportionate to the objectivity of knowledge upon which he is so insistent in his letters, articles, and stories.

Several consequences follow from this pitted narrowness of knowledge. Not to be taken for what you would is daunting, since no one can understand your frames of reference—your allusions are arcane to the general public. It is often difficult to communicate with other people. Is this a part of the problem that Edmund Wilson had with Lovecraft, that Lovecraft was "not a member" of the intellectual community? Wilson's aesthetics—and thereby his implied community—are not simple. First, he assumes a decorum of the genres. If well done, mysteries and horror stories are acceptable as fairy-tales, literature "on a humble but not ignoble level" as he says of the Sherlock Holmes tales (267) but certainly not of equal rank with the novel. Second, he believes that works should be modern, incorporating or in dialogue with the development of literature in the twentieth century; he is a historicist in his judgments without being vulgarly political. Cutting across these criteria, however, he demands that prose be realistic, concise (in this aspect he has reservations about Joyce), and precise without being recherché; he upholds a decorum of vocabulary and style. In addition, he often appeals to such terms as the imagination and humanity of a work (cf. 407–8), but in such a way that we may suspect some unconscious mystification, an argument for taste; no author can fulfill these criteria mechanically.

Now as far as these criteria concern Lovecraft, he certainly has problems with the notion that humanity has priority in the world; and he disagrees with an emphasis upon the assumptions of the realist novel, desiring to write a work that would to a certain extent mask itself as a work not of the twentieth century, and he certainly disagreed with Wilson's decorum of style. His exotic vocabulary functions as a sign of abnormal discourse, of breakthrough, with the slippage and waste to be expected of a language in conflict with itself; it does not function as a vehicle of communication and decorum, the marks of normal discourse, a language content with itself. Lovecraft cannot justify his vocabulary to Wilson, and neither can anyone who has been moved by his stories. On the other hand, as the 1920s gave way to the 1930s Lovecraft came to agree with a number of these criteria. He used fewer and fewer items of the eldritch vocabulary; and increasingly he narrated a story, as Wilson preferred, "with the prosaic objectivity of an anecdote of travel" (289), though his use of normal discourse to characterize his professors is something of a set-up as it reveals its own insufficiency in situations where only an abnormal discourse is possible. Perhaps Wilson's most telling insight was that Lovecraft "rightly regarded himself as an amateur" (289), for Lovecraft was always grateful to the amateur journalists who were a vital part of his education as he left behind the self-absorption of his early years. The amateur movement was the first social group whose language he had to learn in order to develop his skills as a stylist, debater, and imaginative author. Such subcultures are the sort of thing Lovecraft allows Drs. Peck, Waite, and Lyman to imagine when they ascribe the young Charles Dexter Ward's friendship with the elusive Allen to "the tendency of kindred eccentrics and monomaniacs to band together" (*CF* 2.322)—the sort of groups Lovecraftians are liable to form today.

Two further points are useful to make about the community that Wilson represented and Lovecraft's relation to it. Wilson had read widely through most of the major and minor works of post-renaissance fiction, widely enough that he could appreciate Lovecraft's judgment in "Supernatural Horror in Literature." In preference to simplicity, therefore, Wilson emphasizes the complexity of a work, to such an extent that when writing about Gilbert and Sullivan's operettas he can surrender his demand for complexity in favor of a balanced judgment about their complementary virtues in *Pinafore,* the balance of that apparently simple work (363). But Lovecraft's work is not about balance; though to a certain extent he could mime urbanity, it was an urbanity that he had learned from the eighteenth century, into which he could not allow the style of the twentieth century to intrude. He resembles Joseph Curwen, eagerly researching the century in which he finds himself but never quite convincing us that he belongs. The second point is that Wilson had constructed a theory of horror fiction. According to him it represents a "longing for mystic experience which seems always to manifest itself in periods of social confusion" (173); and to this extent we might agree that a deep cause of Lovecraft's fiction, so deep that it lay hidden to Wilson's gaze, was the failure of his family's fortunes and his sense that his New England was being invaded by cultures inimical to its life. In addition, Wilson believed that horror functions to "inoculate" us against our terror at "the real horrors loose on the earth," especially the horrors of totalitarian aggression, to "soothe us with the momentary illusion" that psychic terror can be domesticated as "a mere dramatic entertainment" (173); in this regard we must doubt whether Lovecraft understood the totalitarian threat[1] or believed, except when insisting that he was a gentleman, that he was writing mere entertainment. But Wilson also believes in the possibility that "first-rate modern writers" exist—Hawthorne, Poe, Gogol, Melville, Conrad, James, Stevenson, Kipling, de la Mare, and Kafka—who succeed through "probing psychological caverns" in which the restrictions of contemporary life "have engendered disquieting obsessions" (175). This is the kind of judgment with which Lovecraft might have agreed, but he saw the necessity of escape in more general terms: he desired the escape from space and time, not from the daily toothbrush. And he had his own canon that was both larger and narrower. Wilson's community was Eurocentric (46), Lovecraft's Anglophilic; but this aspect of Lovecraft's community was very much a mask that defined his opposition to contemporary America.

Wilson's community would never admit Lovecraft as a member, regarding him as an entertainer who did not know his own business. He was simple-minded, politically naive, stylistically maladroit, culturally narrow, with no interest in the pressures of living a human life. And though he claimed to be a gentleman, his anti-Semitism had none of the suave cultural or religious pretensions of Eliot that worked so insidiously during the 1930s. To describe Wilson's community negative-

---

1. Lovecraft did, however, believe that Bolshevism was a threat, supported unconsciously by people of "substantial achievement" such as Edmund Wilson (*CE* 5.87).

ly, it is interesting to see how little his collection *Classics and Commercials,* the collection in which he damned Lovecraft, had to say about Addison and Steele, Pope, or any figure of the eighteenth century except Swift and Johnson; and when Wilson discussed ancient authors, the Greeks rather than the Romans concern him. Wilson, of course, was too curious, combative, eccentric to be typical of anything; he resembled the autodidact we shall later describe who undoes his institutional education and reconstructs himself from its fragments. But whereas Wilson was indeed a member of the literary community, often as an adversary, Lovecraft was a pure autodidact which that community could never admit into its midst out of the conviction that he had nothing it wished to hear. And sometimes Lovecraft realized his exclusion. In a letter to Frank Belknap Long in 1931 he wrote:

> We cannot hope to create realistic literature, but must specialize in the literature of imaginative escape, properly tempered with as much of realism as we *can* achieve. We must be the laureates—if of anything—of other circumscribed persons like ourselves . . . that element in society to whom very little happens, but whose imaginations are sensitive to reach wistfully outward wishing that something might happen. If we try to handle life with a greater assumption of experience & sophistication we shall merely make fools or pathetic spectacles of ourselves. (*SL* 3.331)

Lovecraft was quite aware of what his fiction might look like to a littérateur like Wilson.

As a consequence of being excluded, the autodidact is often maladroit, clumsy, socially and bodily inept since he or she misunderstands, almost insists upon misunderstanding, the frames of reference of others. Misunderstanding may become an act of aggression, an increasingly willful exercise in self-segregation since the autodidact does come, through various experiences of the limits that society draws, to perceive those mores that constitute society. Misunderstanding may also become an unconfessed defense. For instance, since Lovecraft shares much of the literary background of Eliot, we must believe that his misunderstanding of Eliot was almost willful, whereas his misunderstanding of Joyce is comprehensible since he did not share Joyce's background in turn-of-the-century narrative.

Granted all these difficulties, autodidacticism has one great advantage, the self-confidence that flows from an area that the autodidact knows. Lovecraft recounted in 1933 a confrontation with an algebra teacher

> who found fault with methods of solving problems, even when correct, if the steps did not agree with his own. He *might* have tried to 'ride' me (he especially disliked me because my methods were unorthodox) if I had not brought him up short the first time he became really offensive; but as it was, I was able to force a showdown—a blackboard demonstration of the actual correctness (which he wanted to deny by forestalling proof) of my method. (*MF* 582)

But later in the letter Lovecraft confessed that mathematics, at least algebra, "repelled and exhausted" him, and he regretted his failure because of his interest in astronomy (*MF* 583).

With these general remarks in mind, let us turn to "The Outsider," Lovecraft's classic story of the autodidact. The career of the protagonist falls into four parts: the education that the Outsider receives; the process by which the protagonist realizes the social consequences of that education; the degree to which the protagonist accepts and does not accept that realization; and the discovery of the protagonist that education, to be fruitful and compelling, must be circular.

What kind of education has it been? In the second sentence of the story the protagonist asserts, "Wretched is he who looks back upon lone hours in vast and dismal chambers with brown hangings and maddening rows of antique books" (*CF* 1.265). The third paragraph is more explicit: "I fantastically associated [bones and skeletons] with every-day events, and thought them more natural than the coloured pictures of living beings which I found in many of the mouldy books. From such books I learned all that I know. No teacher urged or guided me, and I do not recall hearing any human voice in all those years—not even my own; for although I had read of speech, I had never thought to try to speak aloud" (266). The Outsider is within the national tradition of the American Adam, "miraculously free of family and race" (Lewis 41). Certainly miraculous is the claim that books taught him all he knew, for the ability to read is a social ability; we learn to read, just as we learn to talk, within the circuit of others. But Lovecraft claimed that he was "at the age of two . . . familiar with the alphabet from my blocks & picture-books" (*RK* 63); and he had the mythic support of Tarzan who learned to read from the picture books left in his parents' tree-house. Tarzan is a counter-myth to our belief that learning can take place only within a social context—an air myth, we might say, as opposed to a ground myth. But what are we to make of the complete solitary? Is there any possibility that such an individualized person could exist? Does such a person only come to life through conflict and ridicule, as Werner Herzog claimed in his 1975 film of Kaspar Hauser, *Jeder für Sich und Gott gegen Alle?* Frankenstein's monster learned from a family upon whom he eavesdropped; Mowgli had the wolves. But we might say of the autodidact that his community is within, that he holds dialogue with the texts he has read. But with whom does the isolated child hold dialogue? With the archetypes, in Hillman's psychology with the continual drama of the polytheistic being whose very self is one among many of the decentered actors (24–27, 38–42)? In a short passage Buber suggests that already in the womb the baby is striving for dialogue and once born is holding dialogue with its surroundings, the boiling teakettle for instance; and to account for this perception he postulates an inborn Thou which every individual already addresses, one which the later Thous incarnate (31, 76); and later he suggests, in a passage not distant from Hillman, that thought begins not in the empirical self but in "der Genius, der mit mir intendierte Geist, das Bild-Selbst" [the genius, the Spirit occupied with me, the Image of the Self] (178). But the first palpable Thou is the enveloping mother. Tarzan has two mothers, the human Lady Alice Clayton and the ape Kala; he is actuated by love, the beast's and the lady's, each holding a continual dialogue upon his being. Lovecraft, we shall discover, is holding dialogue upon himself as a Puritan and as a Cavalier. Perhaps he took seriously the protagonist of "The Tomb" who claims that no creature can live alone, but lacking the fellowship of the living "draws upon the companionship of things that are not, or are no longer, living" (*CF* 1.39).

No autodidact, however, leaves this solitude undistorted. Many autodidacts will remember how odd as children their pronunciation was of certain words; few people in the rush of learning refer to the dictionary for the sake of correctness. And style is often as antique as the age of the books one reads, not a part of the currency of the larger society. The books become the occasion for another mistake, one about the self: "My aspect was a matter equally unthought of, for there were no mirrors in the castle, and I merely regarded myself by instinct as akin to the youthful figures I saw drawn and painted in the books" (*CF* 1.266–67). If style is the man, the protagonist does not realize that the youthful style of a former age seems merely quaint to the contemporary world. Lovecraft did refer to a dictionary, but in a conscious act of dissociation from the society outside his family's walls not to Webster, not to the American lexicographer drawing a line between England and revolutionary America, but to Dr. Johnson: he went to a different time and a different place.

But education is very dependent upon the learner's motives. In the fourth paragraph the protagonist remembers dreaming "for hours about what [he] read in the books; and would longingly picture [himself] amidst gay crowds in the sunny world beyond the endless forest" (*CF* 1.267). The desire for light and social gaiety becomes a motif of the story, for once arrived in the upper world the protagonist is "determined to gaze on brilliance and gaiety at any cost" (269). The windows of the castle are "ablaze with light and sending forth sound of the gayest revelry" (270); the people inside are "speaking brightly" (270), their wit and knowledge the source of their own light. But in the conclusion the narrator has learned "that light is not for me, save that of the moon over the rock tombs of Neb, nor any gaiety save the unnamed feasts of Nitokris beneath the Great Pyramid" (272). In contrast to the moon's, the light that he desires and must renounce is the sun's, the illuminating power of the Apollonian power of the intellectual mind symbolized by the pyramid that weighs him down.[2] Dr. Johnson lists three meanings for "Gayety": "cheerfulness, airiness, merriment"; "acts of juvenile pleasure"; and "finery" or "show." Lack of gravity—in both senses—youth, and self-display are involved here: Johnson's definition implies the character's ascent from the heavy downwardness of the place in which it found itself originally; the frequent desires and unconscious assertions of youth; and a self-display that once it becomes a display to itself in the close of the story both betrays the protagonist and is itself brutally disappointed. Johnson is of two minds about "revelry." He notes that it may derive from *reveiller,* to wake, re-awake, or remain awake, or from *reveelen,* to

---

2. As I have already discussed, the desire for light also signifies a variety of epistemological concerns.

loosely rove, as in revel-rout, and this looseness is a quality that he emphasizes in several of his examples. Edward Young, however, uses it with all the disapprobation of his moral sense, speaking through the mouth of the free-thinker: "The sum of man, / Of godlike man! to revel, and to rot" (7.733–34), a passage that foresees how the outsider's innocent desire for revelry shall redound upon him.

Before the protagonist has left his castle he has imagined the light and happiness, the beauty, which he desires. His motive is the desire for beauty that Plato identified with Eros, that remarkable translator and mediator between the human and the divine, between Penury and Resource, inability and ability, emptiness and fullness (*Symposium* 202d–204b).[3] We have no such figure in this story at first, but the protagonist is certainly at work making sense of the tracks of beauty he finds in his books, determined to make sense of the tracks that seem to give him a direction.

So in discussing the protagonist's motives for education we see that he has a goal, as becomes explicit when after passing the river he approaches "what seemed to be my goal," a castle that seems the mirror image of the castle he left beneath the crypt (*CF* 1.269). Is it possible that the goal is dependent upon the origin, which the goal represents as a return to where the creature began, but transformed? Education is seldom linear. We turn back upon ourselves again and again, to discover how far we have come, to hibernate, to gather materials again, to set the past in a new key. And we learn in order to create and find ourselves.

The process of the narrator's education is the next point. The original situation is very difficult to leave, not only physically but personally, for in the first attempt to escape "as I went farther from the castle the shade grew denser and the air more filled with brooding fear; so that I ran frantically back lest I lose my way in a labyrinth of nighted silence" (*CF* 1.267). The farther the narrator travels, the more difficult the way, as though the opposing force were both outside and inside, an inner reluctance pulling him back. Opposing his desire for light, darkness becomes increasingly palpable, an emblem for the way that learning seems to increase our ignorance as we become increasingly aware of the edges of our knowledge. The world so large to the child becomes narrower: "Shades of the prison-house begin to close," writes Wordsworth in his Platonizing ode (l. 68). Something of the same pattern arises as the Outsider climbs the inside of the tower, first on a staircase and then clinging "to small footholds leading upward" (*CF* 1.267). Rather than lighter, as he expected, the place becomes darker, so much that "I fancied that night had come suddenly upon me" (267). In addition, the space seems to transform itself, though the narrator does not remark upon the change: inside of the tower he seems "crawling up that concave and desperate precipice" (267) just before he gains "the roof, or at least some kind of floor" (267). Twice he "tests" and "tries" the limits of this journey, pushing at the world around him (267). The climb prepares the major transformation of what he be-

---

3. Plato's word which I have translated as resource is *poros*, which originally meant ford or road and came also to mean the wherewithal to cross the ford; the inability to cross gives rise to an *aporia*.

lieves to be a tower into a crypt, the upper air into a level landscape lit by the full moon. This process mirrors the process of education, especially an education unsupervised by a mentor. As we reach the edge of our knowledge our progress becomes more difficult and we become increasingly suspicious that an internal transformation is imminent that shall feel like a death of the personality. The Outsider's paranoia is revealed in his supposition that new wings were only added to the castle "to confuse the beholder" (269).

But despite his effort and resentment, and despite his ignorance of "who I was or what I was, or what my surroundings might be," he does "become conscious of a kind of fearsome latent memory that made my progress not wholly fortuitous" (*CF* 1.269). Among the many ways we might understand this passage, the most ready to hand is Plato's doctrine of anamnesis. Our recognition of the Platonic reference, in fact, makes us reconsider the events at the top of the tower, the difficulty and release the protagonist experiences, for they are examples of the *aporia* which forms a crucial moment in dialectic learning, what Robert Cushman calls "the Socratic trauma, the induced shock" and "the 'crackingup' of presumption" (21, 50). This is the unsettling moment of transition between normal and abnormal discourse. *Aporia,* often translated as "perplexity" or "confusion," quite literally implies an inability to cross a ford, a loss of road, a cul de sac or a running out of the road; the directionality of the road is no longer there to reassure a traveler. Because the road has run out, the *aporia* forces the traveler to go elsewhere, just as the puzzlement and sense of impoverishment that precedes the *eureka* forces the thinker to change perspective or framework; within its own terms the *aporia* is indecidable. In the *Republic,* faced by such an inability to think, a speaker feels like a person playing checkers who cannot make a move (487c). In the *Euthyphro* it seems as though the words of an argument were moving in a circle or set free to move at random, words which should stay in one place—the art of Daedalus in making statues that move creates vertigo (11b–e). In *Theaetetus* Socrates compares the *aporia* to his role as a midwife who in midlabor inspects whether the child is healthy or not, real or a phantasm, in order to abort the child or deliver it; the *aporia* that confronts us in the birth canal is a question of life and death and only follows much labor (149a–151c). In the *Sophist* the *aporia* feels shameful and demands a purification or a purging; the only solution is an enema. The *aporia* involves an ultimate intimacy in the blocking and unblocking of the person (230b–e). And thus the Outsider uses imagery that suggests an urgent birth of the self as it suffers the constriction and turning round of the self at the top of the tower and a birth, upon which he discovers a wholly new direction, but one that feels like one once known.

In the *Meno* a very different image for the *aporia* is used. The person being questioned suffers a state of numbness that resembles death; it is as though he has been stung by an electric ray or as though he had swallowed a pharmakon very like the nepenthe mentioned at the end of "The Outsider" (80a–b), the significance of which we have already discussed earlier. The only solution for the difficulty in this dialogue, the only way to escape this death-like state, is by sinking further into the self and encouraging the narcolepsis and vertigo further, because all learning according to Plato is a remembering of what has been learned in a past life or in the house of Hades (81c–d). This is the myth raised at the conclusions of both the *Apology* and the *Republic*, the return to the underworld for ultimate knowledge. *Aporia* sets the learner outside every assumption, even the assumption of life, at the least life as we know it, and so true learning feels like death.

If we learn in order to create and find ourselves, the scene in the upper world castle models that individuation as the crowd flees—whether from him the protagonist does not yet dare to imagine. But their flight is extreme. As he enters the room "there descended upon the whole company a sudden and unheralded fear of hideous intensity, distorting every face and evoking the most horrible scream from nearly every throat. Flight was universal" (*CF* 1.270). It appears to the autodidact that his arrival in society occasions an explosion of movement away, as though like a spinning wheel he were the center of a centrifugal force whose cause is opaque; once more we must recall the circular motion that an autodidact suffers. At the same instant as the society disperses, he trembles "at the thought of what might be lurking near me unseen" (270); he is left alone to the thought that someone else is at hand, as though the other were not there until the isolation became apparent— as it was not earlier when he had so desired but not experienced light and gay revelry. Isolation and the other, the mystery of the one and the two, materialize out of the flight, though the creation of the other, the image of the Thou, seems to precede self-creation.

What is the protagonist to make of this isolation and otherness? First, though in great tension with it, so much so that we can hardly say he accepts it, he nevertheless acts as though a part of him confessed that he is a ghoul, a creature who constitutes itself from the dead parts of the past, and that there are other ghouls with which he can live, a micro-society proud to differentiate itself from the macro-society. He does have the light of the moon, which did not shine in the underworld of the uneducated soul and which he shares with "the mocking and friendly ghouls" in "unnamed feasts" (*CF* 1.272). It is not difficult to believe that Lovecraft's friends in the amateur press associations were happy to identify themselves in this account, though it seems to suggest that their activities are ultimately barren. We cannot help but believe, on the other hand, that the tension between the larger and the smaller societies, critical and devouring, may become productive.

The impact of this story, however, depends on the protagonist's confession that he is an outsider; even more, according to the title of the story, he is *the* Outsider, "a stranger in this century and among those who are still men" (*CF* 1.272). In a fashion that exceeds the figure of the ghoul considered within the weird genre simply as a conventional sign of alienage, he is not human, whether we are to say that he is more than human, less, or other. Autodidacticism gives birth to the ability to reflect upon the human state, a distance, irony, and pathos, the ability to recognize in a way that anyone inside light and society cannot how valuable it is to be filled with light and society and to recognize precisely how far that state reaches.

Such a recognition is painful, and nothing assuages the pain.

Nothing assuages the pain. Education is circular, especially for the autodidact forced to reflect upon his education. The Outsider discovers after his flight from the castle that he will always be re-approaching the moment of his intuition, that crucial and definitive as it had seemed it does not in fact possess a limit, and that he is condemned as a learning creature to continue to probe that moment and its limitlessness. Like the Ancient Mariner he discovers that at an uncertain hour the compulsion to replay his story overcomes him.

In noting the circularity of education we raise again Plato's notion of education, but in order to confess that the dialectic may have another effect, different from that which it exercises on the beloved, for Plato does not always present his mentor probing the consciousness of young men like Lysis. He also questions antagonists who without quite realizing it are held up to satire and ridicule. Frequently people in authority, they have ears to hear and cannot hear; normal discourse is sufficient to their needs. What then of the Outsider? As we saw, he is not raised by people who love him. Is he, then, an object of ridicule? Yes, in part. His style, for instance, is ridiculous, an instable mixture of Johnson and Poe from which Lovecraft felt compelled to distance himself.

But the primary impulse of this circularity is love, the energy behind and within motion, coming and going, desire, and speech. Love is involved in Lovecraft's difficulty and shame at repeating the patterns of Johnson and Poe, authors he loved. Having read only the poorest Latin translation of parts of Plato, Dante understood this pattern:

> I, who now bid you on this errand forth,
> Am Beatrice; from a place I come
> Re-visited with joy. Love brought me thence,
> Who prompts my speech. (*Inferno* 2.70–73)

The passage proposes a dynamic pattern echoed in the last lines of the *Commedia:*

> But yet the will rolled onward, like a wheel
> In even motion, by the love impelled,
> That moves the sun in heaven and all the stars.
> (*Paradiso* 33.133–35)

If we think of the *Commedia* as a course of instruction involving a series of advances and returns within a complex pattern of circular and helical motions, with several moments of *ébranlement* and oblivion, even in the final canto, we recognize another aspect of what happens to the Outsider at the conclusion of his story. He comes to a castle that reminds him of something—and it does not. Self-exiled from it, he finds he cannot return to the castle he had deserted. And like Dante when he looked into the three-fold rainbow and saw Jesus, "For I therein, methought, in its own hue / Beheld our image painted" (*Paradiso* 33.120–21), the Outsider becomes an interpreter of the ineffable moment in which he realizes that the face he saw in the mirror is his.

As we come to the conclusion of the story we notice that it is here that the creature claims to be an outsider—outside his century, outside the castle above, and outside the castle below. But how did Lovecraft understand the word? Dr. Johnson is silent on the matter. According to the *Oxford English Dictionary* the word first appears in 1800, when Jane Austen refers in a letter to six people not taking part in the whist table; an outsider does not take part. In 1852 the word appears with a broader semantic range, "one who is outside of or does not belong to a specified company, set, or party, a non-member; hence, one unconnected or unacquainted with a matter, uninitiated into a profession or body having special knowledge, or the like." It is as though it were impossible to be an outsider before society had arrived at a sufficiently specialized state of organization. An outsider is a social phenomenon, not a chronological or ontological one, as the narrator of the story seems to insist.

But there are other possibilities. Partridge notes that in 1870 the word means "a person unfit to mix with good society." It is not simply a question of any society, this or that, from which the outsider feels excluded; it is a question of class; and not inappropriate to this consideration is the meaning of a horse that has long odds against it, not considered likely to win the race, though outsiders do win on occasion. The protagonist of "The Outsider" does not approach just any society but the society of a castle, the upper class of a hierarchical society that finds his presence not only unfit but shocking and shattering; they flee him as though his presence had shattered the coherence of their society. As though he had a revolutionary impact upon the society that he had hoped to enter, the Outsider destroys the race that he had hoped to run. But we must add another connotation of which Owen Barfield reminds us: an outsider displays "caddishness, or original genius, according to the context" (35). Because Barfield's qualification prevents our deciding which side of the possible meanings the word will settle on, "outsider" is capable of meaning either "a person unfit to mix with good society" or a person who considers the space he occupies the only proper space. Donald R. Burleson has shown how the Outsider becomes an insider, and an outsider once again, in a dialectical movement (*Lovecraft* 60–61). R. W. B. Lewis discovered in his analysis of Melville that this dialectic forms an important moment in the fate of the American Adam who unlike European outsiders appears "morally *prior* to the world which nonetheless awaits [him]; as between [him] and the world, it can be questioned who is outside of whom" (128–29). An individual is outside only what he or she perceives as the inside, in the case of Lovecraft's protagonist the inside of the castle that is above ground, the upper castle, a community constituted out of the texts he projected upon it. But from the viewpoints of Partridge, Barfield, Burleson, and Lewis the meaning of "outsider" assumes the indecidable shape of Freud's *unheimlich* and Todorov's fantastic; and this restless nature of the character is one of the sources of its pathos.

We return to the question with which we began: "What is the Outsider's community, with whom does he hold dialogue, whom does he address as thou, who loves him, whom does he love?" But we know the answer: the eyes in the mirror that disgust him.

II

> As Arcturus passes over my smoke-hole
> the excess electric illumination
> is now focussed
> on the bloke who stole a safe he cdn't open (Pound, *The Cantos* 465)

Born only five years before Lovecraft, Ezra Pound illustrates our point that an autodidact need not lack an institutional education, for Pound's career upon arriving in Europe became a slow repudiation of what he had learned and a self-education in what he considered necessary to learn. But his education had been erratic. After two dame schools he entered public school when he was nine (Carpenter 22–26). For secondary education he attended a military academy but does not seem to have graduated; after two years at the University of Pennsylvania he finished his undergraduate life at a private college and returned to Pennsylvania for graduate work (33–58), although he never completed a degree for that work, a failure that rankled so much that in 1920 he tried to receive an honorary degree and in 1932 tried to submit a group of translations for a thesis, both times to no avail, and his rage at the institution for its refusal indicates the degree to which he felt that he was an outsider, an autodidact (Torrey 36–37). At least as important for him were three summers in 1898, 1902, and 1906 that he spent in Europe with a sophisticated aunt. Though he received the college education that Lovecraft yearned for, it would be saying too much to claim that Pound was a product of public education. Except for his verbal dexterity, in fact, much of this education seems to have been devoted to learning as little of normal discourse as possible; his grades were indifferent. And like Lovecraft he spoke in that odd mixture of slang and pomposity that tries to shield itself behind a forced humor.

There are other similarities. Both men were abstemious (Carpenter 73). Both men relied on the power of the rational mind to resolve social hypocrisies. Both men were descendents of old New England families, Pound being related to the Wadsworths, with a grandfather who was a congressman for three terms during the Gilded Age (Torrey 18–19). Both men were disillusioned with democracy. Exclaiming his antique prayer, "God save the King," Lovecraft flirted preposterously with the language of treason, while Pound drifted closer and closer to the indictment for treason from which he was only saved by the presumption of madness; but Lovecraft came to a solidarity with the rest of America during the Depression and appreciated immensely the architect of the New Deal.

And they were anti-Semites. Both Pound and Lovecraft, in the process of their self-education, fell victims to the danger of a violent imbalance. But what is the weakness that left them open to this temptation? It is odd that on this point their biographers fail us; for though they can point to the general atmosphere of anti-Semitism throughout Europe and America in the latter half of the nineteenth century, they seem unable to account for the virulence of Pound's and Lovecraft's language (Carpenter 359–62; de Camp 92–93; *IAP* 112–14). In addition, Pound and Lovecraft use different rationalizations, which we are liable to accept as explanations: for Pound the sore point was financial, his belief that the purity of exchange had been attainted—his biographer E. Fuller Torrey suggests that Pound was in part moved by the extent to which he identified with the financial landscapes of his grandfather and father (131–32); for Lovecraft the sore point was cultural, the fear of assimilation, and the smell—and we may pity the fastidiousness of his habits that so much inhibited him, which the selectivity of his style in part symbolizes. The virulence of the language, however, overpowers all rationalizations and explanations, so that the reader can see no argument behind the torrent of hatred, fear, and loathing. Without in any way suggesting an explanation, that moment in which Lizst realized that Wagner's anti-Semitic rant had the very wide meaning of a generic language (Watson 130) illustrates the problem with Lovecraft and Pound. For both of them the social acceptability of anti-Semitism became the occasion, the mere occasion, through which a pathology could be released, a pathology that remains obscure in part because of the weaknesses to which an autodidact is prone. This pathology harmed Pound's poems in a way that it could not harm Lovecraft's stories, for there is one great artistic difference between them: that despite his critical acumen Pound's poetry, especially *The Cantos,* became increasingly narrow and disfigured by a small range of political and aesthetic doctrines that form the explicit themes of the work, whereas Lovecraft's stories exhibit an increasingly spacious sanity, ceaselessly inventive within the narrow range of each story's purpose and materials.

Pound's case highlights another quality of several autodidacts, remarkable given such weaknesses, the temptation to become teachers themselves. William Carlos Williams became Pound's first, slightly ironic disciple (Carpenter 41), then a group of freshmen while he was still an undergraduate (56), finally the modernists and, he thought, the American troops. Lovecraft assumed the role of teacher first in high school (*IAP* 124–25), then among the amateur movement (165). For all their charm, this is the impulse of many of Lovecraft's letters: the instruction of a correspondent often considerably younger than he, especially toward the end of his life. Not that we should think of Lovecraft in his letters as a dogmatist; he is often trying on ideas, exploring them through the act of writing. This impulse also fulfills itself in a few of the stories as he incorporates utopian elements into "The Mound," *At the Mountains of Madness,* and "The Shadow out of Time," stories in the last phase of his career, as though only during the Depression could pedagogy justify itself within a fictional world.

But how many of his characters are teachers? Not his autodidacts, interestingly. His teachers are the representatives of the institutions that he was not able to enter. It is as though his autodidacts were not to be trusted, whereas the Professors

Angell, Armitage, Wilmarth, Upton, Dyer, and Peaslee, though they learn a number of facts that their science cannot account for, are the only characters capable of recognizing and organizing that knowledge in an effective fashion. But professors are autodidacts in this sense, that after they have devoted years to an institutional process the institution at last licenses them to be autodidacts, to do research; professors are expected, as Bruffee says, "to maintain established knowledge" and, in addition, "to challenge and change it" (650), although research is only proper research when it is done according to the rules of normal discourse. A dynamic tension that may be irresolvable exists both within the teacher and between the teacher and the student, a tension measured by the extent to which normal and abnormal discourses are being employed, a tension to which we must be alert as we read Lovecraft.

This tension between normal and abnormal discourse as far as the teacher is concerned takes another form for Northrop Frye. If one of the tasks of the teacher is to break up "the power of repression in [the student's] mind that keep him from knowing what he knows" (xv), then the questions and more important the answers of the teacher must be elusive and ironic, riddling at times. The reticence of the teacher exists to provoke thought in the student, a reticence that may at certain moments be frustrating for both the teacher and the student: The best thou learnest, in the end / Thou can'st not tell the youngsters" (Goethe, *Faust* 62).[4] The attitude Mephistopheles reveals in these lines becomes an apparent arrogance that in his second confrontation with the student appears purely aggressive; he toys with the older youth who now believes that in Fichte he knows it all, because he has swiftly converted the abnormal discourse of the transcendentalist into a normal discourse. Yet in both these scenes the teacher, an odd combination of Mephistopheles and Goethe, also displays a tenderness for the young man. It is best for the student that certain questions should not be answered, for, as Frye concludes, "to answer a question . . . is to consolidate the mental level on which the question is asked. Unless something is kept in reserve, suggesting the possibility of better and fuller answers, the student's mental advance is blocked" (xv). In addition, it is something of a puzzle for the teacher which questions should not be answered; such a puzzle depends on the teacher being alert to the possibility that the answers he or she has offered in the past may not really be viable. The teacher must, on occasion, abstain from answers, abstain from clarity. Normal discourse is full; abnormal discourse is characterized by gaps, elusiveness, incomplete metaphors, and silence. We should not be surprised, then, if our questions about the Outsider are sidetracked or defeated upon occasion; such a fate is part of the task that the story takes upon itself.

In exploring the role of higher education in the stories we confront what de Camp and Joshi agree was a crisis of Lovecraft's life, his failure to attend college

---

4. Freud was fond of these lines, alluding to them at various points in *The Interpretation of Dreams* (175, 491) when he refers to the difficulty of overcoming repression.

(de Camp 51; *LAP* 126–27). But the reasons for his failure remain obscure. Was his health the reason, or was it an intellectual failure, his inability to master advanced mathematics? The objective reason was his failure to graduate from high school; the public institution of American democratic life could not certify that he belonged. Rosemary Chapman's comment on the role of primary and secondary schools in French life in the first half of this century is all the more true of secondary and advanced schools in American life:

> While the function of primary education was to inculcate civic and nationalist values, that of secondary education was to provide the nation with its cultural elite.... Those who could not afford secondary education were therefore not only excluded from the social and economic life of the bourgeoisie, but also from the culture which the dominant class controlled. (85)

In this regard Lovecraft was no Ezra Pound, just as he was no Edmund Wilson; in Providence before the Great War an autodidact was a person unable to enter college. And despite a variety of rationalizations, he acknowledged that he had failed. His several idealizations of college in the stories always lay beyond him. So in examining the stories we take up the ironies active in the relations of the college and the outside world and the relations of the teacher and the pupil.

An early story, "The Alchemist," contains details that shall recur even in so late a story as "The Thing on the Doorstep": an alienation from the protagonist's parents so strong that it forms the key of the plot as a curse through which every male member of the family dies at the age of thirty-two; a wizard searching for the mysteries of life, "such things as the Philosopher's Stone, or the Elixir of Eternal Life" (*CF* 1.29), and his child whose life after the parent's death is devoted to justifying the parent; an isolation of the protagonist so extreme that it results in a sexual anxiety, for as the narrator insists, "Upon one thing I was absolutely resolved. I should never wed" (31); the triumph of the antagonist over death; and finally, that detail important for us, the autodidacticism of the protagonist. With no parents, raised by a servant who excludes him from the society of other children, Antoine "spent the hours of [his] childhood in poring over the ancient tomes that filled the shadow-haunted library of the chateau, and in roaming without aim or purpose through the perpetual dusk of the spectral wood" (27–28). This pattern, a devotion to books and to the ancient neighborhood, will mark most of the autodidacts Lovecraft portrays, even the Outsider. And, as usual, the studies concern "the dark and occult in Nature" (28). In addition, the autodidact's parents are consistently pallid, only defined through their library, or absent; their love is automatic or purely notional.

In the second paragraph of another early story, "The Tomb," the narrator identifies himself as an autodidact: "Wealthy beyond the necessity of a commercial life, and temperamentally unfitted for the formal studies and social recreations of my acquaintances, I have dwelt ever in realms apart from the visible world; spending my youth and adolescence in ancient and little-known books, and in roaming the fields and groves of the region near my ancestral home" (*CF* 1.39). He believes the ancient books and the neighborhood of his home equal in influence in his education. But he is fairly specific about some of the texts that have formed him. Perhaps most important is Plutarch's *Lives,* but others are Virgil, whose line from the *Aeneid* forms the motto, Chesterfield and Rochester, and "f the sprightliest of the Augustan wits and rimesters" (45). But except for Plutarch and Virgil, these authors are not by implication the authors Dudley reads; instead, they are the authors that Hyde reads, the man whose spirit has possessed Dudley; Dudley has learned them only at second hand.

Dudley learns another work from Hyde, the lyric sung at the height of his possession, "an effusion of eighteenth-century Bacchanalian mirth; a bit of Georgian playfulness never recorded in a book" (*CF* 1.45–46). But though never recorded, it resembles a song familiar to Lovecraft (*IAP* 448), "To Anacreon in Heaven," the model for "The Star-Spangled Banner." The resemblance is not perfect; Lovecraft's poem begins with two couplets rather than a quatrain (in this regard the stanza resembles John Gay's "Newgate's Garland"), but the meters are the same, anapestic tetrameter, concluding in the internal rhyme of the fifth line which forms a couplet with the sixth line and ignoring the last couplet of the anthem that forms a refrain.[5] It is surely a piquant triumph for Lovecraft to subvert American pretensions and retrieve British frivolity. On the other hand, the possessor Hyde has felt the thunder that the original song defied: "Your thunder is useless," a triumphant Apollo sang to Jove (Sonneck 21). But this song and its tension with the belligerent anthem it became reveal a further tension in the story. Dudley's descent into the consciousness of Hyde triggers a multitude of voices, among them "the uncouth syllables of the Puritan colonists" (*CF* 1.44), voices surely at odds with the voice of the Cavalier sensibility. In this discovery of his connection or identity with a stronger personality from the past, this apparently upper-middle-class protagonist reveals the tension between the Puritan and the Cavalier implicit in "The Outsider" and several other of Lovecraft's works. Lovecraft presents hypothetical father figures who are Cavaliers or outlaw Puritans—consider the old man in "The Picture in the House." The name Hyde may refer not only to the alter ego in Stevenson's novella but also to the illustrious family that supported the Stuarts throughout the seventeenth century.

Dudley's interest in the tomb when he is ten years old springs from the "mumbled tales of the weird rites and godless revels of bygone years" (*CF* 1.42). Here again we find that word *revel* that proved so potent for the Outsider. In a hendiadys the word appears a page later, after the twenty-one year old has at last entered the tomb: "Early-rising villagers who observed my homeward progress looked at me strangely, and marveled at the signs of ribald revelry which they saw in one whose life was known to be sober and solitary" (*CF* 1.45), a sentence in which the phrase

---

5. Will Murray relates Lovecraft's song to one by Thomas Morton; but fascinating as the historical material is, Morton's song does not have "a like cadence" (Murray, "A Probable Source" 80).

"sober and solitary" is contrasted to "ribald revelry"—ribaldry is not sober, and revelry is not solitary, though a participation in it may lead to looseness and rot. A further variation is "that charnel conviviality" (48) that he enjoys for a week before the catastrophe. The attraction of Hyde's life for the autodidact lies in an escape from consciousness, which is also to say from the normal processes of bodily life, and from a solitary life. In the climax the mansion resembles the castle of "The Outsider," with "every window ablaze with the splendour of many candles" and "a numerous assemblage of powdered exquisites" (49). "Music, laughter, and wine" excite Dudley to "gay blasphemy"(49). But others call this party a "swinish revelry" (49). In this story the Puritan represents Bruffee and Rorty's normal discourse, whereas the Cavalier represents abnormal discourse. Thus by a deft sleight-of-hand Lovecraft has reversed the usual identifications: the revolutionary Puritan has become the conservative devotee of the dead letter, an empty shell of the Reformation's emphasis upon the word, whereas the monarchical Cavalier, who has drunk a bit too much, makes free of a wide breadth of knowledge that points at the largest community. Is it an accident that the ten-year-old Dudley discovers the tomb when "intoxicated with the surging seas" of summer (40)?

Liquor opposes normal discourse, but Lovecraft distrusted liquor. In 1915 in the *Conservative* he wrote, "Liquor attempts to stir the people against the law" (*CE* 5.16), and characterized intemperance as "the most noxious evil of human life," a threat to civilization (17). This is a threat, however, that civilization invites, for Lovecraft felt forced to believe that "human creatures long atavistically for the levity of an inferior state, and wish to throw off artificially the burden of dignity with which evolution from the simian eye has invested them" (28). Two anxieties, then, intertwined in Lovecraft's mind, are at work in his teetotaling: the several nervous episodes that took him out of public education, and the fate of his father. He must have wondered whether drink would worsen any tendency he had to the *déréglement* that Rimbaud expected of the poet, the intoxication that many believed had destroyed Poe. Would a person who has striven so hard for "the burden of dignity" that should be his natural right ever recover from a debauch?

At least two other characters in Lovecraft's stories besides Hyde drink, the narrator of "Pickman's Model" and Zadok Allen in "The Shadow over Innsmouth," both in order to dull and reveal the horror of their stories, masks of the author who needs the topos of drink as a release of imaginative powers. That Lovecraft condemns drink so unconditionally suggests how distrustful he was of the springs of his imagination. Dreams also he distances from his own responsibility through granting them the myth of a quasi-objective world of their own that he visits through Randolph Carter, probably no drinker though certainly a sophisticate. In Lovecraft's world alcohol comes as a powerful release of the imaginative powers that threaten reason and sanity itself. But his own abstinence has another significance: his mother's people, the Baptist Phillipses, were teetotalers, so that in this regard as in others Lovecraft demonstrates against the world, against his own Anglican father, his solidarity with the family that raised him, even while he renounces their religious allegiance.

In *The Case of Charles Dexter Ward* the protagonist discovers like Jervas Dudley that his personality depends upon the stronger personality of a magician from the past. His education repeats the formula we have seen, but expands it in great architectural detail through Ward's roaming of the neighborhood. The narrator barely mentions Ward's regular schooling, but his attendance at the Moses Brown School during his junior and senior years is odd. He had a number of reasons for attending that private school: its situation "very near his home," his zest in "the military training of the period," and the antiquity of the school, with its "old main building, erected in 1819" (*CF* 2.221). Two of these reasons, however, are a bit odd. Though the school was named after a man hurt in the attack on Curwen and thus provides historical continuity between Ward and Curwen, the historical Moses Brown established his school after his conversion to the community of the Friends. Since the school had been a center of Quaker education from its founding, the military training Ward received could not have been very thorough. Perhaps Lovecraft implies that Brown's conversion was a consequence of his encounter with Curwen. Something of an amateur pharmacist, in that regard rather like Curwen, Brown was also an advocate of temperance and a passionate opponent of slavery (Kelsey 29–32)—no Cavalier he! In addition, however old the main building, the "dignified front porch of Colonial style" which might have appealed to the young Ward had been added quite recently (Kelsey 131). Since Brown and the school named for him in 1904 (Kelsey 127) were famous in Rhode Island history, Lovecraft's choice of the school is something of a hoax, a hoax that clings to Ward's education.

The narrator describes Ward's informal education at greater length. The roaming of the woods, so sketchily mentioned in previous stories, gives way to a roaming of the city, first as a child under the ward of his nurse: he passes through the cultural and material expressions of the past which he resurrects through the resurrection of Joseph Curwen. As he grows older he is increasingly drawn to those older parts of the city near the docks where Curwen had directed his ships, now overtaken by "a riot of iridescent decay" and "polyglot vice" (*CF* 2.223–24) or "the crumbling colonial regions northwest of his home, where the hill drops to the lower eminence of Stampers' Hill with its ghetto and negro quarter" (224). He slums through an architectural education in which the beauties of the past are heightened by being overwhelmed in the decadence of the present. By the time of his senior year at Moses Brown, after he learns of the career of Curwen, school has become "a great bore" and he decides "never to bother with college" (158). Instead, after "a none too brilliant graduation" (277), he undertakes a tour of the continent, rushing through England, Paris, Prague, and Vienna to settle at last in Transylvania—not quite the typical tour (284–85). Now he is ready to read Curwen, to devour that text and be devoured by it. His speech becomes a rasping whisper, and he can no longer handle the affairs or the cultural assumptions of the modern world. Perhaps most sadly he has reached a point of saturation with his most beloved subject, for "regarding antique affairs he soon shewed the plainest boredom" (313); a self-education may lead to a dead end, a point beyond which development is not possible, but at which the return to the context of the larger world becomes problematic. There is little more to say of Ward's development, then, except to note that he completely severs his relation to his mother who is sent away before the final catastrophe and must be assured that her son has died (301); all that has happened to him, in fact, is a transformation through the magic of education.

But this novella also concerns the autodidactic career of Ward's ancestor. When Charles first learns of Curwen his ancestor seems a man who "naturally made acquaintances of the better sort, whose company and conversation he was well fitted by education to enjoy," a man of good birth whose "speech . . . was that of a learned and cultivated Englishman" (*CF* 2.230). Later information, however, implies that this behavior is a sham. Born in Danvers and running "away to sea at the age of fifteen," he returned nine years later "with the speech, dress, and manners of a native Englishman and settled in Salem proper," having little to do with his family (265). Much of his career in Providence is devoted to seeming a proper member of society and failing. Ironically, his attempt to seem a proper Englishman becomes a part of the excuse for the increasingly revolutionary society of America to attack him. It is hard not to say that Curwen becomes a political and social model of what Lovecraft attempted half in jest to accomplish in his self-education and devotion to Dr. Johnson's dictionary. But Curwen is also an individual in rebellion against his Puritan origins in Salem, going first to England and then to Rhode Island in order to escape the orthodox provinciality of his childhood. He does not become a Cavalier, but his taste in poetry, the spells that shall raise and lay Yog-Sothoth, is freer than the common measure of the psaltery.

Curwen's advanced course of self-education, however, lies in his raising of the dead to make them confess *ipsissima verba,* as though the texts they wrote were not enough, too distant for the engaged knowledge that he desires, or as though he agreed with the deconstructionists in denying the intent of the author and then in despair tried to consult the author's very self. But Lovecraft sees any number of problems in this self-education. The text may be too powerful; you may not be able to put it down. "Do not calle up That which you can not put downe," Simon Orne warns Curwen (*CF* 2.263), who becomes such a text for his descendant, drawing him into the past and forcing him to raise the dead letter of his ancestor from the grave (364–65). Ward has no defense. A self-critical reading may not be possible for an autodidact, whose situation lays him open to the sort of misreading that Harold Bloom finds so fruitful. Another difficulty is that something other than human may be raised; the power of such a reading may seem other than the same dull round of normal discourse to which humanity is liable, rather as though the Greeks were correct in seeing that the Muses were other than human in their inspiration, seductive, perhaps misleading, certainly daemonic. And there is the difficulty that a self-educated person may not know whom he is reading, what the social background, cultural implications, and self-interest of the texts are.

"Stopp," again warns Orne, "not to be sure when there is any Doubt of *Whom* you have. Stones are all chang'd now in Nine grounds out of 10. You are never sure till you question" (353). But such a questioning may already involve the learner too deeply; the power of the text may already exert itself over the imagination of the learner and begin the process of devouring. Despite these warnings, however, and despite the failure that Curwen had already experienced in 1766, Orne, Hutchinson, and he continue, just as young Ward continued. In the eyes of the elderly Dr. Willett "illustrious bones were bartered with the calm calculativeness of schoolboys swapping books" (326). After two hundred years "these nightmare ghouls" (326) have still not grown up. Though they are not mature, however, they are still young, with the energy and high spirits of youth. Did not Ezra Pound still seem a child when he leaned over the microphone as Uncle Ez? But the adult mind that yearns for youth disintegrates: Pound disintegrates swiftly in the Pisan cage; and Curwen disintegrates swiftly in "a thin coating of fine bluish-grey dust" (366).

One other problem with Curwen's education is made explicit in "The Shunned House," in which the ghoul Etienne Roulet, a Huguenot whose "ardent Protestantism—too ardent, some whispered—" (*CF* 1.465) lead to his ostracism from the community and the death of his son, returns as a hungry presence to absorb so many people that he appears as "a devil and a multitude, a charnel-house and a pageant ... in the caricatured likeness of legions strange and yet not strange" (476). The passage resembles the conclusion of "The Rats in the Walls" in which voices come pouring out of Delapore. In "The Tomb" as he becomes possessed Dudley hears voices in which "every shade of New England dialect ... seemed represented" (*CF* 1.44). The word *legion* refers to the famous moment in the gospel of Mark when a madman says, "My name is Legion, for we are many" (5:9). But besides a multitude the name suggests also the desire of a book-filled autodidact for a coordination of the voices such as a Roman legion possessed, moving as one. The coordination of voices comes part and parcel with the normal discourse that an institutional education provides; an autodidact is forced to allow the voices a conflict within which, with a bit of luck, a new direction shall arise. Palinurus, whose voice forms the fond hope of the motto to "The Tomb"—"sedibus ut saltem placidis in morte quiescam" (38)—finds no such coordination, for falling into the sea and almost safe on land he is killed by an Italian tribe—the empire of Aeneas and Augustus has not yet come to pass—and now welters upon the waves with no burial (*Aeneid* 6.337–83). The shore rejoices in his name, but he does not, as his body in the waters becomes nameless.[6] A coordination of voices is hard to come by.

"The Dunwich Horror" presents three autodidacts who exhibit different as-

---

6. The clause closing the episode, "Gaudet cognomine terra" [the land, not he, rejoices in his name] (6.383), contains so much irony that some manuscripts read, "Gaudet cognomine terrae" [he rejoices in the name of the land].

pects of the patterns we have been considering. Wizard Whateley is such a figure, but we only see him at the end of his career when he is himself almost totally outside his community. The source of his education is exclusively within the family, since he has inherited books "fast falling to pieces with age and worm-hole" (*CF* 2.422). His daughter Lavinia is the next autodidact of the family, "given to wandering amidst thunderstorms in the hills and trying to read" her father's books (422), a difficult task because of her semi-illiteracy and the condition of the volumes. But Lavinia is more successful than her father, in part because of the importance for her of wandering the hills, for apparently on "those domed hills" with their summits "too rounded and symmetrical to give a sense of comfort and naturalness" (418) she has been impregnated by Yog-Sothoth and received a more intimate, unmediated knowledge than her father or her son ever know. She is the Penury who gives birth to the half-human, half-other Eros and who initiates her son into a knowledge of the hills on Hallowe'en: "they darted almost noiselessly through the underbrush, and the astonished watcher seemed to think they were entirely unclothed" (424). In Lovecraft, the roaming of the hills seems a part of the female province of the autodidact, perhaps as close as to be incestuous; the books belong to the conventional image of the male as rational. But after the death of Wizard Whateley the distance that always seems to grow between the autodidact and his family reaches a violent climax when Wilbur comes to despise his mother so thoroughly that he murders her (432).

We may take Wilbur's swift development both as a result of what an individual is capable of when the area of education is circumscribed and as a result of the isolating forces of autodidacticism. More interesting than his development, however, is his voice, "remarkable both because of its difference from the ordinary accents of the region, and because it displayed a freedom from infantile lisping" (*CF* 2.425). But his voice is strange, perhaps because of "his intonation or . . . the internal organs" (425). He becomes taciturn, muttering "an unfamiliar jargon" and chanting "in bizarre rhythms" (427). We have noted that people who learn from books are liable to have a shaky sense of pronunciation, so that their speech becomes evidence of their alienation; the Outsider does not speak at all. The concrete sign of Wilbur's alienation is his confrontation of Armitage: "I calc'late I've got to take that book home. They's things in it I've got to try under sarten conditions that I can't git here, an' it 'ud be a mortal sin to let a red-tape rule hold me up" (435). Confused by the education he has received in Dunwich, Wilbur is not aware how this combination of substandard English—dialect, colloquialism, cliché, earnest innocence, and solecism—justifies Armitage in never allowing the young man into the library again and in warning every research center in New England against him. Wilbur's naive threat, "Maybe Harvard wun't be so fussy as yew be" (435), hardly helps his case. We cannot but think of Lovecraft, whose learning never received the certification he felt that he needed from a college.

The position that Miskatonic University in the person of its librarian takes to Wilbur is not remarkable. Institutional education has an interest in preserving its prerogatives. The *Necronomicon* like many curious books in their cages is under lock and key; it is often only the autodidact who realizes that they exist, just out of reach. Either the institutional student will be ignorant of their existence or concur in the necessity of not reading them, have indeed no interest in reading them. Only the autodidact has the motive to pursue forbidden knowledge and the cleverness to achieve it, a passion that costs Wilbur his life.

This question of advanced institutional learning and self-learning needs to be understood in another fashion. Lovecraft's characters fall into a small number of groups: the autodidacts; the wizard rebels; and the professors. As for his aesthetes, they do not learn a content but a skill that they apply to their intuitions that originate in a place other than the rational mind. Most of the wizard rebels are autodidacts, but so far off the track of human knowledge that this characteristic is almost unrecognizable. But Lovecraft's professors, especially those with connections to Miskatonic University, are autodidacts also. The two exceptions are Dr. Allan Halsey, a secondary character in the second installment of "Herbert West—Reanimator," and Thomas Olney, the protagonist of "The Strange High House in the Mist." Dr. Halsey is a dean at Miskatonic University, one of those men, writes the narrator, who is "the product of generations of pathetic Puritanism; kindly, conscientious, and sometimes gentle and amiable, yet always narrow, intolerant, custom-ridden, and lacking in perspective," one of those people whom time shall punish for such intellectual sins as "Ptolemaism, Calvinism, anti-Darwinism, anti-Nietzscheism, and every sort of Sabbatarianism and sumptuary legislation" (*CF* 1.299). The punishment visited upon Dr. Halsey, after he dies while treating a plague, is to be reanimated by West and incarcerated for sixteen years in an insane asylum after a murderous rampage. Though the story is something of a joke and a self-parody, that very silliness allows Lovecraft to express an animus against professorial conservatism that in later stories will be carefully qualified. Thomas Olney is a similar conservative, who "taught ponderous things in a college by Narragansett Bay" (*CF* 2.89); he is not on the faculty of Miskatonic. In addition, "With stout wife and romping children . . ., his eyes were weary with seeing the same things for many years, and thinking the same well-disciplined thoughts" (89). He only breaks free when "despite a conservative training—or because of it, for humdrum lives breed wistful longings of the unknown—" (90) he decides to climb a cliff and visit the cottage that overlooks the sea. But perhaps because his training does not prepare him for his experience there, whatever of him that returns is a pale shadow of the man who attempted the height: he is absorbed by "the suitable deeds of a citizen" which are a part of the world of generation, in which "his good wife waxes stouter and his children older and prosier and more useful, and he never fails to smile correctly with pride when the occasion calls for it" (95). The exuberance of the natural world, that for which institutional education prepares us, the education of that college on Narragansett Bay, cannot hide the thinness of its meaning and its gratifications. Despite its pretensions to measure the world totally, normal discourse is poor fare that leaves both Dr. Halsey and Dr. Olney unable to defend themselves against ridicule.

Miskatonic University, on the other hand, is graced by such luminaries as professors Armitage, Wilmarth, and Peaslee, men with minds more speculative than Dr. Halsey, and such students as Derby and Gilman, whose areas of specialization are enriched by their dependence upon the alternate knowledge contained in the rare books room of the university's library. Miskatonic represents an institutionalization of autodidacticism. Its education is oxymoronic; it combats itself as it expands. As Bruffee understands the work of the scholar, "to maintain established knowledge and to challenge and change it," to "perform as conservators *and* agents of change" (650), it is an exemplary university. It offers an *ébranlement* of the mind.

A digression is useful here to examine three such *ébranlements* in the institutional context. In "The Whisperer in Darkness" Henry Akeley is a private scholar, "a recluse with very little worldly sophistication" (*CF* 2.474), though "a notable student" in a wide variety of subjects at the University of Vermont (474), whose methodology appeals to Professor Wilmarth, a teacher at Miskatonic University. But Akeley comes to suffer that affliction of the autodidact that hampered Wilbur, a distortion of pronunciation and an ignorance of modern style that leave the individual isolated. Professor Peaslee in "The Shadow out of Time" complains, "Even my speech seemed awkward and foreign. I used my vocal organs clumsily and gropingly, and my diction had a curiously stilted quality, as if I had laboriously learned the English language from books. The pronunciation was barbarously alien, whilst the idiom seemed to include both scraps of curious archaism and expressions of a wholly incomprehensible cast" (*CF* 3.366). Edward Derby at the conclusion of "The Thing on the Doorstep," a young man educated at home but then doing quite well at Miskatonic University, is reduced to uttering, "Glub glub." Something drastically alters speech at this university. Normal discourse becomes abnormal at such a rate that it seems a language that no one ever spoke; it is the language of the largest community, spoken in another time in which past and future are jumbled, projecting an alternate time, but also the language of corruption, the language that is death to the personality to speak. Wilbur Whateley, speaking such a language, is reduced to "a sticky whitish mass" (*CF* 2.441) on the library floor, and the librarians are justified in placing the texts of such a language under severe control. Wilbur does return from his dissolution, however, as his twin brother in whom his tragedy persists, for neither creature can resemble the father fully, both remain objects of lethe, of that which reveals itself only in part. Wilbur, we are assured, showed himself naked only once, with the mother he comes to murder (424).

Both Lavinia and Asenath are under the influence of their wizard fathers and become teachers of the protagonists of the stories, Wilbur Whateley and Edward Derby. Derby, however, is considerably more slack-willed than Wilbur, though Wilbur has an almost non-existent chin. And Asenath, who seems so strong-willed at the beginning of the story, is revealed to have been more than weak-willed before her father possessed her: *"What devilish exchange,"* Derby asks, *"was perpetrated in the house of horror where that blasphemous monster had his trusting, weak-willed, half-human child at his mercy?"* (*CF* 3.341). As for Derby, because of a vague "organic weakness" (325) his parents give him a private education before he enters Miskatonic University, but they "coddled" (325) him and kept him "closely chained to their side" (325), so much so that the narrator calls them "overcareful" and thinks his friend "retarded" in terms of practical life (326) But besides his precocity Derby maintains "a strange, secretive inner life" (325) that is clearly a defense against his parents, a defense necessary in this story as in "The Dunwich Horror" where some parents, the wizard rebels far sunk in abnormal discourse, are such devourers of their children. But a passive defense is not enough, for once he has graduated his writings suffer from "his lack of contacts" by being "derivative and overbookish" (328). By 1933 when he wrote this story Lovecraft had come to criticize acutely the weaknesses his early education had caused.

We learn little of Ephraim as an autodidact except that he had his own books in Innsmouth, though he had also consulted the library at Miskatonic University more successfully than Wilbur Whateley, and that his daughter was "his morbidly avid pupil" (*CF* 3.329). The suggestion of incest between them becomes this story's version of the suggestion of incest between Wilbur and Lavinia. The love that Plato considered necessary for education takes a perverse turn in these stories, revealing that circularity and return may become regression. Wilbur Whateley, who always knew who he was, dies for the sake of his connection with something that is more outside than he is. But first he has to kill his mother and utterly reject the source of his normal discourse. The process by which Edward Derby severs his connections with the past, mediated in his case by several gender confusions, is more obscure than Wilbur's, but the death of his mother and his murder of his wife are no less a sign of his attempt to join the largest community, an attempt that fails as totally as Wilbur's.

Professor Peaslee in "The Shadow out of Time" is perhaps the most remarkable of our autodidacts for he is not at all one at the beginning of his career, which, like Olney's, is the epitome of the institutional. An instructor of political economy he begets punctually a family of three children. But he is struck by the need to re-educate himself when his possession by the largest community turns him away from his specialization to "history, science, art, language, and folklore" (*CF* 3.367), from the pretension of politics as a science to the *Geisteswißenschaften*, which, at this time, Germans such as Dilthey were placing upon a firm basis of hermeneutics. Peaslee speaks of the future, as though that were an unimaginable turn for a professor of that time, consults the college library at all hours, reading those books for which the library is justly famous, and begins a series of "odd travels, and special courses at American and European universities" (367). His conversation indulges itself in "carefully veiled mockery" (368). He is now a driven reader, swift and blessed with an eidetic memory. Though he frightens some people he also becomes capable of charismatic moments when he can "influence the thoughts and acts" of other people (369). So much has he changed from the kind of academic he had been that two years after his transformation his wife divorces him. The only support he has from his family is from his second son, who in time becomes a professor himself in psychology at Miskatonic University, playing Wilbur and Asenath to his wizard father. For Peaslee is indeed an unwilling wizard, a wise man unable to control the irony of his situation through which his growing lore draws him.

This is the first story to suggest that a self-education proceeds in waves, as though the self were in fugue. Peaslee's first period of intense activity occurs between 1908 and 1913, but when he takes up his classes again in 1914 he discovers that "the outbreak of the World War turned [his] mind to history" (*CF* 3.373); perhaps we need to read this remark backwards, as though the public catastrophe were a part of the impulse to self-education, the kind of event that drives a person from normal to abnormal discourse. In this story Lovecraft refers to the Great War to confirm that no one's language can ever be the same, precisely as had such modernists as Pound, Yeats, and Eliot. Peaslee becomes driven inward to a meditation upon his dreams in which he applies to psychology, anthropology, and history as aids in accounting for his experience. The war and his experience of new sorts of knowledge lead him to a self-reflection in which the "fragments of some hideous memory elaborately blotted out" (378), the "perplexing blank" of his mind that he believes "pseudo-memories" (379) are invading, become increasingly obtrusive on his attention. More and more through the jagged nature of his mental experience he becomes aware of his mental experience as a thing in itself, not simply as a medium of experience. For Peaslee the chief subject of the autodidact is the self, as it had been to the Outsider. But thereby, blessedly, Peaslee grows distanced from the dreams, so much so that he realizes that he is now ignorant of languages that he seems to have learned during the period of fugue (384). The distancing and the new studies that he has taken up for the sake of the self at last become "a really effective bulwark against the visions and impressions which still assailed [him]" (390). The methods of comparative mythology—the triumphs of Sir James Frazer or Dr. Margaret Murray—form an abstraction that protects him against the pain of his learning. Abnormal discourse becomes normal. He has studied so effectively that he becomes absorbed once more into the institutional structure as an instructor in psychology and, in time, an author of scholarly articles concerning his case, not very successful articles until they are answered by the discovery of concrete detail throwing him into a new state of fugue in which, once more, he cannot hold his knowledge at a distance.

In all Lovecraft's stories those about Randolph Carter stand alone as a cycle describing one protagonist, palpably an alter ego of the author, who suffers the great return of Platonic myth. Given his priority in Lovecraft's career, with the first story written in 1919 and the last in 1933, he stands with the Outsider as a measure for the other tales. But the Carter cycle is not only important for its length; Carter is remarkable because he knows Warren, Kuranes, and Pickman, his mentors as Norman Gayford describes them (6), and is familiar with locales like Ulthar in Lovecraft's dreamland, as though the fiction were a part of his education—he functions as an instrument of self-reflection. In three of the stories, *The Dream-Quest of Unknown Kadath* and the two of the silver key, he suffers the great return, "back over well-known years" (*CF* 2.206), with a very intimate association being asserted between New England and his deepest self (207). Though we really know nothing of his education, the "frail nerves" (*CF* 1.135) that his comrade Warren mentions in the first story may be a sign of a private education; he can read certain forbidden books in their original languages, but not all (133). In the second story, "The Unnamable," he is contrasted to his friend Joel Manton, "principal of the East High School, born and bred in Boston and sharing New England's self-satisfied deafness to the delicate overtones of life," a person who believes that artists must work through "accurate, detailed transcripts of everyday affairs" (*CF* 1.398). Manton is an early version of Olney; and the contrast implies Carter's engagement with abnormal discourse, since no discourse is more abnormal than one that consciously gives its allegiance to the unnamable. This story also reveals Carter in a characteristic activity of the autodidact, pursuing his own research in family papers that he compares to Cotton Mather's *Magnalia*, correlating the private to the outré.

"The Silver Key" is not autobiographical. In it Lovecraft traces an alternate life as he describes how Carter between the ages of 30 and 50 educated himself in a way that almost destroyed his imaginative life. Lines from Coleridge's "Dejection: An Ode" lament such a process:

> For not to think of what I needs must feel,
> But to be still and patient, all I can;
> And haply by abstruse research to steal
> From my own nature all the natural man—
> This was my sole resource, my only plan:
> Till that which suits a part infects the whole,
> And now is almost grown the habit of my soul. (ll. 87–93)

The proprieties of philosophy become a disease in the rest of the human being. Modern philosophers, Haeckel for instance, whose impact upon Lovecraft we shall examine in "Lovecraft Born Again," urged Carter to study the discursive order of things as they are; then custom insisted upon "a superstitious reverence for that which tangibly and physically exists" (*CF* 1.73). It was an education into late-nineteenth century physics, removing any ontological basis for the imaginative life. Upon those assumptions Carter passed from aestheticism to traditionalism until he arrived at his salvation, a search for a realized imagining of his childhood that literally returns him to his childhood, just outside Arkham (*CF* 2.413). "Through the Gates of the Silver Key" examines the consequences of that return. At this point the story becomes remarkably geometrical in its imagery, like the imagery of the contemporaneous "The Dreams from the Witch House," in which Walter Gilman also illustrates the great return, for both he and Carter conclude in the roaming of geometrical objects. This fever of geometry may cast light on the Outsider's flight through the pyramids of Egypt, for in them the material constructions of the spirit, the Apollonian impulse, achieve their most refined expression that seems to have little to do with human personality. This imagery functions for Lovecraft as the myth of Byzantium had for Yeats, although the prayer that Yeats had directed to "the singing masters of my soul" Lovecraft must direct to a god that he denies:

> Consume my heart away; sick with desire
> And fastened to a dying animal,
> It knows not what it is; and gather me
> Into the artifice of eternity.   ("Sailing to Byzantium" ll. 21–24)

Despite his love for the landscapes of old New England, Carter like Yeats also desires to "never take / [His] bodily form from any natural thing" (ll. 25–26). But when this imagery appears in the conclusion of "The Outsider," conjoined with the exotic imagery of the catacombs and the ghouls, it is possible that the Apollonian imagination, which is imperfect given the loss of the sun, and the diseased imagination have not assimilated one another; nor can they ever in that story, given the continual shattering of the self that the protagonist undergoes.

Before these geometric adventures can begin, however, the narrative dissolves Carter's identity into an infinite series of possible Carters, human and inhuman, "a legion of selves" spread through "every known and suspected age of earth's history" (*CF* 3.298). But this series possesses a familiar structure, for one of Carter's ancestors is a "wizard Edmund Carter who had fled from Salem to the hills behind Arkham" (305–6), rather like Joseph Curwen. Another Carter is manifested in the Swami Chandraputra whose odd voice croaks because his waxen mask hides the inhuman creature Carter has become, something much worse than the "damned nigger" that Mr. Aspinwall accuses him of being (319). Carter has become the *faker* (320) that so many of Lovecraft's autodidacts and characters become. He has, perhaps, committed a hoax. And the word "faker" is not idly chosen, for it has a number of characteristics in common with "hoax." The origin of each word is obscure. "Faker" of course resembles "fakir," especially in the context of a holy man from the East, which derives from the Arabic "faqir," poor or impoverished, and refers to Muslim mendicant orders, though the West has come to attribute the word to Hinduism also; but for the West it also implies something of the religious charlatan. But we may also hear in the word a relation with "facere," to make, and feel that a faker is a maker, a constructor, a poet. "Fakir," "faker," and "fake" are of recent origin, for Dr. Johnson knows "fake" only as seaman's jargon, "a coil of rope." The *OED* identifies "fake" as thieves' slang, with no citation prior to the nineteenth century. It has such meanings as "to plunder, wound, kill; to do up, put into shape; to tamper with, for the purpose of deception. . . . It has latterly come into wider colloquial use, *esp.* with reference to the 'cooking' or dressing-up of news, reports, etc., for the press." A faker is a writer who consciously falsifies the real world for purely mercenary ends. These meanings place the word in the same provenance as "hoax," which may derive from "hocus-pocus," itself derivable—but only as a speculation—from *hoc est corpus meus,* the words of transubstantiation and identity in the Latin mass. But, again, the *OED* gives no citation for "hoax" earlier than 1796, and Dr. Johnson does not recognize it, though he does grant "hocus pocus," deriving it from Welsh. The words, then, form a complex group. Two have unclear origins; all cast doubt upon the subject, but two also position the subject in a possibly religious and numenous context; and none were accepted into standard English until recently, just as the word *outsider* was not. For Lovecraft, whose language aims at an imitation of eighteenth-century decorum, the words suggest a modernity at odds with that decorum; the recent appearance of the hoaxer and faker and outsider is a sign of the suspicion that contemporary life casts upon its players.

As for Randolph Carter, after his first appearances as a narrator and confidant on the margins of "In the Vault" and "The Unnamable," he became a self-made creature casting doubt upon his own humanity and telling tales about himself that may or may not be true, if it is indeed he in "Through the Gates of the Silver Key"; tales with religious and ontological overtones that attempt to ground his personality in the web of all space and time. But the conclusion of the last story finds him still ungrounded.

In summary, the pure autodidact does not form a large group within Lovecraft's characters, and gradually the nature of the autodidact changed during Lovecraft's career, moving from a person who enjoys an extremely irregular education to a person who breaks out of a regular education, that is to say a professor connected with Miskatonic University. But Miskatonic University, within the larger scale of Lovecraft's fictions, functions as an emblem of the autodidact; its staid professors become extensions of the university and its library, which contains a considerable sampling of the lore of the Outsider; as an institution Miskatonic University belongs to the Puritan, but its library belongs to the Cavalier with a liquor cabinet of forbidden books to which its professors repair in times of stress. And here we find the old opposition between the Puritan's normal discourse and the Cavalier's abnormal discourse: the one is enclosing, the other liberating; the one sober, the other witty; the one discursive, the other lyric; the one reasonable, the other gnomic; the one the King's English, the other exotic, alien, and contemporary, and deathly. The one is a communal discourse, the other often gibberish or silence, an infection of the mind and the tongue from which the autodidact never recovers. In Sartre's *La Nausée* the autodidact is imprisoned as a child-molester and damned by the protagonist for his undigested jargon; but the protagonist has to unlearn his own language and begin the search for another.

Since we have so far avoided the question of what the autodidact of "The Outsider" has learned, we must now consider that learning from various aspects. First, the Outsider has learned the moral lesson enunciated in the first paragraph, a lesson that we ourselves have avoided taking to heart: "Unhappy is he to whom the memories of childhood bring only fear and sadness. Wretched is he who looks back upon lone hours in vast and dismal chambers" (*CF* 1.265). Have we in a previous chapter overlooked the third word of the first two sentences, "he," when we claimed that no evidence existed in the story of the Outsider's gender? Undoubtedly we suffered a moment of lethe, we were negligent; the *lanthanomai* of criticism overtook us, in the same way that any reader overlooks so much through the very act of reading. But the evidence is not decisive. This "he" may be the generalized subject of so much traditional narration; or it may represent an attempt, never to be repeated in the story, at asserting and achieving gender and a denial of the "it" (272) that the Outsider confronts in the mirror. What, then, is the moral? Unhappy and wretched is the person whose content of memory is fear, sadness, solitude, and insomnia in the face of books and trees. The usual space within which a Lovecraftian autodidact begins, the family tradition and the family land, does not make a person happy. This moral does not achieve the limited victories of knowledge that Virgil offered, and Lovecraft on occasion: "Felix qui potuit causas cognescere rerum, / atque metus omnis et inexorabile fatum / subiecit pedibus strepitumque Acherontis avari" [Happy whoever can know the causes of things and casts all fear and immovable fate and the roar of hungry Acheron under foot] (*Georgics* 2.490–92). More strikingly, the Outsider's moral confesses the failure of stoic ataraxia, which Lovecraft frequently offered his correspondents as the summum bonum of moral possibilities.

Another part of the Outsider's content is what it is itself, what it is as its own content. But this problem collapses into the question of style and texts, for "man ist was er ißt"—you are what you eat, and the books you read—but also, in the name of the ghoul, "man ißt was er ist," you eat what you are. This problem, what the Outsider is in itself, the essentialist problem so difficult to surrender given the vulgar evidence of the body's boundary, is the one we are probing throughout this study no matter how provisional our answers. What then of this style compounded from such a variety of texts, most specifically the texts of Poe and perhaps Dunsany on the one hand and of Pope, Addison, Johnson, and Gibbon on the other? As far as Poe is concerned the Outsider employs his vocabulary, but perhaps to the disadvantage of the Virginian for even a slight comparison of the first paragraph of "The Outsider" to that of "Berenice" would demonstrate that the latter is considerably more hectic, though we may have here an instance of that *kenosis* by which an author attempts to empty the self of the style of a precursor (Bloom 14–15). The Outsider reads material that is itself pathological or parodic; and when he reads history, such as Herodotus, he remembers events like the story of Nitokris that lend themselves to the sensational. Lovecraft himself came to dislike "The Outsider" because it imitated Poe too naively and openly. "I couldn't help aping the mannerisms as well as reflecting the spirit," he wrote in 1931 as he reflected on the story (*JVS* 16). Such an anxiety he never felt about Pope, though he admitted that his own poetry was a sterile pastiche because of his adherence to Augustan versification; and, in fact, most of his poetry, despite the early imitation of *The Dunciad* with its unchoice vocabulary (*LAP* 146–47), more resembles the elegiac tone of Goldsmith's "The Deserted Village." But Pope is interesting as an ideal self since he was himself an autodidact, partially because of the alienation that his Roman Catholicism set between his family and British society and partially because of his frail, dwarfish body. As an outsider Pope delineates in *The Dunciad* the deadly effects of an education that deals only in normal discourse:

> We ply the Memory, we load the brain,
> Bind rebel Wit, and double chain on chain,
> Confine the thought, to exercise the breath;
> And keep them in the pale of Words till death.   (4.157–60)

Pope alludes to his self-created nature in "An Epistle to Dr. Arbuthnot" when he wrote, "I lisp'd in Numbers, for the Numbers came" (l. 128). Was Lovecraft aware of the joke involved in these lines that imitate Ovid's biography in the *Tristia*? It is in his dealing with the parodistic and the stupid, the immense energy that is poured into the attacks on Dulness, Cibber, and Tibbald, which Pope provides Lovecraft with an anti-self that appears in his stories and letters. It is on this mythic level that the anti-*Aeneid* of the Outsider follows the trail of Pope's dunces, leaving their cave for the games beside the river and achieving the dissolution of all things through the infection of their own incoherence.

The prose of "The Outsider" also plays off the prose of the eighteenth century. Elements of style that Steven J. Mariconda identified as signs of the age's influence (*Emergence* 19–20), parallelism, inverted syntax, and chiasmus, can be observed in the first paragraph, while parallelism, anaphora, antithesis, and philosophic vocabulary can be observed in the third paragraph. But the Johnsonian rhetoric is also, like that of Poe, exaggerated, one parallelism after another marching across the page as though the terrors of the world could be perceived only through a pattern of controlled duality. The influences of Poe and of the eighteenth-century stylists battle for mastery in the story, a few of the several voices that cannot yet coordinate a voice that Lovecraft could call his own (*ET* 38). The complex attitudes they represent bear witness to the burden Lovecraft assumed in educating himself so deeply in his precursors, when his growth as a writer depended on his taking a stand against the fathers of his life as an author. Is the Outsider's inability to return to the castle a sign of the progress that Lovecraft was beginning to imagine for himself? The great act of his self-making was the decision that his father and home were the landscape of contemporary New England and its depth in historical specificities, rather than this or that author; but he was only able to make that decision by referring to Poe as his only begetter and downplaying the example of Hawthorne.

What, then, does an autodidact read? In Lovecraft, besides reading anything attractive, the autodidact above all reads materials in the family library—those materials that lie nearest to hand, for an autodidact is not a researcher by profession—and in the reserved shelves of libraries like that of Miskatonic University. The autodidact reads the *Necronomicon*. Only the autodidact has the freedom to read and redeem those works that the canon has not recognized, often because those are the books of yesteryear, found only on family bookshelves handed down generation by generation, some of them sophisticated readers and some of them not. And those bookshelves and the family fortunes they represent have a further impact, a political impact, in the autodidact's evaluation of them, constructing a private canon. A believer in democracy like Edmund Wilson, fully aware of the ironies and frailties of the democratic process, constructs a very different canon from the one that Lovecraft constructs, a man insisting on the givens of his New England heritage as the old New England society crumbles around him. The autodidact in Lovecraft's vision revives the frivolities and rhythms of "To Anacreon in Heaven" as an attack upon "The Star-Spangled Banner." And the autodidact reads what he or she will come to write; the Outsider reads the self in the account that we must imagine him writing, justifying the self as he becomes aware of it.

A part of the Outsider's content is its self-understanding of its own methods of learning, the question of its epistemology, both the character's understanding of its epistemology and Lovecraft's understanding of his own. As for the Outsider, learning is certainly to be understood in terms of its books and the entire process that we have already outlined: education, socialization, realization, and circularity. But it is also to be described in terms of its result, the company among whom the Outsider finds itself at the end of the story. Here several readers have felt a certain qualm. The ghouls and the feasts of Nitokris in the penultimate paragraph hardly seem equal to the story or to the ultimate paragraph. The scene is parodistic and frivolous, rather like those Dunsanian stories which Lovecraft was still writing and from which he was slowing extricating himself. The paragraph seems somehow unworthy of the more serious concerns that were to preoccupy the rest of his career.

Such a view is of course wrong-headed, among other reasons because Lovecraft never ceased to write parodistically; his last major story, "The Haunter of the Dark," arose from a parodistic competition with the very young Robert Bloch. But even granted this correction, the observation that the exotica do not feel of the same weight or kind as the rest of the story still bears its own validity. A part of the moral temper of the story is its insight that a creature who has faced its own incompleteness will feel a strong temptation to retreat into a simpler world.

And this retreat is the point of Lovecraft's own Lockean epistemology, which seems so willfully old-fashioned flowing from the pen of a letter-writer in the twentieth century. Having already explored this subject in the context of Lovecraft's reaction to Keats and Newton, let us now explore it further in the context of twentieth-century theories of knowledge, of which Lovecraft was not unknowledgeable albeit unschooled. But as soon as we ask this question we encounter a peculiar problem, for Lovecraft seems more interested in physics than in perception, and in perception than in epistemology. He does not follow the example of the eighteenth-century thinkers who regarded the questions raised by these fields as pressing; and in the twentieth century he does not pursue such questions as quantum mechanics raised, not least in the hands of its practitioners. Though he was aware of the debate between Einstein and Bohr, for he seems to have been aware of Eddington as a popularizer of that debate, he prefers to agree with Einstein's insistence upon causal relations and rejection of any notion that observation and fact participate in one another (*SL* 3.227–29). Lovecraft was the kind of autodidact who preferred to regard certain questions settled. We must confess then that Lovecraft's stories, especially "The Outsider" in which the shattering of knowledge before the mirror is so significant, defeat his epistemology, for the Outsider's method of knowing is hardly Lockean at all.

Another part of the creature's content is its outer appearance, its pure image. All that we know of this content are the words the Outsider uses to describe its image in the mirror, words impressionistic at best. But the description is orderly. The series at the head of the passage, "unclean, uncanny, unwelcome, abnormal, detestable," presents the negativity and absence that the creature experiences at the peak of its self-education. As a "ghoulish shade of decay, antiquity, and desolation" it is a shadow that the past casts, the influence that the past exerts without remission upon the present. It is a "revelation" and "baring," pure truth, pure uncovering of what is overlooked. And that which has been overlooked is a "travesty on the human shape," the autodidact's reflection upon a radical difference from the world of normal discourse which eternally insists upon its humanity. But the words "unclean," "decay," and "putrid, dripping" point at the continual falling away from humanity that is revealed. Most disturbing to the protagonist, however, is the "mouldy, disintegrating apparel"—what a wonderful effort at dignity is placed on that Johnsonian word *apparel*—which will not contain its shame but calls attention to it, for the dead body, our dead body, has no way to protect itself against the accidents of matter it discovers itself at last composed of (*CF* 1.271). Its finery is full of holes; autodidacticism lies open to a continual self-exposure.

Exposed by his father Laios and lame from the cut in his ankle, Oedipus does not know the identity of his father. His anger at the words of the man at the feast may indicate a doubt of his identity before the reveler even speaks; but revelers at even the most polite parties have never cared much for the feelings of others. So Oedipus must ask the man whom he had supposed his father a question crucial to a patriarchal society, who his father might be, and receive an inconclusive answer at best. But we cannot forget that Oedipus is repeating a pattern that several Greek heroes endure, such as Theseus whose story is alluded to in "The Tomb," men doubtful of their origins and social identity. So Oedipus continues to ask the question until he receives an apparently definitive answer from the shepherd, another putative father who would not kill him because he pitied him; the shepherd lets him live, to proceed to the great blind rebellion he commits in the murder of Laios.

Everything that we said of the Puritan and the Cavalier earlier must now be seen in the light of the protagonist's attempt to try on a father: the Outsider tries on the revelers; in terms of the motto taken from *The Eve of St. Agnes* he tries on the Baron. Jervas tries on the figure of the rollicking Cavalier. And Charles Dexter Ward tries on another reckless figure. Trying to bring the birth of his twin brother to fruition Wilbur Whateley steps into the place of both his mother and his alien father. In marrying Asenath, Edward Derby tries on his father-in-law and whatever lies behind him; Peaslee willy-nilly tries on the sexless progenitors millions of years in the past. Randolph Carter quite literally goes backward in time, trying to possess himself more fully as he tries on masks and geometries. All of these gestures to invent an ideal father, the antithesis of the sober self, are recursive, going far backward in time, far before and outside the autodidact's own conception.

And now, once more and at last, we return again to that shadowy moment in "The Outsider," the terminal climax with all its inertia that forces the Outsider and the reader to repeat its recognition interminably, to put into question again what we learned there. What proceeds out of the moment of the polished glass? It is useful to turn to the figure of Tarzan again, who before his formal education in the cabin began received the shock of himself as different from the apes. Two moments are of interest. When he is ten years old he suddenly sees that his body is "entirely hairless, like some low snake, or other reptile" and feels "intense shame" (35). The prepubertal moment contains its phallic recognition. But the second moment is more telling. As he compares his own face and that of another young ape "mirrored" in a pool, his small mouth, teeth, and ugly nose, above all the "blank whiteness" (36) of his eyes, Sabor the lioness crouches behind them and screams, a scream meant to create "a paralysis of terror" that will hold them for her spring. But Tarzan, with "his higher intelligence" leaps into the pool, despite his profound fear of it (37), a fear we can understand for Legion, driven out of the madman, entered a herd of swine that drowned in the Lake of Galilee. Sabor kills Tarzan's cousin, his other. That scream, that paralysis, that leap into the mirror and its shattering, that death and that salvation are all the Outsider's. The autodidact works out his salvation in fear and trembling. The *Nachträglichkeit* of the moment forces the Outsider to reconceive itself, for its prior conception has never been sufficient to its being. Out of the mirror proceeds its idea, its intuition of its image and form; but this essential form is not to be possessed as learning, as a rule or rote by which other knowledge can be conquered. Fakery is involved, and the *ébranlement* will not permit such a possession. Instead, the Outsider discovers, with joy, that the moment is infinitely repeatable, another knowledge of the self, another multiple self always lying beyond its grasp within the glass that is so capable, lovely in its emptiness, to give forth a self again. But only if he breaks it. Working outside of the frameworks of knowledge the autodidact discovers that no end to the act of intuition is possible. The conclusion is, of course, that there is no conclusion.

But we do not see the truth of ourselves in the mirror, at the least because we are reversed, the dexterous becoming the sinister and the sinister the dexterous; we do not see ourselves as others see us. So the conversation with the self in the mirror becomes one that transcends the self. That image of God within the largest community is not quite ours, though it is a Thou with a most intimate connection. Our relation to it is always self-destroying and self-renewing.

PART IV
Materialism, Theology, and Imagination

Lovecraft and Leopardi: Sunsets and Moonsets

I

Ergo vivida vis animi pervicit, et extra
processit longe flammantia moenia mundi
atque omne immensum peragravit mente animoque . . .
Quare religio pedibus subiecta vicissim
obteritur, nos exaequat victoria caelo.

[Therefore a lively power of spirit conquered, and past the flaming walls of the world he went far and walked up and down the immensity in mind and spirit. . . . Hence religion was trampled under foot, and his victory made us the equals of heaven.] (Lucretius 1.72–79)

Strange as it may seem, Lovecraft is not dissimilar to the Italian poet Giacomo Leopardi. Both men hated fish and lusted after ice cream; both suffered bitterly from the cold; and late in life both were neurasthenics, more nocturnal than diurnal in their habits. As they became older both men created larger, more complex structures while writing fewer works, becoming almost silent in their final years. Of course they do differ from each other, and it may seem perverse to compare an Italian poet of the early nineteenth century to an American writer of horror fiction a century later. Leopardi, moreover, is not simply a poet; he is one of the major lyric poets of his country, whereas Lovecraft's reputation is still suspect and shall probably remain so. The comparison is all the more dubious since Lovecraft never refers to Leopardi, though he had some reason to be aware of him. Schopenhauer, whom Lovecraft very much respected (Joshi, *Decline* 30–33), considered Leopardi with himself and Byron one of the three greatest pessimists in the world (6.192) and thought his treatment of the "Nichtigkeit und Leiden des Lebens" [nothingness and sorrow of life] exemplary among authors (2.692–93). But Nietzsche, a figure important to Lovecraft's philosophic life, had problems with Leopardi's pessimism, precisely as he had with Schopenhauer's. In *Unzeitgemäße Betrachtungen* he referred to Leopardi's poem "A se stesso" only in order to illustrate the disgust that he believed historians felt who treated the flow of history from an extrahistorical perspective (1.218). Given Lovecraft's adulation of Nietzsche, his overlooking Leopardi is not difficult to understand. If he pursued Leopardi in the *Britannica,* having seen the poet's name in Will Durant's *The Story of Philosophy* where he appears fleetingly (326, 328), these words might have discouraged him from appreciating the man: "As works of art [the *Operetti morali*] are a possession for ever, as contributions to moral philosophy they are worthless, and apart from their literary qualities can only escape condemnation if regarded as lyrical expressions of emotion, the wail extorted from a diseased mind by a diseased body" (Garnett 457). The notice of Leopardi on the last page of Kuhns's survey of Italian literature, a volume in Lovecraft's library (*LL* #932), asserted that Leopardi was on the level of Dante, Petrarch, Ariosto, and Tasso but added that "the circumstances of his life only added to his morbid tendency, and after a brief existence, passed in sickness, poverty, and gloom, he died" (344). Unless Lovecraft recalled the similar judgment that Victorian optimists passed on Poe, these evaluations were not encouraging. Despite Lovecraft's ignorance of Leopardi, however, their biographies and careers, their presuppositions and assertions, their ways of thinking, system of aesthetics, and the kinds of works they created parallel each other in such a way that a consideration of them should be useful in understanding both in a new light.

Leopardi was born in 1798 in the small town of Recanati, a marginal village of the Papal States, as Lovecraft was born in Providence, a city marginal to New England. Both regarded their contemporary culture with scorn: Leopardi despised the optimistic servility of pre-risorgimento Italy; Lovecraft despised the venal, mechanistic America of the 1920s. Both felt that their ancestries possessed some significance, but both experienced embarrassing poverty. In each case the father failed, facing a financial crisis or dying young, and surrendered the family to the mother. But though Leopardi's mother assumed the finances, she prayed whenever her children were sick that they would die and leave this fallen world; Lovecraft's mother considered him hopeless for practical affairs and, according to one report, thought him "hideous" (*IAP* 131). Both men had smooth chins: Lovecraft preferred to be "a decent, clean-shaven Roman nobleman. . . . How I hate these little Greek barbatuli with their tufts and fringes of sickly fur!" (*SL* 2.224); and Leopardi jeered at the Carbonari who exhibited as the sign of their republican faith "enorme il pelo" [enormous fur] ("Palinodia" 259).[1] For men who believed that very little had meaning, their public habits were fastidious.

Both were autodidacts, though of different orders. Leopardi received a rich education from mentors and his father's library; in Italy at the beginning of the nineteenth century a person educated by tutors at home did not disappoint his social class or his own expectations of himself. Nevertheless there is a strong sense in which Leopardi was an extension of his father's being, so much so that when his father published anonymously a collection of reactionary dialogues many people took them for the work of his son, to the young man's immense shame. The words addressed to the soul in the "Dialogo della natura e di un'anima" have some personal relevance: although the soul will in many ways surpass all its contemporaries "nondimeno ti riuscirà sempre o impossibile o sommamente malagevole di apprendere o di porre in pratica moltissime cose menome in sé, ma necessarissime al conversare cogli altri uomini" [nonetheless it will

---

1. All references to Leopardi's poetry indicate lineation; references to the *Zibaldone,* the journal that he kept for ten years, indicate the original pagination of the manuscript; all other references indicate the volume and page of the Flora edition.

be either impossible or extremely difficult for you to succeed in learning or putting into practice many things small in themselves but very necessary for communication with other people] (1.848). The library of Lovecraft's grandfather was more limited than that available to Leopardi, as was his intermittent, public school education, one that did not meet the expectations of his class, certainly not his own, although Lovecraft gloried in contrasting his education at home to that of his contemporaries. Infatuated with the classics and with astronomy, both men wrote encyclopaedic treatises on the history of astronomy. Leopardi was a trained philologian; and although Lovecraft had no such training he frequently expressed a deeply engaged interest in the details of etymology, dialect, and spelling. Both suffered a physical and moral breakdown that rendered them unable to pursue a public life and defensive about that apparent failure.[2]

Besides those early works, for most of their lives both men wrote immense prose tracts, Leopardi in his intellectual diary the *Zibaldone* and Lovecraft in his letters, works that have come to excite an attention almost equal to that of their creative works. In this regard they further resemble one another, for in the face of his slim yet massive poetic achievement Leopardi's philosophic work has often been discounted, for instance by Benedetto Croce who called it a pseudo-philosophy (105), whereas Giovanni Carsaniga asserts that he was "the greatest Italian thinker of his age" (ix), as well as familiar with contemporary science (ix–x); most of Lovecraft's reputation rests upon a small number of short stories and novellas, against which the letters could well present a forbidding wall if taken with the full seriousness that some Lovecraftians would. But like Schopenhauer and Nietzsche these two writers are to be better understood as critics of cultural tendencies, as moral philosophers than as philosophers in any academic or professional sense; they aspire to a system rather than achieve one. They do not believe in a philosophy which "non piange e non ride, ma attende a indagare le forme dell'essere, l'operare dello spirito" [does not cry and does not laugh, but is intent to investigate the forms of being, the operation of the spirit] (105).[3] Besides these intellectual efforts, both writers in their infatuation for the past were attracted to forgery, hoax, and pastiche; three of Leopardi's early poems were playful imitations of Greek lyrics, which he passed off as originals, and his longest poem, the *Paralipomeni della Batracomiomachia*, is a continuation and pastiche of the Homeric mock-epic that he had translated when a teenager. More to our concern, in the *Operette morali*, a series of dialogues whose dialectical structure he felt developed the main lines of his system, he wrote a

---

2. This is the period that Lovecraft preferred to say least about in later years, and he lied about the reason for his inability to enter Brown University (*LAP* 126).

3. Carsaniga argues that Madame de Staël showed Leopardi "how philosophy, by helping one to grow out of the beautiful illusions of youth, induces in one's spirit a happy melancholy which makes one more sensitive to nature" (30). Leopardi's own meditations were to become more agonistic than this model, but it did partially reconcile for him the complementary functions of poet and intellectual.

few works that resemble Lovecraft's stories insofar as they begin to edge from satire toward cosmic threat, especially those in which certain boundary encounters occur, between Federico Ruysch and his mummies, between a new-born soul and Nature, or between an Icelander and Nature in the center of Africa; in that last dialogue, having crossed continents and oceans to confront Nature, the Icelander at last discovers that she is an indifferent giant, rather like the statues of Easter Island or the forbidding figure at the Cape of Good Hope in *Os Lusiadas,* and dies from the encounter, to be returned to a museum in Europe as a mummy. Though these dialogues do not depart from satire and those dialogues that center more upon lament and consolation, like that between Plotinus and Porphyrius, do not so greatly exhibit cosmic threat, it is possible to perceive throughout his work "la tensione leopardiana verso il macabro, verso una vittoria del pittoresco e dell'idillio nel grotesco carico di razionalistica acutezza e di allibito senso dell'orrore mortuario che tace sotto le verdi zolle" [the Leopardian tension toward the macabre, toward a victory of the picturesque and the idyllic within a grotesque rationalistic sharpness and an astonished sense of mortuary horror that lies silent beneath the green clods] (Binni 161). A part of the power of Leopardi's works lies in the way that he sharply juxtaposes images of elusive beauty and images of imminent destruction, images of human aspiration and images of an indifferent, gross reality.

 Both writers owed a complex debt to Classical culture, above all for its offering a vision of life profoundly different from Christian culture, and that debt was extended to the Enlightenment, which they were accustomed to apply critically against their contemporaries; neither felt a very great affinity for the Renaissance. But the Enlightenment, which behaved as a forward-looking liberator from monarchist and elitist claims in the eighteenth century, meant something different for the anti-democratic Lovecraft in the twentieth century, though both men espoused it against Romanticism, Leopardi against progressivist and philosophic enthusiasms, Lovecraft against a threadbare sentimentality. Leopardi is capable of denouncing Europeans for colonialist adventures ("Palinodia" 59–68) and dissenting from any praise of the noble savage, who eats the flesh of his own children ("La scommessa di Prometeo" 1.862). Because of this Enlightenment orientation, both writers denounce the consolations of religion.

 The impact of the Enlightenment on Leopardi can best be seen in *I pensieri* as he adopts the pose of a disillusioned gentleman of the world dissecting social foibles. Friendship is valuable, though "Più presto si trova chi per un estraneo metta a pericolo la vita, che uno che, non dico spenda, ma rischi per l'amico uno scudo" [More often a person can be found who sets his life in peril for a stranger than one who, I would not say spends, but risks money for his friend] (2.57). A gentleman never reveals his vulnerability because, "Confessando i propri mali, quantunque palesi, l'uomo nuoce molte volte ancora alla stima, e quindi l'affetto, che gli portano i suoi più cari: tanto è necessario che ognuno con braccio forte sostenga se medesimo" [Confessing his own ills, whenever he publishes them a person often injures the esteem and affection that his dear ones bear him; thus it is necessary that each person sustain himself with a strong arm] (2.62). The ideal of *I pensieri* is that familiar figure from La Rochefoucauld who operates independently of any intimate relationship because of his *amour propre*. This is a pose that Lovecraft is fond of throughout his life.

A more profound disillusionment is to be found in Lovecraft and Leopardi's pictures of the universe, which is determinedly mechanistic, without origin and without purpose, certainly without either moral or aesthetic justification, without a stamp of the *valde bona*. In his letters and essays Lovecraft is a frank materialist. Leopardi's attitude is more complex, but certainly distanced. He is bemused that the Judaeo-Christian theology, "che insegnarono ed avvezzarono gli uomini a guardar più alto del campanile, a mirar più giù del pavimento, insomma alla riflessione, alla ricerca delle cause occulte, all'esame e spesso alla condanna ed abbandono delle credenze naturali, delle immaginazioni spontanee ed mal fondate" [which teaches and accustoms men to look higher than the bell-tower, lower than the pavement, in short, to reflect, to search out hidden causes, to examine and often to condemn and abandon natural beliefs, spontaneous and ill-founded notions] (Z 1060), has given birth to atheism; and he exclaims, "Mirabile congegnazione del sistema dell'uomo, il quale non sarebbe irreligioso se non fosse stato religioso" [Wonderful contrivance of the system of man, who would not be irreligious if he had not been religious] (1060). Though divinity is a part of his intellectual apparatus, he tends to collapse God and Nature into one concept (393–94), without taking part in any Spinozistic rationalism.

Both men express moments in which a beautiful scene is suddenly transformed or threatened by a vision of the destruction which the world carries within. For Leopardi the vision takes place in a garden: "Là quella rosa è offesa dal sole, che gli ha dato la vita; si corruga, langue, appassisce. Là quel giglio è succhiato crudelmente da un' ape, nelle sue parti più sensibili, più vitali" [There that rose is offended by the sun which has given it life; it wilts, languishes, withers. There that lily is cruelly sucked by a bee in its most sensitive, vital parts] (Z 4175). That tree is infested by ants, that other by fleas. "Ogni giardino è quasi un vasto ospidale (luogo ben più deplorabile che un cemeterio)" [Every garden is like a vast hospital (a place perhaps sadder than a cemetery)] (4176). The universe in short is "un neo, un bruscolo in metafisica" [a blemish, a mote in the eye of metaphysics] and existence "un'imperfezione, un'irregularità, una monstruosità" [an imperfection, an irregularity, a monstrosity] (4174). The image appears in the poem "Sopra il ritratto di una bella donna," as he compares the disparity between a living face and its putrefaction to what happens when a daydream at a concert is suddenly interrupted by a discord: "in nulla / Torna quel paradiso in un momento" [into nothing / That paradise turns in a moment] (48–49).

For Lovecraft the flaw is closer to home, and he turns the language of the human discord in another direction: "May not all mankind be a mistake—an abnormal growth—a disease in the system of Nature—an excrescence on the body of infinite progression like a wart on the human hand? Might not the total destruction of humanity, as well as of all animate creation, be a positive *boon* to Nature as a whole?" (*Letters to Rheinhart Kleiner* 37). The same vision overtook John Keats, to whom we have already had occasion to refer in this study:

> Dear Reynolds, I have a mysterious tale,
> And cannot speak it. The first page I read
> Upon a lampit rock of green seaweed
> Among the breakers. 'Twas a quiet eve;
> The rocks were silent, the wide sea did weave
> An untumultuous fringe of silver foam
> Along the flat brown sand. I was at home
> And should have been most happy—but I saw
> Too far into the sea, where every maw
> The greater on the less feeds evermore.—
> But I saw too distinct into the core
> Of an eternal fierce destruction,
> And so from happiness I far was gone.   (86–98)

The moral impact of this vision is not blunted by its reminiscence of Albany's realization in *King Lear* that humanity may be no other, no worse and no better than beasts of the sea: "It will come, / Humanity must perforce prey on itself / Like monsters of the deep" (4.2.48–50). But Keats's vision proceeds from the wilderness to the garden:

> though, today,
> I've gathered young spring-leaves, and flowers gay
> Of periwinkle and wild strawberry,
> Still do I that most fierce destruction see—
> The shark at savage prey, the hawk at pounce,
> The gentle robin, like a pard or ounce,
> Ravening a worm.   (99–105)

The language becomes anticlimactic and bathetic, but what other language is possible? It is the same anticlimax and bathos of which Leopardi and Lovecraft are sometimes accused. Keats's vision presents the moment in the garden after nature and humanity have fallen and labor to no point, laboring to make sense and failing.

Lovecraft's experience of the garden is slightly different. After the death of his grandfather, his expulsion from Eden, he planted a garden next to the house to which his family had been exiled:

> I chopped down certain trees and preserved others, laid out paths and gardens, and set at the proper points shrubbery and ornamental urns taken from the old home. My paths were of gravel, bordered with stones, and here and there a bit of a stone wall or an impressive cairn of my own making added to the picture. Between two trees I made a rustic bench, later duplicating it be-

twixt two other trees. A large grassy space I levelled and transformed into a Georgian lawn, with a sundial in the centre. Other parts were uneven, and I sought to catch certain sylvan or bower-like effects. (*Letters to Alfred Galpin* 95)

This attempt to simulate Eden is filled with images of death, urns and a cairn and the sundial, and it looks backward, both to the old home and to Pope's aesthetic of the garden. Like Candide's, the garden that he tends represents a private, fragile order. "Such was the paradise of my adolescent years," but he gave up the garden when he realized "with horror" that he was too old for such activities (*Letters to Alfred Galpin* 95). Adults in Providence didn't do such things. The letter concludes abruptly, "Adulthood is hell" (95). You build the garden in the midst of exile only to discover that you have to desert it. Or you may rediscover it. In 1930 Lovecraft felt that he had found the garden of his dreams in Richmond, reminding his friend Galpin that he has two moments of incantation, one the sight of sunset across a city and the other "the experience of walking (or, in most of my dreams, aërially floating) thro' [. . .] gardens of exotick delicacy & opulence, with carved stone bridges, labyrinthine paths, marble fountains, terraces, & staircases, strange pagodas, hillside grottos, curious statues, termini, sundials, benches, basins, & lanthorns, lily'd pools of swans & streams with tiers of waterfalls, spreading gingko-trees & drooping, feathery willows, & sun-touched flowers" (*JFM* 230), a garden that is an amplification of the garden he lost as a child. He describes the same landscape in "The Gardens of Yin," one of the sonnets of *Fungi from Yuggoth*. But he cannot stay in Richmond, no matter how much it seems to give him this dream, for he has to return to the Providence that is so much an extension of his own being; and perhaps he realizes that no matter how greatly the Richmond garden seems to materialize the lost garden, it can never have the one great lure of that garden, its very lostness.

But even as we look at these passages and compare them to others in which Lovecraft waxes eloquent over the beauties of the Rhode Island landscape, we recognize that they do not contain the terror and rancor of the passages in Leopardi and Keats, whose premonitions in the face of evolution before Darwin's analysis appeared are nothing to the feelings of a man like Lovecraft who has had time to digest the consequences. His anxiety lies elsewhere, not in the brutality of the process but in the kinship it reveals between humanity and beasts.

One aspect of the garden moment is that the scale of the garden, that is to say the scale of the universe, is much greater for Leopardi and Lovecraft than it had been for most writers of the Renaissance,[4] or even for those of the Enlightenment, who were able to tame Newton with the model of the clockwork universe. But Leopardi and Lovecraft differ in their treatment of the infinite. For Leopardi exist-

---

4. The exception would be Giordano Bruno, who had transformed the soul of Lucretius' world (Yates 244–48); but there is no evidence that Leopardi read Bruno, whereas he knew the *De rerum natura* intimately, as well as Fontenelle's *Entretiens sur la pluralité des mondes*.

ence, including all the worlds of the universe that may exist, most probably does not extend to infinity; only that which does not exist, pure nothingness, can accommodate infinity as a mental conception (Z 4174). This universe with its eternal matter and its infinite worlds he refers to in the "Frammento apocrifo di Stratone da Lampsaco" (1.973–4); and although fifty years before Clausius he is capable of playing in that dialogue and in the "Cantico del gallo silvestre" with the notion of the universe running down, he carefully adheres to the eternity of matter in a note (1.1033). More radically, he connects the impossibility of the actual infinite, or at least our impossibility of conceiving it, with the impossibility of our conceiving an infinite intellect that could have framed it; the universe is as it is, not created, with no relation to any conceivable creator (Z 4141–43). Moreover, since time is not a thing but an idea relative to the existence of things, a development of an argument that Lucretius presents (1.459–63), the eternity of a matter that has no beginning and no end does not demonstrate the infinity of time; for that which does not exist except as a word cannot be infinite (Z 4181–82). By the same argument, space does not exist except as a word that expresses the location of matter in the face of nothingness (4233). Infinity is a dream, an expression of the arrogance of our desires (4177–78), and the infinite universe merely an optical illusion (4292). But whereas Leopardi remains Lockean in his conception of infinity, Lovecraft follows Nietzsche and Haeckel in insisting upon the infinity of the universe and of worlds within it, a model that allows him to speculate on the possibility of worlds beyond ours that may transcend our physical laws (RK 140); only by 1930 did he accept the curved space implicit in general relativity, though he did not grant the impossibility of infinite space until 1935 (DW 427). Lovecraft refuses, however, to connect the scale of the universe to his emotional life. In an extended passage he describes how the sight of the stars leads him to meditate upon antiquity, "Thebes and Memphis and Babylon," and concludes, "This, indeed, is *feeling*—but when I approach the same objects as an astronomical student I do so very differently. Then I leave my dreams behind and take along my telescope; and instead of glancing at the lighted town below, I curse it for the smoke and heat-vapours it sends up to obscure telescopic definition" (SL 2.313). This dissociation of feeling and intellect eases some of the tension between the indifference of the universe and his feeling for human transience, but it surely bears other difficulties with it, above all the question of what artistic use, in full integrity, a writer can make of the universe. For Leopardi the prison house is closed, though so vast that humanity is lost within it; for Lovecraft the infinite universe leaves some chinks open, at least to the imagination, but at the price of dissociation.

It cannot be said, however, that either man's vision of the world is as clear-cut as our explication so far may suggest. As far as Leopardi is concerned, he seems to have had two views of Nature that dialectically played upon one another throughout his writing. As Carsaniga expresses this duality, on the one hand Leopardi posits an extra-historical Nature which sustains the human animal, both bodily and instinctually, a Nature that appears good insofar as the individual fits into its processes; on the other hand, to the individual and cultures that have refined their desires and intellects, the individual who can reflect upon Nature, it appears a destroyer (78–82). As Barricelli expresses the duality, the poetic Nature on the one hand and the cosmic Nature on the other, the Nature that sustains and is available to the imagination and the Nature that demands an analysis from the intellect, are both one Nature, two aspects of a reality that transcends every attempt to encompass it (36–43). In the "Dialogo di Cristoforo Colombo e di Pietro Gutierrez" Columbus confesses that Nature, "fornita di tanta potenza" [furnished with such power], is more than any of his theories, "che non solamente non sì può fare giudizio certo di quel che ella abbia operato ed operi in parti lontanissime del tutto incognite al mondo nostro, ma possiamo anche dubitare che uno s'inganni di gran lunga argomentando da questo a quelle, e non sarebbe contrario alla verisimilitudine l'immaginare che le cose del mondo ignoto . . . fossero maravigliose e strane a rispetto nostro" [for not only can no certain judgment be made of what she may have done and does in very distant areas totally unknown to our world, but we can also suspect that anyone greatly deludes himself arguing from this area to those, and it would not be contrary to likelihood imagining that those things in the unknown world . . . would be miraculous or strange compared to ours] (1.955). Lovecraft approaches the question of how far we may comprehend Nature by taking into consideration the limitation of the senses, a favorite topic that we shall investigate in the next chapter. The universe is simply too large and too complex to be understood by such creatures as we are.

Such a theory of the universe has two effects upon both writers, effects visible when Leopardi develops Pascal's famous assertion of human nobility:

> Niuna cosa maggiormente dimostra la grandezza e la potenza dell'umano intelletto . . . che il poter l'uomo conoscere e interamente comprendere e fortemente sentire la sua piccolezza. Quando egli considerando la pluralità de' mondi, si sente essere infinitissima parte di un globo ch'è minima parte d'uno degl'infinite sistemi che compongono il mondo, e in questa considerazione stupisce della sua piccolezza, e profondamente sentendola e intentamente requardandola, si confonde quasi col nulla, e perde quasi se stesso nel pensiero della immensità delle cose, e si trova come smarrito nella vastità imcomprensibile dell'esistenza; allora con questo atto e con questo pensiero egli dà la maggior prova possibile della sua nobiltà, della forza e della immensa capacità della sua mente, la quale, rinchiuso in sì piccolo e menomo essere, è potuta pervenire a conoscere e intender cose tanto superiori alla natura di lui, e può abbracciarsi e contener col pensiero questa immensità medesima della esistenza e delle cose. [No thing more greatly demonstrates the grandeur and power of the human intellect . . . than the ability to know and thoroughly comprehend man and intensely feel his own smallness. When considering the plurality of worlds he feels himself an infinitesimal part of a globe that is the least part of one of the infinite systems that compose the universe, and in this consideration is stupefied by his smallness, and profoundly feeling it and intently observing it is con-

founded as it were in nothingness, and loses himself in the thought of the immensity of things, and finds himself lost in the incomprehensible vastness of existence; then with that act and that thought he gives the greatest possible proof of his nobility, of the force and immense capacity of his mind that closed up in so small and minimal a being has been able to come to know and attend to things so superior to his nature and able to embrace and contain within his thought that very immensity of existence and of things.] (Z 3171–72)

The scale of the universe excites a moral imperative to know and embrace it, through the very infinitesimal scale of the individual to reach out in thought to that apparent infinity of things and contain it; human nobility lies in converting an immense indifferent space into the human, value-charged interiority. Or, as he says in regard to his concept of *noia,* the boredom caused by our realization of the vanity of human life, "L'uomo si disannoia per lo stesso sentimento vivo della noia universale e necessaria" [A man cures himself of boredom through the lively apprehension of universal and necessary boredom] (262). And Lovecraft also, for the very reason that he will insist upon the indifference of the cosmos, hints in his stories at the nobility of attempting to understand that indifference, though in his letters he is considerably more sardonic. In order to imply these two things at once—the nothingness and grandeur of being human—both writers are driven to find a proper syntax and form for such a statement, hence the length, complexity, repetitions, and rhythm of Leopardi's sentence, which reads as though it were a rehearsal for the sinuosity of the late poem "La ginestra," in which the scale of the universe and the moral imperative upon the small human collective is once more announced; and hence the hypnotic repetitions of Lovecraft's vocabulary.

But anyone forced to contemplate the nothingness of what it is to be human is soon forced to contemplate the possibility of suicide. In this regard we certainly find Leopardi stepping aside from the independence projected within *I pensieri* and the indifferentism implied by it. Only a month before writing "Dialogo di Plotino e di Porfirio" in which a confession of weakness becomes the basis of human solidarity in the face of an indifferent nature, Leopardi had written, "Sono stanco della vita, stanco della indifferenza filosofica, ch'è il solo rimedio de' mali e della noia, ma che in fine annoia essa medesima. Non ho altri disegni, altre speranze che di morire" [I am tired of life, tired of philosophic indifference, which is the only remedy of evils and of boredom, but which in the end is boring itself. I have no other plans, no other hopes than to die] (*Lettere* 778). The dialogue is difficult to read because in it Leopardi deploys all his art in a catalogue of the world's ills, especially the horror of *noia* that renders every achievement and every ideal ill-fitted to the mechanism of the physical world and the physical body and mind that lives in it. It is all the more surprising and lovely, therefore, to come to the irrational turn at the close of the work:

> Sia ragionevole l'uccidersi . . .: certamente quello è un atto fiero e inumano. E non dee piacer più, nè vuolsi elegger piuttosto di essere secondo ragione un

mostro, che secondo natura uomo. E perchè anche non vorremo noi avere alcuna considerazione degli amici; dei congiunti di sangue; dei figliuoli, dei fratelli, dei genitori, delle moglie; delle persone familiari e domestiche, colle quali siamo usati di vivere da gran tempo; che, morendo, bisogna lasciare per sempre: e non sentiremo in cuor nostro dolore alcuna di questa separazione; nè terremo conto di quello che sentiranno essi, e per la perdita di persona cara o consueta, e per l'atrocità del caso? [Let suicide be reasonable . . .: certainly the act is proud and inhuman. And it should not be pleasing, nor should one choose, to be a monster according to reason than a man according to nature. And also would we not have any consideration for our friends; our relatives; our children, brothers, parents, wives; people close to us and servants with whom we have been used to live for a long time; whom, dying, we would have to leave forever: and not feel any pain in our heart for this separation; nor take into account what they would feel for the loss of someone dear and familiar nor for the cruelty of the act?] (1.1014–15)

Reason by itself is condemned as monstrous from the point of view of human solidarity, monstrous for its refusal to take account of the pain that others feel because of their love, monstrous because in cutting the individual off from the society that has given birth to it and sustained it suicide is one more manifestation, the final manifestation, of the *causa sui* project. From this point of view, insofar as he refuses to kill himself, Oedipus does not carry out the full implications of the Oedipal drama, and thus he surrenders the reason that had carried him forward so successfully, the reason for which he is known. Reason is insufficient in the face of love and death. The last words of the dialogue speak firmly: "Sì bene attendiamo a tenerci compagnia l'un l'altro; e andiamoci incoreggiando, e dando mano e soccorso scambievolmente; per compiere nel miglior modo questa fatica della vita" [Let us pay attention so well to keep each other company, and go along encouraging one another, and giving each other help, to fulfill in the best way this labor of life] (1.1016). The best compromise to be made of living is by living together, a compromise based upon the tension between reason and friendship.

We can discover the same tension between those passages in Lovecraft's letters in which he counsels disillusionment and self-reliance and those in which he is a ready friend; even more revelatory are such stories as "The Dunwich Horror," in which friends band together against the aliens invading an orderly earth from a chaotic centerless universe. This tension is not a sign of insincerity in either of the authors; quite simply, both construct an ethics that is clear-eyed, valiantly opposed to a universe they think is meaningless.

More compelling than friendship, however, is the memory of the past. When in "The Silver Key" Randolph Carter considers killing himself, having perceived "the hollowness and futility of real things," but discovers that inertia holds him back, he takes down the accoutrements of decadence with which he had dallied and finds himself "refitting the house as it was in his early boyhood, . . . almost glad he had lingered, for his relics of youth and his cleavage from the world made life and sophistication seem very distant and unreal; so much so that a touch of magic and expectancy stole back into his nightly slumbers" (*CF* 2.78–79). Surprisingly these regressive hopes are confirmed by the conclusion of the story when Carter does return to his childhood. This is a frequent theme in the letters:

> In Providence I have never seen a congenial mind with which I could exchange ideas, and even among my correspondents there are fewer and fewer who coincide with me on enough points to make discourse enjoyable. . . . What keeps me alive is the ability to look back to the past and imagine I am still in 1902 or 1903. . . . As long as I can retain the books and pictures and furniture and accessories of those days, as I still do, I have something to live for. (*WBT* 429)

Lovecraft's attempts to explain his failure to commit suicide are often regressive, but sometimes they move toward the future. In 1930 he wrote that the motives holding him back were connected with "architecture, scenery, and lighting and atmospheric effects, and take the form of vague impressions c with elusive memory—impressions that certain vistas, particularly those associated with sunsets, are avenues of approach to spheres or conditions of wholly undefined delights and freedoms which I have known in the past" (*SL* 3.243). Two months later he wrote that he was "always staving off the suicide-line by illusions of some future ability to get down on paper that quintessence of adventurous expectancy which the sight of a sunset beyond strange towers . . . invariably excites within me" (*SL* 3.321). These passages develop statements Lovecraft had made in 1916 and 1918: On the one hand, "To the scientist there is the joy in pursuing truth which nearly counteracts the depressing revelations of truth" (*Letters to Rheinhart Kleiner* 54), although truth is a delusion like religion, ethics, taste, humor, and imagination and although "all rationalism tends to minimise the value and importance of life, and to decrease the sum total of human happiness" (*MWM* 74), statements with which Leopardi would have fully agreed. It is the pursuit of knowledge, not the possession, that brings joy, for the suicidal implications of truth—and Lovecraft seems to experienced the temptation and appeal of suicide from the age of fourteen—are mitigated by the possibility that one is not yet in possession of full truth and may never be. This uncertain pursuit of truth conflates with the aesthetic pursuit to produce the experience of the sunset flight, which may lead to an admission of weaknesses and defects, inabilities to know the truth and inabilities to realize beauty, which must be recognized if one is to live honestly in the world; that is to say, the sunset experience becomes a critical instrument by which an individual can judge the world as it is, one's self as one is, and join and admire others in the recognition of their common weakness. The sunset experience has an ethical corollary; it implies a moral direction within a chaotic universe, a teleological imperative.

The sunset experience has precedents in Lovecraft's reading, one of them in the verse epistle to which we have already referred that Keats wrote to entertain his sick friend Reynolds. In that poem, before the garden moment, Keats exclaims:

> Oh that our dreamings all, of sleep or wake,
> Would all their colours from the sunset take,
> From something of material sublime,
> Rather than shadow our own soul's daytime
> In the dark void of night. For in the world
> We jostle— (67–72)

It is a sudden break, an instant in which Keats hesitates to give full form to the vision of the garden. At the end of the poem he feels that he has betrayed the decorum of a verse epistle to a sick friend. But we, with the dynamic of Lovecraft's passage in mind, can see how the sunset of the imagination becomes a critical manifestation of the "material sublime" that reveals the chaotic, jostling world and opposes it.

Another precedent of the sunset moment takes place in Goethe's *Faust*, following the suicidal moment of the first scene. Standing on a hilltop Faust says to the uncomprehending Wagner:

> The glow retreats, done is the day of toil,
> It yonder hastes, new fields of life exploring;
> Ah, that no wing can lift me from the soil,
> Upon its track to follow, follow soaring!
> Then would I see eternal Evening gild
> The silent world beneath me glowing,
> On fire each mountain-peak, with peace each valley filled,
> The silver brook to golden rivers flowing.
> The mountain-chain, with all its gorges deep,
> Would then no more impede my godlike motion;
> And now before mine eyes expands the ocean. (38)

This passage, shaped by Goethean motifs of the movement to the ocean and the flight of the lark, leads to the famous exclamation, "Two souls, alas! reside within my breast" (39), and the evocation that allows Mephistopheles to appear; once more we can see the critical aspect of the sunset experience, the way in which it responds to a world in which suicide had seemed the only rational response.

The sunset moment also is significant for Lovecraft because of its fragility. In 1923, associating the sunset with his own Dunsanian period that was beginning to die out in him and arguing against T. S. Eliot, he wrote, "An artist must be always a child—that's why I tell you never to grow up!—and live in dreams and wonder and moonlight. He must think of the lives and colours of things—of life itself—and never stop to pick the glittering fabric to pieces. Alas! Who ever caught and dissected the sunset without losing it?" (*SL* 1.230). "Who indeed?" Goethe might have murmured, thinking of Newton. Lovecraft uses rainbow language for the sunset when he speaks of "the iridescent gulfs beyond the sunset" (*DS* 264). Given such fragility, the vision of the sunset moment often served "as the harbinger of the horrors that await the dreamer daring enough to descend to the alluring sunset city below" (Cannon, *"Sunset Terrace Imagery"* 14). In 1923 Lovecraft experienced such a moment while walking with his aunt:

> The scene now became wildly beautiful by reason of one of the most gorgeous sunsets in the history of the province. The whole west flam'd forth as if . . . the door of some Cyclopean furnace had been thrown wide; and the old mansion stood out black against a veritable holocaust of empyreal fire. The spectacle was a chromatick tumult unearthly and iridescent, nearly every colour having its place—even a vivid and sinister green which seem'd to typify the poisonous corrosion and putrefaction of the decaying elder America. It was like the phrensy of hysterical cymbals and brasses translated into light and colour—a screaming, terrible thing while it lasted. And because it was violent and terrible, it was very beautiful. (*JFM* 56)

A number of elements, which occur in different modes throughout Lovecraft's writing, enter into this synaesthetic passage. The sunset imagery is a touchstone for his sense of beauty. But this passage also follows the development of the garden moment that we noted in Leopardi and Keats. The sunset moment is an aspect of Lovecraft's garden moment, for here we see that enormous appreciation of beauty and order abruptly broken off by a sense of unstoppable destruction, which Lovecraft understood as the destruction of a suburban and urban scene. For this is the same language he was later to use in describing his experience of New York. Thus he describes his story "He" as the record of a man "who comes to New-York as to a faery flower of stone & marble, yet finds only a verminous corpse—a dead city of squinting alienage" (*FFF* 346). He describes that experience later, "When I first saw strange and pinnacled New York rising mystic and violet out of its water in April 1922, I got this kick to a stupendous degree" (*JFM* 233), painting that kick in a jumble of ecstatic and terrifying images that include a "sweep of red-gold sun over a luring balustraded hill-crest" (*JFM* 223). But the sunset and the kick did not remain: "as soon as the exotick strangeness lost its *distant mystery;* then all was changed. The very cleavage from the known, sane, world became hideous and engulphing menace, and the very glamour and lure turned to a sense of exile and loneliness" (*JFM* 224). The sunset in the city proceeds disastrously.

But the sunset elsewhere feels more like that which Faust pursues. In a long letter of 1931, attempting to describe his own close connection to Rhode Island, he gave a long catalogue of country scenes throughout the seasons which "all linger unchanged in arboreal twilight since the days when the haughty Narragansetts were its only lords" (*SL* 3.318), suddenly expostulating, "Whatever this unhappy country may some day come to, there is no one who can say that Old Theobald has not known to its inmost depth, & loved to its utmost detail, that first, settled, & homogeneous English America which to the young is half a myth & half a dream" (*SL* 3.318–19), for he has watched it die "as the greedy tentacles of the town overran it bit by bit" (*SL* 3.318). But this sunset, the sunset that lingers over the countryside that is in the process of perishing, unlike the sunset of the city that leads to a gangrenous nightmare, "all this kind of thing," as he says, "joins curiously up with the conception of the cosmic to form a sincere & serious mood of pictorial experience, liberation, & adventurous expectancy" (*SL* 3.319). Nevertheless, it is a countryside that is a garden, a countryside made over to the image of eighteenth-century order, just as the garden that Lovecraft most dreamed of was a jumble of sundials, urns, pagodas, marbles, and termini.

But the countryside is also, as these passages make clear, a landscape threatened by the advance of the twentieth century, symbolized by the monstrous, the tentacular. Under the influence of Edward J. O'Brien and Joseph Wood Krutch, Lovecraft came to see this threat epitomized by the machine, the technological control of nature and arrival of a new kind of humanity which annihilate both the landscape and the ability to appreciate such a landscape (*JFM* 180–81)—to say nothing of destroying the art of the American short story. And this threat is for Lovecraft his garden moment—one which, however, lies in the historical future, not one which has occurred, does occur, and shall always occur, as it does for Leopardi and Keats; Lovecraft historicizes the Fall, but it is none the less for him a Fall that causes a qualitative change in humanity, for the humanity that exists hereafter shall exemplify a culture totally discontinuous with the culture he loves. On the other hand, insofar as it shall be a culture that has absorbed his view of a disinterested nature, there are certainly aspects of his fiction that have as it were a prophetic stake in that culture. But he cannot fall completely. It is as though Lovecraft remained unfallen in Eden, only to see that Eden has begun to wither around him, while the withering of his descendents, those to whom he was the eternal grandfather, could only express itself in his own prematurely withered flesh.

Leopardi also feels the anxiety caused by the rise of the machine in European culture. In the "Proposta di premi fatta dall'Accademia dei Sillografi" he suggests "che oramai non gli uomini ma le macchine ... trattano le cose umane e fanno le opere della vita" [that now not men but machines ... handle human things and do the work of living] (1.835), machines that will turn La Mettrie's *L'Homme machine* upon its head and lead to mechanical men and women who will enact mechanical virtues; and in the "Palinodia" he ironically celebrates the binding together of the globe through iron rails, commerce, the steam engine, and cholera (43–45). These dreams of human perfectibility, he believes, infect literature and lead to the optimistic dreams that he attacks in "La ginestra."

Given these premonitions that oppress both Leopardi and Lovecraft, premonitions of human lives and values threatened by indifferent physical forces and of an increasingly mechanical life that imitates a blind nature, what attitudes can they adopt toward human potential, and what kinds of responses can they find possible toward the state that is increasingly interested in efficient performance? Living during the attempt of the Restoration to return Europe to an imitation of the rigid manners that preceded the Revolution, Leopardi was politically progressive, as the censors were quite aware, especially in his early years before his experience in

Rome and Naples convinced him that liberation was well-nigh impossible. His attitude perhaps most complexly appears in the conclusion to his early poem, "Ad Angelo Mai," dedicated to a man who had recently brought to light new manuscripts by Cicero:

> O scopritor famoso,
> Segui; risveglia i morti,
> Poi che dormono i vivi; arma le spente
> Lingue de' prischi eroi; tanto che in fine
> Questo secol di fango o vita agogni
> E sorga ad atti illustri, o si vergogni.

[O famous discoverer, proceed; wake up the dead since the living are asleep; arm the exhausted language of ancient heroes; so that at last this century of mud either gains life and rises to illustrious deeds, or is ashamed.] (175–80)

Here we can see how Leopardi's politics and metaphysics are connected. The Austrian, Papal, and Spanish domination resembles the operations of Nature, chaotic and maleficent, which the poet has the energy to accuse and feel a moral repugnance for, even though he believes it impossible to oppose effectively; the impossibility does not permit him, or us whom he represents, any excuse for silence. The philological activity of Angelo Mai, the fables, myths, and illusions of our ancestors, the poem now, and the consciousness of shame and remorse in any reader, all these actions oppose the silence. And Lovecraft, radically conservative though he was, has something of the same attitude: the scale and indifference of the universe renders any intense interest in politics foolish and shameful. Only in the last years of his life, during the New Deal, does he come to feel that action is possible and imperative, an experience that Leopardi was never to feel in Naples at the end of his life.

In any case both men feel marginalized from political action; thereby, politics remains one of the few human activities that retains an ideal value against which they find most contemporary politics wanting. But marginalization becomes for them a problem and a glory, which in his poem "Al Conte Carlo Pepoli" Leopardi understands under the concept of "ozio," expanding the "otium" of such marginalized Romans as Horace into the empty life that every human lives, even the busiest and most laborious, and that Lovecraft understands as an eighteenth-century gentleman. A person who is idle has no way to affect the stream of events, though his distance allows him some insight into them, "che conosciuto, ancor che tristo, / Ha suoi diletti il vero" [for when recognized, albeit sad, truth has its own delights] ("Al Conte Carlo Pepoli" 151–52). Whether in Bologna, where Leopardi wrote his verse-epistle while trying to find a position that would allow him to live independent of his parents, or in Providence where Lovecraft was ghost-writing stories in order to make a pittance, an eighteenth-century gentleman does not soil his hands with practical politics.

Like every human activity, politics lies under the judgment of the sense of cosmic space and time, which for both writers bears a certain priority for what one is to think of life. But Leopardi uses this sense in works like "La ginestra" or the "Dialogo di un Folletto e di un Gnomo" (42), in which humanity has vanished with no great consequence to the rest of the earth, to underscore human limitations; for him the cosmic sense is pedagogical rather than sublime. He opposes it rather than acquiescing in it. And because of that imposing scale of the universe, both he and Lovecraft believe that morality is not absolute or external to human concerns (Z 2263–64). Leopardi's conviction of the contextual nature of morality flows directly from his belief that all ideas develop from the experience of the senses, "il che non è più bisogno dimostrare dopo Locke" [which after Locke there is no longer any need to demonstrate] (1339), a conviction that also demonstrates that "le cose stanno così, perchè così stanno, e non perchè così debbano assolutamente stare, cioè perch'esista un bello e un buono assoluto ec." [things stand thus, because they stand thus, and not because they should absolutely stand thus, that is because a beautiful and good absolute exists] (1339–40). But if things are only as they are with no reason, because nothing founds them, if the tabula rasa is truly empty, then "la distruzione delle idee innate distrugge il principio della bontà, bellezza, perfezione assoluta, e de' loro contrarii" [the destruction of the innate ideas destroys the principle of goodness, beauty, absolute perfection, and of their contraries] (1340). What is one to make of things as they are? "In somma il principio delle cose, e di Dio stesso, è il nulla" [In sum, the principle of things, and of God himself, is nothingness] (1340)—which is to say that once we have accepted that there are no innate ideas, no Platonic ideas, and no Kantian categories, nothing preexistent to things as they are, "è distrutto Iddio" [God is destroyed] (1340). For Leopardi the implications of a sensationist epistemology lead directly to an abolition of metaphysics and theology. It is an argument with which Lovecraft would have agreed, though he feels little argument is needed to justify throwing them away.

In addition to being convinced of the relativity of beauty and goodness, they are also dubious whether truth bears any inherent moral worth, since they do not believe that human life is productive of happiness, much less that truth is. In 1929 Lovecraft wrote, "in hard fact we must admit that truth is nothing of intrinsic importance. It doesn't matter a hang whether we know anything about anything or not, so long as we can be contented.... Truth becomes important *only when it is necessary to establish our emotional satisfaction*" (*ET* 102). If Leopardi writes, "Ha suoi diletti il vero" ["The truth has its delights"] ("Al Conte Carlo Pepoli" 152), it is only because he expects that the illusions of art and youth will pass away. Truth is important when a human being can have nothing else. The usefulness of truth seems rather unequally balanced between the possibility of strengthening and comforting the individual who can recognize and confront it or of degrading the individual who cannot. And since the contest between the universe and the individual is unequal, the artistic response becomes torn between lament and satire: "Non so se il riso o la pietà prevale" [I do not know whether laughter or commiseration is greater] ("La ginestra" 201). A further possibility, however, of neither lament nor satire, neither heroism nor degradation, is that unique strength of pity and human piety peculiar to both writers through which lament is strengthened into effectual, moral action by the means of satire, "Che senza sdegno omai la doglia è stolta" [For without scorn sorrow is stupid] ("Sopra il monumento di Dante" 14). Such a complex art, however, is difficult to achieve.

II

>   At mihi per numeros ignotaque nomina rerum
>   temporaque et varios casus momentaque mundi
>   signorumque vices partesque in partibus ipsis
>   luctandum est. Quae nosse nimis, quid, dicere quantum est?
>   Carmine quid proprio? Pedibus quid iungere certis?
>
> [But as for me, through numbers and unknown names of things, and times and various chances and powers of the world, the changes of signs, and parts divided into parts, I have to wrestle. What is hard to know, shouldn't it be hard to say? What is the right song? How to join it to metrical feet?] (Manilius 3.30–34)

In approaching the various aesthetic problems with which Lovecraft and Leopardi dealt, it is useful to begin with the example that Lucretius offered in providing them with a language that can open the enormity of the universe to the human spirit (Joshi, *Decline* 4, 13–15). Dante's system was too scholastic for Leopardi's purposes, and the diction of the eighteenth-century didactic poems too precise (Carsaniga 73–74). It is even more difficult to conceive of a model for Lovecraft, for neither the sublimity of the eighteenth century nor the fantasy of Poe, De Quincey, or Dunsany was at last available for his clinical viewpoint. Only Lucretius created a language precise, intimate, and suggestive enough to bring the universe home to us. Lucretius, however, is one of the first writers to face the paradox of being a thoroughgoing materialist forced to struggle with his vocabulary, because the entities with which he dealt, the "clinamen" and the "semina rerum," were abstractions for which sensory evidence from the material world, the kind of sensory evidence he appealed to, is very slight; and Leopardi was aware of Lucretius' anxiety (Z 748), which Lucretius overcame, he insisted, through sugaring his bitter message with verse (4.11–25)—a solution that can certainly lead to a dissociated sensibility in a modern work. It is an analogous problem that contemporary physicists attempt to solve through referring to such mathematical entities as charm and spin—a charming solution perhaps, baroque but hardly satisfying because so obviously removed from mathematical details. In all these cases, of Lucretius, of Lovecraft, of Leopardi, and of the contemporary physicists (who are not after all fictionalists), the language is necessarily metaphoric.

Leopardi's solution entailed widening his vocabulary by opening it up to its traditional roots in the Latin authors and in Petrarch, as though for him this traditional web of language had necessarily to take upon itself a metaphoric power. But though he widens his diction, it remains selective and simple, as Croce says a style "a volte semplice e immediato, senza abbandanare quella elettezza e solennità di modi" [at times simple and immediate, without abandoning that choiceness and solemnity of modes] (118); and even those moments that Croce believes didactic, arid, and "travagliata" [elaborated] may, he adds, form "quell'impaccio" [that hindrance or embarrassment] that makes a reader feel all the more that miracle of achievement and overcoming (119). That selectivity is no illusion, for the range of diction displayed in the *Canti* is quite restricted; and that very restriction adds to the metaphoric power of the simplest words; but an overcoming does not exist for the reader unless a true hindrance is enacted. The small poem "A se stesso" gives an example of one way that Leopardi can create such a tension, a poem that in fifteen lines moves through ten full caesurae, five semi-caesurae, and six end-stops; no matter what we think of its philosophy, the muscularity of the poem is striking. But in his contemporary context he was certainly not a purist but something of a liberal, for his act of widening his language also allowed contemporary turns of phrase that many felt were too vulgar to be a part of a poetic diction. He claims in fact that a poetic language cannot be distinguished from prosaic language by means of diction at all, only through "la diversa inflessione materiale di quelle stesse voci e frasi che il volgo e la prosa adoprano ancora" [the differing material inflection of the very words and phrases that the people and prose employ] (Z 3009); only through inflection, which is to say the rhythm that arises from the control the poet exercises through meter and sound, does diction achieve aesthetic framing. Leopardi is full-minded in language, for mere modernity in diction would be an expression of Oedipal resentment whereas a purist prissiness would be an act of isolation, as though Oedipus had decided to remain in his false home of Corinth rather than take to the road. At the same time as he was purifying his language, Leopardi gradually loosened the formal structure of the canzone to create a rhythm that increasingly depended upon extremely long periods, subtly modulated through caesuras and irregular line-lengths, counterpointed with complex phonic structures. The music of such stanzas is extended and exquisite.

Lovecraft's solution was at first to allow himself to use the style he had absorbed in his early reading, a style based on the eighteenth-century essayists, laced uncomfortably with Poesque and Dunsanyesque effects; slowly he modulated both to a more sober, factual stance while complicating the narrative structures, increasingly retarding the action and the climax with new qualifications. But he always retained British spelling, which in itself creates an effect of scrupulosity and distance in the midst of horrendous events; and though he modified the eighteenth-century stylistic features—parallelisms, antitheses, doubled words, and anaphora—he never abolished them (Mariconda, *On the Emergence of "Cthulhu"* 19–20). In addition, he never stopped using such words as *eldritch*, which function as marks of the obsessive nature of the material and as a part of the embarrassment that accompanies such fears and apprehensions, an embarrassment that the narrative must slowly overcome in order to achieve its final structure. So Lovecraft like Leopardi always maintains a supple linguistic depth in his works, a sense that behind these events and disasters time lies as an immense background against which human beings, to their shame, are pitiably reduced.

Leopardi and Lovecraft do, on the other hand, follow different developments insofar they are working in poetry and prose. Leopardi is convinced of the difference in diction between the two modes and therefore concerned about the extent to which he can bring the diction of modern argument into his verse without betraying the lyric. It is not a problem that he has in his prose; on the contrary, in the *Operette morali* he enjoys deploying a variety of styles—lyric, biographical, historical, mythic, fantastic—all in tension from one small exercise to another. Lovecraft, who begins with a prose style that is distinctly and consciously lyric, is increasingly concerned to employ the language of the sciences, whereas in his poetry he does not attain any variety or novelty until he writes *Fungi from Yuggoth* with its bewildering variety of styles, fantastic, factual, and lyric. It is as though the two writers only achieve something of common effect when each moves out of his central achievements into the domain of the other, in a work that deploys a variety of exercises and experiments in miniature.

The two writiers do, however, share a stylistic motif very important for their basic thinking, a love for the indefinite, that which lies uncertainly, undeterminably between the finite and the infinite. They are both heirs of the Longinian and Burkean tradition of the sublime. This imagery according to Lovecraft will

> evoke the especial sensations—the complex exaltation of spaciousness, liberation, adventurous expectancy, power, drama, pageantry, symmetry, mystery, curiosity-lure, etc., etc., etc.—whose function it is to make existence seem worth prolonging.... I couldn't get the needed sensations out of any *predicted or predictable* course of events, because such events would lack the glamourous *indefiniteness* and *uncertainty* essential to the fostering of the drama-and-pageantry-illusion; the illusion of being poised on the edge of the infinite amidst a *vast cosmic unfolding* which *might* reveal *almost anything*.... This illusion ... is absolutely necessary to an even tolerable *happiness* on my part. (*JFM* 221)

Such passages in Lovecraft may be matched by several in Leopardi, as in 1820: "Descrivendo con pochi colpi, e mostrando poche parti dell'oggetto, lasciavano l'immaginazione errare nel vago e indeterminato di quelle idee fanciullesche, che nascono dall'ignoranza dell'intiero" [Describing with a few strokes and showing only a few parts of an object, {the classical writers} let the imagination rove in the vague and indeterminate space of those childish ideas which are born from an ignorance of the whole] (Z 100). This reflection from 1827 applies his principle more concretely: "Una voce o un suono lontano, o decrescente e allontanantesi appoco appoco, o eccheggiante con un'apparenza di vastità ec. ec. è piacevole per il vago dell'idea ec." [A voice or a distant sound, either decreasing or going away slowly, or echoing with an appearance of vastness, etc. etc., is pleasing because of the vagueness of the idea] (4293). Leopardi is determined to make his reader cooperate in the aesthetic effect, certain that if the reader does not cooperate the work will be dead, a mere pile of inert details. And so both he and Lovecraft, almost quite literally to their minds, invite the reader beyond the horizon.

This insistence upon the indefinite, however, takes a very different form in the two men's works. In Leopardi's later poems, "Il pensiero dominante," "Canto notturno," "Sopra il ritratto di una bella donna," "Il tramonto della luna," and "La ginestra," we find extended similes whose several elements do not make for a greater clarity of image; instead, sometimes ten, fifteen, or twenty lines long, the similes develop emotional and musical materials that lead away from the objects they ostensibly concern, without leading to any world clear in itself as an Homeric simile does. Lovecraft, on the other hand, instead of breaking up his narrative with a simile is fond of a series of adjectives; but his adjectives disperse details rather than specifying them, as though the adjectives or any adjectival procedure, were by the nature of things incapable of revealing the object being described. He decreases the number of adjectives in any such knot in his later fiction, probably in order to lessen a reader's impression of a stylistic tic he cannot control, and in order to make such passages more of a piece with the material that surrounds them; nevertheless, we still find such passages even in the late work, still deflecting a reader's eyes in a rush away from the horror at which they still attempt to point. Leopardi's similes do not point; they gesture, rather broadly, sinuous and taut at an entire range of experience that nonetheless refuses to come into focus. Lovecraft's conventional vocabulary serves the same rhythmic purpose.

Besides this effect of indefiniteness for which both of them strive, attempting to show and not to show, given the devastating effects on human life which they grant truth, the status of their artworks becomes pressing: both are committed to illusions, because both feel that illusions are a comfort to humanity. But the illusions that they glorify are not the political or religious illusions of a self-aggrandizing modernity; theirs are the illusions of human, individual desire, the illusions committed to human solidarity in the face of death.

Both authors, therefore, exhibit a tendency toward a conscious mythologizing that is supported by their calculated structures. In Leopardi this process can be observed in the gradual construction of so short and seamless a work as "L'infinito," with its several drafts, and the sleight of hand performed in the poem as its voice confuses the potential and the actual infinite. The *Operetti morali* manipulates several fantasias of confrontation in which historical figures, philosophic reconstructions, academic voices, animals, and abstractions take the stage to play out various possibilities of Leopardi's philosophy.

Lovecraft describes to his correspondents his procedure for the construction of his weird tales, but it is a procedure that can be interrupted and fertilized by a variety of inspirations, as we can see in his sketches for "The Shadow over Innsmouth." And as he makes clear, the procedure is always less important than what may happen during the writing of any particular work. "It is invariably the unconscious image-forming which gives the work its real vitality & differentiates it from mere photography & mechanism. . . . It is to be noted that those authors whose habitual methods are most conscious & intellectual are generally weakest in the creation of a convincing atmosphere" (*EHP* 41). In order to play to human desires each writer insists upon the necessity of listening to those desires, no matter how anarchic they may seem.

What do they mean to achieve through their art? Avoiding the Horatian formula of *dulce et utile,* in the 1830 edition of the *Canti* Leopardi wrote that he wished "a consacrare il mio dolore" [to consecrate my sorrow] (1.142). An aspect of this consecration is comfort, for anyone who reads the poetry as well as for himself in his old age. Lovecraft feels something of the same proleptic nostalgia for his stories (*EHP* 48). For Leopardi his poetry is concrete evidence of his solidarity with humanity; if it is sweet, it is so for the purpose of comfort, a comfort that extends horizontally with the rest of humanity and vertically, as a function of memory, with himself. For as he argues, solidarity arises from a love for oneself, perhaps the only innate motive that one can find, the foundation of foundations. The *amour propre* of the Enlightenment loses the Promethean, self-justifying tinge it often had, even for Leopardi in the *Pensieri,* to become a foundation for a new ethics of solidarity. Classical scholar that Leopardi was, this comfort has affinities with Virgilian *pietas* which in its respect for the gods includes the relation of the self to fathers and sons and the depth of the historical community, binding together the living and the dead (Pöschl 40, 150); in addition, *pietas* highlights the destructive impulses of history, the *lacrymae rerum* that include the individuals and nations that perish irrespective of guilt or innocence (Johnson 73).

What then are imagination, art, and the poem within the context of *noia* and *nulla*? Given Leopardi's equation of the tabula rasa with the physical, metaphysical, and psychological void within which the world and the individual exist, he had to answer that they were not much. But he offers another answer, one difficult to read, in a series of metaphors. The poem takes place within "un spazio immaginario" (*Z* 171) that is common to humanity because the innate desire for pleasure that can never be satisfied expands through the imagination into infinity. Propelled by this desire, the imagination continually overleaps the circumscribed conditions of life and creates that imaginary space within which all of the *cari inganni,* the dear illusions, arise (165–72). This élan that bypasses every limitation borne by time and space very much resembles the sunset flight of Lovecraft's imagination. Presumably this is the kind of space within which this surprising fragment makes sense: "Una casa pensile in aria sospesa con funi a una stella" [a house suspended in the air tied with ropes to a star] (256). This entry in 1828 describes that space using a different language and perspective:

> All'uomo sensibile e immaginoso, . . . il mondo e gli oggetti sono in certo modo doppi. Egli vedrà cogli occhi una torre, una campagna; udrà cogli orecchie un suono d'una campanna; e nel tempo stesso coll'immaginazione vedrà un'altra torre, un'altra campagna, udrà un altro suono. In questo secondo genere di obbietti sta tutto il bello e il piacevole delle cose. [To a sensitive and imaginative man, . . . the world and objects are always in a certain way double. With his eyes he will see a tower, a field; he will hear with his ears a sound of a

belltower; and in the same moment with his imagination he will see another tower, another field, hear another sound. In this second class of objects stands everything beautiful and pleasing.] (4418)

A year later he commented upon this passage:

> L'existence des êtres finis est si pauvre et si bornée, que quand nous ne voyons que ce qui est, nous ne sommes jamais émus. Ce sont les chimères qui ornent les objets réels, et si l'imagination n'ajoute un charme à ce qui nous frappe, le stérile plaisir qu'on y prend se borne à l'organe, et laisse toujours le coeur froid. [The existence of finite beings is so poor and limited, that when we only see what is we are never moved. Those are chimaeras that adorn real objects, and if imagination does not add a charm to what strikes us, the sterile pleasure which we take is limited to our organic sense and leaves the heart cold.] (4502)

These passages, of course, explain little if we demand and expect nothing but a rational understanding of the imagination; but the point of these passages lies in the very nature of the explanation they do offer, which is metaphoric, an explanation that is itself an act of the imagination. From the point of view of quotidian living, the imagination offers no more than "chimères," the image that the hard-headed Horace had invoked at the beginning of *Ars poetica*. But Leopardi is not claiming that the imagination creates a new world that abuts upon the finite reality of the senses; according to him the imagination occurs within this world, in an encounter with the tower and the landscape, but discovering within this world a second, infinite, suspended world of beauty and meaning that is rationally unavailable to the senses. He does not require a sunset, Lovecraft's symbol for this moment, but like Lovecraft he sees an expansive world within the real world.

The imaginative space, however, is as unstable as that sunset that may degenerate into horror, for as soon as an object is pictured to any degree of definition its limits become apparent and a profound unrest, the *noia* so much a part of Leopardi's thought, enters the mind. Only an indefinite image that exercises the imagination without limit can be satisfying—a sunset that can never proceed into night. But Leopardi is too much a realist to accept that image.

If he does not require a sunset, however, he has two other moments that resemble the structure of Lovecraft's. One is an image that recurs often in the poetry, the sound of something human dying out in the night, which has the aesthetic virtue of being an indefinite image. On the first page of *Zibaldone*, written when he was seventeen years old, we find a few lines describing a moonlit scene in which a cart is heard "che stritolando i sassi / Mandava un suon, cui precedeva da lungi / Il tintinnio de mobili sonagli" [which striking the rocks sends forth a sound, proceded from afar by the ringing of its swinging bells] (1). This passage reveals an early interest in attempting to render the peculiar dynamic between the half-light of such a landscape and a transient human music within it. In the early poem, "La sera del dì di festa," the image appears as the song that a despairing lover hears in the distance:

> Ahi, per la via
> Odo non lunge il solitario canto
> Dell'artigian, che riede a tarda notte,
> Dopo i sollazzi, al suo povero ostello;
> E fieramente me si stringe il core,
> A pensar come tutto al mondo passa,
> E quasi orma non lascia.

[Ah through the path I hear not far the solitary song of the craftsman returning late at night, after the pleasures to his poor inn; and my heart contracts powerfully, to think how all things in the world pass and leave not a trace behind] (24–30)

Here we find the faint song in the distance semi-logically connected to the transience of earthly affairs, even tacitly the love that the speaker feels. And that song concludes the poem:

> ed alla tarda notte
> Un canto che s'udia per li sentieri
> Lontanando morire a poco a poco,
> Già similmente mi stringeva il core.

[and late at night a song heard along the paths dying away little by little constricts my heart at the same time] (43–46)

Something of the same sign of transience concludes this passage in the middle of a later poem, "Il sabato del villaggio":

> Già tutta l'aria imbruna,
> Torna azzurro il sereno, e tornan l'ombre
> Già da' colli e da' tetti,
> Al biancheggiar della recente luna.
> Or la squilla dà segno
> Della festa che viene;
> Ed a quel suon diresti
> Che il cor si riconforta.
> I fanciulli gridando
> Su la piazzuola in frotta,
> E qua e là saltando,
> Fanno un lieto romore:
> E intanto riede alla sua parca mensa,
> Fischiando, il zappatore,
> E seco pensa al dì del suo riposo.

[Now all the air turns brown, the sky turns dark blue, the shadows return from the hills and roofs, at the whitening of the new moon. Now the ringing tells of the meal to come; and at that sound you would say that the heart was comforted. The boys shouting in a crowd in the piazza, here and there leaping, make a happy noise; and meanwhile the carpenter returns to his meager meal, whistling, and thinks to himself of his day of repose.] (16–30)

This extended passage moves through a series of sounds becoming slowly more quiet, the ringing of the bell—at which you would say the heart took comfort—the shouts which form a joyful rumor, and the whistling muffled as the worker inside his house considers the day of his repose, which is almost over. The next stanza couples the silence with the darkness, "Poi quando intorno è spenta ogni altra face, / E tutto l'altro tace" [then when every torch is extinguished, and all else is silent], though the hammer and saw of carpenter is heard preparing for the next day, "Nella chiusa bottega alla lucerna, / E s'affretti, e s'adopra / Di fornir l'opra anzi il chiarir dell'alba" [in his closed shop under the light, and he hurries, and tries to finish the work before the light of dawn] (32–37). This vigil, however, is one that glides into a sunrise that signals another day of labor. The light of the sun, a sign of definition, is seldom a happy image in Leopardi's poetry.

Lovecraft also employs auditory imagery, but it is of a very different kind from Leopardi's. If it is a music, it is inhuman, issuing from the chaos beyond our universe, and monotonous; if it seems to die away it soon returns, fluctuating erratically, although as his characters hear it they sometimes believe that it has a pattern and rhythm (Mariconda, "Lovecraft's Cosmic Imagery" 191–92). Since it is beyond human senses it is often synaesthetic, a music that is more than music. In opposition to human aspirations and aesthetic appreciation, even when it seems to correspond to them and abet them, it frequently begins as the sunset moment begins to reveal the horror beyond its beauty. Thus though like Leopardi's music it is always vague, an invitation to the infinite, it threatens madness.

The second image that Leopardi uses, closely allied to that of sound dying away, is the moonset. For Lovecraft, the thrilling moment is associated with the transformation of the sun of rationality; for Leopardi the moment is associated with the transformation of the moon of the romantic imagination as it sets into the drab light of the disillusioned world. In the early idyll "Odo, Melisso," a shepherd recounts a dream in which he saw the moon ripped from the heaven and fall to earth, leaving an empty hole in the sky "in cotal guisa, / Ch'io n'agghiacciava; e ancor non m'assicuro" [in such a way that I froze; and I still cannot feel reassured] (19–20). His friend's ironic comment, that it would be so easy for the moon to fall in his own field, and the thought that stars fall, bring the poem to its conclusion: "ma sola / Ha questa luna in ciel, che da nessuno / Cader fu vista mai se non in sogno" [for there is only this one moon in the sky, which no one ever saw fall if not in dream] (27–29). Anomalous though the poem is in Leopardi's verse, an uneasy combination of the pastoral and the cosmic, it represents a genuine remorse and terror for the loss of the moon. That same setting moon accompanies the early poems "Bruto minore" and "Ultimo canto di Saffo," which opens with an address to the "verecondo raggio / Della cadente luna" [modest ray of the descending moon] (1–2). But Leopardi's most powerful use of this image is in the late poem, "Il tramonto della luna," which compares the gradual disillusionment of human life to the light of the setting moon:

> e si scolora il mondo;
> Spariscon l'ombre, ed una
> Oscurità la valle e il monte imbruna;
> Orba la notte resta,
> E cantando, con mesta melodia,
> L'estremo albor della fuggiente luce,
> Che dianzi gli fu duce,
> Saluta il carrettier dalla sua via.

[and the world discolors; shadows vanish, and one obscurity browns the valley and the mountain; the world remains bereaved, and singing with a sad melody, the wagoner salutes upon his way the last gleam of the fleeting light that had lead him before.] (12–19)

The song of the distant traveler parallels the lessening of the light, a tacit but none the less powerful synaesthetic moment; and like the darkening landscape of that moon setting behind the mountain, life darkens:

> Abbandonata, oscura
> Resta la vita. In lei porgendo il guardo,
> Cerca il confuso viatore invano
> Del cammin lungo che avanzar si sente
> Meta o ragione.

[Abandoned, dark, life stays. Watching it, the confused traveler seeks in vain the long road that seems to present a goal or a reason.] (27–31)

The traveler's loss of direction, and the absence of music in these lines, beautifully illustrates the doctrine common to Leopardi and to Lovecraft that the universe has no goal and no purpose. And since for human life, not as for that landscape, no sun shall rise again, human life "Vedova è insino al fine" [is widowed at the end] (66). The light of the moon leaves us *orba, abbandonata, oscura,* and *vedova,* adjectives nicely chosen for their musical and their emotive value, emphasizing the emptiness revealed so dramatically in the idyll of the shepherds.

Finally, we must notice the fusion of these two moments in the late poem, "Canto notturno di un pastore errante dell'Asia," a long poem whose spacious contours perform mimetically to suggest the enormous space, perhaps the perceptually largest of Leopardi's *spazi imaginari,* in which the shepherd's song takes place. It is one of those remarkable works composed from few materials, the shepherd, the moon, the mute animals, and the barren landscape lit by the moon. As an imitation of a simple style it is also perhaps the most studied of Leopardi's poems, another attempt to imitate the Greek poems upon which he had based his hoaxes as a young man (Carsaniga 97). For our purposes, however, the poem is wonderful in the way that its title and the simplicity and musicality of the verses suggest that the song of the shepherd, with its several references to the diminishing of human life, accompanies the moon upon its journey through the sky, so that every *diminuendo* and *poco andante* of the poem functions as an emblem of the gradual loss of beauty and illusion. In addition, like Faust and like Lovecraft yearning for the setting sun, this shepherd yearns to fly with the moon, to become one with this "solinga, eterna peregrina" [lonely, eternal pilgrim] (61) as it moves through the stars, because, he insists, the moon must understand:

> Il patir nostro, il sospirar, che sia;
> Che sia questo morir, questo supremo
> Scolorar del sembiante,
> Il perir dalla terra, e venir meno
> Ad ogni usata, amante compagnia.

[our suffering, our sighs, what they are, what is this death, this final discoloration of the face, this perishing from the earth, and becoming less to every accustomed, loving companion.] (64–68)

Without the shepherd's having to say, nor could he say perhaps in his simplicity, the lessening of the body finds its counterpart in the lessening in the sky toward which the poem gestures as a tacit presence. We should also say of these poems, however, in which the setting moon and the diminishing song appear either as landscape, as simile, or as symbol, that the very indefiniteness of the imagery also means within Leopardi's aesthetic that the poems that hold this bittersweet vision together are very beautiful indeed.

If Leopardi finds himself forced to accept the language of the chimerical, not able to escape the problem of *a-letheia* though the experience of the poetry certainly suggests something other than illusion, Lovecraft, who also believes in the tabula rasa (*SL* 2.273), finds himself forced under the eyes of the everyday world to produce a hoax, the problem that he cannot escape. But what does he mean? Is it a hoax to scare? A hoax to convince the reader that monsters exist? According to several passages it serves instead a double purpose, both to construct a persuasive depiction of the real world, what we have referred to as the real wall, a demand to which Lovecraft felt himself increasingly unequal the more that he felt it was necessary, and to convince a reader that an escape from the prison of this mechanistic world, this real world over which he has expended such careful labor, exists. And to that extent, within the tension of such contrary demands, Lovecraft like Leopardi is offering his reader a comfort. But for Lovecraft the word *hoax* certainly deprecates the comfort he can give much more than Leopardi ever intended in his own works, perhaps because Leopardi was much more confident of his abilities.

A major difference, therefore, between Lovecraft and Leopardi lies in the kind of comfort each man offers, for Lovecraft projects no program that can parallel Leopardi's *pietà*, his covenant with humanity. Lovecraft cannot allow a program of solidarity into his stories, though solidarity does arise in them, because he believes in a stance of indifferentism that conceals his vulnerability. For as Leopardi knew, the covenant lays the heart open to continual disillusioning; it rests upon a purely human ethical construction. Lovecraft tries consciously to draw back from this tension, whereas in his poetry Leopardi faces the tension, which manifests itself as the moral question how at the same time to offer consolation and to tell the truth, consolation without the *cari inganni* and truth without brutality. "Dialogo del Plotino e del Porfirio" and "La ginestra" are central texts that bear witness to this struggle. Something of his answer lies in his solution to the problem of where comfort can arise in a truthful mind. Perfume, sweetness, linguistic depth is a part of the answer, something of a moral category insofar as it implies a Virgilian historicity, an acknowledgment of what happens to human society in time; and so as a libertarian in diction Leopardi frees himself from his early Petrarchism without becoming wholly a modern, just as Lovecraft slowly expands his diction while maintaining the apparent affectation of his English spelling as well as the syntactic structures he absorbed from the eighteenth century. And a further answer to the challenge of truth and comfort lies in solidarity, which seems an exclusively moral rather than an aesthetic category, but solidarity always exists in Leopardi's most successful poems when he takes the part of the suffering mind and flesh against the material world that destroys it; solidarity, therefore, is an aesthetic category insofar as it incarnates the typical turn of *pietà* at the conclusion of his poems, as in these words that introduce the final stanza of "La ginestra":

> E tu, lenta ginestra,
> Che di selve odorate
> Queste campagne dispogliate adorni,
> Anche tu presto alla crudel possanza
> Soccomberai del sotteraneo foco.

[And you, soft flower, that adorns these wasted fields with odorous branches, you too will soon succumb to the cruel power of the subterranean fire.] (297–301)

This address, by acknowledging the beauty that the plant gives to the desert, identifies the poem with the same action. The poet and his poem are one with the plant which "al cielo / Di dolcissimo odor mandi un perfumo / Che il deserto consola" [to the sky lends a perfume of sweetest smell that consoles the desert] (35–37). Personification, repetition, contrast, alliteration and assonance, every musical means of the language is deployed against the certainty of destruction. If such comfort as the plant offers the wilderness is an illusion, as surely it is, it nevertheless vivifies the comfort and solidarity that the poet offers the reader, the only comfort he would dare to offer, which surely is no illusion. No matter how stubbornly a reader might resist the philosophizing of the lines, as Croce did, the reader cannot resist their musicality and suave cadence or the immediacy of such phrases as "dispogliate adorni" which offer without premeditation though surely with art the only comfort a Leopardian lyric can offer.

What are we to say of Lovecraft's treatment of the moral-aesthetic struggle?

First, it seems clear that within a pure indifferentism this struggle would not arise: truth would not permit a person to take the part of human suffering, for human suffering from a cosmic viewpoint is not significant: "All life might well be a trifling pimple" (*SL* 3.229). To Leopardi from this viewpoint Pompeii seems an anthill flattened by an apple grown on the tree of the knowledge of good and evil and on the tree that grew in Newton's garden, and earth a dot, a *nulla* ("La ginestra" 158–230; cf. 2.951). But in his stories, especially those upon his return from New York, Lovecraft does not work from the perspective of indifferentism; that is one reason that he has to create a hoax. He does not simply return *from* New York; he returns *to* Providence, which he loves with a love surpassing that of woman, and his famous exclamation, "I am Providence" (*JFM* 93), reveals only one aspect of that love; his insight transcends narcissism. He loves Providence as an architectural extension of himself and of his family, perhaps of the house that his family had lost, and as an incarnation of history. He loves it also as the style that he had accepted from the eighteenth century but that he found submerged by the pluralistic trends of the twentieth century that break up a homogeneous style, even the style that he crafts with his own hand. Not the least, he loves Providence as an act of civilization committed against Nature, an indication of the only way human beings can stand out against the undifferentiated, destroying indifference of the wilderness. In this respect the Puritans were admirable, having "unconsciously sought to do a supremely artistic thing—to mould all life into a dark poem . . . and in place of slovenly Nature set up a life in Gothick design. . . . On shifting humanity they imposed a refreshing technique, and to an aimless and futile cosmos supply'd artificial values which had real authority because they were not true" (*SL* 1.275). He is not indifferent to Providence, for true, effective authority proceeds from a definite style, a human achievement. Moreover, he had little choice in the matter; he had to love Providence "because I would feel lost in a limitless and impersonal cosmos if I had no way of thinking myself but as a dissociated and independent point" (*ES* 303). Though many of his letters contain an analysis of the mechanistic process by which he had come to love the city of his birth, often as an example of how all individuals come to love the culture and place that has nourished them, his analysis never cools that love.

Given the intensity of his love, the stories that he writes upon his return are different in temper from those he had written before. The tone that he creates in the new stories is cool, circumspect, selective, as precise as it can be about the threats of invasion from that unspeakable place outside the walls of the world. But despite the attempt of the style to render and emulate the indifferentism of the cosmos, the tone implies also a social and historical perspective. The tone is sweet-minded insofar as Lovecraft loves the spirit of the place that is threatened. Contrasting his approach to that of Smith or Wandrei he writes, "With me, the very quality of being cosmically sensitive breeds an exaggerated attachment to the familiar & the immediate—Old Providence, the woods & hills, the ancient ways & thoughts of New England— . . . They despise the immediate as trivial; I know that it is trivial, but cherish it rather than despise it—because everything, including infinity itself, is trivial" (*ES* 288). Leopardi is not of the same mind. He only loves Recanati when he is far away, when as an adult conscious of all that he has lost he is able to reconstitute the *inganni* of the child in his memory.

And, finally, we must also admit that Lovecraft loves and takes the part of his characters, most especially those who are unlovely. The pathos of Wilbur Whateley and his twin brother, poor, insufficient, invisible monster that it is, never to live up to its father, is unmistakable. Not only is Charles Dexter Ward sympathetic in his love of Providence, so is his horrendous ancestor Curwen, because he is an historian obsessed by the idea of finding a proper text. Despite the misogynist doctrines of "The Thing on the Doorstep" Lovecraft cannot prevent his pity for Asenath, devoured by her father. The nameless and faceless narrator of "The Shadow over Innsmouth" receives little characterization until in a fit of terror and ecstasy he realizes that he has at last found his true home and his true city, rather like Lovecraft upon his return to Providence; but before that conclusion Lovecraft has lingered over the architectural filigrees of the decadent Innsmouth and compelled the reader's love for its beauty even in its own decay. He understands the fate of Peaslee, and he has seen his own face in the face of the Outsider. These are points to keep in mind when we are tempted to agree with Lovecraft that he was not capable of characterization. We read Leopardi and Lovecraft because despite the horror and meaninglessness of the world they portray they still find in it so much that moves them; they never come clear of the *cari inganni*, the "local teleology" (*WBT* 379).

Of course anything we read may be simply a matter of taste. *Non disputandum*. As we indicated at the beginning of this chapter, Leopardi had quite definite tastes. According to Ranieri, during the last years of his life when his condition was worsening Leopardi abhorred vegetables and adored sweets: "il caffè, sciroppo di caffè; la limonea, sciroppo di limone; il chioccolatte, sciroppo di cioccolatte (e non senza le vainigie, rigorosamente vietateglì); e così via via. E quanto ai gelati, era un furore" [coffee; coffee syrup; lemon, lemon syrup; chocolate, chocolate syrup (and not without vanilla, strictly forbidden him); and so on and so on. And as for ice cream, it was a mania] (38). Lovecraft was no less excessive: "My 'sweet tooth' has no limit—" he wrote, "I like my cake to be all frosting, & and take five (domino-shaped) lumps of sugar in an average-sized cup of coffee" (*JVS* 84). His victory in an ice cream contest is legendary (de Camp 72). He and Leopardi exhibit an odd combination of fastidiousness and release, of discipline and excess, of prudence and recklessness. Lovecraft's dietary habits (beans and pie, beans and pie) are shaped by poverty, an absence of any gourmandize, and sheer whim; he eats like a starved little boy. The distaste for fish may reveal several traits: fastidiousness, fear of bones, fear of the wild and chaotic, of the thoroughly inhuman, unmammalian life. The desire for ice cream suggests a regression to an artificial, controllable, civilized mother, who is nevertheless as cold as ever.

We must never allow ourselves to ignore the horrendous equation drawn between Nature and the Mother in these works, behind which is acted out Leopardi's relations with his mother who had usurped her husband's control of the house and its finances and whose financial treatment of her son effectively exiled him from his home in his last years, leading him to the experiment of the *sodalizio* with Ranieri and his life in Naples. But the tension with the Mother, the concrete manifestation and symbol of nature, is not thereby ended. In "La ginestra" the womb provides one of the tropes for Vesuvius, the explosive and destroying volcano whose waves of stone flow about its base. Since nature is a destructive mother, the two authors feel that they must erect a hypothetical aesthetic, *causa sui,* in the name of the fictional father. But their fathers differ because Leopardi's is present in charge of his education; in contrast, because Lovecraft's father died very early in his life, his maternal grandfather becomes the source of his autodidacticism, only to die when he is fourteen. This difference in the presence of their fathers may account for the less traditional, more uprooted aesthetic that Lovecraft develops, though the problem of America is doubtless at work also.

In speaking of their relation to the Mother and Mother Nature we must also speak of the Child, of their own self-image, for that self-image becomes one means by which the style actualizes itself: *l'enfant est la style.* In both cases, sometimes impressionistically and sometimes clinically, they view themselves as a monstrosity. Like Pope they find themselves in a body that predisposes them for study and in a body deformed by study. Lovecraft wrote of one of his late characters, "Whether the dreams brought on the fever or the fever brought on the dreams Walter Gilman did not know" (*CF* 3.231); perhaps it was simply his Innsmouth name and perhaps an Innsmouth body. As Helen Deutsch says of Pope:

> The poet's deformity becomes the center of a vicious circle of cause and effect from which Pope in his capacity of author, objectified as an infantilized and feminized cripple, is excluded. Whether readers praise the artist's use of illusion in overcoming his deformity, or exclude him as spectacle from that illusion, they must mark physical aberration as the point of origin, the boundary between art and life. Pope himself, to the letter of his deformity, becomes an ineffable original. (35)

With his passion for the eighteenth century Lovecraft is very aware of Pope as a model, and so is Leopardi. Pope is one of his examples of the modern author who is characterized by a body "esilissimo e sparutissimo" [most weak and most thin] because "la grandezza appartenente all'ingegno no sì può ottenere oggidì senza una continua azione logoratrice dell'anima sopra il corpo, della lama sopra il fodero" [the grandeur belonging to talent cannot be obtained today without a continual consuming action of the spirit upon the body, of the blade upon the sheath] (207). Leopardi's early labors did consume his eyes. Carsaninga has pointed out the constructive use to which Leopardi put his confined circumstances, both physical and geographical, by confining his horizon, purifying his landscape of all extraneous elements until it becomes the deserts of the late poems, in order "to escape into infinity" (39). That purification and constriction takes place in all of his poems, however, for the indefiniteness of the imagery upon which he places such emphasis flows from his own semi-blindness. The moon that he recalls in the poem "Alla luna," "nebuloso and tremulo dal pianto" [cloudy and tremulous through tears] (6) represents the visual field of most of his poetry. His body is present throughout this poetry as a projection into the *spazio immaginario* and as the fulfillment of his aesthetic imperative. His insufficiencies are transformed, but the transformation is a necessity because of the insufficiencies. His weakness becomes a trope for human weakness, but only through the weakness being extreme and being his.

Lovecraft's ugliness, the ugliness that his mother had assured him of, and his illnesses are deeply involved in the free time that he obtained for his erudition, his correspondence, and his fiction. He does not make his illnesses tropes of the human condition, not explicitly, but with some irony they do become models for the spiritual conditions of Henry Wilcox, the far-sighted aesthete of "The Call of Cthulhu," Randolph Carter, Charles Ward, Edward Derby, and Walter Gilman, all men whose alienation from the world is signified by their psychosomatic frailties, just as he makes his ugliness and breakdowns models for the Outsider, Wilbur Whateley, and Nathaniel Peaslee. These projections of identity are possible only through a thorough acquaintance with human askewedness, the signatures of a not-to-be-retrieved "ineffable original."

It is not insignificant that these are situations and reactions that Lovecraft and Leopardi share which their fellow exile from the garden, Keats. After his father had died when he was young, he watched his mother transfer her affections from him and then die from tuberculosis, bestowing upon him his own death. And that body, so frequently reaching out in his poems, was sufficiently monstrous in its size that he overcompensated for it throughout his life. His painful jeer at himself, "I do think better of Womankind than to suppose they care whether Mister John Keats five feet high likes them or not" (*Letters* 1.342), represents the same act of will that slowly transforms the poems into the objective, ambiguous works that continue to alert the mind through their dialectic.

Perforce, therefore, we are concerned with the variety of self-images Leopardi projects in the voices of the *Operetti morali* and the *Canti* and Lovecraft projects in his fiction. One of Leopardi's most striking portraits is of Phillippo Ottonieri, whose version of Socratic irony originates in the discrepancy between the ugliness of the body and the ardency of the heart. Eleandro and Tristano are idealized self-images that justify the completed *Operetti*, the latter divided between defending his work upon "il deserto della vita" [the desert of life] as a philosophy which is "dolorosa ma vera" [sad but true] on the one hand (1.1020) and on the other suggesting that people either burn the book or keep it as "un libro di sogni poetici, d'invenzioni e di capricci malinconici" [a book of poetic dreams, of inventions and melancholic caprices] (1.1026). The split between the philosopher and the artist is manifest. But Eleandro is also important because his pity for humanity projects the moral qualms that modify the pursuit of truth and of aesthetic perfection. The

"Dialogo dello Plotino e dello Porfirio" presents a subtler self-image in which the self is divided into two parts, the one filial and suicidal, consumed by the emptiness of *noia,* the other paternal and consoling. This is the one point in the imaginative works in which Leopardi's desire for a son speaks. Usually in the last works the consoling self is a member of society, a brother; but it could be argued that the consolation that Leopardi offers in his works is that which he much more often desperately needed. The self, then, of the *Operetti* and of the consoling *Canti* is an idealized self, one which creates a son or a community to receive his consolation.

The poems present a different self. In the "Ultimo canto di Saffo," Leopardi's ugliness speaks through the female voice of the Greek poet in love with a handsome man. In a projected preface to the poem he wrote, "La cosa più difficile del mondo e quasi impossibile, si è d'interessare per una persona bruta" [the most difficult thing in the world, almost impossible, is to take interest in an ugly person], and adds that he would never have attempted the subject if it were not for three conditions: her being a woman, since he writes principally for men; her great spirit and fame; and above all her antiquity, the distance set between her and the reader, "l'oscurità de' tempi, l'incertezza ec. [che] introducono quelle illusioni che suppliscono ad ogni difetto" [the obscurity of the times, the uncertainty, etc. {which} introduce those illusions that supplement every defect], conditions which do not apply in his case (1.447). But as a representation of his case the figure of Sappho as a woman, as a famous person, and as a person whose indefiniteness does not allow a reader to see the actual, disillusioning details of her life misrepresents his case, unless we admit the feminine aspects of his poetic life, the fame that he prophecies as inherent to his work, and the unclarity of the self that is dispersed through that work; the aesthetic coherence of the poem highlights his own incoherence. What stands out all the more, therefore, is the ugly, unloved, uninteresting monstrosity of his own life that has no place within nature. In addition we need to keep in mind that Leopardi based his poem upon Ovid's fifteenth epistle of the *Heroides* in which the Latin poet elevates the Greek poet to a mythological status while at the same time presenting her as the victim of a "difficilis natura," not merely a difficult nature but a nature that makes askew when it denies her any beauty despite her genius (1.447; Ovid 31); this discord reminds a reader of the image of the self presented in Sappho's most famous poem, the self sick unto death from love, a sickness that forces the self to dismember itself into a clinical dissection of skin, tongue, eyes, and ears. For Ovid, Sappho's genius originates in the same love that prevents its expression (5–8), or would so if the poem were not a parody of the love-poet, a parody of Ovid himself and the series that this epistle concludes (Jacobson 297–99); she is also a poet who suffers from the present wound, from the shame of her desertion that does not accord with love, and from the contradiction of her present love and the "non sine crimine" of her past (19; cf. 201). Though Ovid draws no consequence from her past, she is a poet who is outcast from her family, an orphan who is deserted by her brother and who no longer cares for her own daughter.

With this material as background, Leopardi begins his poem at moonset. Sappho's ugliness isolates her from a beautiful nature, whether it is pastoral or sublime: "Ahi di cotesta / Infinita beltà parte nessuna / Alla misera Saffo i numi e l'empia / Sorte non fenno" [Alas of such infinite beauty the gods and wicked fate make miserable Sappho no part] (20–23). Within the "superbi regni" [proud kingdoms] (23), she is vile, an illegitimate guest in the natural world because her heaviness of spirit, a sign of *noia*, isolates her from the others. So much is she not a part of natural processes that the world flees her: "al mio / Lubrico piè le flessuose linfe / Disdegnando sottragge" [from my slippery foot the streaming waters disdainful draw away] (33–35). *Lubrico* is a transferred epithet. Sappho takes a word that properly refers to the waters or the riverbank and applies it to her foot; it is not the bank that is weak but her foot, as well as indecent, a further meaning of the word. Because she is flawed and outcast she takes up the complaint of Job and the anxiety of our epithet: "Qual fallo mai, qual sí nefando eccesso / Macchiommi anzi il natale" [what fault, what enormous evil marked me before my birth] (37–38). No answer is vouchsafed her, however, because "arcano è tutto / Fuor che il nostro dolor" [all is arcane except our sorrow] (47–48). She takes up the complaint for everyone, even those who do not realize that they are empty, as her language passes from the first person singular to the plural. Her suicide is thereby a death within which all humanity is rightly involved.

Another picture of the self is in "Il passero solitario," a poem that avoids the *agonismo* of the earlier poetry. The emphasis is in the title: the swallow on its tower and the poet in the countryside, casting his eye on the setting sun, are alone. But this loneliness is accompanied by song that overflows until the day dies. The bird does not take part in the brilliance of spring, in the music of the other birds and beasts, because it is outside the world of generation: "Non ti cal d'allegria, schivi gli spassi; / Canti, e cosí trapassi / Del'anno e di tua vita il più bel fiore" [You do not care for happiness, you avoid the games; you sing and thus pass the most beautiful flower of the year and of your life] (14–16). Leopardi always chooses the slightest, least of creatures as an emblem of the self: the flowering broom, the brown swallow. But the creature is filled with an energy that allows it to ignore happiness—but not quite, given the singular beauty of the first lines—to shy from the common games and flirtations, to give itself up totally to its song and thus pass, trespass, and pass over, to cross the very boundary of the end of the line in a lovely enjambment, to exceed the beauty that belongs to the year and its own life. The regret of the line is fused to a triumph of the artist who has lived beyond the exigencies of instinct. The poem celebrates the singular freedom of the poet.

In his final poem, "La ginestra," Leopardi most nakedly manipulates his self-image as a part of the argument of the poem. The objectivity of the language leaves no doubt that the person being described is the lyric persona:

> Uom di povero stato e membra inferme
> Che sia dell'alma generoso ed alto,
> Non chiama se né stima

> Ricco d'or né gagliardo,
> E di splendida vita o di valente
> Persona infra la gente
> Non fa risibil mostra;
> Ma se di forza e di tesor mendico
> Lascia parer senza vergogna, e noma
> Parlando apertamente, e di sue cose
> Fa stima al vero uguale.

[A man of poor status and infirm limbs, albeit of high and generous spirit, does not call or think himself rich or stylish, and does not make himself ridiculous in society with a splendid life or a strong person; but weak of strength and treasure, he lets himself appear without shame, and names it all openly, and thinks of his things precisely as they are.] (87–97)

This is a consoling self that has none of the authority of the father or of the sage, a naked self, riches, beauty, strength and valiance stripped away to leave the voice that continues to sing through its nakedness; its authority consists of its emptiness. It has sacrificed its egoism to its egoism (Z 3168). The word *mostra*, "show," is very close to *mostro*, "monster"; and the likeness allows the line to suggest that the self, whether show or monster, is not to be ridiculed, belittled, and put aside but must be taken as a serious emblem of humanity's place within an indifferent world. Its emptiness is a mark of its reality. The self is a new Adam, naked but without shame, crippled, a different figure than that of Sappho, attractive despite her ugliness because of her distance; this image is contemporary, engaged in an argument with political consequences. As Helen Deutsch says à propos of the "ugly particulars" that load down Pope's later poems, "This poetic attention . . . is embodied by the author himself. His physical deformity becomes a vehicle for self-reflection, self-representation, and self-legitimation. The poet's body is both a trademark of his poetry's invisible property, and a sign of his own vulnerable visibility, rendering him at once an inimitable original and a faulty imitation" (2). The new self, the hunchback Giacomo, opposes the fool who "di fetido orgoglio / Empie le carte" [with a stinking pride fills his pages] (102–3) with promises of a happiness that exceeds earth and heaven, a person the opposite of the self's nakedness, fat and profuse and filling mere pages with something that does not exist. It is possible to see that fool as the poet's father who in an anonymous publication supporting the papal states seemed to steal from the poet, from his son, all that he owned, which was not much, the fruit of his imagination, the *Operetti morali* and his poetry. If he then, as Deutsch expresses the matter, reappropriates himself as an "inimitable original," does he yet have any hope of recovering from the disease of being "a faulty imitation" of the father whose library had given birth to him, the father who had written "quell'infame, infamissimo, scelleratissimo libro" [that infamous, horribly infamous, most wicked book], the confusion all the more likely and bitter because "mio padre è sconosciutissimo, io sono conosciuto" [my father is absolutely unknown, I am known]? With a convoluted irony, half conscious and half unconscious, he remarks, "Lo stesso mio padre troverà giustissimo ch'io non mi usurpi l'onore ch'è dovuto a lui" [My own father will find it totally just that I do not usurp the honor due him]; for since he believes that no honor is due the book he finds it very easy to grant his father that dishonor (3.1029). Shame is inevitable, unavoidable, for even when he writes as many disclaimers of the book as he can he is nevertheless forced to admit that he was begotten by the man who wrote that *scelleratissimo* book. Only one action is possible for the naked self, in the words of "La ginestra," "che con franca lingua, / Nulla al ver detraendo, / Confessa il mal che ci fu dato in sorte" [that with a frank tongue, taking away nothing from the truth, confesses the evil given us in fate] (114–16). A part of this confession is the admission that his parents are that bigoted, stingy pair.

    Last in this list of self-images is that presented in the figure of Dedalo in the *Paralipomeni*. Here is the archetypal exile who built the labyrinth in order to contain the monstrosity that has resulted from the usurpation of male lineage by a monstrous female lust, a creature whose very name, the Minotaur, identifies its double nature and testifies to its cuckolded foster-father. It is useful to view this myth from the angle Marie-Hélène Huet used in examining the process by which "the vision of the Romantic artist as creator borrowed a metaphor of creation from the theory that long ascribed the birth of monstrous progeny to the maternal imagination" (9), so that the typical Romantic "reflected on the dark desire to reproduce without the other and rehabilitated the resulting monstrosity as a troubling but unique work of art" (126). In this version of the myth of monstrous female lust that eradicates paternity, Pasiphae requires the aid of the artist in order to fulfill her desire, and so Daedalus builds the artificial cow into which she climbs, accepting the mask of an artifice in order to deceive the bull with the appearance of natural love. So Daedalus is involved in arousing the bull, as well as complicitous in the containment of the monstrous offspring; and Dedalo in Leopardi's poem is self-exiled through his sympathy with animals. Joyce must have appreciated this part of the myth when he claimed in his poem "The Holy Office" to render the same "service" to virgins as the cathartic function he served for the good Catholics who were his schoolmates (*Portable Joyce* 659). This is one version of the primal event. Another version in which the primal event is made explicit occurs in Gabriele D'Annunzio's "Ditirambo IV." Here Icarus, in love with Pasiphae, watches voyeuristically as his father fabricates the heifer and as she, the daughter of the sun, enters it: "Splendea divinamente / la sua carne quand'ella penetrava / nel simulacro per imbestiarsi" [her flesh shone godlike as she penetrated into the simulacrum to make herself bestial] (196). In this version the artist finds himself implicated in the bestiality of the imagination when as an act of revenge upon her father the sun it conceives both the artificial heifer, the wings, the self and the labyrinth that shall contain it, a self that in this case is the Minotaur, "il figlio suo bovino e umano" [her son, bovine and human] (205)—rather like what happens in "The Dunwich Horror" since Lovecraft suffers from this primal event of the imagination also, abetting the conception of monsters. As a writer of weird fiction, especially a weird fiction concerned with such matters as these, Lovecraft realizes that he can only arouse the fear that he considers basic to human emotions (and the desire concomitant with that fear which he cannot admit to) by short-circuiting the reader's rational qualms; the shame he feels as a writer of these paltry things is in part the shame of the pander who must labor to exhibit the virtues of his merchandize. It is a lonely business, an extended foreplay to produce the monstrous fiction in which he only half believes. The only comrade Daedalus has is his son, for we hear nothing of the woman who we presume begot Icarus; the myth encapsulates both the eradication of the father in its first part and the eradication of the mother in its second part, the full range of the monstrous imitations that Marie-Hélène Huet details. Given such a dialectically threatened begetting, Icarus suffers the fate that in the eternity of myth he is one of those figures who is always-about-to-fall and always-fallen, back to the sea from which the bull arose. But Dedalo does not even have the grace of having lost a son, for he is not Daedalus, or probably not Daedalus; in something of the same jest that Goethe enjoys when Chiron says that mythological figures are free from the chronological anxieties of scholars (*Faust* 7426–33), Leopardi suggests that only his friend Niebuhr—if he were still alive—could truly decide whether Dedalo were anachronistic or not (7.2). But outside time, prior as it were to giving birth, Dedalo has no son, and so the Son is lost by the allusion. The labyrinth of Dedalo is the underworld of the animals to which he directs the magnanimous rat-hero of the poem, the anti-climactic scene in which Leccafondi confronts the inert dead; but Dedalo himself cannot enter the underworld because he is too large (8.3–4). In the contemporary world, after all, the mythic world is mere fable. The only underworlds that Leopardi can enter are the contemporary landscapes of the Austrian and Spanish dominations or the peculiar worlds of the *Operetti morali;* the only underworlds that Lovecraft can enter are immigrant ghettoes of Providence or New York or the peculiar worlds of his fictions, such mazes as Curwen's laboratory, Innsmouth, or the city beneath the Antarctic.

Though the myth represents Daedalus as the archetypal artisan who through his double Talos invents the saw, the potter's wheel, and the compass,[5] besides the wings, there is much that he cannot do, for he is an artisan who pays for the daring of his art twice over, both times in the fall of a person near to him, an extension of him, the fall of his nephew Talos and the fall of Icarus, falls implicated in the fall of Hephaestus who has limped ever since the day that his father Zeus cast him out of Olympus. Is that limp a part of the price that Oedipus pays for the brilliance of his mind, his reconstruction of his past, a payment he makes before he gives proof of his brilliance? Is he like the pre-existent Jesus whose heel has been bruised by the serpent (Gen. 3:15), slain before the foundations of the

---

5. The story of Talos is manifold, for one story tells of the Talos whom his uncle Daedalus killed out of jealousy for his skills and another tells of the Talos who was either an artificial man forged by Hephaestus or the last representative of his race, in either case the protector of Crete. Robert Graves suggests that they represent one figure (1.311–18).

world (Rev. 13:8)? It is a part of Joyce's myth of Stephen Dedalus that the artificer always bears a wound for the intricacy of the work, a myth worked out definitively in his treatment of Shem in *Finnegans Wake*. As for Lovecraft, his wound is obscure, a complex knot of his father's death, the family exile from its paradisal home and status, and the anti-Semitism, all of which creates the aggressions, failures, and successes of his fiction.

What kind of a monsters, then, are Daedalus and his son? In the discrimination that Jane Harrison drew, is he peloric or teratic, an omen of the earth or of the sky (458–59)? He attempts to be a teratic monster, an omen in flight, but the falseness of his assertion is revealed in the fall of his son. For that matter, if we ask how the Outsider rides "with the mocking and friendly ghouls on the night-wind" (*CF* 1.272), this consideration reveals the falseness of that aspect of his situation at the conclusion of that story, for he is in fact a peloric apparition, himself a Daedalus who has risen in flight from the labyrinth in which he finds himself at the beginning of the story, a tomb as static as the underworld to which Dedalo points Leccafondi, and which for all we know or the Outsider knows he has himself built in a supreme flight of overlooking the truth. And the falseness of the Outsider's flight may indicate what is wrong with Lovecraft's attempts to emulate Dunsany; here is a fiction without either weight or solidity, without gravity, an attempt to escape the blood-history of the monstrous, that erasure of the maternal and paternal, and so it fails because the monstrous still exerts itself upon the shape of the world and deforms it; Lovecraft's stories and the story of Lovecraft perform a peloric myth. The modernist version of this myth, the figure of Stephan Dedalus, not only suffers from the question of his reality as an artist and an exile in terms of the question whether he is the Father or the Son, but he also suffers from his monstrosity, his awareness of how much he falls outside the norm that society constructs for sexual and bodily behavior, and he creates monsters thereby in his own breast, "goatish creatures with human faces, hornybrowed, lightly bearded and grey as indiarubber" (137), that testify to the power church and state still exert upon him. His flight lies in his ability "to forge in the smithy of my soul the uncreated conscience of my race" (253), which is not only to create that conscience, that solidarity of mind, through an artifice, the minutely considered work that the reader is almost to complete, but also to counterfeit that conscience, since Joyce was suspicious of any possibility of being of one mind with his Dubliners and his Irish; so the story of Stephan Dedalus testifies to his isolation, as do the stories of Leopardi and Lovecraft.

As we earlier intimated Daedalus is responsible for two monsters, the hybrid creature hidden in the labyrinth and his double Talos, the bull-headed bronze man who beats the bounds of Crete in service to the imperial demands of Minos; in *The Faerie Queene* Spenser chose the figure of Talos to represent the punitive justice that England wielded over Ireland, quite properly in Spenser's eyes. And so there is an ambiguity in Daedalus, who is forced to serve Minos as the artificer of a police state and as the confessor who puts aside the fruit of Minos' impotence. In the opening poems of the *Canti* Leopardi encourages a renascence of Italian glory, a contrast of Roman grandeur against the present oppression of the decadent Austrian and Spanish empires, but finds himself forced in his late poems to construct the labyrinth of the *Paralipomeni* to conceal his monstrous parody of contemporary history and to forge wings for his flights into the imaginary spaces of "Canto notturno del pastore errante dell'Asia" and "La ginestra." Lovecraft spends his early years using the ancient glories of King George and Caesar Augustus to flail the pretensions of the expanding American democracy and his late years speculating on the possibility of an American utopia constructed along socialist-fascist lines, while sending his spirit into more and more massive outsides and more and more massive insides, an imperial space of the imagination to control the chaos that his system demands, an increasing appropriation of cosmic space and time. And both these efforts at imperial control begin within relative degrees of isolation, though it should be acknowledged that all three writers, Leopardi, Lovecraft, and Joyce, were able to construct a domesticity in their later years that represented a comfort and a human solidarity, however problematic these domesticities were (the peculiar nature of Leopardi's *sodalizio* with Ranieri; the epistolary compulsions, poverty, and depletion of spirit that Lovecraft suffered living with his aunt; and the complication of Lucia's psychosis in the multiple incests of *Finnegans Wake*). Though Daedalus lost his son, he came to dry land himself, where his attempt to resurrect his son in art failed, for "bis conatus erat casus effingere in auro, / bis patriae cecidere manus" [twice he tried to draw the affair in gold, / twice the paternal hands fell] (Virgil, *Aeneid* 6.32–33), lines that Aeneas' attempt to embrace his father in the underworld later in the sixth book faintly echo. All attempts at control, all attempts at establishing a more intimate piety, even the attempts in art, fail. The monstrous work of art that Daedalus begins he cannot complete. The ideal father Dr. Willett descends into the labyrinth that his dark double Curwen has constructed in order to hide his "monstrous fruits" (*CF* 3.342), but like Daedalus Willett cannot resurrect Charles Dexter Ward, only free him from the powerful shadow father who has absorbed his son's identity. Leopardi certainly concludes his poems; but the *Operetti morali*, that jumble of different styles and genres, which he requires two dialogues to conclude, never in fact concludes; and the system remains monstrous and an embarrassment.

Lovecraft like Leopardi images himself in his work, attempting to establish an authority upon the basis of his deformity. "The Outsider" is an early attempt in which appearance, mentality, self-creation, and an ambiguous sexuality combine to mark the conviction of the story and its witness, qualities we find also in Wilbur Whateley and Asenath Derby; for Wilbur is too human, unable to achieve the total alienness of his brother, and as a woman Asenath is not human enough, according to the feelings of her father who can only perpetuate himself in her. Not only is the sexuality of the protagonist in question, so is the size. Wilbur is growing too big and too fast, "teratologically fabulous, . . . sheer phantasy" below the waist (*CF* 2.439), and Asenath is short, perhaps one of her Innsmouth failings, concealing her father Ephraim within; each is treated as though out of scale with the world that surrounds them. Early in his career Lovecraft was anxious because of his size, since "some of the greatest men have been the smallest," men like Newton, Poe, and Pope (*SL* 1.121), to say nothing of Keats. But both those who are too large and those who are too small are monstrous, for they do not fit into the monolithic normality of society. The most remarkable fact about Lovecraft's monsters, however, is the fact that they exist, that we can identify them as other. According to Emita B. Hill's analysis of d'Holbach's materialism, monstrosity is an empty concept (cited in Huet 89), for every phenomenon is explicable in a mechanical system, certainly a philosophy with close connections to Lovecraft's thinking. But despite his system Lovecraft restores the monstrous to its existence and its dignity, and thereby restores the human to its dignity. "Monstruosus homo est tamen homo" (Huet 33). Since it is the very identity of the monster as human that implies the monstrosity, Wilbur remains human, as do the Outsider and even the Old Ones; only the shoggoths Lovecraft attempts to exclude from humanity because of their ability to imitate the human, and not even that exclusion can be fully successful since the persistence of the shoggoth, despite the anti-Semitic code, is a human persistence.

One of Lovecraft's last self-images is that of Professor Peaslee whose comfortable world, an ideal self-image of the Lovecraft that might have been had he learned mathematics, attended college, attained a doctorate, and become a professor, is shattered because of his nightmares. Though colleagues, friends, and wife desert him, however, his sons remain faithful, for Lovecraft created sons all around him, in part through the strategy of presenting himself as an old man, perhaps so old as to have arrived at that age where sex becomes generalized once more and the feminine aspect of the self can once more step forth; and one aspect of his surviving his death has been the gratitude of those sons, people like Frank Belknap Long, Fritz Leiber, and Robert Bloch—though some sons rebelled, like Samuel Loveman who burned Lovecraft's letters when he realized the full extent of Lovecraft's anti-Semitism. Lovecraft saved his Icarus by consenting to his own death. Peaslee, the man who had attended college and become a part of its community, is shattered into the shape of his creator, the autodidact who never achieved such things, who certainly never achieved the success of his sons but whose imagination, obsessed with the monstrous and for a time giving birth to itself before its self-doubt made it abdicate paternity, gave birth to monsters who attest to the indelible monstrosity of their maker.

It is probably not a monstrosity that Leopardi could have ever saluted; he did not approve of the Gothic productions of his day. And we doubt that given his prejudice against Italian culture Lovecraft could have appreciated the solemn playfulness of the *Operetti morali,* much less the extended lament of the poetry. They are different kinds of monsters, after all; Leopardi is teratic, a man of the air who like the sparrow lives in the air and who constructs walls to the horizon in order to leap off into a different space, whereas Lovecraft is peloric, a man whose imagination is continually descending. But they approach one another in the creation of a world that human beings must oppose, though much of that opposition finds its strength in the monstrous.

Lovecraft Born Again: An Essay in Apologetic Criticism

I

> There is nothing unscientific in the idea that, beyond the lines of force felt by the senses, the universe may be—as it has always been—either a supersensuous chaos or a divine unity, which irresistibly attracts, and is either life or death to penetrate. (Adams 487; ch. 33)

The 1991 exchange between K. Setiya and S. T. Joshi (*LS* 24) highlighted a series of problems for our understanding of Lovecraft. For many years Joshi has argued that Lovecraft is important because his fiction embodies a structure of concepts that Joshi calls cosmicism; in contrast to Lovecraft's fiction, Joshi condemns the fiction of M. R. James because it lacks any apparent conceptual structure (*The Weird Tale* 133–42). Given his insistence on such criteria, Joshi very nearly suggests that Lovecraft is only of interest to readers who share his cosmicism and that readers who do not share it, especially any readers with a religious faith, simply cannot understand the force and direction of the work. Joshi constructs a monolithic Lovecraft, always in agreement with himself, always logical, always reasonable, a Lovecraft such as Lovecraft would have liked to be. Something of the same results has been achieved by Paul Montelone's ingenious essays examining Lovecraft's stories from a rigorous viewpoint informed by Lovecraft's appreciation of Schopenhauer and such materialists as Haeckel.[1]

Setiya's Lovecraft is rather different. He is, as Setiya half-jestingly suggested, "schizo" (*LS* 24); he is that Lovecraft that early biographers constructed, a divided man who built his fiction from his nightmares and dreams, a man who set himself as consciously as he could against his inheritance of an absent father, an overly possessive and mad mother, and a family cast out of the security of a Victorian home into the financial chaos of the contemporary world. This is the Lovecraft of de Camp's biography, of St. Armand's archetypal study, and of Lévy's study. But more specifically in Setiya's interpretation, Lovecraft was a man torn in his view of knowledge, at the least a man with a more complex concept of knowledge than Joshi, with his view of a materialist Lovecraft, can quite make room for; Setiya's

---

1. I have in mind Paul Montelone's essay on "The Outsider," which concludes that the story "gives a picture of the blind willing of life, the affirmation of life, that informs the whole world and results in this scene of despair and death" and that the protagonist is "a sprawling heap of dust, that dreams the endless and suffering world" (21), and his essay on "The White Ship," which concludes that its theme "may be regarded as Schopenhauerian because desire is represented as primary in human nature and as destined for frustration" (13).

arguments resurrect the possibility that the philosophic dregs of religion tainted Lovecraft.

The possibility of such a taint has certainly existed in the past. As a part of the background to this debate, we must recall a third understanding of Lovecraft, the man whom August Derleth delineated in his essays and pastiches. This Lovecraft was religious, rather schematically so: he had created a mythos in which forces divine and demonic warred above the heads of the human race in a combat always decided in favor of divinity. As has sufficiently been argued, this is a Lovecraft shaped by Derleth's conservative Roman Catholicism, with little resemblance to the Lovecraft who attempted to combine a classic ataraxia with a Nietzschean amoralism. On the other hand, Derleth was a capable man, familiar with Lovecraft through his fiction and letters, and he loved that fiction deeply, enough to devote a good deal of his life to its promotion. Although his view of Lovecraft has been rightly criticized, we must not ignore the possibility that Derleth might have seen in Lovecraft's work elements of the kind of mythos that Derleth constructed upon his own, an heretical mythos that nevertheless bore a sort of congruence with that more complex world that Lovecraft had created. I do not mean to raise the banner of a neo-Derlethian reading; but it is possible to appreciate how Derleth came to read Lovecraft as he did, because there are religious elements in Lovecraft's world-view.

He was raised a Baptist. Lovecraft's mother was a member of the historic First Baptist Church of Providence; and though he thought her agnostic like him (*ET* 364), her name was entered on its list of members in 1905 as were his aunt Lillian's and his aunt Anne's. Lovecraft's name is conspicuous for its absence, though he always respected the antiquarian splendors of the building.[2] *The Case of Charles Dexter Ward* mentions it as "the exquisite First Baptist Church of 1775, luxurious with its matchless Gibbs steeple" (*CF* 2.223), and "The Call of Cthulhu" features the Fleur de Lys house "which flaunts its stuccoed front amidst the lovely colonial houses on the ancient hill, and under the very shadow of the finest Georgian steeple in America" (*CF* 2.42). Lovecraft was never an apostate to the beauties of his mother's church, though he did have a certain nostalgia for St. John's Episcopal Church a few blocks to the north, in part for the sake of its cemetery that figures in *The Case of Charles Dexter Ward* and in part for the sake of his father, who had been Episcopalian—Anglican, we should say, for in his letters Lovecraft refers to the Anglican church or the Church of England but almost never to the Episcopalian church, since it is the pre-Revolutionary establishment that appeals to him, represented by St. John's original name, King's Chapel; one of his epistolary friends, Henry S. Whitehead, was an Episcopalian deacon (*LAP* 806). On the other hand, we cannot say that his image of the Anglican was always positive, for the main character of "The Evil Clergyman" is an Anglican priest whom the narrator

---

2. Some names on the List of Members were to recur throughout Lovecraft's fiction: Angell, Bicknell, Brown, Dexter, Durfee, Dyer, Lyman, Peirce [not Pierce], Potter, Slocum, Tillinghast, Ward, Weeden, Wheeler, Whipple, Whitman, and Wilcox.

sees in the mirror at the climax and realizes, with the same terror as the Outsider, "For all the rest of my life, in outward form, I was to be that man" (*CF* 3.514); although popery is often the threat and lure of the English Gothic, it transforms itself in this story into the threat, for Lovecraft, of religion itself. Nevertheless, Lovecraft was raised a Baptist and taught to pray to "the bland proper god of Baptists" (*CF* 2.94).

In 1931 Lovecraft wrote, "[N]o sane adult, confronted with the information of today, could possibly think up anything as grotesque, gratuitous, irrelevant, chimerical, and unmotivated as 'immortality' unless bludgeoned into the ancient phantasy by the stultifying crime of childhood orthodox training" (*MWM* 306). What might the little Lovecraft have learned of the bland god of the Baptists? Four tenets are normative in Baptist confessions. The first is the priority of the Bible, especially the New Testament, as opposed to any ecclesiastical set of historical creeds, though not all Baptists would confess the inerrancy of the Bible as contemporary Fundamentalists understand the doctrine; the book is important to Baptists. The second tenet is the insistence upon the baptism of the reborn individual; negatively, this tenet denies any sacramental value to baptism and forbids the baptism of infants as superstition. One of the consequences of this tenet and the first is the denial of sacraments, most crucially the denial of the mass and of any grace bestowed through material forms, mere words and gestures, or on the authority of a priest. As a consequence the third tenet, the priesthood of all believers, refuses to draw any distinction between priests and laity and establishes the authority of each congregation; this tenet and the first account in part for the animus against Roman Catholicism often expressed by Baptists, an animus expressed in Lovecraft's letters and fiction—an animus that Henry Melville King, the minister during Lovecraft's childhood, expressed against Italian immigrants (121–22). The final tenet is an insistence upon the religious freedom of each individual and the demand for a separation between church and state, a salient contribution to the Bill of Rights (Tobet 15–34). Certainly these assertions, the freedom of conscience of the individual, the self-governing structure of each congregation, and the independence of the church from the state, virtues represented by Roger Williams when he left Massachusetts and founded the first Baptist Church of Providence, were virtues of which Lovecraft was proud (*SL* 3.348–55) and which he exemplified all his life. The general impact of the demystifying nature of Baptist theology on his thinking should be clear.

A tenet not found here is the doctrine of election, for Baptists were divided between Calvinist predestination to damnation and Arminian free will, of which Lovecraft was aware (*JFM* 247, 250); the church in "The Haunter of the Dark" was originally a Free Will Church (*CF* 3.463), a member of the Free Will Baptists whose heyday fell about the time that the church was sold to Enoch Bowen (Tobet 273–78). But without any explicit change, by the mid-1800s the First Baptist Church had dropped its adherence to the belief in predestination unto damnation, present in the first Baptist confession of 1646 (Lemons 78–79; Bettenson 351), though the second confession of 1677 had asserted that "infants dying in infancy are regenerated and saved by Christ, through the Spirit; who worketh when, where and how He pleaseth; so also are all elect persons, who are incapable of being outwardly called by the ministry of the Word" (Bettenson 354). This remarkable article suggests that the grace of God is always superior to, or at least strongly qualifies the force of, those typical Baptist doctrines of regeneration and of immersion that emphasize the rationality of an adult believer. In 1914, Free Will churches merged with the Northern Baptist Convention (Lemons 81). So broad was the belief in general salvation that Henry Melville King could write that in Christ's sacrifice "the provisions are ample for all nations and for all ages of the world" (*Thinking* 216). On the other hand, extreme versions of Calvinist themes are the materialist doctrine of the Two-Seed-in-the-Spirit Baptists, who believed that God and Satan had placed two seeds in Eve, which have since become the Elect and the Reprobate (Tobet 279), or the doctrine of the Landmark Baptists who asserted the purity of the saved through the ages by insisting that Baptists always existed in their own unbroken succession, despite the presence of the Antichrist in Rome and despite other congregations that call themselves Baptist but are not (Ahlstrom 722; Tobet 298–99). Though both groups were Southern, they exerted a critical force throughout the Baptist tradition; the tension between Arminian and Calvinist thought reappears transformed in Lovecraft's thought and fiction.

Given such a background, what kind of knowledge did Lovecraft have of the Bible? To his disingenuous comment that he "read much in the Bible from sheer interest" (*MWM* 51) we need to add that in a Baptist Sunday School, which he probably attended until his twelfth year (*RK* 158), he would have been obliged to memorize Bible verses, no great task for a mind with the kind of memory he later exhibited. His stories overflow with Biblical names, even if we allow for such common names as Thomas, John and Jonathan, James, Matthew, Luke, Paul, Joseph, Joshua, Joel, Simon, Stephen, Daniel, Nathaniel, Hiram, Silas, Ebenezer, Maria, Martha, Elizabeth, Sarah, Hannah, Abigail, Benjamin, and Samuel, even if we allow for Lovecraft's habit of sitting in graveyards, reading the old New England names with his fidelity to the tradition they represent, and even if we allow for his knowing such stories as those of Abel, Enoch, Noah, Moses and Aaron, Abraham and Lot, Eli, and Delilah. Such names as Ephraim, Asenath, Ammi, Zadok, Asa, Nehemiah, Eleazar, Naphthali, Zebulon, Amasa, Zechariah, Seth, Jabez, Obediah, Nahum, Thaddeus, Simeon, Isaiah, Jedediah, Elkanah, Peleg, Abijah, Esek, Elam, Jephthah, Hepzibah, Barnabas, Obed, Esra, Ezdras, Asaph, and Elihu are embedded in the stories, testifying to Lovecraft's familiarity with the Bible. Some names that look Biblical are not, though they may be suggested by Biblical names, such as Benijah (Benaiah), Nabby (Tabitha), Adoniram (Adonijah), Nahab (Nadab), Zenas, Zaman, and Keziah. There are the names of devils—Abaddon, Dagon, Azazel, Ashteroth, Beelzebub, Belial, Moloch, and Satan—names that Lovecraft could also have read in Milton. Finally, there are a few place-names which are Biblical in origin, such as Ophir, Rehoboth, Zion, Salem, and Arkham (the town of the Ark of the Covenant). Lovecraft's stories are immersed in the Bible, especially in the Old Testament.

In addition to these names, the stories often allude to the Bible. James Egan surveys several passages that he argues are constructed as satires of Christian beliefs, though many of them seem more generally satires of several Western beliefs of the nineteenth century that are liberal parodies of actual Christian thought. A number of passages have been identified, however, as direct allusions. Kadesh and Zin may provide the context of a wilderness and the destroying, revealing wind for Kadath and Zin (Num. 13:26 and 27:14; Ps. 29:5–9), both in *The Dream-Quest of Unknown Kadath* and in "The Dunwich Horror" (Price, "Two Biblical Curiosities" 12–13). Egan notes the parodies running through "The Dunwich Horror," that of the virgin birth and that of Jesus' last words from the cross, "My God, my God, why have you forsaken me," which finds its echo in the cry, "Help! Help! Father! Father! Yog-Sothoth!" (464). He also notes how the phrase "the great priest Cthulhu" echoes the assertion in Hebrews that Jesus is "a great high priest, that is passed into the heavens" (4:14), who was "called of God an high priest after the order of Melchisedec" (5:10). Robert M. Price believes that the story of Sodom and Gomorrah provides several of the details for "The Colour out of Space," especially Ammi's name, the fire from heaven, and the looking back at the disaster ("A Biblical Antecedent" 24–25). In addition, the scientists from Arkham are three wise men, with some irony since they do not know what they are dealing with; yet the phrase and other details in the story suggest that this epiphanic moment is a visitation of a force from outside our universe (Burleson, "Prismatic Heroes" 14). The simplicity of the sentence in the last paragraph, "I shall be glad to see the water come" (*CF* 2.399), though it ostensibly refers to the reservoir probably alludes to a second Flood. "The Dunwich Horror" also plays with material from the Bible. This passage, "*Yog-Sothoth* knows the gate. *Yog-Sothoth* is the gate. *Yog-Sothoth* is the key and the guardian of the gate. . . . *Yog-Sothoth* is the key to the gate, whereby the spheres meet" (*CF* 2.434), clearly refers to passages in the gospel of John, "I am the door: by me if any man enter in, he shall be saved" (10:9), and Jesus' answer to the apostles, "I am the way, the truth, and the life: no man cometh unto the Father, but by me" (John 14:5–6). In *The Case of Charles Dexter Ward* we have the reference to Job 14:14, "If a man die, shall he live again? All the days of my appointed time will I wait, till my change come" (*CF* 2.271), a remarkable verse that forms the climax to a lament for the predestination of individual fate: "Seeing his days are determined, the number of his months are with thee, thou hast appointed his bounds that he cannot pass" (Job 14:5). Finally there is the conclusion to "The Shadow over Innsmouth" when the narrator, who has just discovered that he is connected to a world thousands of years old, a world in which dreams connect him to his ten-thousand year old grandmother, intones, "And in that lair of the Deep Ones we shall dwell amidst wonder and glory for ever" (*CF* 3.230), the *we* including the speaker and his cousin but also including, through such a heightened language, all humanity. As Joshi has pointed out, this passage probably alludes to the conclusion of the 23rd Psalm. But how are we to hear the passage in "Innsmouth," what is its tone? Joshi believes that it parodies its original (Joshi and Schultz, *The Shadow over Innsmouth* 102). It is possible, on the other hand, to hear the words of the narrator as ecstatic, especially if we feel that his fate is not wholly evil, that his standing outside the human community implies a justified critique of the every-day *So-sein* that otherwise he would have lived, the hopeless desireless world of bicycling about on genealogical quests that lead nowhere. All these allusions play with eschatological-epiphanic moments in which a hidden power or coherence of the world is revealed, moments in which suddenly narrator and reader find themselves upon the way to truth. A further aspect of such allusions is the play upon the figure of the Antichrist that forms a part in the apocalyptic myth of Nyarlathotep, so basic to much of Lovecraft's fiction. Such moments, therefore, are analogies to a typically Christian process of pilgrimage. Where is the way? The way in front of you (Phil. 3:8–14). This belief calls upon the language of *mellein*, "about to be," a construction frequent in the epistles, especially Romans and Hebrews, and which parallels the moment when Moses learns that he confronts an I-am-that-I-am, or more exactly, an I-shall-be-that-which-I-shall-be. The Judaeo-Christian God is never finished, always open-ended; it is in that unfinished, not yet to be defined quality that the critique of the world most powerfully resides. And Lovecraft knows that language because despite his materialist certainties he yet writes stories of a world suddenly opened up to epiphany. But if these are moments that open up to truth, our evaluation of that truth is still to be judged. Egan, Price, and Joshi regard these allusions as parodies, as devaluations of Christian claims; we may regard them, however, as potential witnesses to the power of the Christian claims, passages that gain a good deal of their poignancy from the context of the allusions within which they are formed. Among these several uses of the bible we should add that Lovecraft knows how it can be misused; when the old man in "The Picture in the House" reads how "them Midianites was slew," probably a reference to Judges 6–7, he does so to "tickle" his appetite (*CF* 1.215).

Lovecraft's stories are embedded in the context of the Bible, and thereby embedded in a context of faith. Our problem with those stories concerns what it is in his fiction to which any reader responds that is broader than either his beliefs or our beliefs, at the same time that we remain faithful to both beliefs and allow such aggressive material to work upon us. It is the same problem that Croce faced in the *Commedia*, whether a contemporary reader could respond to a poem embedded in a world-view of the Catholic Middle Ages; Croce thought it at least very difficult, so much so that he thought it best to separate the poetry from the theology, just as some attempted to do in their reading of the materialist Leopardi, though it is in practice difficult to say where to draw the line between poetry and content. What are the dynamic relations between religion, belief, and art? Although we cannot deal with such large questions, we must recognize that we do raise them and that they are yet to be settled.

More narrowly we must ask whether Lovecraft's understanding of religion is equal to the understanding of religion held by contemporary philosophers and theologians and whether a theology today will misunderstand Lovecraft. We need also to ask whether Lovecraft's fiction contains elements that speak to a religious understanding of the world, a question in part answered in the fact that these arguments of belief have arisen. In asking such questions, we do not argue from the point of view that thinks the value of art indifferent to belief; our questions affirm with Geoffrey Hill, à propos of Ezra Pound, that an artist's word is his bond and that, as Joshi argues, the world-view of an author has a significant bearing upon the impact and complexity of a work. Art is not religion, but it does have the power to raise eschatological questions. By insisting that the stories are other than philosophy, though they handle philosophic themes, and also saying that they are something other than psychological case histories, though they certainly spring from Lovecraft's own psychological structure and handle psychological themes, we are simply claiming that they are aesthetic works, objects that orchestrate vocabularies, sentences, and narratives, the color of vowels and consonants, irrational elements recalcitrant to rational handling, in addition to philosophic and psychological themes—and religious themes also.

    I have little doubt that Joshi's reading of Lovecraft's philosophy is in the main correct, but with one qualification: the difference between the tone of his letters and the tone of his fiction. Tone is not unimportant for meaning. The two Lovecrafts are quite different, and given such a difference it is not surprising that Joshi's Lovecraft is the writer of the letters, for he is the most aggressively philosophic, the Lovecraft most eager to proselytize. He is that "monstrous species of man," according to Addison, a zealot in atheism, propagating his infidelity "with as much fierceness and contention, wrath and indignation, as if the safety of mankind depended upon it" (2.460–61; No. 163). The tone of this Lovecraft varies: he is sage, precise, careful, complex; he is also aloof, that is to say stoic, though he is also involved and certainly compassionate; but he is also a cracker-barrel philosopher, eager to assume that his arguments are apparent to common-sense if only the idiots would listen. He hectors. This tone he shares with Mark Twain, Ambrose Bierce, H. L. Mencken, and Ezra Pound. It is the tone of Ernst Haeckel, the German scientist whose book *The Riddle of the Universe* Lovecraft often alludes to in his letters, a book that chapter after chapter proves a fervent polemic against the Christian, especially the Roman Catholic, world, for "the popes are the greatest charlatans that any religion ever produced" (284). Haeckel may well have been the source of the grosser blasphemies associated with Buck Mulligan in *Ulysses,* for the phrase "gaseous invertebrate" is his (12; cf. 9.487) as is the story of the paternity of Jesus by the Roman soldier Panthera (327); the latter story is a part of the evidence Richard Noll advances for Haeckel's anti-Semitism (85–86). We understand why Joseph Wood Krutch, one of Lovecraft's favorite authors in the 1920s, asked, "Who reads Haeckel now or who, having read him, fails to find the complacency of his atheism even more antiquated than his facts?" (194–95). The answer to this rhetorical question remained—Lovecraft. Unfortunately this tone has its dangers beyond becoming outdated, as Pound discovered after he delivered his common-sensical radio broadcasts to the American troops during the Second World War, doing incomparable damage to the complex poet in him. Despite the assumption of these authors their tone is not natural; it is constructed, rhetorical, with a particular kind of prejudice in mind.

Foremost among these assumptions is the emptiness of metaphysics. The material constitution of the world is beyond argument, apparent to any one who need look; and if the uselessness of metaphysics is so apparent, it is also clear that religions, as Haeckel said, are the business of charlatans. It seems a concomitant of this assumption that ethics need not present any great difficulties, so that political questions are also open to easy solutions and so that, if seemingly unsolvable situations do exist, they exist for the benefit of political shysters. From the viewpoint of the frontier and of rural America, political and religious institutions, all institutions of power and traditional knowledge, are at best to be met with a stubborn skepticism, at worst with an aggressive ridicule.

This tone has a good deal to do with how Lovecraft divides his discussion of Christianity into two subjects, the theological and the ethical. As for theology, he thinks it all ridiculous; the Christian system is absurd, a Semitic invention that makes less sense than paganism. And having said so much, he says very little about Christianity, because he attacks it not for its theology but for the fact that it is a religion, a theism, in which he fiercely sees no reason to believe; it is divinity that he finds incredible, let alone a trinity (*SL* 3.341). He has much more to say about the ethics of Christianity because of its cultural embedding; thus he treats the difference between Roman Catholicism and Protestantism as the difference between Italian and Anglo-German culture, that is to say in terms of his cultural prejudices. This passage about Puritans, his own forebears, is representative: "Instead of running away from consistency & honesty as those coprophagous little sewer-rats of papists did, they faced courageously—like white men & Romans, by god!—the blank wall of absurd & impossible myth which their limited vision led them to regard as reality" (*SL* 3.339–40). His cultural background formed his opinion of Christian ethics, and he would have had it no other way.

This tone is not the tone of the stories, in which the constitution of the world is considerably more difficult to ascertain and in which religions, though they are certainly mistaken, are mistaken for good reason, the opacity of the world that human experience faces. Within this tone the intellectual difficulties of the world are freely admitted: rural America is superstitious, though it is a superstition that may preserve important facts otherwise overlooked by the power-structures of society; given its potent nature, lore must be treasured and treated very carefully by the libraries of the world. Human particularism—our languages, cultures, and rites—is not to be explained away by common sense.

If this tone has anything in common with religion, to what religion shall we compare it? It is hard not to be tendentious; art calls to the most basic and most particular aspects of our identities, to which religion also speaks. I am not surprised to read an argument comparing the work to aspects of Zen Buddhism, as Dirk Mosig has done (95–102), or to Calvinism, as St. Armand has done (31–32), likely comparisons when we consider how often in Lovecraft's narratives paradox and preterition abound. But we are concerned with the way in which the stories approach the central perceptions of the main religious tradition of the western world; orthodox Christianity, therefore, needs to be investigated for such traits as Lovecraft might evidence. I am not concerned with the theology of a militant orthodoxy whose questions of chastity or the priesthood might prove ephemeral nor with a fundamentalism whose inerrant readings so often prove marginal—though we must admit that when Lovecraft ridicules religion he frequently has such extremes in mind. We need instead to address the perennial questions of creation and incarnation, free will and original sin, death and resurrection, justification and salvation, and sacrament. To do so, I will utilize the radical Protestantism of Karl Barth that seems in retrospect to represent most thoroughly that moment in which European existentialism became appropriated by a rigorous Christian orthodoxy and the recent theologizing of the Roman Catholic Edward Schillebeeckx, not because of his correctness, which the Vatican has so vigorously denied, but because his position seems to represent what is at present most solidly shared by both Catholic and Protestant traditions, what seems now most representatively orthodox.

Such a reading has an ancient tradition within the church, the tradition of apologetics through which various patristic thinkers attempted to demonstrate the compatibility of dogma with certain elements in paganism. The first moment in apologetics occurred when Paul pointed at the altar of the unknown god and alluded to lines from Epimenides and Aratus, "Yet in fact he is not far from any of us, since in him we live and move and have our being, as some of your own writers have said, 'We are all his children'" (Acts 17:28); and Aratus is apt to Paul's purpose, for the proem to his poem on the stars and the weather depicts a Zeus who fills the whole earth, streets and markets, seas and harbors, vitally involved in the daily life of every individual (Aratus ll. 1–7). Christianity defends such an apologetics by insisting upon the global, unitary nature of a god revealed as the creator, redeemer, and mover of the world. The danger of such an apologetics is the temptation of an imperialist attitude toward pagan culture, an attempt at erasing differences to prove the inherent Christianity of the pagan viewpoint, because Christianity is committed to the belief that every word, every intelligible and incommensurable structure, is conceived through the holy spirit; but such an imperialism has to admit the stubborn reality of Odin, who even though he rode the world-tree Yggdrasil is nevertheless a gallows-god to whom living victims were strung up; and it has to admit the reality of Lovecraft also. My exploration separates itself from apologetics in not aiming at any imperialism; it simply attempts to show that this reading of Lovecraft is not willful, that it does reveal aspects of the text that may reasonably move even a Christian reader.

But we are not only concerned in such a discussion with theology. Schillebeeckx makes clear the degree to which his theologizing depends upon and utilizes the hermeneutic tradition of Husserl, Heidegger, and Gadamer, which has already been absorbed into contemporary theology (*Christ* 30–79). Religion has always relied upon the language and categories of philosophy: neoplatonism affects the gospel of John, Aristotle the *Summa* of Aquinas. Aware of its reliance, theology has had to declare the degree of its independence, those aspects by which philosophy does not affect the credal content (Aquinas 1–2.40).

Most Christian apologetics begin with the work of the Father, the creation and nature of the visible and invisible world; so we will begin with the given world, a subject we have already touched upon when we treated the wall to which documents attest and when we drew the distinction between the real wall and the true wall. And we will deal with this subject from the perspective of the anxieties science fiction experiences in dealing with physical law, one of its most defining concerns; for despite the trappings of the weird and of horror, Lovecraft increasingly wrote the kind of story that seems science fictional in its assumptions. In identifying God with physical law, however, the modern age has already played false with the understanding of God in orthodoxy, for it is only since the Enlightenment that the intricacies and autonomy of physical law have become a part of the description of God, not incidentally removing God from any intimate relation with the creation (Borg 38). In Genesis, however, God creates the world with an immense ease, a simple *fiat*, in order to labor over Adam and Eve with more care and foresight. The anxiety that science fiction and Lovecraft exhibit in the face of physical law and the insistence that this law has something to do with the existence of God misread orthodoxy.

On the other hand, given his prejudice against the assumptions of deism and the ethics of Christianity, Lovecraft is most interesting when he argues the details of his materialist mechanical position and the indifferentism to which he felt it led, for his attitude toward physical law is crucial to any understanding of him. He begins where Haeckel left off, affirming the oneness of the physical world and agreeing that the materialist description of the universe exhausts what it is possible to say of the universe. This monism that Haeckel so fervently insisted upon Barth associates with the monotheism of Islam and its iconoclasm (3–2.458–73); but Lovecraft is no iconoclast, and as we shall see he is no monist either. He does believe in the existence of physical law, its coherence, rationality, and uniformity—but breaking with Haeckel he also entertains the idea that the universe is so large that areas might exist where the universality of law breaks down, and he feels impelled in his fiction to witness this breakdown and our human inability to endure it. His classic expression of this theme is the opening of "The Call of Cthulhu": "The sciences, each straining in its own direction, have hitherto harmed us little; but some day the piecing together of dissociated knowledge will open up such terrifying vistas of reality, and of our frightful position therein, that we shall either go mad from the revelation or flee from the deadly light into the peace and safety of a new dark age" (*CF* 2.22). In this passage he resembles the Isaac Asimov of "Nightfall," another rationalist who entertains the notion that hard as the mind may try in the face of a Lucretian breaking through the walls of the world it cannot sustain a rational vision: "We thought six stars is a universe is something the Stars didn't notice is Darkness forever and ever and ever and the walls are breaking in and we didn't know" (181–82). Under the impact of this revelation the people of the planet burn its civilization and crawl off mad into caverns from which their children will emerge to begin the cycle once more. Asimov did try to dissociate himself from "Nightfall," as though it were only an entertainment; like Orson Welles at the end of the *War of the Worlds* broadcast he insisted, "You will be relieved, I hope, to learn that we didn't mean it" (Cantril 42). Of course neither Lovecraft nor Asimov go far enough in the view of a theologian like Barth who scorns all half-way physicist attempts to transcend the world, all astral bodies, supernaturalisms, and paranormalisms, all jargon about dimensions and anti-Euclidean geometries. From Barth's point of view these are false transcendences, because the language and models they employ always return the subject to the world as it is, attempts to make God an object (cf. *Römerbrief* 78, 246). But if neither Lovecraft nor Asimov nor most readers believe the literal assertion of these stories, how do we read them unless the complexity of the universe functions as a metonymy for that which transcends it, that against which we measure the insufficiency and critical nature of the material world and of any intelligent entity within it? Such stories suggest that we are not sufficient to ourselves and that we must be judged.

In reading these stories we also need to put aside their implication that there are certain things mankind is not *meant* to know—presumably not meant by the authority of a creator who jealously preserves the signs of his power, though even Lovecraft allows his narrator to use this language: "We live on a placid island of ignorance in the midst of black seas of infinity, and it was not meant that we should voyage far" (*CF* 2.21). Orthodoxy considers this anti-intellectualist stance a misreading of the prohibition in Eden against eating the apple. More crucial to stories of this sort is the belief that standing against human endeavor something exists against which our doings appear existentially insufficient; these stories articulate the judgment against humanity that any person would wish to escape. And in this judgment of human insufficiency Lovecraft stands in close agreement with Christian orthodoxy.

A further anxiety that science fiction exhibits in the face of the laws of nature concerns the nature of those laws. Upon its most basic level this anxiety reveals itself as an attentiveness to the kinds of understanding that proceed from scientific inquiry, whether in scientific enquiry we have to deal with an explanation or a description and whether we substantially encounter the heart of things as they are. Science fiction cannot avoid these problems; it cannot ignore them, be ignorant of them, or dismiss them without some rationalization that admits their just claims. It may certainly oppose some kinds of understanding to other kinds, but when it does this it still plays the game that the day-by-day practice of the sciences and the history and philosophy of science play, for science fiction is under no more constraint than they to believe that the scientific endeavor is monolithic. Science fiction has in fact admitted a variety of philosophic assumptions, as Daniel Born illustrated in his history of the positivistic assumptions of the Golden Age writers, who like Lovecraft believed in the emptiness of metaphysics, assumptions that yielded in the 1960s to a reliance upon the relativistic claims of linguistic analysis (252, 268). The genre has learned to be leery of its biases.

Given the non-monolithic nature of science, it is no surprise that science fiction interprets physical laws broadly and that a part of the history of the genre can be traced through an analysis of what laws science fiction pays heed to. Prior to physics was the position that geography occupied in Jules Verne's work. Now thermodynamics, biology, even the soft sciences such as sociology interest authors—for H. G. Wells a Fabian sociology was of thematic importance—or linguistics. Whatever society considers a body of organized knowledge may become the model of law for science fiction. In any particular work, then, we need to pay attention to whatever understanding of science was prevalent when that particular work was written; it is certainly important as far as Lovecraft is concerned that we learn of his admiration for the world-views of Ernst Haeckel and Hugh Elliot (Joshi, *Decline* 7–20, 42–44).

These struggles for the interpretation of science reveal that more than knowledge is involved in the fidelity that science fiction brings to the sciences, for the genre is written by men and women swayed by the values of their society, values that arise from a constant strife of desire and fear. Finding ourselves within a universe to which we must bring some measure of understanding if we are to live, we are necessarily affected by the kind of universe that we feel we have come to understand, a universe desirous and fearful. In science fiction these desires and fears are thematized in terms of law and its imposing order. Science fiction, then, does more than pay respect to law; it approaches law with an anxiety that because under law we live threatened by the universe we should pay attention to in order to live, we must pay attention in order to manipulate the world into the shape of the heart's desire.

Despite these considerations some authors are inclined to say that law is law. Tom Godwin's classic story "The Cold Equations" presents physical law as an unalterable structure, uniform throughout space and time. In that story physics and biology, questions of spatial and temporal dimensions, velocities, and metabolism, in addition to the legal questions of murder and suicide, economic constraints, and a myth of the American West projected into the future through historiological assumptions, form a complex structure within which human choice is steadily reduced. The pilot and stowaway can act in only so many, restricted ways; and their actions are motivated by an ethics that also constrains them, a fairly traditional ethics of the greater good. This story thereby reveals that some form of continuity exists between scientific law and human law and that this continuity may constitute a resemblance, perhaps even an identity. Both have such qualities as order, impassivity, progressive modification, and ideality; their greatest difference lies in the way that most natural law is based upon a concept of number. Yet human law is often expressed in terms of gradations, payments, and years; human law is not shy of quantification. These characters act for the good that is greater. Lovecraft's heroes, Dr. Whipple, Dr. Willett, Professor Armitage, and Daniel Upton act also within such physical and moral constraints; only a certain set of words are of any use.

Given the notion that law is impassive, science fiction expresses our anxiety in the face of things as they are; explanation gives way to description, a development that lay at the heart of the argument over the Copenhagen interpretation of quantum mechanics. That anxiety increases as interpretation becomes necessary; the meaning of law, if that law is merely descriptive, becomes a matter for a contentious, dialogical hermeneutics, as though we were once more back in court. One of the great arguments of quantum mechanics, whether we are to accept its non-causal picture as descriptive or as ontological, resembles a difficulty that arises in one of Elliot's marks of materialism, "the denial of any form of existence other than those envisaged by physics and chemistry" (142), which he supports by an appeal to Occam's razor, "Entia non sunt multiplicanda praeter necessitatem" (144). Rather, however, than employing the principle of economy as an indication that such entities do not exist, Occam used it in a purely methodological manner; the *necessitas* is logical rather than ontological. More significant, however, is his use of the principle to underline the immediacy of God's power and the contingency of the world as God made it: the world is as it is, though it could have been quite other since this is as it is as God chooses, with no other cause or *entia* between God and the creature. To press the principle of economy in this way is to insist upon the immediate dependency of the creature upon its creator and to argue that only a close attention to what is self-evident, to experience and revelation, can justify asserting that something exists; Occam makes human experience peculiarly naked to God, who cannot be experienced according to any category (Leff 17, 423–31). The non-causal ontology of the Copenhagen interpretation recapitulates the novelty of existence in Occam's theology.

As far as orthodoxy is concerned in one regard, Lovecraft's Faustian characters do not transgress physical law, for the power of the magician and his demon lies in the manipulation of natural powers; according to Aquinas such power is not miraculous, not outside the order of the universe (1.110.4, 1.114.4). On the other hand, for Aquinas the demon can manipulate nothing more than natural law, whereas in Lovecraft it is possible that in several instances such figures as Yog-Sothoth and Nyarlathotep represent a trespass from areas in the universe where the universality of physical law, as we have understood since the Renaissance, does not exist.

As to the breakdown of physical law as we know it, Lovecraft is quite remarkable and appears to be outside the tradition of science fiction, as it was practiced by Verne and Wells and by the authors of *Astounding*. But he also breaks with the model of Haeckel and Elliot, for each espouses a radical monism that according to Elliot professes the uniformity of law, especially the law of causality exemplified by the Laplacean billiard balls, the non-teleology of the universe, and the exclusive materiality of the universe, expressed as the conservation of matter and energy (138–43); in addition Elliot insists upon the irreversibility of time expressed in the second law of thermodynamics and the gradual degradation of the universe (60–68), in this regard parting from Haeckel who believes the universe infinite and eternal (191).

Lovecraft agrees with most of these tenets, especially the materiality and non-teleology of the universe. But he does not believe that the physical laws of space and time discovered within the range of our senses necessarily hold outside that range. He takes a hint from Elliot, but extends it considerably further than Elliot ever intended, who early in *Modern Science and Materialism* had argued that "all our knowledge of the Universe is based on sense-impressions; nor can we so much as imagine or conceive of anything that is beyond the sphere of our senses" (4), but added, "For so long as we have anything less than an infinite number of senses, there must always remain unknown aspects of the Universe, which might be disclosed by the possession of other senses" (5). This sensist notion of understanding, a Lockean notion as far as Lovecraft is concerned, leads Elliot in his concluding chapter that attacks Kantian idealism to employ the language of outside and inside—"matter is outside and permanent, sensation is inside us and fleeting" (180)—only to dissolve them through insisting that both are "sensations like the others" (180) and indistinguishable. All is sensation for Elliot. The wall exists, insofar as it represents the barrier of the senses, and does not exist, insofar as no outside is perceptible. The argument parallels the argument in Lucretius that all images of the mind, whether in the eye, memory, dreams, or hallucinations, result from the imprint of particles emitted as simulacra by every object in the world; all images enjoy the same level of being and may be considered indistinguishable (4.722–822), though Lucretius refuses to draw the conclusion that one cannot distinguish fantasy and reality. So many are the images, in fact, that assail the mind that Lucretius raises the possibility that within the instant that a sound is uttered other times lie, "tempora multa" (4.796), which provide space for the images, "tanta est mobilitas et rerum copia tanta" [so great is the speed and number of the things] (4.799). This passage may have given Lovecraft the hint that time need not be considered a linear phenomenon.[3]

For Elliot the argument of the limitation of the senses, an agnostic argument that Lovecraft liked, leads to the possibility that the outside and its *multa tempora*, that which is outside our senses and the laws which become perceptible through them, do exist, or at least exist for the purposes of speculation and of fiction. If, however, an outside exists beyond our senses and beyond the coherence of those laws, those laws then seem purely contingent, something which we may describe but for which we can never discover an internal, coherent principle. Their fragility is patent. Only one scientist, Karl Pearson, went as far as this claim though we

---

3. Although there is no evidence that Lovecraft read Hume (cf. Joshi, *Decline* 4), he did read Will Durant's *The Story of Philosophy*, which summarized Hume's ideas in this way: "He proposed [. . .] to destroy science by dissolving the concept of law. [. . .] We never perceive causes or laws; we perceive events and sequences, and *infer* causation and necessity; a law is not an eternal and necessary decree to which events are subjected, but merely a mental summary and shorthand of our kaleidoscopic experience" (281). Does this passage lie behind Lovecraft's use of the word "kaleidoscope"? In his discussion of law and causation Elliot does not address Hume's arguments.

have no indication that Lovecraft read him; nevertheless, Elliot refers to Pearson's book *The Grammar of Science,* as does Henry Adams, whom Lovecraft seems to have read (*JFM* 56).[4] According to Adams, Pearson believes as strongly as Elliot in the sensory limits to human knowledge:

> "In the chaos behind sensations, in the 'beyond' of sense-impressions, we cannot infer necessity, order or routine, for these are concepts formed by the mind of man on this side of sense-impressions"; but we must infer chaos: "Briefly chaos is all that science can logically assert of the supersensuous." The kinetic theory of gas is an assertion of ultimate chaos. In plain words, Chaos was the law of nature; Order was the dream of man. (451; ch. 31)

At this abrupt revelation of Azathoth, Adams continues dispiritedly, "For himself he knew, that, in spite of all the Englishmen that ever lived [Bacon, Newton, and Kelvin], he would be forced to enter supersensual chaos if he meant to find out what became of British science—indeed of any other science" (451). This entry into the supersensual chaos is precisely what Lovecraft attempts in such stories as "From Beyond" at the beginning of his career and "The Dreams in the Witch House" and "Through the Gates of the Silver Key" near its end. But more frightful than these stories, and more typical, are those in which alien laws and alien entities enter our coherent universe from an unimaginable place beyond to reveal the fragility of life and infect it with their incoherence. In one of Adams's striking metaphors, Pearson had taken our universe, wrecked by the incoherence of new discoveries, and "cut the wreck loose with an axe, leaving science adrift on a sensual raft in the midst of a supersensual chaos" (452). Within our cosmos we hypothesize the uniformity of law; such laws as causality, the three-dimensionality of space, and the irreversibility of time are graffiti on the walls of the world.

This chaotic outside of the universe, unapproachable through our senses, has another consequence for Lovecraft's stories, in that it expands Lovecraft's universe farther than any telescope can reach, situates that immense distance no farther away than a person's elbow, and emphasizes the plenitude of the universe; Lovecraft's universe is fuller of being than the universe of Newton or Haeckel because it has more dimensions. Certain passages describing that multiverse resemble theological passages describing angels, for one purpose of angels is to emphasize the ordered plenitude and immediacy of the created world. This is the point of these lines in the hymn, "What Wondrous Love": "Ye wingèd seraphs fly, like comets through the sky, / Fill vast eternity with the news, with the news" (Christ-Janer 1.299). So many angels dance on the head of a pin because they are incommensurable in comparison to the material world and contain space rather than being circumscribed by it (Aquinas 1.50.3, 53.1–2). The difference between angels and Lovecraft's creatures lies in the moral dimension; for Lovecraft this difference undercuts the *valde bona* of Genesis,

---

4. Barton St. Armand devotes a few pages to resemblances between Adams and Lovecraft (78–80, 102n36).

which in any case is as Barth argues a matter of faith rather than of evidence (*Römerbrief* 120). On the other hand angels, insofar as they are created beings that under certain conditions are sensible to the human senses, distinguishable and discussable in rational terms (cf. Aquinas 1.50–53), are no more extranatural than the entities that fill Lovecraft's universe.

The language of Elliot, Pearson, and Adams goes back to Lucretius, who imagines an infinite chaos of atoms within which an infinity of cosmoses come into being as those atoms randomly collide, cohere, and disperse (2.1044–89): "Sic igitur magni quoque circum moenia mundi / expugnata dabunt labem putrisque ruinas" [Thus the atoms around the walls of the great world battled down will sicken into putrid ruins] (2.1144–45). Unlike Lovecraft's model, these cosmoses resemble one another, for Lucretius does believe in their coherence owing to the given shape of the atoms. But his picture of worlds besieged and battered down by immensely energetic forces surely has much in common with Lovecraft's world threatened by incomprehensible purposes. Like Pearson, Lucretius develops a sensist epistemology that becomes an instrument of rather unbridled speculation. The walls of the universe are weak. So Lovecraft finds himself justified in asserting, "The precise mechanism of the cosmos was not then [in 1900], is not now, and never will be understood" (*SL* 2.271). He had, however, drawn a more radical conclusion earlier, that "since the entire plan of creation is pure chaos, and wholly devoid of values, we need draw no line betwixt reality and illusion" (*SL* 1.261), a conclusion at work in several of the stories. The comment of the narrator in "The Silver Key" that Randolph Carter has forgotten, though he is about to uncover the truth that "all life is only a set of pictures in the brain, among which there is no difference betwixt those born of real things and those born of inward dreamings, and no cause to value the one above the other" (*CF* 2.73), is one more version of these speculations, now phrased as a materialist rewriting of Schopenhauer. The theme that Burleson identifies as oneiric objectivism ("On Lovecraft's Themes" 136, 142), then, is constructed from several sources and one that we should understand as seriously and as ambivalently as Lovecraft meant it, for it asserts the plenitude and immediacy of the universe on the one hand and on the other its incoherence, its distance, and its transparency.

An aspect of Western thinking in this matter may be read in the broad meaning of the Latin word *res,* which has the solidity of matter, the generality of the matter at hand, and the infinite interpretability of a matter at law. To the Roman mind *res agere* is as much a part of reality as the *res naturae* and the *res publicae;* to the Roman mind one may proceed with reality in as hortatory a manner as one proceeds in a court of law.[5] Very broadly, whenever we consider attitudes toward the creation, we shortly find ourselves understanding it as law, but as physical law, moral law,

---

5. According to Pokorny, *res* may connote "order" and "number" (1.60) as well as "case," "matter," and "ownership," hence its connection to matters of law (1.860). *Reri* means "to reckon" or "to lay out," hence "to think" (Tucker 205). Over the years a thought has become a thing in the Western mind.

and natural law. From this vantage of historical experience, then, the real wall is not necessarily so matter-constituted as we have often assumed.

This understanding of law can now be translated to terms of the real wall and the true wall. Those physical laws of a material, deterministic nature, those moral laws of prohibition, and inescapably within the natural law of Lovecraft's upbringing those laws of racial segregation form in Lovecraft's world a real wall that imprisons every possibility of a fuller life. Their extension and trespass, the kick as he called it, forms the true wall for which he yearns and which, of course, he fears. The real wall is grossly present, like the stone that Dr. Johnson so triumphantly kicks to reject the speculations of Bishop Berkeley, whose argument was so impressive and exasperating for the very reason that it had so pressed the prerogatives of the senses. Do we sense an anxiety in Dr. Johnson's toe?

The anxiety that science fiction feels in the face of natural law, therefore, confronts another form of law entirely, the constraints and orders of which bear upon humanity a much sharper obligation than mere human law. This is divine law, by which we now mean both the creation and institution of the physical world, the physical law that the West has pursued since the Greeks in the faith that a *logos, nous,* and *ratio* would lie at the base of it, and the institution of the divine promise with the human world, in pursuit of which the Judaeo-Christian culture has been transforming itself through the notion of history, institutions that Barth considers as two moments of one act (*Kirchliche Dogmatic* 3–1.261ff.). *Torah, Shekinah, Sophia,* and *Logos* bring to theology peculiar problems. Above all, insofar as science fiction and Lovecraft are concerned, the promise that human life may mean something brings a distinctive crisis to human affairs.

II

> I kan noght parfitly my Paternoster as the preest it syngeth,
> But I kan rymes of Robin Hood and Randolf Erl of Chestre.
> (Langland 5.395–96)

All that we have said so far about law and boundary-experience might be said merely of deism. It takes us not much further than Otto Rank's theory that religion begins in awe. It does take us further to agree with Schleiermacher that religion begins in a sense of dependence upon the transcendent, for it is in that dependence that a personal relation with the transcendent both begins and overcomes that transcendent. We have still to ask in what fashion Lovecraft's stories can satisfy a Christian who believes in the triune godhead, a transcendent creator out of which a savior is born and a spirit proceeds, a personal godhead in which one aspect is experienced as law and creation, the *natura naturata,* and as the Torah which is the way one shall go; a second aspect as a son, god's word and gesture in whom suffering and resurrection are experienced; and a third aspect as a spirit, as a rush or stir of wind or as the maternal and anima, the *shekinah,* the *natura naturans,* in which inspiration, knowledge, and community are experienced. If we consider godhead as a trinity,[6] Lovecraft certainly commits a heresy in the enormity of the father's manifestation in his stories; more precisely, in his stories the *natura naturata,* Chaos and its daughter Dulness, has usurped the place of the *natura naturans* and reduced the order of the creation to the aggressive world as human limitation too often experiences it, the real world and nothing else, not the true world. In this real world, suffering and resurrection count for nothing. The holy spirit is reduced to a chill wind that pursues the characters who have ventured forth to discover the sunset moment in the underworld.

But there are other answers to our question of what kind of sense Lovecraft's stories make to a Christian, one part of which rests in the particularity of the stories; their settings are new within the canon of horror fiction, the Providence and New England that he loved and gave a narrative life. In addition, the stories pose new goals and problems for the horror story and solve their dilemmas in new and ingenious ways. In these ways the stories are a part of an incarnational world, important enough, at least that very local manifestation of it "with its clustering gambrel roofs that sway and sag over attics" (*CF* 3.232), for his characters to move heaven and hell to save it. And because the incarnate world is important so is the particularity of a word such as "gambrel." The logos at work in Lovecraft's fiction reveals that he does believe in the *valde bona* of his world.

A further aspect of Christianity in Lovecraft's work is the conviction of guilt. Such a conviction can be understood in several ways, whether as debt or as erring or as an existential standing-out in the world. Lovecraft denies that any guilt and thereby any justification exist; in an indifferent universe sin does not exist. But the stories provide rather different evidence. Within Christianity there are other aspects of guilt than one in which a person is conscious of a particular wrongdoing. Omission, darkness of will, the unforgivable sin, and the scandal of damnation from never hearing the word are other modulations of having been found wanting than simply those listed in the ten commandments and the seven deadly sins. Guilt is a manifold under which all nature groans.

> Sünde ist das spezifische Gewicht der menschlichen Natur als solcher. Sünde ist nicht ein Fall oder eine Reihe von Fällen im Leben des Menschen, sondern *der* Fall, der mit seinem Leben als Mensch schon geschehen ist. Sünde *geschieht,* noch bevor sie sich im Bewußtsein oder Unterbewußtsein dieses oder jenes Menschen *ereignet* hat, Sünde ist *Macht,* noch bevor sie dieses oder jenes Menschen Wille und *Gesinnung* geworden ist. [Sin is the specific weight of human nature as such. Sin is not an event or a series of events in the life of an individual, but *the* event that has already occurred with one's life as a person. Sin *happens,* before it *arises* in the consciousness or subconsciousness of this or that

---

6. In this passage I am following the example of Dorothy L. Sayers as she investigates the degree to which various writers are father-ridden, son-ridden, or ghost-ridden, though I am more concerned with the world that the author projects (141–65).

person, sin is *power*, before it has become this or that person's will and intention.] (Barth, *Römerbrief* 164)

"The Outsider" concludes in the realization that the monstrous is in fact the self, a monstrousness that lay before it and that it carried with it long before it becomes aware of the terror that others feel for it and their flight and long before it turns to the empty archway that is a mirror.

The old law and the new law are not opposed as the early heretic Marcion had argued; the wrath of God is a real aspect of his grace, a protest against the *Da-sein* and *So-sein* of the world insofar as we do not make that protest our own (Barth, *Römerbrief* 19). In terms of predestination, in which God is the God of Jacob and of Esau, as limited subjects in time we can only understand God as the God of Esau, the God of wrath, who is yet the God of no "and," not a twofold God but a divinity in whom this opposition, our determination to count ourselves as lost, is suspended and transcended,[7] because we can only understand the grace and election of God as an event that implies damnation also. For how, asks my limited humanity that believes in the law of the excluded middle, could God freely choose me unless he could also freely unchoose me (362–65, 374)? According to orthodoxy, however, God transcends all oppositions, heaven and hell, day and night, life and death (Ps. 139:8–12; Rom. 8:38–39). It is not simply that the conceptual space of God encompasses every space, as though divinity were a Venn diagram of infinite dimensions; God embraces every being, even the damned, and protests against their will to damnation.

When we do not take part in that protest against the world as it is, the world of limitation and necessity, we find ourselves face to face with the nothingness that Barth calls sin; this is chaos, the abnormal, measureless, lawless, deviate trespass. It is something that cannot be dealt with rationally or systematically, not even within the bounds of a dialectical system such as Barth aspires to in his theology (*Kirchliche Dogmatik* 3–3.407–09). From the viewpoint of resurrection and return it is "das *Alte*, nämlich die alte Drohung, Gefahr und Verderbnis, das alte, Gottes Schöpfung verfinsternde und verwüstende Unwesen" [the *old*, namely the old threat, danger, and ruin, the old non-existence that darkens and wastes God's creation] (3–3.419). From this point of view we must question Lovecraft's penchant for choosing old men as his cultural heroes, not only in his fiction but in his letters, because his old men very much stand for the status quo that attempts to repress ancient knowledge. We have already expressed some irony about their attempts to seal away the *Necronomicon* in the special collections of Miskatonic Library; it is not

---

7. "Suspended" is a translation of *aufgehoben*, a technical word in phenomenology for a bracketing or suspension of experience; it represents Husserl's epoche. It may imply an annulling or an overcoming. "Transcended" is a translation of *übergestiegen*, "to step over" or "to surpass," in the idealism of Kant and Hegel. By juxtaposing them I do not mean to equate them but to suggest that the hendyadis may do some justice to the attitude God takes toward the human will to nothingness.

wrong of a reader to sympathize with the attempts of men like Wilbur Whateley to liberate such texts, for from the point of view of the Pauline epistles all things are lawful.

A darker aspect of sin is its temptation to *Trägheit*, a heavy inaction or omission, a ponderous rottenness, backwardness, heedlessness, or belatedness characteristic of the world in nothingness (Barth, *Kirchliche Dogmatik* 4-2.452), which Aquinas pointed to as a *languor naturae* in original sin (1-2.82.1). We are belated, unable to catch up with ourselves and unable to catch up with God. The antithesis of pride, unheroic and trivial, insistent upon insignificance, *Trägheit* forces us to reconsider the *Nachträglichheit* we examined in the terminal climax, for in *Nachträglichkeit Trägheit* discovers its own inwardness; the traumatized person never clarifies the original trauma but shatters and reinvents, as though something in the self forbade its ever coming to closure. This is the sin that Lovecraft in his posture of old age and in his frequent, fruitful inabilities was particularly prone to. Through the compulsion to repeat and reinvent the past we experience the inert sluggishness of all matter in which the darkening of the intellect takes place (cf. Joyce, *Ulysses* 9.461–76, 1002–9), the turbulence at the heart of original sin that prevents ever eradicating itself. Matter, the matter of the world in nothingness, the matter of Esau that appears as a mess of pottage rather than as a birthright, matter that strikes us in retrospect as guilt, is actively opaque. This is the *Trägheit* and *Nachträglichkeit* of the dog that returns to its own vomit. From this perspective one of the conditions of modern science, the possibility of repeating an experiment, becomes suspect. The lack of repeatability has often been seen as a stigma of such pseudosciences as extrasensory perception; yet certain fields of knowledge such as sociology, philology, or Darwinian evolution lack repeatability and must be content with seeing the extent to which theory offers the possibility of uncovering new data from the undifferentiated mass of experience. Repeatability is a protection against the pain and liberation of a new paradigm and thereby reveals itself as a constitutive part of the *Trägheit* of the world, in the view of Freud tending to death.

Barth's *Trägheit* is an analysis of the scholastic sin of acedia, a consent to spiritual dryness that is one of the seven deadly sins, indeed to some theologians the chief of them rather than pride. Aquinas regards it as directly opposed to caritas (2–2.35.2), originating in that moment when reason assents in a hatred of the divine good, "carne omnino contra spiritum praevalente" [the flesh totally prevailing against the spirit] (2–2.35.3). Thus acedia is a particular sin against the joy, inspiration, and vivification of the Holy Ghost. For Barth *Trägheit* is characterized by the stupidity that denies God (thus it is the sin in which atheism originates), the refusal to be human (and thus that sin in which the individual becomes monstrous), the determination to waste (and thus that sin that attempts to reduce the world to chaos and nothingness, the sin that attempts to undo creation), and the consent to sorrow and *Angst* (and thus that sin that refuses to have any joy in the creation). But unlike pride, the pride that delights in its own expansion, acedia refuses to acknowledge itself; it is characterized by its attempt to hide, cover, deny itself, especially to itself, the sin of hypocrisy that sharpens, compounds, and repeats the original sin upon a new level (*Kirchliche Dogmatik* 4–2.452–546). Despite the medieval figure of sloth, however, acedia and *Trägheit* are not slothful, neither for Aquinas nor for Barth (cf. *Summa* 2–2.35.4 and *Kirchliche Dogmatik* 4–2.534). For both of them this sin has an immense energy, especially insofar as it resolutely opposes joy and perpetuates its own concealment and repetition.

Given this analysis, we understand how for Lovecraft acedia and *Trägheit* is more significant than pride; for though he has characters in a state of Luciferian or Promethean rebellion, such as Curwen or Wizard Whateley or Waite, his exemplary characters are Charles Dexter Ward, Wilbur Whateley, or Edward Derby, souls whose experiments at escape can proceed only so far before they collapse, revealed to be not the equal of the others, not as much the son of the father or ancestor as the dark double or the invisible brother or the incestuous sister is. Lovecraft is the prophet of matter, a matter so dense that it exerts its own inertia upon his characters.

Thus this quick sketch of Christian notions of evil and nothingness surely has analogies with the world of dead matter at work in Lovecraft's fiction, a world threatened by ancient forces within a universe of chaotic particles, always measureless and lawless, a world that ceaselessly exceeds human norms and traditions, the only consolations we have. This living presence of damnation is the subject of the couplet from the *Necronomicon:*

> That is not dead which can eternal lie,
> And with strange aeons even death may die. (*CF* 2.40)

This couplet refers to Paul's exclamation, "Death is swallowed up in victory. O death, where is thy sting? O grave, where is thy victory?" (1 Cor. 15:54–55),[8] though the couplet turns that passage on its head because it does not deny the second death of hell but the first death of material corruption that through its life asserts its presence in human experience. Thereby the couplet still affirms damnation, the second death that Lovecraft meant to deny, death alive, meaninglessness alive and perdurable; the couplet denies the good news Lucretius had preached, "Nil igitur mors est ad nos neque pertinet hilum" [Death, therefore, is nothing to us and matters not at all] (3.830). According to the couplet death matters very much, for it exists in such a fashion that it seems to act upon us. Not only does it seem to possess a positive existence, it acts upon us as a liar, deforming the impulse of life to increase and incorporate further experience; the couplet deforms the sunset experience. Lovecraft's solemn assurance at the beginning of "Supernatural Horror in Literature" that fear, a fear that has close affinities to Barth's *Trägheit* and *Angst*, is the most basic of human emotions, is a part of this insistence upon the fact of damnation because it assumes that the unknown is a veil upon the dreadful rather

---

8. This verse looks back to passages in Hos. 13:14 and Is. 25:8 and inspires passages in Spenser's *Faerie Queene,* Donne's *Holy Sonnets,* and Milton's *Paradise Lost.*

than upon the hopeful and that it harbors the destroyer.

"The Colour out of Space" is the story that most sharply expresses the Christian paradox that evil, that which opposes human fulfillment, is nothing and yet feels like something. It was merely a color, as the narrator insists, yet it destroys the Gardners as though it were purposive. Orthodoxy affirms the privative nature of evil yet also affirms the myth of Satan as the accuser who probes human nature through the pressures of psychological and physical pain. But when in the story Nahum wonders whether he has done wrong and thus brought this "stony messenger" upon himself (*CF* 2.373, 384), he is voicing that need for a simple explanation that Jesus rejects when to the question whether a man was blind because of his sin or the sin of his parents he responds, "Neither hath this man sinned, nor his parents: but that the works of God should be made manifest in him" (John 9:3). Difficult as it is, orthodoxy affirms that the border experience of destruction is itself for the purpose, if the individual will have it so, of the glory of God. "The Colour out of Space," the story that most often alludes to Biblical parallels, affirms the universe that so incomprehensibly transcends human categories and thus affirms the world of damnation that the Gardners stoically accept, "as if they walked half in another world between lines of nameless guards to a certain and familiar doom" (*CF* 2.381).

Since a transcendent grace is ridiculous in this world of *Trägheit* and damnation, the world of the real wall, the only possible consequence is a rejection of the life that feels like a rejection, a damnation in which purposeless forces overwhelm the individual; thus so many of Lovecraft's stories conclude with a scream that seems to occur outside time, a scream enshrined in the old aeon of our suffering world (Schillebeeckx, *Christ* 899). This world of the real wall and the damnation that it confronts are not presented in Lovecraft's fiction without protest, and a part of that protest is his loyalty to the damned. Lovecraft is on the side of the hopeless. It is not inappropriate to recall how Tolkien, no liberal Catholic, defended Germanic poetry, arguing that it is possible to affirm imaginatively a "faith in the value of doomed resistance" (23). A world-view in which defeat is certain and all combat is a holding-action, even the intellectual combats of Lovecraft, highlights the possibility of certain virtues like fortitude, endurance, fidelity, and *pietas* (23–24); clearly one of the strengths of Lovecraft's fiction, not to be discounted, is its dramatization of the risk of failure which the love of knowledge, the thirst for exploration, and the delights of the imagination all face.

But what are we to say of salvation? Certainly there are few Christ-figures in Lovecraft's fiction, nor do I read it for such figures—though it is important to realize how fully and how blasphemously in "The Dunwich Horror" Wilbur is such a figure as is his father Yog-Sothoth. But this realization is a richer answer to our question, because Christianity has come to realize how central to its endeavor is its understanding of the creative place of blasphemy in the Christian world; it takes up the endeavor of Job and the hard sayings of Jesus and Paul.

A component of salvation, a corollary of the incarnation because the incarnation is limited in history, in space and time, is the particularity of salvation as it reaches out to this or that individual soul. Such a particularity is one of the scandals of Christianity—a scandal to the Greeks, an anxiety to Schillebeeckx (*Christ* 764). Because salvation depends upon particularities, the damnation seems to follow of anyone who has refused the Christ or of anyone who never having heard of the Christ has not even had the opportunity to refuse him. In the *Paradiso* Dante responded to this anxiety by insisting that God can transcend even dogma and redeem the Trojan Ripheus whose faith intuited the invisible world (20.94–99, 118–38; cf. *Summa* 2-2.3.7 and 1-2.109.5 and Barth, *Kirchliche Dogmatik* 4-3.1052–55). Salvation is a larger category than damnation. Ripheus lives—and I now use the present tense not as an instance of the grammar of narrative but as an article of belief in his full mythic being—lives at the point where the real wall of God's law gives way to the true wall of God's grace and the state of eternity.

There is another way to understand salvation, when we recall that according to normal discourse law and religion imply a binding of human possibilities, whereas the abnormal discourse of salvation implies health, wholeness, and solidity, or more positively a release and expansion, the possibility of breaking through the determinist world-view of our experience. And that is precisely the effect at which Lovecraft aimed in his fiction, the kick of suddenly creating the possibility for the reader of believing in such a release. Repeatedly in his letters Lovecraft said that in his stories he strove to describe the moment in which physical law seems lifted, "one of my strongest and most persistent wishes being to achieve, momentarily, the illusion of some strange suspension or violation of the galling limitations of time, space, and natural law which forever imprison us" (*CE* 2.176). His stories consciously aim at the transfiguration of the deterministic world that he believed in, "upsetting none of [the laws of time, space, matter, and energy], yet superior to their limitations" (*ES* 302). Whenever Lovecraft speaks of the story, the indifferentism of his philosophy transforms itself into the language of desire as the structure of the universe is reconstrued as a prison or a wall, so much so that his description of art often bears the signature of freedom. In 1924 he wrote, "I think anything based on low instinct necessarily tawdry, local and limited to a vast degree. Freedom—the lofty freedom that puts a great imagination outside mankind, outside the world, outside the universe—that I take to be the true godlike inspiration" (*SL* 1.305). In 1929 he developed these themes at length:

> Art is the gateway of life—and in the opinion of many, myself included, the only reason that any highly developed man of sense has for remaining alive. Life without art ... is simply an animal or mechanical process, even when dully diversified by sterile thought We only live as human beings in proportion to our receptiveness to impressions of beauty. (*SL* 2.300)

Through art a person overcomes the analysis of the world that denies free will, not through denying the denial but by coming into an intimate experience of an autonomous self freed from the compulsions of instinct. But besides liberating the self, the experience of art also joins the self to others, bestowing "the sense of expansion and adventure inherent in viewing Nature through a larger proportion of the total eyes of mankind" (*SL* 2.300), language that parallels the language Lovecraft always uses to express his sunset moment and that explicates further the meaning of that moment for him: it truly is a model for the aesthetic experience. In addition, that experience of expansion through the eyes of others reacts upon the self and refines it: "we ourselves are impelled to 'be ourselves' more thoroughly and poignantly than might otherwise be possible" (*SL* 2.300). Through art authenticity becomes possible. And through this expansion of both the self and the other Lovecraft sees it possible to make an epistemological claim for the aesthetic experience: "the constant discovery of different peoples' subjective impressions of things, as contained in genuine art, forms a slow, gradual approach, or faint approximation of an approach, to *the mystic substance of absolute reality itself*—the stark, cosmic reality which lurks behind our varying subjective perceptions" (*SL* 2.301). Lovecraft immediately qualifies this claim; the experience of knowing reality is an illusion, for "absolute reality is for ever beyond us" (*SL* 2.301), mainly because Lovecraft believes in the fortuitous nature of our senses that cannot encompass reality, but also because an achieved reality allows no more "gradual approach" or expansion toward it. Despite this inability, however, which is the true sign of freedom, he does not believe that any person, at least any truly developed human being capable of experiencing such a freedom, can ever wish to refuse the gifts of art, for "the search for ultimate reality is the most ineradicable urge in the human personality—the basis of every real religion" (*SL* 2.301). This religious desire, then, the desire to be recognized as an autonomous, authentic self, Lovecraft finds enshrined in the liberation and self-definition afforded by the aesthetic experience. In art we find ourselves, as self and other, freed for a moment from the compulsions of space and time, from *Trägheit* and *Nachträglichkeit*.

It should be no surprise, however, that the theme of freedom bears a strong ambivalence for a man who despises democracy, yearns to turn back the clock to Colonial times, and despises the Marxist demand for proletariat freedom. So the freedom symbolized by the sunset and the horrors to which that sunset might lead requires a definite qualification: "My wish for freedom is not so much a wish to put all terrestrial things behind us & plunge forever into abysses beyond light, matter, & energy. That, indeed, would mean annihilation as a personality rather than liberation. My wish is perhaps best defined as a wish for *infinite visioning & voyaging power*, yet without loss of the familiar background which gives all things significance" (*SL* 3.214). After all, Lovecraft never sees only the sunset; it always lies across the landscape that is either explicitly or implicitly Providence, because only thus, with a direction for the sunset, the setting of a directional relationship, can meaning arise. We must never claim, despite the context of Lovecraft's indifferentism, that no meaning exists in the world where Lovecraft lives and writes, for "although meaning nothing *in the cosmos as a whole*, mankind obviously means a good deal *to itself*" (*RB* 209). Thus Lovecraft's remark about "local teleology" (*WBT* 379). And so in speaking of his wish for freedom Lovecraft writes of his mooring: "I want the familiar Old Providence of my childhood as a perpetual base for these necromancies & excursions—& in a good part of these necromancies & excursions I want certain transmuted features of Old Providence to form parts of the alien voids I visit or conjure up" (*DS* 263). This paradoxical basing of his flight in Providence, both leaving and not leaving, may account for his odd language in describing what happens in the breaking of physical law in his stories, for he comes to say that what he really wants is an extrusion or extension of this world. But clearly it is not so much the physical law that is extended as this local expression of law manifested in Providence, the time and place and culture that give his own life meaning, the only life he feels that he has any claim to speak of. Such an account of Lovecraft's aesthetics may resolve, but only partially, the doubleness that St. Armand saw as basic to Lovecraft, "at once a defender and upholder of a strict universe of natural law as well as its secret saboteur" (36), for Lovecraft's defense of such a universe only had relevance to his intellect, not to his love of Providence that he made the basis of his aesthetics. Salvation lay to hand in the world that he loved and energized in his fiction. The word as narrative has the freedom to move out of the actual, day-by-day belief-system of the author-creator, of course with the author's consent, and out of the thematic prison that it had seemed to create and affirm.

The theme of freedom has another qualification, more personal and difficult to resolve, a qualification that strikes at the heart of his ability to write such stories as his aesthetics projects. In the early 1930s Lovecraft began to experience a crippling self-doubt that to a certain extent curtailed the rest of his creative life, though during this period he wrote such things as "The Shadow over Innsmouth" and "The Shadow out of Time." A number of factors contributed to his condition, a major one being a series of rejections by *Weird Tales, Strange Tales,* and Putnam's in 1931 and by Knopf in 1933, and another being the increase of self-consciousness caused by the research that went into his writing "Supernatural Horror in Literature." A further factor, however, one in which converged his mechanistic understanding of the universe, the question of free will, and his position as a writer for the pulps, was probably his reading of Edward J. O'Brien's cultural critique, *The Dance of the Machines,* published in 1929 from material that had earlier appeared in the *Modern Quarterly.* Lovecraft was familiar with O'Brien, an anthologist of short stories who in 1927 had asked Lovecraft for biographical details (*SL* 2.202); and Lovecraft owned O'Brien's collection, *The Best Short Stories of 1928 and the Yearbook of the American Short Story* (*LL* #715). Lovecraft felt some chagrin when O'Brien decided not to reprint "The Colour out of Space," but he continued to respect O'Brien's judgment (*DS* 153).

The Dance of the Machines is a timely book, picking up ideas that were in the air as Chaplin's *Modern Times,* Capek's *R.U.R.,* and O'Neill's *The Hairy Ape* demonstrate. According to O'Brien, the world is becoming a place where the use of machines will increasingly cause mechanistic structures to manifest themselves in business, warfare, and the short story, in America exaggerated through Puritanism. Just as the machine is predetermined and predetermining (24), so the short story is as predestinarian in its plot as a watch (117–19). In the same way, the deterministic nature of modern war, because of the ideologies of Darwinism and Marxism, subverts a faith in free will, which O'Brien understands as responsible, effective action (105–7). The machine scorns creativity, intelligence, taste, and leisure, all of them qualities despised by contemporary editors, and subverts all tradition (46–95). Like machines modern short stories are made up of interchangeable parts and are interchangeable with each other (123–28); in addition, editors demand quick stories, with snappy dialogue and climaxes (135), optimistic glorifications of human progress (128–30, 177–78). As Heidegger argues, human affairs become objectified through *Technik*.

Several of these themes Lovecraft develops in the late 1920s. In 1927 he wrote, "Mechanical invention has so appallingly divorced us from the soil & from those conditions of our forefathers around which the aesthetic feelings of the race are entwined" (*DS* 122). Early in 1929 he wrote, "I find existence tolerable—because I keep aloof from the rising machine-culture and remain a part of the old New England civilization which preceded it. But nothing good can be said of that cancerous machine-culture itself," which "crushes relentlessly with disapproval, ridicule, and economic annihilation, any sign of actually independent thought and civilised feeling which chances to rise above its sodden level. . . . It is wholly a material body-culture" (*SL* 2.304); the degree to which this passage resembles O'Brien's themes and tone make it probable that Lovecraft had read him by this time. By the end of the year he recommends O'Brien in order to substantiate this argument:

> There's no use pretending that a standardised, time-tabled machine-culture has any point in common—any area of contact—with a culture involving human freedom, individualism, & personality; so that it seems to me all one can do at present is to fight the future as best he can. . . . Men can use machines for a while, but after a while the psychology of machine-habituation & machine-dependence becomes such that the machines will be using the men—modelling them to their essentially efficient & absolutely valueless precision of action & thought. (*JFM* 180)

Here we find Lovecraft, the atheist who denies free will, on the side of human freedom, a man who does not believe that any absolute value in the universe exists defending traditional values against the value-destroying world-view that is on the rise, represented by the blind mechanisms of the machines. The result for an author will be "quantity-production devoid of individualities and subtleties, or of genuine personal vision" (*JFM* 181). Two months later he sums up this threat:

> I think machine-culture is inferior to ours because it exalts an *absolute meaningless* group of qualities—speed, quantity, industry *per se*, wealth, ostentation, etc.—to the position of primary virtues, because it destroys normal memory-relationships with environment & folkways, because it emphasises uniformity in place of individuality, & because its net effect is a vicious circle of activity leading nowhere & sapping continuously at the normal ideals of quality, adven-

ture, personality, & the full expansion of the human spirit in poignant & complex realism remote from animal simplicity. (*SL* 3.64–65)

It is as though the mechanistic universe were suddenly visible in the form of machine-culture, manifest in aimless motion and animal instincts, and as though to oppose it Lovecraft were taking up the defense of tradition, virtue, quality, and expansion, taking up the defense of the illusions he so loves to debunk and defending them because the mechanistic universe is attacking him where he lives, in the creation of his art. In 1934 he makes the point once more: "We must save *all that we can,* lest we find ourselves adrift in an alien world with no memories or guideposts or points of reference to give us the priceless illusions of direction, interest, & significance amidst the cosmic chaos" (*WBT* 392–92). It is certainly not that Lovecraft is defending the Christianity that he began his career by attacking; but he is defending a number of the same things that Christianity defends, the structure of history, the worth of personal interest, and the effective existence of meaning in the face of a chaos that cannot be willed away.

There is no need to accuse Lovecraft of being inconsistent; as a writer he knows what he is talking about. His next mention of O'Brien's book, however, when he bought a remaindered copy, becomes the sign of a personal crisis: "Between popular junk and actual literature there is only war to the death"; and he confesses his inability to write for "high-grade" magazines because "the cheap tricks I have unconsciously picked up from [*Weird Tales*] writing were instrumental in causing Putnam's to reject my MSS. last year" (*WBT* 214). A month later he calls the book "a splendid exposé of the vulgar shallowness, insincerity, and worthlessness of American commercial fiction under the false-standarded conditions of the present"; and turning to the question of his recent "The Dreams in the Witch House" he adds, "I think I need a long fallow period during which to purge my mind of the popular-fiction formula" because "I have allowed the popular forms to infect my work more than I realised" (*EHP* 20). A year later he still laments his inability to measure up to O'Brien's standards, but concludes, "Of course I realise that there are infinite gradations between the purely charlatanic concoction & the purely aesthetic tale. One must not expect perfection, but must merely do the best one can" (*EHP* 103). The self-forgiveness is encouraging, but the threat of the charlatan, the threat of bad habits, the continual possibility of returning to the *Trägheit* of American commercialism cannot be laughed away; Lovecraft had lost his innocence. At the end of 1933 he feels that "when I come to put anything on paper the chosen symbols seems forced, awkward, childish, exaggerated, & essentially inexpressive. I have staged a cheap, melodramatic puppet-show without saying what I wanted to say in the first place" (*DS* 494), as though there were an inertia within him preventing him from doing what he wishes to do. "The Whisperer in Darkness," written in 1930, had proven prophetic. Its vision of brains preserved in metal cylinders, speaking through radio hookups, their thoughts reduced to tape recordings, is a reaction to the machine culture Lovecraft was living. O'Brien woke him up to realize the nightmare of that life.

More dreadful than the loss of his innocence is the loss of his freedom, which he had made the goal of the sunset moment. He discovered that his writing was itself involved in and perhaps constituted by the very acts of mechanical repetitions and indifferentiations that O'Brien had identified, so that the new beginning that seemed possible in 1926 began to disintegrate. Writing is not enough for freedom, not in itself. His attempt to move forward despite his unfreedom, his determination, a year after his disgust over the puppet-shows he cannot help but write, to write stories like "The Shadow out of Time," whose protagonist discovers the extent of his own unfreedom, is an act of courage that attempts to overcome his own inertia. But in O'Brien's terms, what are the sins he has to expiate? In certain ways he writes stories of which O'Brien would approve, for his stores are not optimistic, not indulgent in silly patter or in adventure for its own sake, and not slavishly realistic; they believe in the preservation of tradition and are acts in that preservation. But in two ways they are lacking, for they do not create characters that move beyond type, a problem Lovecraft certainly felt, enough to attempt to justify the atmosphere that he considered the heart of the weird tale; and they do not avoid the ending that snaps, tying together the plot as a very considered plot. Lovecraft's stories are deterministic, despite his attempts to allow them their freedom, and several display that typical ending, the terminal climax, which above all carries the *Trägheit* and remorse of the world within its structure. His culpability, then, is both technical and substantial; the tendency of his characters to disappear into the landscape that has given them birth and the tendency of his plots to lie in wait for those weak characters constitute an unfaith in the power of the imagination to expand beyond its bounds and an unfaith in the world, in the possibility for such an expansion to carry the soul forward. But he recognizes this culpability, and his stories represent an internal conflict in which the expansion and the failure, the material body of the world and the spiritual achievement of the fiction are in combat.

We must return to the point that Lovecraft is faithful to his home; he serves it, and Christianity has always identified freedom as a service to God, as a total submission to the ground of being (Küng 181–85), and Providence is Lovecraft's ground of being. When my word is my bond, as Geoffrey Hill reminds us (*Lords of Limit* 153–59), it not only binds and buys me, it also enables me. Lovecraft's theology of the sunset moment is orthodox insofar as its postulation of an infinite approach to truth resembles the moment at the end of the *Paradiso* when Dante feels that not only does his vision more and more approximate the complex face of the trinity, it is also a moment at which the circle has been squared—God squares the round world in the human figure, the incommensurable in the measured (33.127–38). But if my word, the logos in my mouth that is my bond, enables me it also judges me; my word in my mouth takes the measure of how far I fall short. So we take Lovecraft at his word when we ask what is the unfreedom in his fiction, how far it mars its promise. And with that question we return to his phobias. The failure of the fiction is the degree to which it does not surprise or expand us, the degree to which our boredom increases in the presence of those tentacles, those orifices and slime, those imitations, the degree to which it mechanically repeats the stereotypes that editors expected as faithful mediators of public expectations; and in the last regard, though O'Brien speaks of the tendency of the magazines toward typical characters and a lack of artistic and moral responsibility, he says nothing of stereotypes and the slack morality that perpetuates them (122, 160–61). Though I believe Lovecraft's fiction in its specific virtues would have been impossible without his anti-Semitism, racism, and sexism, we also realize how its constriction sins against the freedom of biblical tradition, more concretely against the freedom of his Baptist tradition, which implies social and political freedom in addition to religious and moral freedom (Küng 181); and we have to judge him no matter how severely the institutions of Christianity have themselves sinned against this freedom.

We cannot allow our knowledge of the letters and our knowledge of Lovecraft's actual beliefs to blind us to the broader aspects of the stories. This is not at all to accuse him of insincerity, frivolity, or any inartistic manipulation of his materials. Stronger as an artist than as a philosopher, though in no way is the philosopher unimportant, he is aware of an additional world; the problem is that because he has rejected all philosophic developments since Locke he does not have the language to describe that world. He writes, however, *as if* there were another world, an unknown in which we live and move and have our being (Acts 17:28), and this *as if* comprehends the narrative core without which no story could exist. In this additional world it is impossible to approach or to experience the cosmic chaos without perceiving it as Azathoth, sluggish in pipes and dance, and impossible to approach that place without a mediator, Nyarlathotep, who looks like us, with all the moral ambiguity of our being, impossible to approach without feeling the threat of dissolution and impossible not to feel the objective and subjective compulsion of approach.

As an artist, Lovecraft has to use the tone of this metaphoric language that suggests that a constitutive encounter is about to occur. He and Aquinas are in agreement: "Est autem naturale homini ut per sensibilia ad intelligibilia veniat: quia omnia nostra cognitio a sensu initio habet. Unde convenienter in sacra Scriptura traduntur nobis spiritualia sub metaphoris corporalium" [It is natural to human nature that we arrive at intelligible things through sensory things; because all our knowledge begins in the senses. Thus by convenience sacred scripture gives us spiritual things through corporal images] (1.1.9). A metaphoric language is not constitutive of reality; either Godhead does not exist and language can do nothing about that absence, or Godhead exists and extends beyond any attempt of language to exhaust it. Aquinas cites Gregory to this point, that while scripture "narrat gestum, prodit mysterium" [narrates through gesture and action, it brings forth a mystery] (1.1.10). But language does constitute an effective reality, one by which a person could live; it constitutes belief. This attitude toward the metaphoric nature of religious language becomes a major theme of Barth's *Römerbrief*, in which he insists upon the command to behave in this world hypothetically, as though all its works were under the *as if*. The conclusion of Goethe's *Faust*, "Alles Vergängliche

/ Ist nur ein Gleichnis" [all passing things are only a likeness] (12104–5), implies that out of the world that is daily corrupt proceeds all of the doublenesses called image, metaphor, parable, narrative; and this proceeding is imperative, both factual and burden, for "Dasein ist Pflicht, und wär's ein Augenblick" [existence is a pledge, if only for a moment] (9418). Stephan Dedalus is not unorthodox when he insists that all flesh must become the word (Joyce, *Ulysses* 14.292–94).

Steven J. Mariconda has written persuasively about the nature of the imagery Lovecraft developed throughout his career, though I believe that this imagery transcends his cosmicism. According to Mariconda key words of the imagery are *kaleidoscope, vortex, pattern, rhythm,* and *symmetry* (*On the Emergence of "Cthulhu"* 189–94). The odd aspect of Lovecraft's use is that he both postulates these qualities as necessary to aesthetic work and attributes them to the universe, often suggesting that they transcend our local teleology and are to be discovered in the fundamental chaos: "One of the fixed conditions of this infinite & eternal entity is pattern or rhythm—certain regular relationships of part to part" (*ET* 115). This assertion of a pattern is remarkable from a man who believes in the chaos of the universe. The kaleidoscope creates a beautiful shape through rotation and doubling. The vortex has a long history connected with the philosophic tradition with which Lovecraft aligns himself, the tradition of the atomists and Descartes: the cosmos arises through the structure of the vortex. Rhythm also gives shape to otherwise indistinguishable events, but more than shape it bestows direction; it is purposive and impelling. When Lovecraft emphasizes these qualities, therefore, he is envisioning a universe that is beautiful, structured, and purposive, qualities that otherwise he denies strenuously. It is possible that he means only that these are qualities bestowed by human perception, rather than paradoxically inherent in the infinite chaos; but since he also insists, as we have seen, upon there being no way to distinguish between reality and human imagination the attempt to deny purpose to the universe seems fated to fail. The instinct for symmetry that he postulates as arising from the regularities and rhythms of earthly life (*CE* 5.79) finds its satisfaction in the more complex rhythms of the universe beyond us. And thus a freedom from the chaos is really possible; the monolithic wall transforms itself into architecture.

Lovecraft is convinced of the efficacy of the word upon another level; and this is to say more than that he lives within the Reformation world-view. It is true that his devotion has a Gnostic overtone, for he has a certain elitist attitude toward knowledge, often in his stories hinting that knowledge should be kept hidden away in libraries for the delectation and frisson of scholars; he would have approved of such passages in the Loeb translations where Greek obscenities are translated into Latin rather than into English. But this efficacy of the word is apparent in other forms. If as Proust claims it is faith that prepares, guides, and shapes the aesthetic experience, or as Gadamer argues that it is prejudgment that allows experience, the art of reading in Lovecraft's stories always moves upon the presumption that the word, that knowledge, will shape the world for the reader; a person who reads the *Necronomicon* and runs the risk of being damned by it must read attentively, responsibly, in fear and trembling. The unforgivable sin lies in those pages like a disease. When Lovecraft created a history for that book he confessed that it lies in the vicissitudes of history and is therefore as much about human souls, their closing themselves down to the literal word or their opening themselves up to the broad spirit and context of the word, as it is about the extrahuman gods who come to this earth, out of all the indifferent worlds of the universe, in order to annihilate it. The swoop and ecstasy of the word, *Iä Iä!* is understandable in the light of its effectual nature.

III

But at night the god stood by my bed smiling, and said: "Even though I am a god I have learnt to serve the times."
(Palladas of Alexandria, *Greek Anthology* 9.441)

Despite these several points, Joshi is certainly not wrong to establish Lovecraft's philosophy as a normative guard against the excesses of the critical mind run rampant, eager to demonstrate whatever may please it; Joshi's reading of the letters has been absolutely necessary as a means of approaching the daily Lovecraft, the man who had to wrestle every time he set pen to paper with his particular heritage of Providence, horror, and the world, every time he bore up under the insult of writing for *Weird Tales* and failing to live up to the dignity of writing within this genre that he thought important for the moral life of America. For as much as the letters reveal a man struggling to piece together a great diversity of experience, they also reveal a man becoming more aware of the constrictions of his moral life. We have insisted upon saying "Lovecraft the story-writer" and "Lovecraft the thinker," for the sake of our argument; but there is only one Lovecraft. Even the thinker must cope with his desire for escape, redemption, being made sense of in the world.

Lest the creative Lovecraft disappear in the scholarship that concerns his biography, let us turn now to the stories to see how these several considerations work out aesthetically. Four of these stories I wish to examine under one narrow rubric that of salvation, before turning for a more exhaustive examination of "The Call of Cthulhu," because in Christianity salvation is all-important, certainly from the point of view of the purposes of God; despite all difficulties, pains, and manifestations of evil, Christianity asserts that God intends salvation for humanity. What, then, does salvation mean in "The Outsider," *The Case of Charles Dexter Ward,* "The Thing on the Doorstep," and "The Shadow out of Time"?

The Outsider is redeemed from his grave to achieve the prophetic voice, "a stranger in this century," for he is not only a stranger in the semi-medieval century of the story; through our determination to read the story autobiographically and through the present tense of the "I am," he is a stranger in our century that needs this critical voice. It is true that he does not receive light and revelry, but he does receive the light of the moon and the companionship of the mocking friendly ghouls; and he does receive the critical truth about himself. Not only is he a rotting corpse; he is also his hand on the mirror. Charles Dexter Ward is redeemed from his genealogical pursuits by the discovery that he has an ancestor who mattered in the world. Genealogy is both an objective study and a study powered by its ability to give us material through which we can dream about ourselves; and thus it is extremely important for the story that although Charles dies, as it were offstage, he lives a transformed life in the alienated figure of his ancestor who finds it difficult to make sense of the modern world and thereby brings to it a lively, critical eye. Edward Derby also dies offstage, but his return has more to say about the effect of the story. Again it is his hand, his peculiar knock, his turn of phrase, through which he is known, his way of speaking that brings him release from the body of this death (Rom. 7:24). We may also say that both Ward and Derby bring to life itself a critique that asserts that life is not in and of itself an absolute value; the release of the blue dust and of the puddle on the doorstep signifies a release from a life that is insufficient. And finally, Peaslee finds a release from a life that is merely a life into a shattered life that drives him forward into a moment at which his hand returns the truth to him. In all these stories salvation reveals itself as a shattering, a liberation, and a hand; the *via regia crucis* becomes an aesthetic substitution for the reader who faces the self in the broken mirror.

Let us now see the degree to which such considerations play themselves out in "The Call of Cthulhu," not Lovecraft's best story and not his most centrally representative, but certainly the breakthrough that allowed him to write the stories of his later years. The aspects of the story that strike us first, however, the very conscious frames he constructed around the story and the language of those frames, we will first put aside in order to consider the very remarkable shape of the plot itself, the articulation of the hoax.

"The Call of Cthulhu" is articulated in two ways. One is the division into three chapters, which represent an odd pattern of approach and retreat from the ultimate encounter with Cthulhu, the other the pattern of repetitions that give a musical rhythm to the work. The titles of these chapters, "The Horror in Clay," "The Tale of Inspector Legrasse," and "The Madness from the Sea," may be understood as a reflection upon the reader. That which is clay, that which is grass (or fat), and that which proceeds from the sea is the human race: Adam is made from the red clay, like a pot on a potter's wheel; all flesh is grass; and we now admit the procession of all life from the sea, and it lies within our experience that each person proceeds from the breaking of waters. As we have so often believed in this study, the monstrous at the heart of Lovecraft's fiction, even the high priest Cthulhu, reflects a particular aspect of ourselves, for is not Cthulhu upon R'lyeh a distorted image of us who "live on a placid island of ignorance in the midst of black seas of infinity" (*CF* 2.21), from which we struggle to arise. We are that which cannot die; we are that which rises again; we are that which is cut apart and pieces itself together once more, at the same time that we affirm our mortality and see that we sink again into the tomb, though we are also that which pictures us forth and sustains us in dreams and that which sends forth emissaries to slay us, instruments of our lust after knowledge, as our hand gives testimony. These are realizations that we necessarily approach and retreat from.

Against the pattern of the three chapters runs a pattern of repetitions. The story is written in a ruminant, fugal style; motifs, events, descriptions, and phrases recur that the narrator refuses to overlook, returning to them obsessively, sometimes redundantly. Some of the words are cosmic or geometric: "stars," "cycles," "angles." Some are mythic, especially R'lyeh and Babylon; the image of the city is in fact frequent in the story, thus the reference to "Irem, the City of Pillars" (*CF* 1.242) and the narrator's comment that Johansen's home lay "in the Old Town of King Harold Haardrada, which kept alive the name of Oslo during all the centuries that the greater city masqueraded as 'Christiania'" (49). But no matter what the repetitions, the cause for their repetition has to be assigned to the narrator who seldom reports the actual words of the characters. He prefers indirect discourse, because he distrusts the styles of Wilcox, Legrasse, Galvez, Castro, and Johansen, for Wilcox is "slightly affected" (43), Legrasse is perhaps too minute, Galvez too "distractingly imaginative" (37), and Castro too old; Johansen is perhaps the most distrustful of all, for though his style is "simple, rambling," it also suffers from "cloudiness and redundance" (49). So Thurston attempts to translate all the reports into his own language, but it is a language that edges toward repetition and mystification. It is not necessary, for instance, as far as our comprehension of the story is concerned, that we given three descriptions of Cthulhu, the description of Wilcox's statue, the description of the Esquimaux statue, and the description of Cthulhu himself as reported by Johansen and reworked by Thurston. As for that description, it is probable that the comparison of Cthulhu to Polyphemus is not that of the sailor but of Thurston as he attempts—but what is it that he is attempting with all these repetitions and variations? What is it that Lovecraft is attempting? And does he believe in the attempt?

This last question really has to do with what he might have believed when he looked back at the story. One of the characteristics of the American short story, according to O'Brien, was repetition, which in the words of Walter B. Pitkin, one of the men he holds accountable for the disease of contemporary fiction, "breaks down credulity. Belief is induced by the mere habit of hearing or seeing," as in advertisements (156). Pitkin thought that if such a technique were not employed the story "would fall to pieces like an old rag" because nearly all its situations were absurd; but a writer who uses this technique will have performed "a legitimate and highly artistic hoodwinking" (170). What, in retrospect, is Lovecraft to think of his own work, especially since he so often argues that it is the business of a writer of a weird tale to perpetrate a hoax? Does he find himself guilty of the contamination of the machine against which he has inveighed? Does the story like Cthulhu "fall to pieces like an old rag"?

The story begins in Providence, the center of Lovecraft's universe from which he begins his extension of reality, a reality that exists solidly in these opening pages because Lovecraft has carefully excluded the contemporary life that exists outside the charmed circle of his childhood in East Providence and its own, private connection to the outside world. This is the Providence that actuates the beginning of the story, Brown University, the Newport boat, the hillside, the waterfront, Williams Street, all the scenery witness to Dr. Angell's death, the Rhode Island School of Design, and the Fleur-de-Lys house, a bizarre piece of architecture that seems an extension of reality; for reality does try to extend itself. The young artist Wilcox lives in that house, a genuine extension not so much because he is an idealized and parodied character of the decadent self-image that Lovecraft was leaving behind as because he is a dream that Lovecraft had dreamt in which he saw himself as such a man creating just such a sculpture (*RK* 162–64; *CE* 5.220 [#25]), which Wilcox does because he has dreamed of it, a dream that extends itself as he shares it with sensitives around the world and a dream that extends itself outside the dimension of the earth to R'lyeh where "dead Cthulhu waits dreaming" (*CF* 2.34).

This extension into dream only succeeds because of Lovecraft's faith in the language of dreams. "The Call of Cthulhu" is in part a witness to his years of jotting down his dreams, his faith in their possibilities as imaginative material. He really does take his dreams seriously; he pays attention. In this matter he disagrees with Haeckel, who regarded dreams as no better than hallucinations, religious delusions, and "the fantastic notions of the transcendental dualist philosophy" (122). For Lovecraft dreams represent a remarkable evasion of the appearance of things; Burleson's theme of oneiric objectivism is for Lovecraft a matter of personal experience and a matter of faith, which his art presupposes in order to exist. For him as well as for Wilcox dreams "are older than brooding Tyre, or the contemplative Sphinx, or garden-girdled Babylon" (*CF* 2.25), reaching backward in time and eastward of Providence into the heart of the monuments that circle the original garden. And through his dreams Wilcox sculpts a figure that works upon Thurston precisely because he cannot put a limit upon it. It is "a sort of monster, or symbol representing a monster" and produces within his mind "simultaneous pictures of an octopus, a dragon, and a human caricature" (23). A caricature, one of those words of travesty with which we have been concerned throughout this study, is a drawing that exaggerates a feature of its subject, that "overloads" or overweights what already seems an abnormality in the subject, or so, at least, the caricaturist would persuade us; and if successful we agree that the abnormality was always there. All noses bear the curse of caricature. What, then, is the deformation that to the eye of Thurston Cthulhu further deforms? Our misplaced images, our dreams? The imaginary space is overloaded with images that cannot give place to each other; and as so often in Lovecraft's fiction, the last image, "a human caricature," returns us to ourselves displaced, nearly misplaced. From the Fleur-de-Lys house to Wilcox to Babylon to Cthulhu to ourselves, the swift and provocative extension circles like a nightmare.

But Henry Anthony Wilcox is not alone in the beginning of the story. With his sculpture he challenges George Gammell Angell, Professor Emeritus of Semitic Languages, whose age is emphasized by his title and by his middle name, which means "old" in Scandinavian. "Angell" connects him to Lovecraft's childhood home on Angell Street and to his function, after his death, of being a messenger to his nephew. But above all his sober, agèd rationalism, as though it were the dragon-slayer St. George, confronts the young aesthete Anthony, a type of the saint whose interior retreat to the desert provoked demons, the Anthony who sculpts the monstrosity of a dragon that caricatures humanity. The contest is drawn between characters more connected and more differentiated than they realize. Age and youth, institutional authority and artistic authority, stiffness and sickness, they seem unable to join. But because of the connection between them, this contest is not the fabled conflict between Good and Evil, which many people mistake for the world-view of Christianity. It is a contest within a good but injured world between two people who find themselves facing the compulsion to be less than they are, to surrender to that caricature of the self that Cthulhu represents, to suffer *Trägheit*. But in order to face that compulsion Dr. Angell discovers that he must learn more of its manifestations throughout the world, through keeping a firm hold on the dreams and legends, acts of imagination that give us a dangerous but necessary access to the no-thing that lies on the other side of our compulsion.

At the beginning of the story we face an anxiety of "piecing together." The "piecing together of dissociated knowledge" will reveal terror (*CF* 2.22), as the narrator has experienced from the mere "accidental piecing together of separated things," simple newspaper articles; and thus he hopes that no one else will accomplish this "piecing out" (22). At the conclusion also the narrator gathers together the various manuscripts that compose the story, along with his own account, "this test of my own sanity, wherein is pieced together that which I hope may never be pieced together again. I have looked upon all that the universe has to hold of horror, and even the skies of spring and the flowers of summer must ever afterward be poison to me" (55). The lust to piece together, which realizes itself as a rhetorical and literal repetition and which Angell and his nephew the narrator exemplify, cannot be restrained, and so the original fear of the introduction is met. Several piecings together occur during the story. Angell pieces together the accounts of the Cthulhu cult. Legrasse pieces together some of those accounts before him. Thurston pieces together the scraps of paper his uncle has left; by accident, at the beginning of the third section, he discovers a "stray piece of shelf-paper" that gives him the final clue he needs to the existence of Cthulhu (44). The inexorableness of things being pieced together is revealed in Cthulhu, which as "the scattered plasticity of that nameless sky-spawn was nebulously *recombining* in its hateful original form" (54). We do what the monster our caricature does, piece things together. And what we piece together is a vision of the fallen garden, of the created world and every creature within it that groan in labor to be free (Rom. 8:22). What we are unable to do, except through madness or the collapse of civilization, is to flee "into the peace and safety of a new dark age" (*CF* 2.22). The paradox of the story is that even when pieced together we remain in pieces.

In a fairly obvious fashion the lust to piece together produces something monstrous. In his preface to the *De Revolutionibus* Copernicus complains that the experiece of the Ptolemaic astronomers "was just like some one taking from various places hands, feet, a head, and other pieces, very well depicted, it may be, but not for the representation of a single person; since these fragments would not belong to one another at all, a monster rather than a man would be put together from them" (4). Dr. Frankenstein cast his shadow before him onto the heavens, a shadow that Copernicus could not quite dispel by moving the sun into the center. The monstrous nature of that composite being arises from its exemplification of eikastiken art, a literal-minded art that attempts to present an image without interpretation, without a foreshortening or a lengthening that takes into account the position of the audience.[9] This is the kind of art that seems to provide Lovecraft a model for his mature art, a scrupulous piecing together of diverse materials in order to produce a hoax, a monstrous accusation of the reader. But always moving against that effect is the rhythm of his repetitions and the anxiety that accompanies them.

This lust to piece together has a more sinister aspect, however, something more than tragedy, and that is its aspect as an evil action. There is no concrete evil in Lovecraft's fiction, just as there is no concrete evil in Christianity; the adjective "evil" does not signify a substantial thing (Aquinas 1.48.1–2). But we can certainly say that there are characters in these stories who do evil things, Curwen, Ephraim, the Innsmouthers, the Old Ones, and Cthulhu. This evil takes a particular form in the fiction, the lust to piece together that proceeds from an anxiety of not being whole and that manifests itself as an exploitation of other souls, a sending forth of others to piece the world together. Thus Cthulhu sends forth his dreams to take over the imaginations of others, to make them his sensoria. Curwen subjugates dead matter to assume coherence again and speak for their past experiences; he vampirizes their lives in order to see beyond the world as it is, a world of fragments. Ephraim subjugates Asenath and Edward in order to increase in experience and knowledge. The Old Ones subjugate humans and others, intelligences throughout the history of the universe, in an attempt to piece the universe together, which through such an attempt reflects an anxiety about its fragmentary nature. The lust to trespass the fragmentary nature of the world and to obliterate the private outlook of others reveals a form of evil that is peculiar to Lovecraft's fiction because it is an evil that he sees as common to all. More than that, it is an evil that

---

9. I depend on Huet's development of Plato's distinction between eikastiken art, "a reproduction without interpretation," and phantastiken art, a rendering of appearances for the sake of beauty. In the one case, things are liable to fall apart monstrously because of their mere reality; in the other case the truth of the thing is achieved through unfaithfulness (24–27). As Delacroix put the matter, speaking of the daguerreotype, it makes "a copy of the real *that is fake, in a way, because it is so exact* (ctd. in Huet 188). Belloc drew the same distinction between the marble bust, which "can never be more than a symbol," and the wax effigy, as in Madame Tussaud's, which "aims at exact reproduction" (ctd. in Huet 213), an interesting distinction for our concerns given Lovecraft's frequent use of the wax mask that renders the person who wears it monstrous.

is inextricably constitutive of his aesthetics, for as we have seen he postulates an approach to the monolithic reality of things through an expansion of sensory experience; the only consideration that saves his soul in this attempt is his awareness of its impossibility and, even more, the freedom that his attempt grants to the aesthetic objects—he does not subjugate but enters into a free association with other artists. This is not, however, to say that the temptation to subjugate does not remain and that the temptation to piece the world together does not thereby represent a moral danger. Despite Lovecraft's assertions in his letters, the moral universe constructed in his fiction is not indifferent.

But a further frame should be noted, one that frames this frame, the frame of survival. Twice at the beginning the word *survival* appears, once in the epigraph from Blackwood and then in the second paragraph, when the narrator speaks of the "strange survivals" Theosophists hint at (*CF* 2.22). And the story concludes: "Who knows the end? What has risen may sink, and what has sunk may rise. Loathsomeness waits and dreams in the deep, and decay spreads over the tottering cities of men. A time will come—but I must not and can not think! Let me pray that, if I do not survive this manuscript, my executors may put caution before audacity and see that it meets no other eye" (55). The answer to the speculation that puts conclusions into question is the chiasmus that asserts a cyclic history, one upon a vertical axis of sinking and rising, in which horror is renewed; for rising, the traditional language of resurrection, is transvalued here as a horror. The next sentence explicates this vertical axis further as loathsomeness and dream in the deep and decay above, establishing an identity between the depth and the height, confirming the first action of the story in which Cthulhu has risen through the dreams of Wilcox and taken its first incarnate form in his sculpture. Finally we must say that survival has occurred; it occurs as we confess that the death of the narrator, which a footnote at the bottom of the first page of the story had assured us of, has been transcended by his manuscript, which has risen to our eyes, which is rising to our eyes as we read it. And insofar as we experience an aesthetic reaction to these several plottings and framings of the entire story we are pleased that this resurrection takes place.

Lovecraft is an atheist, advancing the godlessness of the world with conviction. He is religious in the sense that Barth employs the word, as a part of the dogmas and culture of European history; his saints and texts have a long tradition. Some might ask whether Lovecraft attacks God or the God of religious people, but such a question has no sense if we agree with Barth that religion and all religious people, every person complacent in his or her relation to God, must be attacked in order to be on the side of God. God's loyalty to humanity only appears at the moment when religion becomes a transcendence of human religion (*Römerbrief* 69), because the church, especially the righteousness of Christianity, represents the continual attempt to make God human, temporal, substantial, worldly, something practical, all for the good of humanity (346). Against that progressive, optimistic co-option of divinity Barth resolutely sets his face. And is it not possible to see under such a light what Lovecraft does in his stories?

We have so far in these chapters treated the fate of Lovecraft's characters as the fate of Oedipus that Sophocles reveals in *Oedipus Tyrannos;* but there is another Oedipus, one more enigmatic, into whom the first Oedipus transforms himself, the Oedipus of Sophocles' *Oedipus at Colonus*. And in this investigation of Lovecraft and Christianity it is not inappropriate to use the typological language that Paul employed to center human life on its way from Adam to the Christ (cf. Rom. 5:14–19; Eph. 4:22–24; and 1. Cor. 15:22–49). The old Oedipus who found himself caught in the seamless web of fate is put aside by a new identity that he slowly begins to realize, just as the Lovecraft who upheld the laws of physical and evolutionary determinism is put aside. The old Oedipus is a peloric monster, a creature of the earth in precisely the sense that all the Greek heroes are the snake sons of the Great Mother (Harrison 277–88); he is an outsider. But he is a twofold monster, in his limp and in his actions. The limp leaves him crippled, a man of the mind and not of the body; he is not whole like Achilles or Odysseus, who both despite the accents of their heroism, warrior and plotter, are also wise and valorous. The only violence we see Oedipus capable of is his response to the attack of the man where the three roads meet, his killing of his father. The limp is not merely a symbol of castration; it leaves him a man who needs to be known through his cleverness, his ability to solve a problem. But he is also monstrous in his actions; within the broad context of things that he does not know, he becomes monstrous by acting as anyone would act; when he is attacked he defends himself, and when he has the chance of marrying the queen of Thebes he does. He cannot help but defend himself by saying he did not know; but to society and to the gods he remains monstrous, the incestuous patricide who must be expelled from society in order to return it to its health. And no matter how much he has wandered and suffered, to his last hour he remains aware of his monstrosity.

The old Oedipus is also the monstrous apparition who brings the Minotaur home to his own cradle; he is the Minotaur, the monster, which no history of his lineage can account for. In this sense, as the monster and original of his race, he is the Adam of Thebes who has revolted against his god and father. And so he becomes the first detective of literature, tracing the clue of the labyrinth that he himself has built through his life only to find himself, the monster, at its center, to whom his own mother plays Ariadne, his sister. And so like Theseus he deserts Ariadne and departs, and like Daedalus he flies from the labyrinth but loses his son, both of his sons, upon the way, just as Adam loses Cain and Abel; original sin, that which we have in common with Adam and the race of Adam, inexplicably becomes the individualizer that damns the soul in all its isolation.

Let us not, therefore, overlook the Theseus to whom he appeals, the kind of ruler who he might have been, a confident hereditary king, the solver of a famous puzzle. But their intellects are not quite the same: Oedipus is rational, Theseus reasonable. The ruler of Athens is his contrary, not his double. Theseus is an idealization, a gentleman, but his promise to Oedipus to protect his daughters fails to prevent Antigone, at the end of the play, from returning to Thebes to save her brothers, to die, as the audience knows (Winnington-Ingram 273–75); and so Theseus, like many gentlemen, has a moral life that extends a reasonable distance. Theseus lives his life the way that Lovecraft claimed that he lived his; he maintains order. He is almost Roman in the way that Lovecraft idealized, appealing frequently to Virgil's imperial line, "Parcere subjectis, et debellare superbos" (cf. *SL* 2.189 and 3.313; *JFM* 281), a line that he also associated with his Anglophile ideals. His remark in 1933, "I think of Greeks as cultivated but somewhat sycophantic aliens—good tutors of rhetoric & philosophy, but a little servile, unctuous, ratlike, sharp, & effeminate—in a word, not quite as much *men* as real ROMANS" (*DS* 498), echoes his words in 1923, "Our province is to found the cities and conquer the wilderness and people the waste lands—that, and to assemble and drive the slaves, who tell us stories and sing us songs and paint us pretty pictures" (*SL* 1.276). One of those stories is the one Oedipus has to tell, from which Theseus can benefit as a man who maintains order within his boundaries.

A measure of Theseus' success is his conquering of the Minotaur, the issue of bestiality, with the help of Ariadne whom he then deserts. We receive the impression of Theseus throughout his stories that he succeeds in part through the distance he imposes between himself and sexuality, precisely the attitude that Lovecraft strikes, though of course Lovecraft cannot use his sexuality as a weapon as Theseus does. A half year before his death Lovecraft writes this bit of advice to the teenager Robert H. Barlow:

> We'd all *like* to kiss pretty girls to our dying day—but we know damn well that it would be only a repellent & sordid mockery except with the very few women who really have affection for us when we are young. Therefore the man of taste & dignity cuts off that side of his personality in toto as he ages—until the excision comes to be really natural, & he is able to converse with young women just as coolly & impersonally as if they were lamp posts, hydrants, men, old women, or no-parking signs. (*OFF* 366)

We must, however, wonder whether Lovecraft was so successful in this excision since he then writes of the "repulsion & contempt" one must feel for a man who "lets a woman pull him down to *profound depths* of humiliation & degradation" (*OFF* 366) and then adds that "a very old or very ugly man ought to *know* that no woman could care for him, hence to suspect the advances of any affable beauty who says that she does" (*OFF* 366). Lovecraft does not here make of love "a game, a joke, a ribaldry even," as Joseph Wood Krutch thought perhaps the only possibility for the modern temper (104); and insofar as Lovecraft cannot, insofar as his words are in excess of the occasion, they seem an expression of bad faith. We cannot avoid considering them in the context of his feeling for his own ugliness and in the context of his marriage; the only way to behave reasonably and invulnerably is through excision, the conscious attempt to deny sexual feelings. Ariadne remains on Naxos to meet Dionysos, the wine-bibber. And Theseus returns to Athens to wed several ladies, but the last is Phaedra; and because Theseus is a reasonable man, a friend to his friends, willing to descend to the underworld with Perithous, whose shrine at Colonus reminds us of their inviolable pact to abduct Persephone (ll. 1593–94), he leaves his friend behind and returns only to destroy his own life through suspecting that his son has visited the Oedipal situation upon him. Self-castration and a reasonable life protect no one; neither the life of Oedipus nor its contrary defends a person against the life of desire and the sudden assertion of meaning. Without knowing it, Theseus lives the life of the old Oedipus.

Let us admit, however, that all this talk of Oedipal fate, if by it we mean exclusively the attack on the father, is beside the point for Lovecraft who probably did not see his father after he was three years old (*LAP* 25–26); he was victorious. For him the mother is the target for aggression, or rather women are the target, as when Lovecraft insists that young women should be regarded as "lamp posts, hydrants, men, old women, or no-parking signs." These are attacks upon the anima, in Christian terms upon the Holy Ghost, attacks upon the psychological roots of the imagination. Within the context of Marie-Hélène Huet's history of the imagination in the West, his work represents a further stage in the attack upon the maternal imagination (9) and is thereby reduced, as he feared, to being an art of mere reproduction, a disproportionate, lifeless, uninterpreted, meaningless hoax (24–26; 132). His anxiety about his art is bottomless. Jocasta hangs herself because Oedipus's desire demands it, and Theseus leaves woman after woman behind. Does he will his son to approach Phaedra so that she will be compelled to kill herself? Is that the way reasonable men behave with lamp posts and no-parking signs? Thus Theseus remains king of Athens.

As for Oedipus, the new Oedipus has put himself outside Thebes and rejects every attempt of his sons to bring him back inside. He will not authorize the fraternal suicide they have begun to commit; and he will not countenance them or endure beholding the acts for which they are beholden to him. In a series of curses and prophecies he claims that his body in the earth will drink the blood of his sons and appeals to the paternal darkness of Tartarus and to his own destroying spirit, in common with the Erinyes whose grove he stands in, to confirm his curse (ll. 621–23, 787–90, 1389–92); that destroying spirit is the *alastor* that will never overlook the blood that brings retaliation, although its never overlooking, its truth, is so thoroughly mechanical that it seems a manifestation of mere reality.[10] Thus, as Karl Reinhardt says, "his fluctuations between mortal and daimon become more enigmatic" as his death approaches (219) and thus the more difficult it is for the audience to place his liberty upon a scale. Thebes and his sons, therefore, are left outside the sacred space of the grove of Colonus. As much because of this curse as because of its own acts, as much because of Oedipus' prophetic spirit that cuts to the moral heart of the situation, Thebes becomes the city above all others, even the Argos of the Agamemnon cycle, of blood-

---

10. The alastor (*a* privative, *lanthonomai*) is a pursuing spirit who never forgets or who never overlooks (Liddell and Scott 31). It is the dark side of *aletheia*.

shed; and the audience is aware that this is also the historical Thebes that is on the verge of destroying Athens. But Oedipus in putting himself outside that deterministic cycle of blood has come to Athens where a different kind of law obtains, a law in which blessings can be given.

Among the several reasons for this possibility one is the emphasis that Sophocles gives to this place; beyond any question of dramatic propriety he exhibits a fidelity to his own *deme,* his own country that has nourished him and that receives such a loving treatment in the play, just as Providence receives such a loving treatment in Lovecraft's stories. We cannot say that Oedipus is saved or that he enters into heaven; he is "raised to power and not to happiness" (Winnington-Ingram 255). Nevertheless, despite his past whose horror still resonates within his own heart, the gods justify him in his new place, so new that he defines it through bestowing a blessing. He becomes a source of sacrality and blessing. In his study of the limping hero, Peter Hays recognized that the figure is two-sided by devoting a chapter to the sterility figure and a chapter to the fertility figure. Sophocles mentions Oedipus' wound once, in passing, in *Oedipus Tyrannos* but not at all in *Oedipus at Colonus*. It seems clear, however, that the man who caused the devastation with which the first play began is the same man with the same wound—and a new wound, his blinded eyes—who founds a new fertility in the second play. Nothing at all to look at, as he confesses to the handsome Theseus, he still benefits his new home (ll. 576–78). The old Oedipus, the tyrannos whose rule is not hereditary, as soon as he discovers that he is in fact the legal ruler of Thebes, but blood-soaked, leaves to become a different kind of ruler, one whose authority originates in his claim to blessing. But we must not sentimentalize this blessing; its corollary is his ability to curse his sons, externalizing the deterministic world of self-slaughter to which they have committed themselves. Damnation and salvation, self-loss and self-origination, find themselves as facts in this world as soon as the old city of destruction has been left behind.

Another aspect of this death to consider is that it is one more version of the *causa sui* project. Oedipus has discovered the enormous consequences of his first attempt at giving birth to himself by literalizing the motions of killing his father and bedding his mother. Now he leaves behind the arrogation of his birth by arrogating his death and imposing his own meaning upon it, at the same time calling upon the gods and Theseus, the representative of the community, to authorize it; and all this without committing the solipsistic act of suicide, for the calling upon the gods and Theseus moves out from the self both vertically and horizontally; his death connects the world, gods above and gods below and the mortal community, through placing himself at its center.

All this is true, of course, only if we believe the new Oedipus. But what if all this talk of being elected by the god at Delphi were a hoax? When Tiresias accused the old Oedipus of killing his father and marrying his mother, the old Oedipus very properly accused the prophet of being a fake, of attempting to perpetrate a hoax; their mutual recriminations originated in attempts to establish authority. For what else, feeling innocent as he did, was he able to suspect? But many readers have felt in his accusation that he is himself uneasy about his position, anxious that he himself is in a place where he should not be. He feels that the old world is reaching out to threaten him, the old accusation back in Corinth and the words in the old man Tiresias' lips. Something is returning upon him with an enormous enertia, an enormous *Nachträglichheit* that he is forced to reconsider, retrace, and retell. Tiresias was not preparing a hoax, as the old shepherd confesses, who would not take part in the hoax that Oedipus's parents attempted to commit in the eyes of the gods. But is the new Oedipus attempting to pull the wool over the eyes of Theseus? What of Christianity? Does it attempt to perpetrate a hoax? Don't we feel that it does, when its first apologist, Tertullian, finds himself dealing in such paradoxes as the *credo quia impossibile est?* Is it any wonder that the critics of Christianity throw up their hands? And so it is not surprising to find Lovecraft accusing it of dealing in a hoax. But Lovecraft is accustomed to make such accusations freely. Bolshevism, modernism, free verse are all attempts to put something over on us, just as Tiresias, Creon, and the Shepherd appear as hoaxers to Oedipus. Thebes is the city of the hoax.

And Lovecraft in his fiction has left behind such a city, the city of his ancestors where his father and mother died in madhouses and where he had been unable to find himself artistically, to return and affirm it as the city of beauty and affection, within which he reaches out to ask his readers and his correspondents to witness his affection and his dread. He is not its son until he takes the burden of sonhood upon himself consciously. And then he is able to bless it, in such stories as "The Call of Cthulhu" and *The Case of Charles Dexter Ward* and in such a free recreation of it as its *Doppelgänger* in Arkham; for though Salem and Marblehead were its conscious models, the center of Arkham is Miskatonic University and its library. No doubt the self-loss, the damnation, in these stories is real; we could not take them seriously if damnation were not a possibility. They would not have the solidity of the world as we know it if they did not have its resistance to us. But the damnation of those stories is only as real as the blessing that extends beyond it, just as God's mercy extends from beyond God's anger, from God's ability to stand back from law and reflect upon it, because it is his. And Lovecraft learned how to reflect upon law as he knew it also, because law is his by an act of the imagination under siege. Thus, in his stories, he is continually reborn as he confesses his faith, on his way from the city of destruction.

Works Cited

A. Works by Lovecraft

The Ancient Track: The Complete Poetical Works. Ed. S. T. Joshi. 2nd ed. New York: Hippocampus Press, 2013.
Collected Essays. Edited by S. T. Joshi. New York: Hippocampus Press, 2004–06. 5 vols.
Collected Fiction: A Variorum Edition. Edited by S. T. Joshi. New York: Hippocampus Press, 2015, 2021. 4 vols.
Dawnward Spire, Lonely Hill: The Letters of H. P. Lovecraft and Clark Ashton Smith. Edited by David E. Schultz and S. T. Joshi. New York: Hippocampus Press, 2017.
Essential Solitude: The Letters of H. P. Lovecraft and August Derleth. Edited by David E. Schultz and S. T. Joshi. New York: Hippocampus Press, 2008. 2 vols.
Letters to Alfred Galpin. Edited by S. T. Joshi and David E. Schultz. New York: Hippocampus Press, 2003.
Letters to Alfred Galpin and Others. Edited by S. T. Joshi and David E. Schultz. New York: Hippocampus Press, 2020.
Letters to C. L. Moore and Others. Edited by David E. Schultz and S. T. Joshi. New York: Hippocampus Press, 2017.
Letters to E. Hoffmann Price and Richard F. Searight. Edited by David E. Schultz and S. T. Joshi. New York: Hippocampus Press, 2021.
Letters to Elizabeth Toldridge and Anne Tillery Renshaw. Edited by David E. Schultz and S. T. Joshi. New York: Hippocampus Press, 2014.
Letters to F. Lee Baldwin, Duane W. Rimel, and Nils Frome. Edited by David E. Schultz and S. T. Joshi. New York: Hippocampus Press, 2016.
Letters to Family and Friends Friends. Edited by S. T. Joshi and David E. Schultz. New York: Hippocampus Press 2020.
Letters to J. Vernon Shea, Carl F. Strauch, and Lee McBride White. Edited by David E. Schultz and S. T. Joshi. New York: Hippocampus Press, 2016.
Letters to James F. Morton. Edited by David E. Schultz and S. T. Joshi. New York: Hippocampus Press, 2011.
Letters to Maurice W. Moe and Others. Edited by David E. Schultz and S. T. Joshi. New York: Hippocampus Press, 2018.
Letters to Rheinhart Kleiner. Edited by S. T. Joshi and David E. Schultz. New York: Hippocampus Press, 2005.
Letters to Rheinhart Kleiner and Others. Edited by S. T. Joshi and David E. Schultz. New York: Hippocampus Press, 2020.
Letters to Robert Bloch and Others. Edited by David E. Schultz and S. T. Joshi. New York: Hippocampus Press, 2015.

Letters to Wilfred B. Talman and Helen V. and Genevieve Sully. Edited by David E. Schultz and S. T. Joshi. New York: Hippocampus Press, 2019.
Letters with Donald and Howard Wandrei and to Emil Petaja. Edited by S. T. Joshi and David E. Schultz. New York: Hippocampus Press, 2019.
A Means to Freedom: The Letters of H. P. Lovecraft and Robert E. Howard. Edited by S. T. Joshi, David E. Schultz, and Rusty Burke. New York: Hippocampus Press, 2009.
O Fortunate Floridian: H. P. Lovecraft's Letters to R. H. Barlow. Edited by S. T. Joshi and David E. Schultz. Tampa, FL: University of Tampa Press, 2007.
Letters to Samuel Loveman and Vincent Starrett. Ed. S. T. Joshi and and David E. Schultz. West Warwick, RI: Necronomicon Press, 1994.
Lovecraft at Last (with Willis Conover). Arlington, VA: Carrollton-Clark, 1975.
Marginalia. Ed. August Derleth and Donald Wandrei. Sauk City, WI: Arkham House, 1944.
Selected Letters. Ed. August Derleth, Donald Wandrei, and James Turner. Sauk City, WI: Arkham House, 1965–76. 5 vols.
The Shadow over Innsmouth. Ed. S. T. Joshi and David E. Schultz. Rev. ed. West Warwick, RI: Necronomicon Press, 1997.

B. Biographical and Critical Writings

Boerem, R. "The First Lewis Theobald." In Schweitzer, *Essays Lovecraftian* 36–40.
Buchanan, Carl. "'The Outsider' as an Homage to Poe." *Lovecraft Studies* No. 31 (Fall 1994): 12–14.
Burleson, Donald R. "Humour beneath Horror: Some Sources for 'The Dunwich Horror' and 'The Whisperer in Darkness.'" *Lovecraft Studies* No. 2 (Spring 1980): 5–15.
———. *Lovecraft: Disturbing the Universe.* Lexington: Univ. Press of Kentucky, 1990.
———. "On Lovecraft's Themes: Touching the Glass." In Schultz and Joshi, *An Epicure in the Terrible* 139–52.
———. "Prismatic Heroes: The Colour out of Dunwich." *Lovecraft Studies* No. 25 (Fall 1991): 13–18.
Burleson, Mollie L. "The Outsider: A Woman?" *Lovecraft Studies* Nos. 22/23 (Fall 1990): 22–23.
Cannon, Peter. *H. P. Lovecraft.* Boston: Twayne, 1989.
———. *"Sunset Terrace Imagery in Lovecraft" and Other Essays.* West Warwick, RI: Necronomicon Press, 1990.
Cox, Arthur Jean. "Some Thoughts on Lovecraft." In Schweitzer, *Essays Lovecraftian* 51–56.
Davis, Sonia H. "The Private Life of H. P. Lovecraft." In Joshi and Schultz, *Ave atque Vale* 119–51.
de Camp, L. Sprague. *Lovecraft: A Biography.* Garden City, NY: Doubleday, 1975.
Dziemanowicz, Stefan. "Outsiders and Aliens: The Uses of Isolation in Lovecraft's Fiction." In Schultz and Joshi, *An Epicure in the Terrible* 165–95.
Egan, James. "Dark Apocalypse: Cthulhu as Parody of Christianity." *Extrapolation* 23 (1982): 362–76.

Fulwiler, William. "Reflections on 'The Outsider.'" *Lovecraft Studies* No. 2 (Spring 1980): 3–4.

Gayford, Norman. "Randolph Carter: An Anti-Hero's Quest (part 1)." *Lovecraft Studies* No. 7 (Spring 1988): 3–11.

Jackson, Forrest. "The Reflection of Narcissus." *Crypt of Cthulhu* No. 87 (Lammas 1994): 9–13.

Joshi, S. T. *H. P. Lovecraft*. Mercer Island, WA: Starmont House, 1982.

———. *H. P. Lovecraft: The Decline of the West*. Mercer Island, WA: Starmont House, 1990.

———. *I Am Providence: The Life and Times of H. P. Lovecraft*. New York: Hippocampus Press, 2010. 2 vols.

———. "Introduction." In Schultz and Joshi, *An Epicure in the Terrible* 11–38.

———. "Lovecraft and the *Regnum Congo*." *Crypt of Cthulhu* No. 28 (Yuletide 1984): 13–17.

———. "Topical References in Lovecraft." *Extrapolation* 25 (1984): 247–65.

———. *The Weird Tale*. Austin: Univ. of Texas Press, 1990.

———, and David E. Schultz. *Lovecraft's Library: A Catalogue*. 4th rev. ed. New York: Hippocampus Press, 2017.

———, ed. *H. P. Lovecraft: Four Decades of Criticism*. Athens: Ohio Univ. Press, 1980.

———, and David E. Schultz, ed. *Ave atque Vale: Reminiscences of H. P. Lovecraft*. West Warwick, RI: Necronomicon Press, 2018.

Lauterbach, Edward J. "Some Notes on Cthulhuia Pseudobiblia." In Joshi, *Four Decades* 96–103.

Leiber, Fritz. "A Literary Copernicus." In Joshi, *Four Decades* 50–62.

Lévy, Maurice. *Lovecraft: A Study in the Fantastic*. Trans. S. T. Joshi. Detroit: Wayne State Univ. Press, 1988.

Loveman, Samuel. "Lovecraft as a Conversationalist." In Joshi and Schultz, *Ave atque Vale* 240–42.

Lovett-Graff, Bennett. "Shadows over Lovecraft: Reactionary Fantasy and Immigrant Eugenics." *Extrapolation* 38 (1997): 175–92.

Mariconda, Steven J. "Lovecraft's Cosmic Imagery." In Schultz and Joshi, *An Epicure in the Terrible* 196–207.

———. *On the Emergence of "Cthulhu" and Other Observations*. West Warwick, RI: Necronomicon Press, 1995.

Montelone, Paul. "The Inner Significance of 'The Outsider.'" *Lovecraft Studies* No. 35 (Fall 1996): 9–21.

———. "'The White Ship': A Schopenhauerian Odyssey." *Lovecraft Studies* No. 36 (Spring 1997): 2–14.

Mosig, Yôzan Dirk W. *Mosig at Last: A Psychologist Looks at H. P. Lovecraft*. West Warwick, RI: Necronomicon Press, 1997.

Murray, Will. "A Probable Source for the Drinking Song from 'The Tomb.'" *Lovecraft Studies* No. 15 (Fall 1987): 77–80.

———. "Do Shoggoths Lurk in *The Case of Charles Dexter Ward?*" *Crypt of Cthulhu* No. 37 (Candlemas 1986): 37–39.

———. "In Search of Arkham Country." *Lovecraft Studies* No. 13 (Fall 1986): 54–67.
———. "The Trouble with Shoggoths." *Crypt of Cthulhu* No. 32 (St. John's Eve 1985): 35–38, 41.
Penzoldt, Peter. "From *The Supernatural in Fiction*." in Joshi, *Four Decades* 63–77.
Price, Robert M. "A Biblical Antecedent for 'The Colour out of Space.'" *Lovecraft Studies* No. 25 (Fall 1991): 23–25.
———. "St. Toad's Revisited." *Crypt of Cthulhu* No. 20 (Eastertide 1984): 21–22.
———. "Two Biblical Curiosities in Lovecraft." *Lovecraft Studies* No. 16 (Spring 1988): 12–13.
———. "What Was the 'Corpse-Eating Cult of Leng'?" *Crypt of Cthulhu* No. 2 (Yuletide 1981): 3–8.
Quayle, Thomas. "The Blind Idiot God: Miltonic Echoes in the Cthulhu Mythos." *Crypt of Cthulhu* No. 49 (Lammas 1987): 24–28.
St. Armand, Barton Levi. *The Roots of Horror in the Fiction of H. P. Lovecraft*. Elizabethtown, NY: Dragon Press, 1977.
Schultz, David E. "The Lack of Continuity in *Fungi from Yuggoth*." *Crypt of Cthulhu* No. 20 (Eastertide 1984): 12–16.
Schultz, David E., and S. T. Joshi, ed. *An Epicure in the Terrible: A Centennial Anthology of Essays in Honor of H. P. Lovecraft*. 1991. New York: Hippocampus Press, 2011.
Schweitzer, Darrell. "Abnormal Longevity in 'The Picture in the House.'" *Crypt of Cthulhu* No. 28 (Yuletide 1984): 10–12.
———, ed. *Essays Lovecraftian*. Baltimore: T-K Graphics, 1976.
Setiya, K., and S. T. Joshi. "Lovecraft on Human Knowledge: An Exchange." *Lovecraft Studies* No. 24 (Spring 1991): 22–23, 34.
Sterling, Kenneth. "Caverns Measureless to Man." In Joshi and Schultz, *Ave atque Vale* 404–18.
Vaughan, Ralph E. "The Story in *Fungi from Yuggoth*." *Crypt of Cthulhu* No. 20 (Eastertide 1984): 9–11.
Waugh, Robert H. "Landscapes, Selves, and Others in Lovecraft." In Schultz and Joshi, *An Epicure in the Terrible* 230–55.

C. General Works

Adams, Henry. *The Education of Henry Adams: An Autobiography*. Intro. D. W. Brogan. Boston: Houghton Mifflin, 1961.
Addison, Joseph, and Richard Steele. *The Spectator*. Ed. Alexander Chalmers. New York: Appleton, 1864. 6 vols.
Adorno, Theodor. *The Jargon of Authenticity*. Tr. Knut Tarnowski and Frederic Will. Evanston, IL: Northwestern Univ. Press, 1973.
———. *Minima Moralia: Reflections from Damaged Life*. Tr. E. F. N. Jephcott. London: Verso, 1978.
Aeschylus. *Tragoediae*. Ed. Gilbert Murray. 2nd ed. Oxford: Oxford Univ. Press, 1960.
———. *The Seven Plays in English Verse*. Tr. Lewis Campbell. London: Oxford Univ. Press/World's Classics, 1906.

Ahlstrom, Sidney E. *A Religious History of the American People*. New Haven: Yale Univ. Press, 1972.
The American Heritage Dictionary of the English Language. Ed. Anne H. Soukhanov. 3rd ed. Boston: American Heritage; Houghton Mifflin, 1992.
Anderson, Sherwood. *Winesburg, Ohio: A Group of Tales of Ohio Small-Town Life*. Ed. Ray Lewis White. Athens: Ohio Univ. Press, 1997.
Aquinas, Thomas. *Summa Theologiae*. Madrid: Bibliotecas de autores cristianos, 1955. 5 vols.
Aratus. *Phainomena*. Trans. G. R. Mair. In *Callimachus, Lycophron, and Aratus. Hymns and Epigrams, Alexandra, and Phainemona*. Tr. A. W. Mair and G. R. Mair. Cambridge: Harvard Univ. Press/Loeb Classical Library, 1955.
Asimov, Isaac. "Nightfall." In Silverberg, *The Science Fiction Hall of Fame* 145–82.
Bachelard, Gaston. *The Poetics of Space*. Tr. Maria Jolas. Fwd. Etienne Gilson. Boston: Beacon, 1969.
Bacon, Francis. *The Complete Essays*. Intro. Henry LeRoy Finch. New York: Washington Square, 1963.
Barfield, Owen. *The Rediscovery of Meaning and Other Essays*. Middletown, CT: Wesleyan Univ. Press, 1985.
Barnard, John, ed. *John Keats: The Complete Poems*. 2nd ed. Harmondsworth: Penguin, 1976.
Barricelli, Gian Piero. *Giacomo Leopardi*. Boston: Twayne, 1986.
Barth, Karl. *Der Römerbrief*. 2nd ed. 1922. Zürich: Theologisher Verlag, 1989.
———. *Kirchliche Dogmatik*. Zürich: Zollikon, 1932–65. 4 vols. in 12.
Bate, Walter Jackson. *John Keats*. Cambridge, MA: Harvard Univ. Press, 1963.
Baudelaire, Charles. *Baudelaire: His Prose and Poetry*. Ed. T. R. Smith. New York: Modern Library, 1919.
Bennett, Andrew. *Keats, Narrative and Audience: The Posthumous Life of Writing*. Cambridge: Cambridge Univ. Press, 1994.
Bersani, Leo. *The Culture of Redemption*. Cambridge, MA: Harvard Univ. Press, 1990.
———. *The Freudian Body: Psychoanalysis and Art*. New York: Columbia Univ. Press, 1986.
Bettenson, Henry, ed. *Documents of the Christian Church*. New York: Oxford Univ. Press, 1947.
The Bible. Authorized King James. Akron: Saalfield, n.d.
Binni, Walter. *La nuova poetica leopardiana*. Firenze: Sansoni, 1962.
Blake, William. *The Complete Poetry and Prose*. Ed. David V. Erdman. Com. Harold Bloom. 2nd. ed. New York: Doubleday/Anchor Press, 1988.
Blavatsky, H. P. *Isis Unveiled: A Master-Key to the Mysteries of Ancient and Modern Science and Theology*. 1877. Pasadena: Theosophical Univ. Press, 1976. 2 vols.
Bloom, Harold. *The Anxiety of Influence: A Theory of Poetry*. New York: Oxford Univ. Press, 1973.
Bobrick, Benson. *Labyrinths of Iron: A History of the World's Subways*. New York: Newsweek Books, 1981.

Borg, Marcus J. *Meeting Jesus Again for the First Time: The Historical Jesus and the Heart of Contemporary Faith.* New York: HarperCollins, 1994.
Born, Daniel. "Character as Perception: Science Fiction and the Man of Faith." *Extrapolation* 24 (1983): 251–71.
Brillat-Savarin, Jean-Anthelme. *The Philosopher in the Kitchen.* Tr. Anne Drayton. Harmondsworth: Penguin, 1970.
Brown, Norman O. *Life Against Death: The Psychoanalytical Meaning of History.* New York: Vintage Books, 1959.
Browning, Robert. *The Complete Poetic and Dramatic Works.* Boston: Houghton Mifflin, 1895.
Bruffee, Kenneth A. "Collaborative Learning and the 'Conversation of Mankind.'" *College English* 46 (1984): 635–52.
Buber, Martin. *Das Dialogische Prinzip: Ich und Du; Zwiesprache; Die Frage an den Einzelnen; Elemente des Zwischenmenschlichen; Zur Geschichte des dialogischen Prinzips.* 5th ed. Heidelberg: Lambert Schneider, 1984.
Burke, Edmund. *A Philosophical Enquiry into the Origin of Our Ideas of the Sublime and the Beautiful.* Ed. James T. Boulton. Notre Dame, IN: Univ. of Notre Dame Press, 1968.
Burroughs, Edgar Rice. *Tarzan of the Apes.* 1912. New York: Ballantine, 1963.
Calasso, Roberto. *The Marriage of Cadmus and Harmony.* Tr. Tim Parks. London: Vintage, 1994.
Campbell, Joseph. *The Masks of God: Creative Mythology.* New York: Viking Press, 1970.
Cantril, Hadley, with the assistance of Hazel Gaudet and Gerta Herzog. *The Invasion from Mars: A Study in the Psychology of Panic.* New York: Harper & Row, 1966.
Carpenter, Humphrey. *A Serious Character: The Life of Ezra Pound.* Boston: Houghton Mifflin, 1988.
Carroll, Lewis. *Alice in Wonderland.* Ed. Donald J. Gray. New York: Norton, 1971.
Chapman, Rosemary. "Autodidacticism and the Desire for Culture."*Nottingham French Studies* 31 (1992): 84–101.
Christ-Janer, Albert; Hughes, Charles W.; and Sprague, Carleton. *American Hymns Old and New.* New York: Columbia Univ. Press, 1980. 2 vols.
Cicero. *De natura deorum. Academica.* Trans. H. Rackham. Cambridge, MA: Harvard Univ. Press; London: Heinemann/Loeb Classical Library, 1979.
Coleridge, Samuel Taylor. *The Poems.* Ed. Ernest Hartley Coleridge. London: Oxford Univ. Press, 1912.
Copernicus, Nicholas. *On the Revolutions.* Tr. and com. Edward Rosen. Baltimore: Johns Hopkins Univ. Press, 1992.
Cooke, George Albert. "Palmyra." In *The Encyclopaedia Britannica.* 9th ed. Vol. 18. Edinburgh: Adam & Charles Black, 1885. Vol. 18. 198–203.
Cowper, William. *The Poems.* Ed. John D. Baird and Charles Ruyskamp. Oxford: Clarendon Press, 1980. 2 vols.
Croce, Benedetto. *Poesia e non poesia, Note sulla letteratura europea del secolo decimonono.*

Bari: Laterza, 1923.
Cushman, Robert E. *Therapeia: Plato's Conception of Philosophy*. Chapel Hill: Univ. of North Carolina Press, 1958.
D'Annunzio, Gabriele. *Alcyone*. Verona: Mondadori, 1966.
Dante Alighieri. *La Divina Commedia*. Ed. E. Moore. Oxford: Oxford Univ. Press, 1900.
———. *The Divine Comedy*. Trans. Henry Francis Cary. Garden City, NY: Doubleday, 1946.
———. *The New Life*. Tr. Dante Gabriel Rossetti. Ed. Oscar Kuhns. New York: Thomas Y. Crowell, 1897.
Delany, Samuel R. *The Einstein Intersection*. New York: Ace, 1967.
Democritus. "Die Atomisten: Leukipp und Demokrit." In *Die Vorsokratiker*. Vol. 2. Ed. Jaap Mansfeld. Stuttgart: Reclam, 1986. 230–345.
Derrida, Jacques. *L'Écriture et la différence*. Paris: Editions du Seuil, 1979.
Deutsch, Helen. *Resemblence and Disgrace: Alexander Pope and the Deformation of Culture*. Cambridge, MA: Harvard Univ. Press, 1996.
Dick, Philip K. *The Man in the High Castle*. New York: Vintage, 1992.
Dobie, Charles Caldwell. *San Francisco's Chinatown*. New York: Appleton-Century, 1936.
Donne, John. *Complete Poetry and Selected Prose*. Ed. John Hayward. London: Nonesuch, 1929.
Dumézil, Georges. "Comparative Remarks on the Scandinavian God Heimdall." Tr. Francis Charat. In *Gods of the Ancient Norsemen*, ed. Einar Haugen. Berkeley: Univ. of California Press, 1977.
Durant, Will. *The Story of Philosophy*. 2nd ed. Garden City, NY: Garden City Publishing, 1927.
Encyclopaedia Britannica. 9th ed. Edinburgh: A. & C. Black, 1875–98.
Euripides. *Works*. Trans. A. S Way. London: Heinemann/Loeb Classical Library, 1916. 4 vols.
Fordyce, C. J., ed. *Catullus: A Commentary*. Oxford: Oxford Univ. Press, 1987.
Freud, Sigmund. "Aus der Geschichte einer infantilen Neurose." In *Gesammelte Werke Chronologisch Geordnet*. Vol. 12. Ed. Anna Freud. Frankfurt am Main: S. Fischer Verlag, 1947.
———. *The Interpretation of Dreams*. Tr. and ed. James Strachey. New York: Avon, 1965.
Frost, Robert. *Complete Poems*. New York: Holt, Rinehart & Winston, 1949.
Gadamer, Hans-Georg. *Wahrheit und Methode: Grundzüge einer philosophischen Hermeneutik*. 5th ed. Tübingen: J. C. B. Mohr (Paul Siebeck), 1986.
———. *Wer bin Ich und wer bist Du? Ein Kommentar zu Paul Celans Gedichtfolge 'Atemkristall.'* Frankfurt am Main: Suhrkamp, 1986.
Garnett, Richard. "Leopardi." In *Encyclopaedia Britannica*. Vol. 14. 463–66.
Gerard, John. *Gerard's Herbal*. Ed. Marcus Woodward. New York: Crescent, 1985.
Godwin, Tom. "The Cold Equations." In Silverberg, *The Science Fiction Hall of Fame* 543–69.

Goethe, Johann Wolfgang. *Faust.* Tr. Bayard Taylor. New York: Modern Library, 1912..

———. *Sämtliche Werke.* 1st Abt. 27 Bd. Frankfurt am Main: Deutsche Klassiker, 1989.

Gradman, Barry. *Metamorphosis in Keats.* New York: New York Univ. Press, 1980.

Grimm, Jacob. *Deutsche Mythologie.* 4th ed. Intro. Leopold Kretzenbacher. Graz: Akademische Druck- und Verlagsanstalt, 1968. 3 vols.

Haeckel, Ernst. *The Riddle of the Universe at the Close of the Nineteenth Century.* Trans. Joseph McCabe. New York: Harper, 1900.

Harrison, Jane Ellen. *Themis: A Study of the Social Origins of Greek Religion.* 2nd ed. 1912. Cleveland: World Publishing Co., 1962.

Hays, Peter L. *The Limping Hero: Grotesques in Literature.* New York: New York Univ. Press, 1971.

Heidegger, Martin. *Being and Time.* Tr. John Macquarrie and Edward Robinson. New York: Harper & Row, 1962.

———. *Holzwege.* Frankfurt am Main: Vittorio Klostermann, 1950.

Herodotus. *The History.* Tr. A. D. Godley. Cambridge, MA: Harvard Univ. Press/Loeb Classical Library, 1926. 4 vols.

Hesiod. *The Homeric Hymns and Homerica.* Ed. and tr. Hugh G. Evelyn-White. London: Heinemann/Loeb Classical Library, 1929.

Hill, Geoffrey. *Collected Poems.* New York: Oxford Univ. Press, 1986.

———. *The Lords of Limit: Essays on Literature and Ideas.* New York: Oxford Univ. Press, 1984.

Hillman, James. *A Blue Fire: Selected Writings.* Ed. Thomas Moore. New York: HarperPerennial, 1991.

———. *Re-Visioning Psychology.* New York: HarperPerennial, 1992.

Hogan, James C. *A Commentary on the Plays of Sophocles.* Carbondale: Southern Illinois Univ. Press, 1991.

Huet, Marie-Hélène. *Monstrous Imagination.* Cambridge, MA: Harvard Univ. Press, 1993.

Hugo, Victor. *La Légende des siècles; La fin de Satan; Dieu.* Ed. Jacques Truchet. Paris: Gallimard, 1950.

Huxley, Thomas Henry. *Man's Place in Nature and Other Anthropological Essays.* 1896. New York: Appleton, 1929.

Irving, Washington. *Tales of a Traveller by Geoffrey Crayon, Gent.* Ed. Judith Giblin Haig. Vol. 10 in *The Complete Works of Washington Irving.* Ed. Richard Dilworth Rust. Boston: Twayne, 1987.

Jacobson, Howard. *Ovid's* Heroides. Princeton: Princeton Univ. Press, 1974.

Johnson, Samuel. *A Dictionary of the English Language.* 4th ed. London: W. Strahan, 1773. 2 vols.

Johnson, W. R. *Darkness Visible: A Study of Vergil's* Aeneid. Berkeley: Univ. of California Press, 1976.

Joyce, James. *Finnegans Wake.* New York: Viking, 1939.

———. *The Portable James Joyce*. Intro. Harry Levin. New York: Viking, 1966.

———. *A Portrait of the Artist as a Young Man*. Ed. Chester G. Anderson. New York: Penguin/Viking Critical Library, 1977.

———. *Ulysses*. Ed. Walter Gabler, with Wolfhard Steppe and Claus Melchior. New York: Random House, 1986.

Julius, Anthony. *T. S. Eliot, Anti-Semitism, and Literary Form*. New York: Cambridge Univ. Press, 1996.

Keats, John. *The Complete Poems*. Ed. John Barnard. 2nd ed. Harmondsworth: Penguin, 1976.

———. *The Letters: 1814–1821*. Ed. H. E. Rollins. Cambridge, MA: Harvard Univ. Press, 1958. 2 vols.

———. *Poems*. Ed. Jack Stillinger. Cambridge, MA: Harvard Univ. Press, 1978.

Kelsey, Rayner Wickersham. *Centennial History of Moses Brown School, 1819–1919*. Intro. Rufus Matthew Jones. Providence: Moses Brown School, 1919.

King, Henry Melville. *Thinking God's Thoughts After Him: A Retired Man's Meditations*. Boston: Gorham, 1914.

Krutch, Joseph Wood. *The Modern Temper: A Study and a Confession*. New York: Harcourt, Brace, 1929.

Küng, Hans. *Justification: The Doctrine of Karl Barth and a Catholic Reflection. With a Letter by Karl Barth*. Tr. Thomas Collins, Edmund E. Tolk, and David Granskou. New York: Thomas Nelson & Sons, 1964.

Kuhns, Oscar and Frank Justus Miller. *Studies in the Poetry of Italy: I. Roman, and II. Italian*. Cleveland: Chautauqua Assembly, 1901.

Langland, William. *The Vision of Piers Plowman: A Critical Edition of the B-Text*. Ed. A. V. C. Schmidt. London: Dent, 1978.

Laplanche, Jean and J.-B. Portalis. "Appendices." *Yale French Studies* 48 (1972): 179–202.

Leff, Gordon. *William of Ockham: The Metamorphosis of Scholastic Discourse*. Manchester: Manchester Univ. Press, 1975.

Leith, John H., ed. *Creeds of the Churches: A Reader in Christian Doctrine from the Bible to the Present*. Garden City, NY: Doubleday/Anchor Books, 1963.

Lemons, J. Stanley. *The First Baptist Church in America*. East Greenwich, RI: Charitable Baptist Society, 1988.

Leopardi, Giacomo. *Tutte le opere*. Ed. Francesco Flora. Milano: Mondadori, 1937–40. 5 vols.

Lewis, R. W. B. *The American Adam: Innocence, Tragedy and Tradition in the Nineteenth Century*. Chicago: Univ. of Chicago Press, 1955.

Liddell, Henry George, and Robert Scott. *A Lexicon: Abridged from Liddell and Scott's Greek-English Lexicon*. 1871. Oxford: Clarendon Press, 1958.

Loveman, Samuel. *The Hermaphrodite and Other Poems*. Caldwell, ID: Caxton, 1936.

Machen, Arthur. *Tales of Horror and the Supernatural*. New York: Pinnacle Books, 1973. 2 vols.

———. *The Three Impostors*. Intro. Lin Carter. New York: Ballantine, 1972.

Manilius, Marcus. *Astronomica/Atrologie*. Tr. Wolfgang Fels. Stuttgart: Reclam, 1990.
Marlowe, Christopher. *Complete Works*. Ed. Fredson Bowers. 2nd ed. Vol. 2. Cambridge: Cambridge Univ. Press, 1981.
Meeks, Wayne A., ed. *The Writings of St. Paul*. New York: W. W. Norton, 1972.
Merritt, Abraham. *The Moon Pool*. 1919. New York: Collier, 1961.
Meyrink, Gustav. *Der Golem*. Frankfurt am Main: Ullstein, 1993.
Miller, Karl. *Doubles: Studies in Literary History*. Oxford: Oxford Univ. Press, 1987.
Milton, John. *Complete Poems and Major Prose*. Ed. Merritt Y. Hughes. New York: Odyssey, 1957.
Newton, Isaac. "An Hypothesis Explaining the Properties of Light Discoursed of in My Several Papers" [Letter to Oldenburg, 25 January 1675/76]. In *Newton's Philosophy of Nature: Selections from His Writings*. Ed. H. S. Thayer. Intro. John Herman Randall, Jr. New York: Hafner, 1953.

———. *Opticks, or A Treatise of the Reflections, Refractions, Inflections and Colours of Light*. Fwd. Albert Einstein. Into. Edmund Whittaker. Pref. I. Bernard Cohen. Contents, Duane H. D. Roller. New York: Dover, 1979.

———. *Philosophiae Naturalis Principia Mathematica*. 3rd ed. Ed. Alexander Koyré and I. Bernard Cohen. Cambridge, MA: Harvard Univ. Press, 1972.
Nietzsche, Friedrich. *Werke*. Ed. Karl Schlechta. München: Carl Hanser, 1956. 3 vols.
Nicolson, Marjorie Hope. *Newton Demands the Muse: Newton's "Opticks" and the Eighteenth Century Poets*. Princeton: Princeton Univ. Press, 1946.
Noll, Richard. *The Jung Cult: Origins of a Charismatic Movement*. New York: Free Press, 1997.
O'Brien, Edward J. *The Dance of the Machines: The American Short Story and the Industrial Age*. New York: Macaulay, 1929.
Ovid [Publius Ovidius Naso]. *Heroides and Amores*. Tr. Grant Showerman. Cambridge, MA: Harvard Univ. Press/Loeb Classical Library, 1914.

———. *Metamorphoses*. Ed. W. S. Anderson. Stuttgart: Teubner, 1991.
Palladas of Alexandria. In *The Greek Anthology*. Tr. W. R. Patton. Vol. 3. Cambridge, MA: Harvard Univ. Press/Loeb Classical Library, 1917.
Partridge, Eric. *A Dictionary of Slang and Unconventional English*. 8th Ed. Ed. Paul Beale. New York: Macmillan, 1984.
Petrarca, Francesco. *Secretum*. Ed. Enrico Fenzi. Milano: Mursia, 1992.
Pindar. *The Extant Odes*. Tr. Ernest Myers. London: Macmillan, 1912.
Plato. *Opera*. Ed. John Burnet. Oxford: Oxford Univ. Press, 1907. 5 vols.
Poe, Edgar Allan. *Collected Works*. Ed. Thomas Olive Mabbott. Cambridge, MA: Harvard Univ. Press, 1969–78. 3 vols.
Pokorny, Julius. *Indogermanisches Etymologisches Wörterbuch*. Bern: Francke, 1959. 2 vols.
Pope, Alexander. *The Poems*. Ed. John Butt. New Haven: Yale Univ. Press, 1963.

———. *The Odyssey of Homer*. In *Poems*. Ed. Maynard Mack. Vol. 9. London: Methuen, 1967.
Pöschl, Viktor. *The Art of Vergil: Image and Symbol in the* Aeneid. Tr. Gerda Seligson. Ann Arbor: Univ. of Michigan Press, 1970.

Pound, Ezra. *Personae: The Shorter Poems of Ezra Pound.* Ed. Lea Baechler and A. Walton Litz. New York: New Directions, 1990.

———. *The Cantos.* New York: New Directions, 1970.

Praz, Mario. *The Romantic Agony.* Tr. Angus Davidson. 2nd. ed. Cleveland: World Publishing Co., 1956.

Quintilian. *Institutio Oratoria.* Tr. H. E. Butler. Cambridge, MA: Harvard Univ. Press/Loeb Classical Library, 1920. 4 vols.

Ranieri, Antonio. *Sette anni di sodalizio con Giacomo Leopardi.* Pref. Vittorio Russo. Napoli: Arturo Berisio, 1965.

Reinhardt, Karl. *Sophocles.* Tr. Hazel Harvey and David Harvey. Intro. Hugh Lloyd-Jones. New York: Harper & Row, 1979.

Rilke, Rainer Maria. *Gesammelte Gedichte.* Frankfurt am Main: Insel, 1962.

Rimbaud, Arthur. *Oeuvres.* Ed. Suzanne Bernard. Paris: Garnier, 1960.

Roethke, Theodore. *Collected Poems.* Garden City, NY: Doubleday, 1966.

Rogers, Eugene F., Jr. *Thomas Aquinas and Karl Barth: Sacred Doctrine and the Natural Knowledge of God.* Notre Dame, IN: Univ. of Notre Dame Press, 1995.

Rohmer, Sax. *The Insidious Dr. Fu Manchu.* 1913. New York: Pyramid Books, 1961.

Rorty, Richard. *Philosophy and the Mirror of Nature.* Princeton: Princeton Univ. Press, 1979.

Sayers, Dorothy L. *The Mind of the Maker.* New York: Meridian, 1956.

Schillebeeckx, Edward. *Christ: The Experience of Jesus as Lord.* Tr. John Bowden. New York: Crossroad, 1983.

———. *Jesus: An Experiment in Christology.* Tr. Hubert Hoskins. New York: Vintage, 1981.

Schleiermacher, Friedrich. *Ueber die Religion: Reden an die Gebildeten unter ihren Verächtern.* Nachw. Carl Heinz Ratschow. Stuttgart: Reclam, 1989.

Scholem, Gershom. *Kabbalah.* New York: Dorset, 1987.

Schopenhauer, Arthur. *Sämmtliche Werke.* Ed. Eduard Grisebach. Leipzig: Reclam, 1891. 6 vols.

Scott, Sir Walter. *Letters on Demonology and Witchcraft.* 2nd. ed. Intro. Henry Morley. London: Routledge, 1885.

Seneca [Lucius Annaeus]. *Oedipus.* In *Tragedies.* Vol. 1. Ed. and trans. Frank Justus Miller. Cambridge, MA: Harvard Univ. Press/Loeb Classical Library, 1979.

Sepper, Dennis L. *Goethe Contra Newton: Polemics and the Project for a New Science of Color.* Cambridge: Cambridge Univ. Press, 1988.

Shakespeare, William. *Complete Works.* Ed. Alfred Harbage. Baltimore: Penguin, 1969.

Silverberg, Robert, ed. *The Science Fiction Hall of Fame.* New York: Avon, 1970.

Skeat, Walter K. *A Concise Etymological Dictionary of the English Language.* 1910. New York: Putnam, 1980.

Smith, Clark Ashton. *The Hashish-Eater; or, The Apocalypse of Evil.* West Warwick, RI: Necronomicon Press, 1989.

———. "The Tale of Satampra Zeiros." In *The City of the Singing Flame.* Ed. Donald Sidney-Fryer. New York: Pocket Books, 1981. 66–78.

Sonneck, Oscar George Theodore. *Report on "The Star-Spangled Banner" "Hail Columbia" "America" "Yankee Doodle."* Washington: Government Printing Office, 1909.
Sophocles. *Fabulae*. Ed. A. C. Pearson. Oxford: Oxford Univ. Press, 1928.
Spenser, Edmund. *Complete Poetical Works*. Ed. R. E. Neil Dodge. Boston: Houghton, Mifflin, 1908.
Sperry, Stuart M., Jr. "Keats and the Chemistry of Poetic Creation." *PMLA* 85 (1970): 268–77.
Stesichorus. "The Palinode." In J. M. Edmonds, ed. and trans. *Lyra Graeca*. 2nd ed. London: Heinemann/Loeb Classical Library, 1931.
Stillinger, Jack. *The Hoodwinking of Madeline and Other Essays on Keats's Poems*. Urbana: Univ. of Illinois Press, 1971.
Suvin, Darko. *Metamorphoses of Science Fiction: On the Poetics and History of a Literary Genre*. New Haven: Yale Univ. Press, 1979.
Swift, Jonathan. *The Writings*. Ed. Robert A Greenberg and William Bowman Piper. New York: W. W. Norton, 1973.
Swinburne, Algernon. *Swinburne Replies*. Ed. Clyde Kenneth Hyder. Syracuse: Syracuse Univ. Press, 1966.
Tennyson, Alfred, Lord. *The Poetic and Dramatic Works*. Boston: Houghton Mifflin, 1927.
Thomas à Kempis. *Imitazione di Cristo*. Intro. Elémire Zolla. Tr. Carlo Vitale. Milano: Rizzoli, 1974.
Thomson, James. *The Complete Poetical Works*. Ed. J. Logie Robertson. London: Oxford Univ. Press, 1908.
Tolkien, J. R. R. *The Monsters and the Critics and Other Essays*. Ed. Christopher Tolkien. Boston: Houghton Mifflin, 1984.
Torbet, Robert. G. *A History of the Baptists*. Frwd. Kenneth Scott Latourette. Philadelphia: Judson, 1952.
Torrey, E. Fuller. *The Roots of Treason: Ezra Pound and the Secret of St. Elizabeths*. New York: Harcourt Brace Jovanovich, 1984.
Trimbur, John. "Consensus and Difference in Collaborative Learning." *College English* 51 (1989): 602–16.
Tucker, Harry, Jr. "Introduction" in Rank, *The Double*.
Tucker, T. G. *Etymological Dictionary of Latin*. Chicago: Ares, 1985.
Vergil [Publius Vergilius Maro]. *Opera*. Ed. Frederick Arthur Hirtzel. Oxford: Oxford Univ. Press, 1900.
Wagner, Richard. *The Ring of the Nibelung*. Tr. Andrew Porter. New York: W. W. Norton, 1977.
Wandrei, Donald. *Collected Poems*. Ed. S. T. Joshi. West Warwick, RI: Necronomicon Press, 1988.
Watson, Derek. *Richard Wagner: A Biography*. New York: Macmillan, 1981.
Webster, John. *The Complete Works*. Ed. F. L. Lucas. London: Chatto & Windus, 1927.
Wells, H. G. *Seven Science Fiction Novels of H. G. Wells*. New York: Dover, 1950.

White, Ray Lewis, ed. "Introduction and Commentary." In Anderson, *Winesburg, Ohio.*
Wilson, Edmund. *Classics and Commercials: A Literary Chronicle of the Forties.* 1950. New York: Random House, 1962.
Winnington-Ingram, R. P. *Sophocles: An Interpretation.* Cambridge: Cambridge Univ. Press, 1980.
Wolfe, Gary K. *The Known and the Unknown: The Iconography of Science Fiction.* Kent, OH: Kent State Univ. Press, 1979.
Wordsworth, William. *The Complete Poetical Works.* Ed. Alice N. George. Boston: Houghton Mifflin, 1932.
Wu, William F. *The Yellow Peril: Chinese Americans in American Fiction 1850–1940.* Hamden, CT: Archon Books, 1982.
Yates, Frances A. *Giordano Bruno and the Hermetic Tradition.* New York: Random House, 1969.
Yeats, William Butler. *The Poems.* Ed. Richard J. Finneran. New York: Macmillan, 1983.
Young, Edward. *Night Thoughts.* Ed. Charles Cowden Clarke. Edinburgh: James Nicholl, 1865.
Young-Bruehl, Elisabeth. *The Anatomy of Prejudices.* Cambridge, MA: Harvard Univ. Press, 1996.

Index

"A se stesso" (Leopardi) 219
"Ad Angelo Mai" (Leopardi) 216
Adams, Henry 86, 241, 255, 256
Addison, Joseph 10, 36, 134, 135, 169, 194, 247
"Adventure of the German Student, The" (Irving) 20–21
Aeneid (Virgil) 120–21, 136, 181, 185
Aeschylus 114, 130
Agamemnon (Aeschylus) 114
"Al Conte Carlo Pepoli" (Leopardi) 216
"Alchemist, The" 180
Alhazred, Abdul 23
"Allerdings: Dem Physiker" (Goethe) 135
"Amy Levy" (Loveman) 89
Anderson, Sherwood 21, 47–48
"Antarktos" (*Fungi from Yuggoth*) 107
Apology (Plato) 174
Aquinas, Thomas 249, 253, 260, 261, 269
Arabian Nights 23
Arendt, Hannah 49
Aristotle 249
Ars poetica (Horace) 223
Asimov, Isaac 250–51
Astounding Stories 253
At the Mountains of Madness 9, 18, 20, 22, 24, 25, 29, 33, 36, 41, 55, 56, 61, 79–108, 137, 178, 240
Augustus (Emperor of Rome) 114, 239
Austen, Jane 176
Azathoth 35, 64, 255, 269

Bachelard, Gaston 99–100
Bacon, Sir Francis 74–75
Bamford, Mary E. 84
Barfield, Owen 176
Barlow, Robert H. 279
Barricelli, Gian Piero 209
Barth, Karl 249, 250, 251, 256, 257, 259, 260–61, 269, 277
Baudelaire, Charles 49, 121
Beardsley, Aubrey 141
"Becalmed" (Loveman) 89

Beckford, William 20
Being in Time (Heidegger) 49
"Belle Dame sans Merci, La" (Keats) 134, 142
Belloc, Hilaire 276n9
Bennett, Andrew 128, 150
"Berenice" (Poe) 146, 160, 194
Berkeley, George 133, 135, 257
Bersani, Leo 10, 153, 156
Best Short Stories of 1928 (O'Brien) 265
"Beyond the Wall of Sleep" 117
Bible 19n2, 57, 243, 244
Bierce, Ambrose 247
Bishop, Zealia 81, 125
Blackwood, Algernon 277
Blake, William 133, 141, 158
Blavatsky, Helena P. 60
Bloch, Robert 29, 196, 240
Boats of the "Glen Carrig," The (Hodgson) 47
Bohr, Neils 196
Book of Dzyan 29
Born, Daniel 251
Bowen, Enoch 243
"Bride of Corinth, The" (Goethe) 143
Brillat-Savarin, Jean-Anthelme 69
Brown, John 81
Brown, Moses 183
Brown, Norman O. 106
Browning, Robert 39
Bruffee, Kenneth A. 164, 179, 182, 188
Bruno, Giordano 207n4
"Bruto minore" (Leopardi) 225
Buber, Martin 164, 170
Buchanan, Carl 115
Burke, Edmund 46, 220
Burleson, Donald R. 17n1, 56, 71, 176, 256, 274
Burleson, Mollie 115
"By the North Sea" (Swinburne) 25–26
Byron, George Gordon, Lord 201

Calasso, Roberto 10, 113, 139, 147, 154

Callimachus 125
"Call of Cthulhu, The" 18, 20, 23, 25, 32, 34, 35, 38, 39, 44, 50, 52, 73, 95, 117, 232, 242, 250, 271, 272–77, 282
Cannon, Peter 11
Canti (Leopardi) 219, 232, 233, 238
"Cantico del gallo silvestre" (Leopardi) 208
"Canto notturno di un pastore errante dell'Asia" (Leopardi) 221, 226, 239
Cantos, The (Pound) 178
Capek, Karel 265
Carsaninga, Giovanni 203, 208, 231
Case of Charles Dexter Ward, The 18, 19, 20, 25, 26, 28, 29, 33, 34, 35, 36, 39, 41, 44, 50, 52, 56, 59–60, 95, 97, 98, 99, 100, 113, 167, 168, 183–85, 197, 230, 239, 242, 245, 271, 272, 282
Catullus (C. Valerius Catullus) 125
Chaplin, Charlie 265
Chapman, Rosemary 180
Chaucer, Geoffrey 128
Chesterfield, Philip Dormer Stanhope, earl of 181
"Childe Roland to the Dark Tower Came" (Browning) 39
Christianity 10, 82, 241–82
Cibber, Colley 195
Cicero (M. Tullius Cicero) 216
"City in the Sea, The" (Poe) 26
Classics and Commercials (Wilson) 169
Clausius 208
Cleopatra 114, 141, 157, 158
Codrescu, Andrei 88n3
"Cold Equations, The" (Godwin) 252
Coleridge, Samuel Taylor 103, 134, 191
"Colour out of Space, The" 20, 24, 25, 29, 37, 52, 56, 57–59, 60, 64, 106, 108, 117, 130, 137, 138, 245, 262, 265
Commedia divina (Dante) 175, 246
Commonplace Book 26, 116
Comus (Milton) 132
"Conqueror Worm, The" (Poe) 144, 145
Conservative 182
Conversation (Cowper) 44
Cooke, George Albert 104
"Cool Air" 18, 36
Copernicus, Nicolaus 276

Cowper, William 10, 39, 44
Cox, Arthur Jean 30
Crane, Hart 88, 89
Croce, Benedetto 203, 218–19, 228, 246
Cthulhu 50, 75, 76, 91, 245, 273–77
Cthulhu Mythos 17, 75, 242
Cultes des Goules (d'Erlette) 29
"Curse of Yig, The" (Lovecraft-Bishop) 117, 124, 125
Cushman, Robert 173
Cymbeline (Shakespeare) 157

Daedalus 236–38, 239
"Dagon" 17, 18, 19, 24, 25, 26, 38, 46, 49
Dance of the Machines, The (O'Brien) 42, 265
D'Annunzio, Gabriele 236
Dante Alighieri 175, 218, 263, 268
Darwin, Charles 72, 81, 129, 260, 266
Davis, Sonia. *See* Greene, Sonia H.
De Bry, Brothers 76
de Camp, L. Sprague 9, 88, 146, 179, 241
De Quincey, Thomas 121, 218
De Revolutionibus (Copernicus) 276
De Vermis Mysteriis (Prinn) 29
Delacroix, Eugène 276n9
Delany, Samuel R. 62
Democritus 31, 58
Derleth, August 29, 42, 75, 242
Derrida, Jacques 52, 119
Descartes, René 270
"Deserted Village, The" (Goldsmith) 194
Deutsch, Helen 231, 235
"Dialogo della natura e di un'anima" (Leopardi) 202
"Dialogo di Cristoforo Colombo e di Pietro Gutierrez" (Leopardi) 209
"Dialogo di Plotino e di Porfirio" (Leopardi) 210, 228, 233
"Dialogo di un Folletto e di un Gnomo" (Leopardi) 217
Dick, Philip K. 53
Dilthey, Wilhelm 189
"Ditirambo IV" (D'Annunzio) 236
Donne, John 261n8
Dream-Quest of Unknown Kadath, The 21, 28, 34, 37, 39, 44, 47, 48, 93, 94, 97,

137, 191, 245
"Dreams in the Witch House, The" 18–19, 34, 35, 36, 38, 41, 43, 46, 81, 117, 118, 191–92, 231, 255, 257
Dryden, John 129
Du Chaillu, Paul Belloni 75, 76, 77
Duchess of Malfi, The (Webster) 18
Duino Elegies (Rilke) 140
Dunciad, The (Pope) 23, 132, 194–95
Duns Scotus 23
Dunsany, Lord 79, 90, 114n1, 194, 196, 213, 218, 219, 238
"Dunwich Horror, The" 18, 19, 22, 25–26, 28, 29, 34, 60, 95, 117, 122, 130, 185–87, 188, 189, 197, 211, 230, 236, 239, 240, 245, 262
Durant, Will 201, 254n3
Dybbuk, The (Anstey) 86
Dziemianowicz, Stefan 69

Eddington, Arthur 196
Edwards, Jonathan 19n2
Egan, James 245, 246
Einstein, Albert 129, 196
Einstein Intersection, The (Delany) 62
"Elgin Marbles, The" (Keats) 128
Eliot, T. S. 86, 91, 168, 169, 190, 213
Elliot, Hugh 252, 253, 254–55, 256
Encyclopaedia Britannica 104, 201
Endymion (Keats) 128
Epicure in the Terrible, An (Schultz–Joshi) 69
Epicurus 31, 54
"Epistle to Dr. Arbuthnot, An" (Pope) 195
Essay on Criticism, An (Pope) 132
Euclid 35
Euripides 113
Euthyphro (Plato) 173
Eve of St. Agnes, The (Keats) 116, 120, 127, 129, 130, 143, 144, 147–53, 155, 157, 197
"Evil Clergyman, The" 242–43
"Ex Oblivione" 53

"Facts Concerning the Late Arthur Jermyn and His Family" 25, 81, 117, 125
Faerie Queene, The (Spenser) 143, 238, 261n8
"Fall of the House of Usher, The" (Poe) 27–28, 145, 146
Faust (Goethe) 213, 269–70
"Festival, The" 18, 25, 44, 45, 95–96
Fichte, Johann Gottlieb 134, 179
Fife, Ernelle 11
Finnegans Wake (Joyce) 160, 238, 239
Flame Dancer, The (Mathews) 84
Flaubert, Gustave 124
Fontenelle, Bernard de 207n4
"Frammento apocrifo di Stratone da Lampsaco" (Leopardi) 208
Frazer, Sir James George 190
Freud, Sigmund 10, 72, 118, 119, 124, 128, 176, 179n4, 260
"From Beyond" 25, 255
Frost, Robert 52
Frye, Northrop 179
Fulwiler, William 116, 127, 145
Fungi from Yuggoth 53, 93, 107, 207, 220
Fuseli, Henry 58

Gadamer, Hans-Georg 63, 115, 249, 270
Galpin, Alfred 207
"Gardens of Yin, The" (*Fungi from Yuggoth*) 207
Gass, William H. 24
Gauguin, Paul 139
Gay, John 181
Gayford, Norman 11, 190
Gerard, John 57
ghouls 20–21, 36–37, 47
Gibbon, Edward 194
Gilbert, W. S. 168
Gilgamesh 125–26
"Ginestra, La" (Leopardi) 210, 215, 217, 221, 228, 231, 234–35, 236, 239
Godwin, Tom 252
Goethe, Johann Wolfgang von 113, 115, 133, 135–36, 140, 143, 148, 149, 159, 179, 213, 237, 269–70
Goldsmith, Oliver 194
Golem, Der (Meyrink) 84, 86
Goya y Lucientes, Francisco de 78
Grammar of Science, The (Pearson) 255
Gravity's Rainbow (Pynchon) 106
Greene, Sonia H. 49, 80, 86–87, 88, 89, 133
Guéhenno, Jean 164

H. M. S. Pinafore (Gilbert-Sullivan) 168

Haeckel, Ernst 191, 208, 247, 248, 250, 252, 253, 255, 274
Hairy Ape, The (O'Neill) 265
Haldeman-Julius Weekly 134n3
Halley, Edmond 152
Hamlet (Shakespeare) 76, 156
"Hands" (Anderson) 21–22
Harrison, Jane 238
"Haunted Palace, The" (Poe) 144, 145
"Haunter of the Dark, The" 18, 26, 46, 81, 113, 196, 243
Hauser, Kaspar 170
Hawthorne, Nathaniel 195
Hays, Peter 281
"He" 26, 44, 95, 214
Hegel, G. W. F. 134
Heidegger, Martin 10, 19, 42–43, 49, 58, 249, 266
Helen (Euripides) 113
Henry V (Shakespeare) 93
"Herbert West—Reanimator" 31, 38, 39, 43, 44, 49, 80, 117, 118, 187
Hermaphrodite, The (Loveman) 88–89, 121
Herodotus 114, 194
Heroides (Ovid) 233
Herschel, Sir William 129
Hesiod 139
Hill, Emita B. 240
Hill, Geoffrey 10, 92, 94, 247, 268
Hillman, James 10, 105, 170
Hitler, Adolf 19
Hodgson, William Hope 47
Hoffmann, E. T. A. 37
Holbach, Paul Thiry d' 240
"Holy Office, The" (Joyce) 236
Holy Sonnets (Donne) 261n8
Home Brew 24, 49, 80
Homer 221
Homme machine, L' (La Mettrie) 215
Horace (Q. Horatius Flaccus) 216, 222, 223
"Horror at Red Hook, The" 25, 92–93, 96
"Horror in the Museum, The" (Lovecraft-Heald) 117
"Hound, The" 18, 20, 22, 24, 25, 28
Howard, Robert E. 39
Huet, Marie-Hélène 10, 236, 237, 276n9, 280

Hume, David 254n3
Husserl, Edmund 49, 249, 259n7
Huxley, Thomas Henry 75, 76, 77, 83, 166
Huysmans, J.-K. 37
Hyperion (Keats) 129
"Hypnos" 45, 88, 117, 121

"In a Station of the Metro" (Pound) 79
"In the Vault" 193
Inferno (Dante) 139
Infinito, L'" (Leopardi) 221
Irving, Washington 20–21, 28, 37
Isis Unveiled (Blavatsky) 60

Jackson, Forrest 154n7
James, M. R. 241
Jaspers, Karl 19
Jeder für Sich und Gott gegen Alle (film) 170
Jews 42, 48, 49, 76, 81–87, 91, 104
Johnson, Judith 11
Johnson, Samuel 20n3, 46, 169, 171, 175, 176, 184, 192, 193, 194, 195, 197, 257
Joshi, S. T. 9, 10, 56n1, 75, 79, 88, 179, 241, 245, 246, 247, 271
Joyce, James 133, 160, 167, 169, 236, 238, 239
Julius, Anthony 10, 86, 87, 91
Junzt, Friedrich von 64

Kalevala 132
Kant, Immanuel 54, 134, 217
Keats, John 17, 116, 124, 127–61, 196, 206, 207, 212–13, 214, 215, 232, 240
Kempton, Dan 11
King, Henry Melville 243, 244
King Lear (Shakespeare) 206
Knopf, Alfred A. 265
Krutch, Joseph Wood 42, 215, 247, 279
"Kubla Khan" (Coleridge) 103, 107
Kuhns, O. 202

La Mettrie, Julien Offray de 215
Lamb, Charles 131
Lamia (Keats) 124, 128, 129–31, 135, 138, 142, 143, 146, 151, 152, 157–58
Langan, John Paul 11
Langland, William 257
Laplace, Pierre Simon, marquis de 54, 253

Index 301

"Legend" (Loveman) 89
Leiber, Fritz 111, 116, 117, 124, 240
Leprière, John 145
Leopardi, Giacomo 10, 201–40, 246
Lévy, Maurice 64, 85n1, 241
Lewis, R. W. B. 176
Lives (Plutarch) 19, 181
Lizst, Franz 178
Locke, John 134, 196, 197, 203, 217, 254
Long, Frank Belknap 86, 240
Longinus 220
Lopez, Eduardo 76, 77
Lovecraft, H. P.: anti-Semitism of, 48–49, 76, 81–83, 85–86, 90–92, 104, 177–78; and authenticity, 41–44, 52, 75; and documents, 52–54, 55–58; and doubles, 28; education of, 162–63, 166–67, 169–70, 179–80, 202; and grotesque, 45–47; and handwriting, 18–19; on hoaxes, 23; and homosexuality, 88–89; language of, 30–41; on liquor, 182; marriage of, 86–87; and masks, 44–45; narrative voice of, 28–29, 60–61, 64–65, 69–72; narrators of, 24–25; and New York, 80–81, 84, 85, 92–93, 214; philosophy of, 134–35, 196–97, 205–6, 208, 212, 216, 217, 228–29, 253–57, 265–67; and Providence, R.I., 80, 212, 229–30, 264–65; racism of, 81, 83–85, 103, 141; recognition of, 9, 167–69; religious views of, 241–82; on Romantic poets, 127–29; and science fiction, 250–53, 257; style of, 29–30, 195, 219–20; and terminal climax, 116–18, 120–24; and water, 25–27
Loveman, Samuel 49, 80, 86, 88–89, 121, 240
Lovett-Graff, Bennett 92
Lucretius (T. Lucretius Carus) 10, 31, 54–55, 58, 201, 207n4, 218, 254, 256, 261
"Lurking Fear, The" 20, 22, 39, 97, 117
Lusiados, Os (Camoens) 204

Macbeth (Shakespeare) 56, 157
Macleod, Fiona 24
Magnalia Christi Americana (Mather) 191

Mai, Angelo 216
Man in the High Castle, The (Dick) 53
Manetho 113
Manilius, M. 218
Man's Place in Nature and Other Anthropological Essays (Huxley) 75
Mariconda, Steven J. 31, 59, 195, 270
Marlowe, Christopher 113
Marxism 264, 266
"Masque of the Red Death, The" (Poe) 144–45, 157
Mather, Cotton 191
Mathews, Frances Aymar 84
"Medusa's Coil" (Lovecraft-Bishop) 81, 117, 124–25, 130, 133, 137, 138–44, 145, 146, 152, 153, 155, 159–60
Melville, Herman 24, 176
Mencken, H. L. 247
Meno (Plato) 173
Metamorphoses (Ovid) 112
Meyrink, Gustav 84, 86, 92
Midsummer Night's Dream, A (Shakespeare) 157
Milton, John 43, 64, 128, 132, 261n8
Modern Quarterly 265
Modern Science and Materialism (Elliot) 254
Modern Temper, The (Krutch) 42
Modern Times (film) 265
Montelone, Paul 241
"Moon-Bog, The" 25, 43
Morton, Thomas 181n5
Mosig, Dirk W. 248
"Mound, The" (Lovecraft-Bishop) 55, 75, 94, 97–98, 99, 117–18
Mulhall, Stephen 49
Murray, Margaret A. 190
Murray, Will 93, 181n5
"Music of Erich Zann, The" 18, 26, 46
Mystères de Paris (Sue) 141

"Nameless City, The" 20, 95
Nausée, La (Sartre) 193
Nazism 49, 82, 85
Necronomicon (Alhazred) 17, 19, 22, 23, 29, 34, 108, 187, 195, 259, 261, 270
"Newgate's Garland" (Gay) 181
Newton, Sir Isaac 10, 129, 131–34, 135, 136, 137, 138n4, 140, 142–43, 144–45, 146, 149, 152, 153, 156, 160, 161, 196, 207, 229, 240, 255

Nicholson, Marjorie 132
Nietzsche, Friedrich 82, 102, 134, 201, 203, 208, 242
"Nietzscheism and Realism" 133
"Nightfall" (Asimov) 250–51
"Night-Gaunts" (*Fungi from Yuggoth*) 93
Night Land, The (Hodgson) 47
Night Thoughts (Young) 40, 154
Nitokris, Queen 114, 116, 122, 125, 155–56, 159, 171, 194, 196
Noll, Richard 247
"Notes on Writing Weird Fiction" 115
Nyarlathotep 24, 37, 39, 43, 50, 58, 73, 76, 88n2, 137, 246, 269

O'Brien, Edward J. 42, 215, 265–68, 269, 273
Occam, William of 253
"Ode. Dejection" (Coleridge) 191
"Ode on a Grecian Urn" (Keats) 128
"Ode to Melancholy" (Keats) 140
"Odo, Melisso" (Leopardi) 225
Odyssey (Homer) 112–13
Oedipus 10, 27, 34, 56, 118, 119, 124, 154, 160, 161, 165, 197, 211, 219, 237, 278, 280–82
Oedipus at Colonus (Sophocles) 161, 278, 281
Oedipus Tyrannos (Sophocles) 278, 281
Olsen, Tom 11
"On First Looking into Chaopman's Homer" (Keats) 128, 129
"On Sitting Down to Read *King Lear* Once Again" (Keats) 129
"On the Creation of Niggers" 84–85
"On the Pleasures of the Imagination" (Addison) 134
O'Neill, Eugene 265
Operette morali (Leopardi) 203–4, 220, 221, 232, 233, 235, 237, 239, 240
Opticks (Newton) 135, 137
Ottonieri, Phillippo 232
"Outsider, The" 9, 17, 20, 24, 26, 28, 29, 30, 36, 50, 90, 111–98, 230, 238, 239, 240, 241n1, 243, 259, 271
Ovid (P. Ovidius Naso) 10, 112, 132, 136, 137, 139, 154, 156, 166, 195, 233
Oxford English Dictionary 176, 193
"Ozymandias" (Shelley) 40

"Palinodia" (Leopardi) 215

Palladas of Alexandria 271
Paradise Lost (Milton) 19, 40, 43, 56n1, 131, 143, 157, 261n8
Paradiso (Dante) 263, 268
Paralipomeni della Batracomiomachia (Leopardi) 203, 236, 239
Partridge, Eric 176
Pascal, Blaise 209
"Passero solitario, Il" (Leopardi) 234
Paul, St. 249, 261, 278
Pearson, Karl 254–55, 256
Pensieri, I (Leopardi) 204–5, 210
"Pensiero dominante, Il" (Leopardi) 221
Penzoldt, Peter 28
Petrarch (Francesco Petrarca) 111, 117, 218, 228
Phillips, Whipple Van Buren 70–71, 76, 77
"Pickman's Model" 19–21, 24, 25, 26, 28, 36–37, 78, 92, 96–97, 105, 117, 121–22, 165, 182
"Picture in the House, The" 9, 19, 20, 21, 24, 36–37, 39, 45, 46, 52, 69–78, 81, 165, 181, 246
Pigafetta, Filippo 75, 76, 77
Pindar 139
Pitkin, Wlater B. 273
Plato 172–75, 189, 217, 276n9
Plutarch 19, 159, 181
Pnakotic Manuscripts 29
Poe, Edgar Allan 24, 25n5, 26, 30, 45, 71, 90, 104, 144, 145–46, 160, 175, 182, 194, 218, 219, 240
"Poetry and the Gods" (Lovecraft-Crofts) 127
Pokorny, Julius 256n5
"Polaris" 39
Pope, Alexander 10, 23, 46, 64, 112, 132, 136, 163, 169, 185, 194–95, 207, 231, 235, 240
Pound, Ezra 79, 91, 92, 94, 177–78, 180, 190, 247
Praz, Mario 140
Price, Robert M. 245, 246
Principia (Newton) 135, 138n4, 152
Prior, Matthew 181
"Proposta di premi fatta dall'Accademia dei Sillografi" (Leopardi) 215

Index 303

Protocols of the Elders of Zion, The 48
Proust, Marcel 140, 270
Putnam's Sons, G. P. 265, 267
Pyke, James 162
Pynchon, Thomas 24
Pythagoras 112

Queen's Enemies, The (Dunsany) 114n1
Quintilian (M. Fabius Quintilianus) 162

R.U.R. (Capek) 265
Rainbow 133
Ranieri, Antonio 230, 231
Rank, Otto 257
Rape of Lucrece, The (Shakespeare) 158
Rape of the Lock, The (Pope) 139
"Rats in the Walls, The" 24–25, 28, 37, 96, 160, 185
Regnum Congo (Pigafetta) 74–75
Reinhardt, Karl 280
Republic (Plato) 173, 174
Rhodopis 113
Riddle of the Universe, The (Haeckel) 247
Rilke, Rainer Maria 140
Rimbaud, Arthur 121, 182
Roberts, Dorothy 87
Rochefoucauld, François, duc de La 205
Rochester, John Wilmot, earl of 181
Roethke, Theodore 144
Rohmer, Sax 84
Rorty, Richard 182
Rosa, Salvator 58

"Sabato del villaggio, Il" (Leopardi) 224–25
St. Armand, Barton Levi 25n5, 50, 94n4, 100, 241, 248, 255n4, 265
Saison en enfer, Une (Rimbaud) 121
Salammbô (Flaubert) 124
Sappho 233–35
Sartre, Jean-Paul 193
Saturn Devouring One of His Sons (Goya) 78
Sayers, Dorothy L. 258n6
Schelling, Friedrich Wilhelm Joseph von 134
Schillebeeckx, Edward 249, 263
Schleiermacher, Friedrich 163, 257
Schmidt, Jan 11
Schopenhauer, Arthur 134, 201, 203, 241, 256
Schultz, David E. 11
Scott, Sir Walter 72
Searight, Richard F. 89
Seneca the Younger (L. Annaeus Seneca) 160, 161
"Sera del dì di festa, La" (Leopardi) 223–24
Setiya, K. 241
"Shadow out of Time, The" 18, 22, 25, 28, 33, 34, 37, 39, 40–41, 44, 52, 54, 55, 56, 60–64, 98–99, 99, 100, 101, 117, 123–24, 138n4, 178, 188, 189–90, 197–98, 240, 265, 268, 271, 272
"Shadow over Innsmouth, The" 17, 19, 20, 24, 26, 28, 29, 34, 52, 55, 56, 59, 60, 81, 91, 92, 94, 107, 124, 125, 141, 182, 221, 230, 245, 265
Shakespeare, William 56, 93
Shapley, Harlow 129
Shelley, Percy Bysshe 27, 40, 127, 128, 140
"Shunned House, The" 37, 95, 97, 185
"Silver Key, The" 47, 191, 211–12, 256
Simmons, Dan 128n2
"Sin-Eater, The" (Macleod) 24
"Sinners in the Hands of an Angry God" (Edwards) 19n2
Sleep and Poetry (Keats) 157
Smith, Clark Ashton 73, 93
Smith, William 75
"Some Notes on Interplanetary Fiction" 23
"Sopra il ritratto di una bella donna" (Leopardi) 205, 221
Sophist (Plato) 173
Sophocles 278, 281
Spengler, Oswald 63
Spenser, Edmund 129, 132, 238, 261n8
Spinoza, Benedict de 205
Staël, Madame de 203
"Star-Spangled Banner, The" 181, 196
"Statement of Randolph Carter" 20, 38
Steele, Sir Richard 10, 46–47, 169
Sterling, Kenneth 93
Stesichorus 113, 138, 161
Stevenson, Robert Louis 181
Stillinger, Jack 151, 155, 159
Story of Philosophy, The (Durant) 201, 254n3

"Strange High House in the Mist, The" 187, 189, 191
Strange Tales 265
Sue, Eugène 141
Sullivan, Sir Arthur 168
Summa Theologica (Aquinas) 249
"Supernatural Horror in Literature" 18, 27, 47, 128, 168, 261, 265
Swann's Way (Proust) 140
Swift, Jonathan 94, 169
Swinburne, Algernon Charles 25–26

"Tale of Satampra Zeiros, The" (Smith) 93
Tarzan of the Apes (Burroughs) 171, 198
Task, The (Cowper) 39–40
Taylor, Bayard 148n6
"Tell-Tale Heart, The" (Poe) 71
"Temple, The" 18, 46
"Terrible Old Man, The" 71
Tertullian 282
Theaetetus (Plato) 173
Thel (Blake) 158
Theobald, Lewis 23, 195
"Thing on the Doorstep, The" 18, 28, 36, 37, 41, 50, 94, 107, 108, 124, 125, 130, 138, 142, 180, 188–89, 197, 230, 239, 271, 272
Thomson, James 132–33, 134, 144, 160
"Through the Gates of the Silver Key" (Lovecraft-Price) 18, 23, 44, 138n4, 191–92, 193, 255
Ti: A Story of San Francisco's Chinatown (Bamford) 84
Tibetan Book of the Dead, The 116
"To Anacreon in Heaven" 181, 196
"To the Memory of Sir Isaac Newton" (Thomson) 132, 144
Todorov, Tzvetan 116, 176
Tolkien, J. R. R. 262
"Tomb, The" 25, 37, 117, 120–21, 171, 180–81, 185
Torrey, E. Fuller 178
"Tramonto della luna, Il" (Leopardi) 221
Trimbur, John 164
Tristia (Ovid) 195
Tsathoggua 73
Tussaud, Madame 44, 276n9
Twain, Mark 24, 247

"Ultimo canto di Saffo" (Leopardi) 225–26, 233–34
Ulysses (Joyce) 247
Unaussprechlichen Kulten (von Junzt) 29, 64
"Under the Pyramids" (Lovecraft-Houdini) 96, 113, 117, 119, 124
United Amateur 86
"Unnamable, The" 24, 28, 117, 191, 193
Unzeitgemäße Betrachtungen (Schopenhauer) 201

Vathek (Beckford) 20
Verne, Jules 252, 253
"Vice" (Loveman) 89
Vico, Giambattista 63
Virgil (P. Vergilius Maro) 10, 99, 137, 181, 194, 222, 228, 279

Wagner, Richard 91, 127, 178
War of the Worlds, The (radio broadcast) 251
Waste Land, The (Eliot) 24, 166
Webster, Noah 171
Weird Tales 24, 32, 70, 141, 265, 267, 271
Welles, Orson 251
Wells, H. G. 79, 252, 253
"What Wondrous Love" 255
"Whisperer in Darkness, The" 18, 19, 20, 24, 28, 29, 31, 34, 37, 38, 44, 50, 52, 61, 117, 122–23, 128–29, 188, 267
"White Ship, The" 241n1
Whitehead, Henry S. 242
Whitman, Sarah Helen 25n5
Wilde, Oscar 88
Williams, Roger 166, 243
Williams, William Carlos 178
Wilson, Edmund 9, 23, 167–69, 180, 196
Winesburg, Ohio (Anderson) 21, 47–48
Wordsworth, William 133, 172
Wright, Farnsworth 165

Yeats, W. B. 190, 192
Young, Edward 10, 40, 154, 172
Young-Bruehl, Elisabeth 10, 26–27, 81, 85, 89–90, 107

Zibaldone (Leopardi) 202n1, 203, 223

www.ingramcontent.com/pod-product-compliance
Lightning Source LLC
Chambersburg PA
CBHW070634160426
43194CB00009B/1462